HUMAN IMPACT
ON
MOUNTAINS

Edited by

**Nigel J. R. Allan
Gregory W. Knapp
Christoph Stadel**

Rowman & Littlefield
PUBLISHERS

ROWMAN & LITTLEFIELD PUBLISHERS, INC.

Published in the United States of America
by Rowman & Littlefield Publishers, Inc.
4720 Boston Way, Lanham, Maryland 20706

British Cataloging in Publication Information Available

Library of Congress Cataloging-in-Publication Data

Human impact on mountains.
Bibliography: p. 277
Includes index.
1. Man—Influence on nature.   2. Mountains.   3. Mountain people.
I. Allan, Nigel J. R.   II. Knapp, Gregory W.   III. Stadel, Christoph.
GF57.H85   1987
910'.0943   86–31471

ISBN 0–8476–7459–2 (cloth : alk. paper)
ISBN 0–8476–7755–9 (pbk. : alk. paper)

Printed in the United States of America

Contents

Tables and Figures

Acknowledgments

Five chapters are reprinted with minor revisions by permission of the authors and publishers: Stephen B. Brush, "Traditional Agricultural Strategies in the Hill Lands of Tropical America," *Culture and Agriculture* 18 (Winter 1983):9–16; Jack D. Ives, "Mapping of Mountain Hazards," *Impact of Science on Society* 32 (1982):79–88; Sylvia H. Forman, "The Future Value of the 'Verticality' Concept: Implications and Possible Applications in the Andes," *Actes du 42 Congrès international des Americanistes (Paris)* 4 (1977):234–256; Walter Moser and Jeannie Petersen, "Limits to Obergurgl's Growth," *Ambio* 10 (1981):68–72; Carl Troll, "Vergleichende Geographie der Hochgebirge der Erde in landschaftsoekologischer Sicht," *Geographische Rundschau* 27 (1975):185–198; Harald Uhlig, "Problems of Land Use and Recent Settlement in Thailand's Highland-Lowland Transition Zone," in *Conservation and Development in Northern Thailand,* edited by J. D. Ives, S. Sabhasri, and P. Vorauri, 33–42 (Tokyo: United Nations University, 1980).

Preface

Twenty years ago when I enrolled in a course entitled "Peoples and Cultures of the Himalaya" I was struck by the dispersion of the literature I read for the course. The English language materials were scattered and often conflicting, and French and German sources were often buried in obscure places. Since that time matters have improved somewhat through the establishment of the International Mountain Society and the provision of a forum through the pages of its journal, *Mountain Research and Development*. In addition to the established mountain research centers in Munich, Innsbruck, Bern, and Grenoble, bibliographic centers on the Himalaya have sprung up in Paris (CNRS) and in Kathmandu at the newly established International Centre for Integrated Mountain Development (ICIMOD).

Despite the tremendous proliferation of information on mountain societies in journals, no single book in the English language has brought together a review of studies of mountain societies around the world. This book is designed to fill that void by emphasizing humans and their life in mountains. It is not intended to be a survey of the world's mountains, as the focus is on the traditional patterns of mountain occupance and the mountain peoples' transition into a modern world. For a comprehensive survey of the literature about the physical or environmental aspects of mountains, the reader is advised to consult Larry Price's *Mountains and Man*.

As undergraduate courses in mountain studies continue to increase in the disciplines of anthropology and geography, this text will provide the college student with a synopsis of mountain societies. It can also be used as a reference volume for those involved in cross-cultural studies or by physical scientists who require a measure of human life in the mountains. A cumulative bibliography is provided that will direct the reader to further sources, especially in the non-English literature.

My coeditors, Professors Stadel and Knapp, who conduct research in the Andes, collated and translated the contributions from Latin America. Stadel also translated two manuscripts originally written in German and checked other German language materials.

The gestation period for this book was longer than for most volumes. Either the editors were conducting extended research in inaccessible places, or the contributors were mailing in manuscripts from mountain locations around the world. Our editors at Rowman & Littlefield, Paul A. Lee and Janet S. Johnston, kindly tolerated this state of affairs.

The editors were supported in their mountain studies over the years by a variety of research fellowships and grants. Without this support this book would not have been created. Thanks go to the National Geographic Society, the National Science Foundation, the National Academy of Sciences, the Fulbright-Hays Program, the Ford Foundation, the American Institute of Pakistan Studies, and the Canadian Social Science and Humanities Council.

The excellent illustrations in the book were produced by Mary Lee Eggart and Clifford Duplechin. Maudrie Monceaux produced the typescript, and Linda McQueen edited several of the manuscripts. I would also like to thank Colin Rosser, director of ICIMOD, who has provided me with quiet and the excellent facilities of this mountain research center amid a long period of field research.

Nigel J. R. Allan
Kathmandu, Nepal
November 1986

PART I
The Mountain World

1
Introduction
Nigel J. R. Allan

The chapters in Part One are written to give the reader insight into the mountain world. After teaching a course on that topic for several years I realized how inadequate is our knowledge of mountains as the habitat of people. Scholars, especially in the English language, have not greatly helped to expand that knowledge because they have frequently misused or poorly translated material written in another language. This book is designed to assist the English reader in comprehending traditional mountain societies while it provides a contemporary look into the forces of change which are altering mountain societies and the natural environment.

Chapters by Groetzbach, Troll, and Bharati address the fundamental nature of life in the mountain environment. Later chapters by Rinschede, Penz and Brush describe traditional mountain livelihoods. Whiteman's chapter is inserted into the middle of Part One to provide a bridge between the mountaineers and their natural environment.

Hewitt's opening chapter highlights the current debate facing many Westerners and local Western educated scholars and administrators who are engaged in mountain activities. One can cite a litany of particularistic field studies or failed projects in reviewing the efforts of people from "downcountry" who have tried to "improve" the lot of mountaineers. Hewitt's comments are especially valuable as they come at a time when traditional livelihoods of mountaineers are shifting from being influenced by geoecological conditions to the more human concerns of integration into capitalistic and socialistic societies. The geoecology paradigm is less successful in elucidating formerly selfsupporting mountain societies that are becoming dependent on outside lowland dwelling people and institutions. The effect of this transition is everywhere visible on the mountain landscape. Ski resorts, parking lots, dams and power lines, roads and scruffy new towns constitute the litter of modern civilization. The chapter provides a valuable counterpoint to the dominant geoecological view of those who study mountain life.

Nowhere has mountain geography received greater emphasis than in the German-speaking countries, a fact which is reflected in the contents of this book. Groetzbach, for example, begins by tracing the theme of a "high mountain culture" as it has been developed in Europe by decribing and defining the terminology used by European scholars in studying alpine areas. He then extends this typology to high mountains elsewhere in the world. Whether or not mountain development in the non-Western world will emulate the modernization processes of Europe remains to be seen.

To clarify the German developed geoecology paradigm used in studying mountains, Stadel has translated one of the late Carl Troll's review articles. While no one has dominated research like Carl Troll, we now see from a reading of Hewitt's chapter that this paradigm, well exploited in the past, is less suitable for examining mountain societies today. In Troll's time the natural environment influenced much of mountain life; now modernization is underway and forcing us to develop human oriented modes of inquiry. This chapter will assist English speakers because it provides a succinct summary of Troll's method of looking at mountain environments, while it also gives a review of its associated literature.

Few visitors to mountains are aware of the environmental complexity that confronts mountaineers when they are extracting a livelihood from the soil. In Chapter Five, Whiteman elucidates the mountain farmer's agrosystems in three localities. A prominent feature of his work among mountain agriculturalists is his effort at producing greater agricultural production via methods selected by the cultivators. Standardized prescriptive remedies often conflict with local cultural and agronomic practices; therefore Whiteman would argue for a "smorgasbord" approach in which the farmer is provided with choices, is free to organize his own labor, to try new cultigens, and to choose an appropriate technology. All these components of the agrosystem are manipulated within the fixed bioclimatic environment.

Earlier, Hewitt had written about his concern for local mountain folk trying to maintain their identity and particular way of life in the face of increasing pressure from lowlanders. A frequent cause of friction between these people is the opinion lowlanders have of mountain folk. Pejoratives abound. The "Highlanders" of Scotland, "Oberwalder" of Austria, "Kohestani" of Afghanistan, "Rohilla" of India and "Hillbilly" of America are only a few of the names used by lowlanders in describing mountaineers. Nowhere are the distinctions of social geography more pronounced than in the South Asian mountain rimland. Professor Bharati's essay focuses on that social and environmental interface. Formerly only a few pilgrims visited remote Himalayan enclaves but now masses of tourists, both native and foreign, trek into the mountains, bestowing upon them an almost mystical identity.

The last three chapters in Part One discuss the livelihoods of mountain communities in Europe and the Americas with applications elsewhere. Terms such as transhumance and almwirtschaft are almost invariably misused by English speakers. The chapters by Rinschede and Penz define these terms and provide examples for those unfamiliar with basic types of mountain livelihoods. Brush concentrates on one vital component of the agrosystem, strategies, in examining traditional hill farm systems in the New World. These chapters conclude Part One which provides a guide to the current human impact on mountains.

2

The Study of Mountain Lands and Peoples
A Critical Overview

Kenneth Hewitt

Introductory Remarks: Mountains and "Big Science"

To focus one's studies on mountain regions is, presumably, to accept that they define a distinct and meaningful area of specialization. The boundaries, technical or geographic, need not be exact nor inviolate. As with national geographies or histories, law and economics, or the civil and military, independent study is sometimes useful without implying their separation in the "real world." Nevertheless, those choices that define or imply a special subject matter in terms of regional differences and habitats, need careful reflection by the geographer.

It is not difficult to find experiences and conditions that seem peculiarly well-developed in, if not unique to, mountain lands. That is especially so of activities within the compass of human senses and physique. When we examine the geographical patterns of a variety of geophysical, biotic and cultural kinds, they reflect or seem to highlight the arrangement of mountain lands. These are also uniquely associated with geotectonic processes or orogenic zones and altitudinal vegetation zones. That does not mean we have no difficulties defining the limits of orogenic and vegetation belts, the scale at which accidented topography becomes or ceases to be "mountainous," nor exactly what widespread features, if any, are actually unique to mountain societies (Thompson 1964; Hewitt 1972; Troll 1972c; Soffer 1982; Uhlig 1984). One merely discovers that there are issues in which these difficulties are minor compared to the advantages of concentrating upon mountain conditions. There have been numerous essays and introductory passages describing or defending such specialization (Peattie 1936; Troll 1972a; Price 1981; Ives and Messerli 1984).

"Natural regions" once provided, if they no longer do, one of the favored ways of organizing the subject matter of geography. Although surviving in introductory texts, they have fallen into disrepute as a means of organizing human geographic study, mainly because of the association with environmental determinism and a change in our preoccupations (Soffer 1982). They do remain a significant concern in climatology, plant, soil and even crop geography.

There is also, largely inspired outside of geography itself, a resurgent "natural regions" approach associated with environmental concern and the ecology movement (Parsons 1985). It is identified especially with regional environments marginal to the urban-industrial heartlands, or in so-called Third World countries. Moreover, it is a growth area for studies associated with international cooperation and agencies such as UNESCO. The latter's "Man and Biosphere" Programme is a prime example, which divides up most of its projects in terms of natural regions, including the "Arctic and Alpine" (UNESCO 1974). Such regions are also commonly those that recent ecological works have identified as "fragile," at least in relation to the contemporary development pressures and as being "in crisis." That has been an impetus for recent mountain studies. It seems to me that regional or biosphere studies in this vein raise issues for geographers going well beyond the mountains or their environmental problems.

My purpose here, however, is to critically review what seems a prevalance of poor and inappropriate definitions of the mountain problem field. I am concerned with both the ideas that are employed to divide off and to unify mountain land studies. The problem is primarily a failure to deal adequately with the human dimensions of mountain lands. But it is also reflected in a debatable choice of concerns in the physical or environmental dimensions. The weaknesses become most acute where this knowledge is employed to assess and recommend action in relation to the so-called crisis in the mountains (Eckholm 1975; UNESCO 1974; Pitt 1978; Ives and Messerli 1984).

In the first place I would argue that what are commonly presented as the unique or special problems of mountain lands are less and less a real outgrowth of mountain land experience and mountain studies. Rather, they revolve around a quite different intellectual and institutional environment, albeit "applied" in the mountains. From a scholarly point of view, it reflects the terrain and targets mapped out by particular disciplines. These might be geophysics, plant ecology, or cultural anthropology. Likewise the expertise in mountain problems today is largely drawn from and evaluated in terms of such disciplines, and their cutting edge in the more prestigious schools. It is not something greatly changed by the rise of interdisciplinary studies. The choice of expertise is similarly based. Their problem realms also tend to reflect fashionable concerns of the wealthiest nations. A similar prejudging of the issues arises from the role of agencies, national or international, charged with specific tasks. They might be in crop improvement, world conservation, famine relief or rural water supply. In themselves these are, of course, worthy and needed concerns. It is just that they further help the emergence of a field of studies that is defined in a highly partial and abstracted sort of way. They tend to see only what their mission prescribes. Scholars tend to favour the currently fashionable issues and techniques that seem most fruitful for development in the mountains.

To a great extent this is also at the heart of recent efforts to define the mountain field and complaints of its relatively poor degree of development. The difficulties raised are really those of establishing viable territorial boundaries within the bureaucracy of science, or a distinctive professional expertise within the technocratic divisions of established agencies and problem fields. There is little sense of an intellectually curious and open-ended response to experience. There is little or no penetration of other actors or sources of wisdom into this "citadel of expertise."

Specifically where "man and mountains" are concerned, I find the basic if often unspoken assumptions are environmentalist. That is to say they define problem and explanation in terms of the (local) associations of people and habitat, and hence, essentially by what is supposed to be peculiar to the mountain environment. Typically, understanding hinges upon physical conditions, whether the geo-, bio- or techno-physical. The natural environment, and hence the more refined sciences and institutions studying it, underpins or looms largest in explanation and practice. For geographers and ecologists, this has recently converged into a broad description of our interest as being in "mountain geoecology" (Troll 1972). This gives pride of place to physically based process and pattern, even in the defining of human phenomena. And that describes most of what appears in a series of publications representing the mainstream of work by geographers for example in recent decades (Troll 1972a; Ives and Barry 1979; Webber 1979; Ives and Messerli 1981). I hasten to add following this citation of such impressive "offenders," that the issue is not the quality of the work as science, nor do I challenge the validity of the approaches in all contexts or for certain purposes. I have done and do work of this kind myself. Still, the materials here reflect mountain conditions and experience, as noted earlier, only in partial and indirect way. Most directly they reflect the preoccupations and technocratic spirit of the societies and institutions of the wealthiest (urban-industrial, lowland?) states. And yet, this same style of work and expertise is perceived to be the most relevant to the human and habitat problems of all the world's mountain lands.

An interesting case is the two impressive volumes of the International

Karakoram Expedition (Miller 1984). The first volume represents conference proceedings given before most of the participants carried out field
work in the Karakoram. The second volume is essentially the results of a
summer's fieldwork. The latter certainly has new data and a refinement of
understanding of various aspects of the region. The essential content and
frameworks are unchanged. They are merely an application of standard
practices and ideas. And one suspects that the assumptions of today's
"big science" here as elsewhere more or less ensure this must be so. Yet
one may wonder how anyone who has never visited this remarkable and
complex mountain region could really know ahead of time what they
needed to know to understand it. Nevertheless, such is the style of work
and expertise widely believed to be the only adequate approach to habitat
and social problems in the mountains.

"Mountains and Man": The Limitation of Mountain Geoecology

Recently, the geographer Larry W. Price has provided a comprehensive
overview of the field of mountain studies in his book *Mountains and Man:
Study of Process and Environment* (1981). This is in many ways a
landmark in the development of the field, and the first such overview
since Peattie's *Mountain Geography* (1936). Most of the remainder of this
essay will review those aspects of Professor Price's book that relate to the
issues noted above. An earlier version of the review entitled "Human
geography and mountain environments" appeared in *The Canadian Geographer,* Vol. 23(1983):96–102. And although my remarks are mainly
critical, it is not because I have picked an unrepresentative, let alone a
poor example. On the contrary, this book very competently constructs a
picture of the mainstream of mountain studies in English at least. It
reflects very well the preoccupations of the past several decades, and
what is and is not novel since Peattie wrote. One expects, and I would
recommend, that the book should be used to introduce advanced students
and other scholars to our field.

The general content of Price's book will not surprise anyone familiar
with parallel work on arid lands, island ecosystems, the tropical rain
forests or wetlands. Moreover, my reservations have a familiar, almost a
deja vu quality, for anyone aware of the history of geographical thought.
These reservations almost wholly concern the "Man" aspects. In contrast to the geoecological materials, the treatment of human behavior and
societies seems stereotyped and conceptually weak. Much of it slips into
a crudely environmentalist view. And yet, Professor Price's discussions
strike me as less insensitive to the elements of human understanding than
much of the environmental science or "man and biosphere" work he
draws upon. At the risk of some unfairness to his other achievements, I

feel my review must dwell in some detail upon the poverty of human understanding here, which has some serious implications for human geography, and still more for action on mountain land problems.

Before turning to that I must emphasize that the bulk of the book provides an excellent introduction to high mountain *environments*. It is a good guide to the literature and state-of-the-art in mountain geoecology. Its scope is global. It provides insight into the diversity of habitats and a sense of the regional complexities more detailed work must consider. The breakdown of material is broadly that of a conventional regional text. There are chapters on orogeny, mountain climate, snow and ice, land-forms, soils, vegetation and wildlife. Climate and landforms receive the lion's share of discussion and illustration. This is typical of the literature quoted and reflects the main interest and contribution of physical geographers. Topics such as orogeny and plate tectonics are lavishly treated in other accessible publications.

My only serious quarrel with this part of the text is the devoting of nearly all attention to timberline and above, or "high alpine" (Price 1981:4) conditions, while other parts of mountain lands (80–90%) are barely sketched in outline (Soffer 1982). Now these neglected areas happen to be where human settlements are concentrated, just as, even in high areas, temporary human occupancy tends to favor patches of gentler slope. The skimpy treatment here does less than justice to mountain lands *as habitats*. That is surely part of the reason why the physical background is such a poor guide to the human condition in them. Again, however, this is quite typical of the bulk of the literature in the field and especially in its geoecological vein. Rather than being a genuine response to mountain lands in and of themselves, I suppose it reflects the preoccupations—scientific, aesthetic and recreational—of wealthy classes in wealthier states.

It is the aura of romance and the coffee table book, rather than a deep sense of the role of culture in all human circumstances, that fills an introductory chapter concerning attitudes to mountains. The subject itself is welcome. It is seriously neglected in most of the sorts of work Price is reviewing. However, it is dealt with quite superficially. The content largely reflects its origins in the drawing rooms and college courses of urban-industrial, Western society. Interestingly, these manage to get by with essentially the sorts of sentiments, albeit watered down, that the *anarchist* geographer Elisée Reclus expressed in his little classic *The History of a Mountain* (1881). But like most notions classed as aesthetic, cultural or moral in the West, this is virtually irrelevant to and absent from the scientific and technical material in the rest of the book.

We are told that (until now) "Mountains have never been so much in demand [sic!] or regarded with such favor in all the history of man" (p. 23). It would be very interesting to see a critical summary of the evidence for this sweeping view and the statement that follows it that mountains are "universally viewed as havens of retreat and symbols of freedom." That may well strike a responsive chord in undergraduates after a mountain vacation, a Walt Disney movie, or Sierra Club book. A scholar with a global approach is, however, obliged to help them see that their perspectives can be rather less than universal, even, perhaps, that the human experience of mountains as here conveyed is swiftly dissolving into a fog of sentimental cartoons and media "hype." Meanwhile, evidence such as appears in chapter 12 might make the opposite assertions easier to defend: namely, that the distinctive qualities and adaptive problems of mountains have never been so ignored, distorted or casually swept away as today. Are their "havens" not being laid bare momently by highways and megaprojects or ravaged by guerillas and counterinsurgency operations? Is not the independence and uniqueness of mountain peoples being everywhere sacrificed to mining, dam building, tourism and central government policy or expediency? Is not the "freedom of the hills" being increasingly confined by regulations and surveillance, by parks management and biosphere reserves?

The book will, of course, go on to deal with mountains as though everything there is dominated by natural processes. However, on the ground, rather than being "favored," one witnesses, even here, the final disappearance of mountain forests, widespread extermination of wildlife, vast tracts of accelerated erosion and abandoned land. Once "proud" mountain people by the hundreds of thousands have been uprooted and are in urban slums. Wherever I have been, the more evident contemporary physical processes are often the work of bulldozers, dynamite, chain saws and helicopters. From the Japanese Alps to the Pyrenees one sees massive concrete form-work confining slopes and streams, and marching into the havens and wildernesses. Few indeed of the classic sites of the picturesque experience bear much resemblance to what Ruskin described or what the tourist photographs still try to show. One thinks of the dense "suburb" on the Reider Alp of the Aletsch, the smogs of Grindelwald, or the construction site that was once Japan's sacred Mount Tateyama. Although I care for few things as much as visiting remote mountain wildernesses, in light of present developments the points Professor Price makes seem more accurately termed *false consciousness*. In any case, this short, pleasant sortie into the language of the Romantic Revival bears little relation to the rest of the book and its source materials. For "man" as well as environment, they are unashamedly mechanistic. One can only ask why it is that the most profound and far-reaching of all the activities of intelligent life—how it conceives and values its world—has become the stuff of pleasant titillation or dusty scholarship? Meanwhile, even the muck in a solifluction terrace receives a fierce commitment to precision and generality.

My difficulties with the rest of the human material spring, despite his protests to the contrary, from an almost unwavering environmental determinism. This is supported by examples and generalizations that turn upon quite extraordinary compressions of geographic and historic diversity. That is reinforced by a sense that the meaning of the mountain environment is typified by processes in the alpine wilderness—the zone with the least history or ecological diversity! This applies to many small observations throughout the text. However, it is the last three chapters (10–12) that focus upon "Man" and most fully show this style of interpretation at work.

Chapter 11, on agriculture and settlement, is replete with the telescoping of geography and history that bothers me. Take the statements on p. 393, such as: "Sedentary agriculture in mountains reaches its finest development and is most widely practiced in the tropics." First, one is nagged with thoughts of counter-examples. The agriculture of, say, the Val d'Aosta in the Italian Alps, parts of the Pontus Range or Japanese mountains has struck me as rich and diverse. On the other hand, one thinks of extensive areas of impoverished tropical mountain agriculture and the large tracts where sedentary cultivation is not practiced. Perhaps my experience is unrepresentative. We do need fairly substantial illustration and data to support this sort of global generalization. Again: "highland areas of the humid tropics characteristically support denser population than do lowlands."

There are ample counter-examples from New Guinea to West Africa. Presumably he has in mind the population-altitude graphs for Peru and Ecuador (Little 1981). But are altitude and humidity the decisive or the only ecological variables at work there? Is the social and economic history of the region unimportant? That has been anything but an unruffled story of adaptation to natural conditions. Meanwhile, the tropics are said to contrast with "middle latitudes" where "the lowlands are the focus of intensive, sedentary agriculture and mountains [of] comparatively sporadic use." I thought there were areas of intensive land use of mountain lands in the European or Japanese Alps, the Carpathians and mid-latitude China. Meanwhile, are there not large and ancient tracts of "intensive, sedentary cultivation" in lowlands of S.E. and S. Asia, or a long history of intensive plantation agriculture in other tropical lowlands? And what of the "sporadic" use and "shifting cultivation" widespread in tropical highlands such as New Guinea's?

However, it is easy to trade counter-examples in this sort of discussion. Until some means of composing a representative overview is available, what is more at issue is the logic of such statements and the urge to make them. Also, as categories for explaining human affairs "the tropics," "lowlands," or "middle latitudes" are labile as well as simplistic. I often had the feeling, too, that Professor Price forgets that valley floors, piedmonts, or intermontane basins and terraces are part of mountain environments. But he does accept findings from extensive high altitude flatlands like the altiplano of Peru or Tibetan plateau.

As his discussion proceeds, one must ask, too, what it means to identify the influence of the physical environment in such elements as terracing, nomadism, "compact agglomerations of settlement" (p. 393), or "sporadic" use? Are these not themselves labels for matters of great internal complexity? Are they not, without more precise definition, as much in evidence outside mountain lands as here discussed? And what does it imply when examples of these phenomena are detached from material life in widely separated places and times, as though they represent the action of identical forces? The environmental and societal significance of terracing, for instance, surely differs greatly with the ethno-ecological and historical context, no less than does the presence of books in societies widely different in literacy, in what is published and sells well.

What the logical structure of the statements quoted and most of the other material in the book serve to do is preclude or ignore social understanding. Here, we even slip back beyond the mechanistic environmentalism of Ellsworth Huntington or Griffith Taylor. This is the world of Ancient Greek geography, where habitat and mankind are explained by a system of zones "torrid," "temperate," "frigid," also used to explain regional differences of the second order physical pattern of highland and lowland life. In detail, the basic paradigm of explanation is that used to relate, say, plant growth to heat, moisture and other biophysical variables, though without comparable rigor. Professor Price is aware of the problem here, and occasionally hovers on the brink of quite different structures of explanation, essentially when he happens to quote the work of social scientists (e.g., pp. 416–17). That fails to affect the bulk of his thought. At the beginning of the chapter *Implications for Man,* he says: "While the physical features of environments are paramount for those who live in mountains, it is unsafe to attribute cultural features solely to them" (page 346, my italics). I suggest it is not only "unsafe," but untenable. Moreover, most of my experience and the situations described in the last three chapters here argue persuasively for the antithesis of his proposition. In effect, events today commonly reflect the fact that the "physical features" are not, and are not being treated as, "paramount." Rather the habitat, and well-tried practices for dealing sensitively with it, are being sacrificed in desperate efforts to adapt them to relentless pressures of political economy. Most of the latter stem from outside the mountain lands being discussed.

However, I would also suggest that, while the intensity of external pressures on mountain lands today is unprecedented, hardly any of the cultures or practices of mountain peoples I have encountered or read about had evolved as an isolated symbiosis of "man" and "mountains";

quite the contrary. Even in the rare cases exhibiting a still sensitive and robust accommmodation to the mountain habitat, contact with and events in the wider world around has exercised a more or less decisive influence.

Professor Price does say that "historical and social conditions," even "human inscrutability" and the way men do things "because they feel like it" (p. 347) cannot be ignored. But they are ignored. Moreover, there is a vast range of organized, determinate, intentional and repetitive activities in every society that lie between the extremes of biophysical reflex and mere whim. That is the essence of the human geography of settlement. It is central to understanding human adaptation at the social level and the ecological crises of our time. Neither environmentalism nor a sentimental feeling for mountains can deal with those questions.

There is a still deeper, perhaps "ideological," problem here. Environmentalism, ever since we first find it in ancient Greek science, has usually been a cloak for Western ethnocentrism and self-congratulation. Environmentalists have invariably found their own and closely related cultures to have emerged in the most favorable habitats for enterprise, knowledge and power. In the last couple of centuries, environmental arguments always pass over or diminish the achievements and worth of societies lacking urban-industrial technology and often enough, because they live outside that geographical fiction called "the temperate zone" (Huntington 1945; Stefansson 1922). Their adaptations to environment may be fascinating but, unlike ours, are represented as fundamentally archaic, outmoded and "unfree" (Peattie 1936: 225–228). This is, after all, another phase of the social Darwinist view of human evolution: the biological and ecological explanation of "success" as justification for the right to expand, and to determine the fate of others (Hofstadter 1959).

By something resembling a Freudian slip, the big problems of material life and environment are always located in those other "adverse" habitats, as they are located in the parallel economic fiction of "The Third World" rather than the "first." This sort of attitude is convenient, of course, because it also fosters a technocratic citadel of expertise in the "favored lands." The forces of nature, especially in non-Western settings, are seen to be manageable only by the application of "advanced" technological counterforce. Such an underwriting of the priorities of science is further served by the way it hides the political and economic preoccupations of dominant states and institutions in assumed problems of impersonal natural forces and the dictates of survival. It is a pattern of assumptions present in much of the environmental science and biosphere projects Professor Price is reviewing, and it creeps into the tenor of his book as well.

At the most general level first, take the reassertion of that old chestnut of environmentalism: "Mountains tend to separate and impede, while level tracts facilitate exchange and interaction" (p. 369). That may seem reasonable to a timid, armchair geographer but is odd for one well traveled in mountains. Governments and pioneers struggling to open up the vast *lowland* tracts of the Amazonas or Siberia might take note too, and the thoroughly balkanized peoples around the margins of the Arabian and Mesopotamian flatlands. However, one could also develop a detailed historical case for showing how the Alps, Caucasus, Himalaya or Central Andes have encouraged and fully shown the benefits and risks of inter-communication, trade, travel, and borrowings among diverse peoples. Of course, the suggestion (p. 369) that the cultures of Mediterranean and Northern Europe have been separated because of the mountains is absurd. They have been continuously in one anothers' pockets or at one anothers' throats since before the Romans. A glance at the "Italian connection" in Shakespeare's plays gives one the idea. And the mountain "barriers," like the equally "treacherous" seas, have proved very permeable. Their constant use for trade, travel and war is evidenced in the innumerable castles and walled towns of the Alpine or Pyrenean foothills, spanning three millenia of history (Braudel 1972).

The same may be said of the still more rugged landscapes of the Karakoram and other ranges of "The Roof of the World." Since the Emperor Asoka sent his emmisaries into and through them to preach peace and Buddhism two hundred years before Christ, their routeways have been in almost constant use. Their history is fully bound up in the interactions of the Middle East, India, China, Inner Asia and Russia. But here we come to the nub of this barriers and boundaries business. In the Inner Asian mountains it was the predatory interests and mutual mistrust of the Russian, British, and Chinese Empires that closed the ancient arterial trade routes, notably of the Himalaya. It was they who sent officials and geographers scurrying in search of "natural boundaries" and placed garrisons to guard strategic passes and close them to traffic. Mountain barriers are largely a political fiction, albeit a powerful one (Curzon 1908: 13–23). With that too goes the overblown interest in passes, which receives an exceptional four-page discussion here (pp. 371–74). By collapsing the mountain communication problem on the pass, that precarious breach in a potential rampart for separating peoples, one identifies one's interest with political security and the-view-from-the-capital, not a balanced sense of natural obstacles . This was fascinating to a colonial geography answering the call to define territorial limits to sovereignty and the points where access might more readily be denied. For the merchant, the traveller or, indeed, today's mountaineers, crossing the highest point on a route has some significance. But the major obstacles usually occur in the long, populated valley tracts leading to the passes, unless the latter are indeed invested by soldiers. Even more risks sometimes exist in the piedmont towns that are the "gateways" to the mountains where taxes are levied, papers examined, bribes required and expropriation possible.

On questions of detail, there is one all-weather road and at least two summer roads for vehicular transport across the Western Himalaya, which Professor Price says has no highway (p. 369). Moreover, trans-Himalayan travel has been by far the more enduring and probably the commonest form of communication between India and China. A word must also be said for the "ruthless local tribesmen (around the Khyber Pass) who have long exploited their strategic location between Afghanistan and . . . Pakistan" (p. 374). The amazing thing is that these "tribesmen,"—whom it is now more fashionable to see as "freedom fighters"!—have managed to keep any kind of a distinct, let alone a robust, defiant culture together. It is not they, but the military and economic adventuring of surrounding civilizations that have brought centuries of ruthlessness and bloodshed here, and devastated the environment such that none of it is "natural." The Pathans (Pashtuns) are a clear case of mountain folk whose use of the mountain lands is largely an adjustment to pressures from surrounding human societies, rather than intrinsic forces of their habitat. Their problem continues! There are many even more tragic examples of what John Bodley calls *The Victims of Progress* in the world's mountain lands (Bodley 1975).

An unusual and welcome aspect of Professor Price's discussion is the several places where he introduces military questions. These are conspicuous by their absence from most human geography, as they are so often overwhelming on the ground, not least in so-called "harsh" or "fragile" places like coral islands, arid lands and mountains (Westing 1980). It is hard to find a long-settled mountain region that has not suffered periodic or enduring transformation by military activities; whether in the form of actual warfare, enforced conscription, rebel bands and counter-insurgency, or the permanent presence of exogenous military forces. Here, his discussion does recognize the function of the geopolitical strategies of states who find mountains logical boundaries, and their "peripheral environments" better sacrificed in warfare than richer lowlands (p. 374). He does not recognize the sometimes devastating significance of that for the life and environmental relations of mountain people. Elsewhere, he confines himself to narrow, technical problems of mountain warfare (e.g., p. 353–54). But as von Clausewitz argued 150 years ago, the military significance of mountains, from Hannibal to Napoleon and, we may add, the Soviet presence in Afghanistan, is open. The final roles of altitude, terrain, weather, accessibility depend upon the intentions and the relations of the opposing forces. The latter decide the pattern of advantage in and significance of mountain conditions.

Over the past century, wars and other armed violence in remote lands and against peoples seen as on the frontiers of civilized life, have not just been what von Clausewitz called "a continuation of policy by other means." They have been a continuation of biology by other means. From the highland clearances in Scotland (Prebble 1963) and the United States' army operations in the West (Slotkin 1985) or French colonial operations in the Atlas mountains (Gottmann 1943), to recent events in the mountains of Vietnam, Ethiopia, Afghanistan, and Peru, wars have accepted or intended the total disruption if not the extermination of indigenous mountain cultures. And even those societies that have survived, to be treated by geographers and anthropologists as archetypically adapted to their mountain fastnesses, usually turn out to have undergone multiple, often recent devastations through armed conflicts and the demands of military activity (see below). But we are here concerned with styles of scholarship and evaluation that rarely recognize that such peoples or regions even have a history, or that their condition could reflect it.

Now let us focus down, and look at what is said about mountain peoples, specifically those more or less well removed from Western industrialism. Characteristically, we find them being explained by factors of "remoteness" and inaccessibility (pp. 365–67); by lives bound to a hard-won, thin resource base (chapter 11); by "particularly dangerous environments" (p. 377) and habitat "fragility" (p. 419). Similar notions were also present in Peattie (1936). They seem to encourage a dominant thrust of anthropological research on mountains emphasizing physiological stress and a general preoccupation with "stability" and "instability" (Ives and Messerli 1984), "impacts" and "corrective measures" (Glaser and Celecia 1981). Again, these concerns may have their place. But the result of emphasizing these general constraints and specific operations of high mountain processes, are said to produce people who resemble "mountain plants and animals" (p. 419). They are as bound by the dictates of their environment as flies set in amber. For these reasons, too, we are told they tend to be conservative, "clannish," "suspicious," and resistant to the benefits of modern technology. Perhaps I am overly inclined to see the main problems of mountain peoples and habitats today as stemming from the behavior of the dominant, urban-industrial heartlands, and the cities of the plains everywhere (Allan 1986). But what is the evidence for and substance of the view of remoter mountain peoples being mountain-bound, and hence inward-looking, inbred and plant-like?

Take the Balti villagers of the Karakoram Himalaya whose image represents "Man" on the dust jacket of the book. I cannot say if they are typical. It would be difficult, however, to find a case of seemingly greater remoteness, of village economies more dependent upon their habitat for material resources, and in a more extreme setting of "deep, narrow valleys separated by precipitous alpine ridges" (p. 367). One can agree that overall, the valleys of the Karakoram are homes of "diverse cultures," and have often been described as "refuges," though I would add that refugees are a complex human phenomenon. However, we also know the Baltis are devout Muslims, mostly Shiites, converted in the fifteenth to sixteenth centuries from Buddhism. They use much of any cash they earn to send menfolk on pilgrimage to Mecca and Iran. In villages of more than 50–100 folk, you will find two or three who read and speak Persian and Arabic. Most can converse in Urdu, the language of Pakistan. Many have sufficient English and Italian to shame, say, the French of my anglophone Canadian undergraduates. Meanwhile, their own language, Balti, is Tibetan, not Indo-European, but with a Persian script. Now, even Griffith Taylor thought language a decisive guide to human geography!

Not surprisingly, external historical factors have played a large role in Balti life. Islam is of primary importance, but notable too were the impacts of colonial rule. During the nineteenth century period of Kashmiri Dogra (Hindu Rajput) rule, ruthless conscription of menfolk, heavy taxes, and repeated military adventures or parasitic garrisons throughout the region had disastrous socio-economic results. It was the beginning of the "Kashmir problem" that continues to bring turmoil and violence to this region. There was a precipitous population decline that still seems to be reflected in abandoned terraced land and homes in some villages, in unused high pastures and summer villages and, I suspect, in many of the health and "inbreeding" problems.

Western observers commonly attribute such things to a combination of Balti "backwardness" and Professor Price's "physical factors," but the effects were further reinforced when the machinations and self-interest of British, Russian, and Chinese imperialism closed the trade routes through the Karakoram. Many villagers participated in that trade. They sold food and services and sent goods and porters with caravans. They travelled to see their kinfolk in Chinese Xinjiang or practiced those age-old techniques for redistributing wealth, robbery and extortion!

In the 1960s there were still old men who remembered spending their youth laboring on road and rail projects for the British in the plains of India. In recent decades enterprise of that sort has turned to Pakistan's towns and army, while nowadays, young men are off earning petrodollars in the Persian Gulf states. At home, since the 1890s, frequent mountaineering expeditions have attracted hundreds of porters in most summers. This, in the mainly subsistence economies of the villages, represents a major leverage on the use of labor, cash, prestige and the influx of industrial goods. Such relationships, the external pressures and internal responses, whether of dislocation or villager enterprise, are major ingredients if they do not dominate material life and its environmental relations here. The mountain habitat with which they articulate is a great ingredient too. But it is not an exclusive preoccupation of the Balti nor is it unamenable, for all its vastness and the tremendous geophysical energy, to alternative choices of use and priority. In that highly geographical aspect of occupancy, the spatial texture and intensities of use prove very flexible.

It might seem unfair to challenge Professor Price with an example he barely mentions otherwise. But what is lacking throughout is a sense of mountain communities as living worlds, and at least one rounded examination, rather than a collection of one-dimensional references that supposedly demonstrate universal principles. How else can we test such principles? How can one grasp human ecology without grasping the detail of human as well as geophysical contexts? But this is again typical of the style of work on which his discussion is based. Hence, I find it generally symbolic that those Balti porters on the dust jacket are shown in shadow, passive and dwarfed by the brilliantly lit, snow-covered crags of the Central Karakoram.

There is very little here of a sense of the histories, the ethno-ecological complexities, the extensive cultural contacts and enterprise of such mountain folk. And they are by no means relevant to only a few cases like the Balti. Yet, even close to home, we have the Appalachian folk caricatured as typical products of isolation and inbreeding in a mountain fastness, but no sense of their having been at the "sharp end" of a rapacious political economy, such as Harry M. Caudill (1962, 1973) has described, and of Hollywood's skills in stereotyping.

For environmental geography these are not small matters. Though the smaller concern of the text, the interpretations of mountain life are not minor aberrations. This is an otherwise soberly competent study, and one likely to be much used to educate and inspire concern for mountain lands. Unlike so much of recent biosphere research, Professor Price does attempt to deal with its most vital task: the interpretation of biophysical conditions in relation to human need, past adaptations and present environmental damages. However, he does this largely by grafting a 1920s environmentalism onto a rigorous biophysical and geophysical stem that simply overwhelms it.

If the net effect is fully in accord with the ethos of international science, there are specific "social constructions" at work in knowledge of the mountains that serve to exaggerate it here. First, as noted, there is a uniform tendency to focus upon and seek answers in the high alpine zone. Since I am also a mountaineer of sorts and enjoy getting "high" (p. 33) above timberline, I am not unaware of the attraction, but also of how Western culture is at work here. From a human perspective, however, it is essential to see that nearly all of the uses and problems of the mountains lie lower down and are deeply embroiled in a wider world. Hardly anyone lives in the alpine wilderness. The visitors are often oddities in a global social sense, and arrive according to schedules independent of alpine ecology. Contacts there are transient. Mountain land residents, no less than hikers and skiers, come from far downslope if not the towns of piedmonts and plains. Now the further downslope one goes the more muffled, modified and compounded are processes found in, and downslope effects of, the alpine zone. They are not absent. Sometimes they are decisive along an avalanche track or stream gully. Moreover, one might legitimately use "alpinification" if the term were less ugly, by analogy with "desertification." This is the progressive expansion to lower altitudes of processes and land forms of the alpine zone due to habitat abuse—mainly the destruction of vegetation. But the prime movers bringing that about rarely stem from the physical environment at all, but from socio-economic stresses and responses to them. Failure to recognize and reflect upon the patterns of human influence and response here seem to me why Professor Price shows the role of the mountain environment largely in discussion of human minutae, and details amputated from living culture in a gratuitous fashion. I do not say the high alpine is lacking in subjects worthy of study or in human significance, only that far too much is being said about and asked of it in relation to the human issues being assessed.

Finally, Professor Price's remarks on solutions to mountain region problems strike me as, again, fully symptomatic of today's international "Big" science. They are typically lacking in social or ecological understanding. I refer to strategies for coping with abuses to the interwoven fabric of the ecosphere that would cordon off areas to "preserve" them and their contents. This is, at least, a patently un-ecological solution to an ecological problem. Perhaps biosphere reserves have some value, but can never be large enough. Even if themselves preserved, they are likely to have the same effect as local erosion control on a beach, concentrating and greatly increasing the problem elsewhere. And it seems to me that any argument that can be made for "saving" the alpine wildernesses— and I would like to see them saved—is vastly more persuasive in relation to the ecologically richer environments of the fertile and settled areas lower down.

Technocracy in the Mountains

Whether one thinks in terms of "process and environment" or geoecology, the style of work reviewed above presents a special and very partial view of mountain lands. It is one clearly identified with the places where such terms are *de rigueur,* and perceived to be full of deep meaning. And despite its partiality, we seem to have here an emerging consensus that is both more widely accepted and conformed to than a host of other possible styles of work on the mountains.

In fact, my response to the bulk and the most widely available work in the field is much the same as to another related interest, natural hazards research (Hewitt 1983). The state of mountain studies seems to me to exhibit identical symptoms and predelictions. This is hardly surprising. The same general hierarchies of authority and learning, of institutions and agencies, are at work. The same "social construction of knowledge" is to be expected (Berger and Luckman 1967). The same convergence of the wealthiest, scientifically most "advanced" institutions around an "academic-research-consensus" is present (Said 1978).

In itself, this is such a commonplace of the pursuit and uses of science it may seem at once unavoidable and irrelevant. However, it is something that becomes acutely part of "the problem" and not merely "the solution," when such a consensus is deployed to deal either with questions whose frameworks are very different from those of the sub-disciplines of science, or that arise in environments and cultures other than those of the urban-industrial heartlands. At least, that has become a major concern of various students of natural hazards (Hewitt 1983), and for reasons that seem to apply equally in the mountain context.

We have noted the same "hidden hand" of environmentalism due to the patterning of most descriptions and explanations in terms of physical science models. In international work there is the same "natural sciences" approach that Burton et al. (1978) see as prevailing in United Nations studies concerned with hazards. But the highly partial, "First World" and technocratic perspectives of the dominant consensus on mountain lands, as with hazards, works strongly to inhibit or demean even experiments with alternative frames of reference. Rather, what we may call the "source discipline" frameworks are seen to prescribe all possible developments. Only work advancing in their terms is thought rational. This leads, in the contexts of "man and mountains," to the scientism—an imposing of forms common in a science, rather than the emergence of scientific understanding from substantive enquiry—of which Waddell has accused natural hazards research (Waddell 1975).

Soffer (1982) seems to share my sense that a human geography of the mountains fails to emerge because of an absence of mountain-based experience in its formulation. He also explains it as being due to an acceptance of a view of mountains essentially defined by physical geography. I think one might add that physical geography has become an increasingly poor contributor to understanding in general geography. In part that stems from another substrate in the patterns of dominance over scientific enquiry. This involves the pressures and rewards for less refined or prestigious fields that imitate or adopt the forms of more refined ones. Thus there has been a major preoccupation in areas like geomorphology with reconstructing their concerns in terms of notions and methods of other earth sciences or more technically specialized fields. This has, no doubt, much increased the technical sophistication of our work. It has, however, been achieved at the price of a great erosion of any distinctive sense of problem and a conspicuous lack of imagination or intellectual curiosity. With that comes a loss of identity as a branch of geography. Since most of physical geography's basic stock of ideas and practices are now borrowed from and measured against still more specialized fields—it might be soil mechanics, network analysis or dynamic models of the atmosphere—its sensitivity to broader problems, especially those of society's environmental relations, or of particular regional settings, is at an all time low. No doubt this intellectual "social climbing" was the proper course in terms of certain problems defined by geographers early in this century and perhaps the survival of these sub-fields in the academic "pressure cooker." But it only reinforces the underpinning of studies such as mountain geoecology with an environmentalist bias and formulations derived from physical sciences. The scramble for "expertise" here has left us unable or unwilling to think through other, and perhaps more appropriate frameworks or concerns.

Unfortunately, Soffer's response to the problem strikes me as essentially cut from the same cloth, albeit at different points. He speaks of "socio-economic" zones definitive of the mountain context. They turn out to be homologous with the altitudinal zones of the physical geographers. Indeed, they are not significantly different from those in the "geoecology" papers (Ives 1978). Soffer says, "the altitudinal division is the most outstanding characteristic of the mountain" (p. 395). No doubt vertical patterns of difference exist in most mountains, as do lateral and aspectual ones. Sometimes they are graphically reinforced by timberlines, cloud seas and *gipfelfluren*. As "divisions" they are a technical and sometimes useful fiction. As a *general* underpinning of *human* life in the mountains they are open to serious question. They serve to reinforce the emphasis upon physical and physiological difference and a static mapping of "physical" resources as the paradigm of "human use"! As a formal scheme no doubt it belongs equally with the "zoning" approach typical of urban and other planning fields; function classifying and deploying procedures embedded in the technocratic ethos. To imagine it is, or ever has been, the definitive structure in socio-economic life in mountains begs more questions than it answers.

Meanwhile, such ways of seeing the problems, and proposed solutions to them, call into question the whole idea of mountain regions as a meaningfully separate area of investigation. This relates to at least two false assumptions. The first is that the problems of so many mountain lands today are essentially a function of what mountain conditions are like. Hence the environmentalist tendency even of studies that do not give much emphasis to physical factors. Second, the direction of those influences that are distinctive and that create the special problems of mountain lands today is missed or reversed. Studies start with what is special in the mountain context and, if they do so at all, look outwards from these to surrounding areas or influences. Yet I would think that most if not all the major problems today are triggered and shaped by developments outside the mountains (Allan 1984, 1986). The linkages with outside areas are powerful in such problems as deforestation, accelerated erosion, "over-population" and depopulation. The initiative here is with outside socio-economic forces rather than mountain geoecology. Moreover not only the science being applied, but the statement of what are the problems of the mountains emanate from outside of them! There is little or no opportunity for either the questions or the answers in this "citadel of expertise," to be influenced let alone decided by those whose lives are most directly dependent upon mountain lands.

An apt description of these mainstream studies is "technocratic" in the broad sense. They presuppose a style of work requiring technical proce-dures and language worked out by specialized professionals in well-established fields. They usually articulate closely with professional orga-nizations, whose members work within bureaucratically regulated institutions of professionally trained "experts." Without doubt this is the prevailing style of scientific endeavor today. In its home situations it has developed powerful and persuasive orderings of knowledge. It is no coincidence that the particular technocratic views that predominate today emanate from the most powerful and wealthy states. Yet it surely takes no great wisdom to expect that these formations of enquiry will channel study into a particular view of "the facts," or "relevance" and acceptable "results." Is it not also conceivable that there are many problem-fields which these formations either failed to anticipate or willfully dismiss? Is it not likely that this will become more evident as we move into environ-ments and cultures removed from the industrialized heartlands where such technocracy arose and flourishes?

3

High Mountains as Human Habitat

Erwin F. Groetzbach

General Characteristics

The high mountains of the world exhibit remarkably similar geographical traits. This statement not only applies to their natural environment and thus to the ecological characteristics of high mountains as human habitat, but it is also applicable to certain forms of society, economy and settlement, which can be interpreted as results of an adaptation to the extreme conditions of the high mountain environment.

Jentsch (1977:65) considers the natural environment in high mountains so dominating that he proposes the recognition of a relatively uniform "high mountain culture" which he describes on a world-wide basis as a form of human existence near the upper altitudinal limit of the ecumene resulting from the adaptation of man to the high mountain environment. Besides such forms of adaptation which show remarkably uniform characteristics, even over large areas, there are also considerable regional modifications due to climate (e.g., inner tropics and non-tropics), but especially due to culture (adherence to different cultural realms) or socioeconomic characteristics (most notably the contrast between industrialized countries and developing countries). The concept of a globally prevailing "high mountain culture" should definitely not lead to the assumption that these regionally effective factors are of minor importance. The following is an attempt to, first, present the common characteristics, and then some of the important differences in the cultural geographic structure, organization and situation of high mountains of the world and to demonstrate the determining forces.

The human habitat in high mountains is above all determined by its vertical dimension (Troll 1966; Uhlig 1976a; Jentsch 1977). The mountain inhabitant is living permanently within and with this third dimension. Almost daily he has to overcome more or less pronounced altitudinal differences, and there are still many mountain regions that are not serviced by major roads and railway lines, cable cars or lifts. (The same hardship is also experienced by the mountain geographer, particularly in mountains of the Third World. Perhaps this explains why we do not encounter many cultural geographers in these regions!) The vertical dimension, however, does not only entail natural disadvantages and risks for the inhabitant of mountains, but also opportunities, as we shall demonstrate later. The most important environmental factors inherent in all high mountain regions are briefly characterized as follows.

Among the major threats to human existence and economic activities in the high mountains the *alpine elemental events* should be mentioned first, with "alpine" standing for high mountain regions in general (Matznetter 1958). These events comprise among others avalanches, rock and mud flows, major rockfalls, and hangslides, which can, at times, have catastrophic dimensions and effects. These hazards have increased with the extent of deforestation in high mountain regions. The large-scale deforestation does not only lead to catastrophic events, but also to a gradual soil destruction by increased washouts (soil erosion). All these processes, which occur increasingly in high mountain regions that are overstressed by agricultural and tourist activities, are now being intensively studied within the framework of the "natural hazard" research (Ives and Messerli 1981).

Apart from these irregularly occurring elemental events, human activities in the mountains are even more determined by the constraints of altitude and relief, which particularly hinder economic activities. This hindrance consists in the marked relief energy of high mountains and the resulting steepness of the terrain. This limits agriculture and transportation, to mention these two sections only briefly. Mountain agriculture is affected by two major constraints. With increasing incline of the slopes, the energy input rises while at the same time productivity declines (Loehr 1971). This results in a natural disadvantage for the mountain farmer in comparison to the farmer in the foreland. Within the industrialized countries there is a definite attempt made to equalize these income disparities by means of support measures, particularly for mountain agriculture, through different types of subsidies for mountain farming operations. The altitude and relief constraints are further manifested by the extraordinarily high investments for the construction of modern lines of transportation, in particular transmountain freeways and railway lines that are safe in winter. On the other hand, relief and altitude have recently also been proven to be particular assets for tourism, especially for modern alpine skiing. As a result, numerous high mountain regions have become important centers of recreation, a development which will be referred to subsequently.

The third characteristic of the natural environment of high mountains— the altitudinal zonation—should be mentioned here. From the perspective of cultural geography, this represents the most important characteristic of high mountains. The altitudinal belts in human geography relate to the climatic ecological zonation of the mountain region. With increased elevation this zonation establishes limits for agricultural land use and human settlement related to it.

The following general trend can be established. With increasing altitude, agricultural land use in high mountains becomes more uniform and extensive. The highest belt of agricultural land use is always the zone of high pastures, mostly located above the forest line (Groetzbach 1980). In this zone only grazing cattle can be kept, while field cultivation is not possible or profitable. The use of high pastures exploits an additional potential area for the provision of fodder for livestock farming; without the use of high pastures, the number of cattle in a high mountain region would have to be considerably reduced (Lichtenberger 1979:416).

With respect to the temporal utilization of the high pasture belt, the high mountains of the inner tropical regions are totally different from the non-tropical regions. The day climate of the inner tropics has no distinct temperature seasons, i.e., no summer and winter. Where the high regions of tropical mountains are at all pastorally used, grazing activity is possible throughout the year. This, for example, is the case in the South American Andes from Peru to Colombia. The situation is totally different in the mountains of the non-tropics with their seasonal climate, i.e., the change from summer to winter. There the stay of men and livestock in the high pastoral belt is limited to the warm season. Therefore, a seasonal pastoral economy similar to that of the Alps prevails with summer pastures and their related summer settlements (alps) forming the highest belt of agricultural land use and settlement. Below this zone, in some parts of the Alps, a belt of spring and fall settlements exists. Only below this zone follows the belt of permanent or winter settlements. It can be subdivided into further belts of land use according to the altitudinal limits of cultivated plants.

The vertical arrangement of the different parts of agricultural land results in a highly complex farm operation which is characterized by a system of seasonal echelons of land use and settlement (Uhlig 1973b). It existed formerly in the Alps, for example, the six part echelon system in the Val d'Anniviers (Fig. 3.1). Similar complex systems have been described in the Afghan Hindukush and in the Himalaya (Groetzbach 1972; Uhlig 1976a). Common to all these systems is the dominant vertical component from which American social anthropology developed the concept of verticality or vertical control (Forman, this volume; Sanchez 1977). These echelon-like systems (Ger. *staffelsystem*) of seasonal land use and settlement result in *regularly re-occurring migrations of men and livestock* over, at times, large altitudinal differences and horizontal distances. In traditional agrarian societies, a large part, even at times the

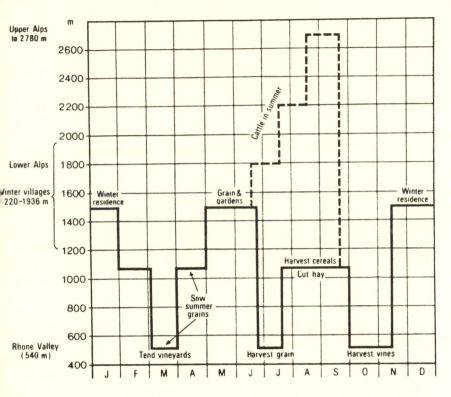

Figure 3.1 Seasonal Movement in the Val d'Anniviers, Switzerland. (After Peattle 1936: 140.)

majority, of the population participates in these movements. Such mountain populations are highly mobile, as was the case until the beginning of the twentieth century in the Alps, and still is in other mountains regions of the world (Peattie 1936:134). Therefore Blache (1933: 177) considers exchange and continuous mobility as the essential expression of life in the mountains.

The second major aspect of our theme lies in the variety of phenomena found in the cultural geography of high mountains. Whereas the extreme conditions inherent in the nature of high mountains challenge highly diverse population groups to rather uniform forms of adjustment, other factors tend to lead to different types of adaptation. These regionally different cultural influences appear in specific forms in the high mountains. Consequently, our perspective cannot be limited to the high mountains proper but has to include their forelands, the whole respective country, and even the higher-order framework of the cultural realm.

A Tentative Cultural Geographic Typology of High Mountains

The form, the organization, and the change of phenomena in the cultural geography of high mountains may vary so greatly within small areas that they can be hardly portrayed in a short overview for an individual mountain region like the Alps, let alone on a global scale. A further difficulty for a global analysis lies in the regionally different state of research. Our knowledge of the overseas mountain regions is highly different. Some of these regions have been closed for international research, as, for example, the mountains of China and the Soviet Union, of which little is known about the cultural-geographical situation; others, in contrast, experience a true boom in scientific exploration, as, for example, the Nepal Himalaya. These differences alone in the actual knowledge of individual high mountain regions make it necessary to limit a comparison to a few and very general characteristics. This will be attempted by a comparative typology of high mountains.

There is a great variety of characteristics which can be used. A cultural-geographical typology should not be derived from physical-geographical characteristics because these are—except for the contrast inner tropical/nontropical—essentially contained in a general definition of high mountains. In this paper those characteristics were chosen which were easily available, were ubiquitous, and had a cultural-geographical relevance. Above all, the demand for easy availability excludes statistical data, as even population number and density are not known for all the high mountain regions of the earth. In lieu of this the term "settlement density" is introduced by way of substitution, and is related to permanent settlements. Accordingly one can distinguish relatively densely and sparsely settled mountain regions, a distinction based on the existing literature, on maps, and on satellite imagery. An important additional characteristic is the age of settlement, which has an effect on the population and settlement densities as well as on the type of land use. P. and G. Veyret (1962:25) similarly distinguish primarily between "populated mountains" and "empty mountains" (Fr. *montagnes peuplées* and *montagnes vides*), as well as between "old settled mountains" and "mountains of new countries" (Fr. *montagnes anciennement peuplées* and *montagnes des pays neufs*). As further criteria they use the altitudinal zonation: high mountain, medium mountain, low mountain (Fr. *haute montagne, moyenne montagne, basse montagne*), as well as the climatic latitudinal position: cold mountains, temperate mountains, desert mountains, and tropical mountains (Fr. *montagnes froides, montagnes tempe-rées, montagnes désertiques, montagnes tropicales*). To indicate, at least roughly, the respective level of the socio-economic development, development research frequently uses the contrast of "traditional versus modern" to portray dominant economic and social forms of living. It is not possible to discuss here the problems inherent in this approach. The special situation of high mountains in Communist countries is given by the collectivized or nationalized mountain agriculture. A final characteristic lies in the distinction of the major population groups which use the living space of high mountains, according to their origin, namely autochthonous mountain farmers on the one hand, and, on the other hand, nomadic people and tourists having no other similarities than coming from regions outside the mountains.

The schematic typology (Table 3.1) with a total of five major types (A1a, A1b, A2, A3, B) is derived from a combination of the characteristics mentioned above. Primarily, two basic types may be distinguished, namely A, old and relatively densely settled high mountains; and B, young and relatively sparsely settled high mountain regions.

The majority of high mountains in Europe, Asia and South America exhibit the common characteristics of an old and relatively dense settlement. The term "old" means that it dates back to pre-historic times; and it contrasts with the high mountains of North America and New Zealand which were not settled until the nineteenth century, and even then only in sporadic clusters. Whereas these mountains of the New World represent a distinct type, the old and relatively densely settled high mountains are quite different in their cultural geography and their socio-economic organization. High mountains as refuge regions with old, traditional forms of living are found in particular in the underdeveloped regions of the world.

Table 3.1 Typology of High Mountain Regions from a Human Geographical Perspective

A. OLD AND RELATIVELY DENSELY SETTLED HIGH MOUNTAINS
 1. Largely intact traditional subsistence agriculture and a tendency toward overpopulation:
  a) Population of mountain peasants.
   (Large parts of the Himalaya–Karakorum–Hindukush; Andes)
  b) A population of mountain peasants, overlain by nomads.
   (High Atlas; mountains of the Middle east; western parts of the Hindukush and Himalaya.)
 2. Strongly declining traditional agriculture and expanding new activities (tourism, among others)
   (High mountains of Europe, especially the Alps and Pyrenees)
 3. Largely collectivized or nationalized agriculture, in parts with new activities (island-like scattered tourism)
   (High mountains of the Soviet Union and China; parts of the Carpathians)
B. YOUNG AND RELATIVELY SPARSELY SETTLED HIGH MOUNTAINS
 In areas of European overseas colonization, with extensive market-oriented agriculture and forestry and recent tourism.
 (High mountains of North America and New Zealand.)

Niches of a traditional mountain peasantry remain also in the mountains of Europe, but this peasantry is in complete recession since World War II, as Lichtenberger (1979) has demonstrated.

The mountain regions with a predominant old established population of mountain peasants and a dominant traditional agriculture (A1) encompass the system of mountain ranges in Southwest and South Asia from Turkey to the eastern Himalaya, and in addition, a large part of the Andes in South America and the island-like High Atlas. In Southwest Asia, these mountain peasants are seasonally "overlaid" with nomads who take their herds to the high summer pastures (subtype A1b). This competition between sedentary and nomadic population groups over the naturally meager living space of high mountains is known from the Taurus, the mountains of Iran and Afghanistan (Balland, this volume), and from the western Himalaya. De Planhol (1975) interpreted this competition as a consequence of a rapidly expanding "bedouinization" since medieval times and of an expansion of nomadism in the wake of Islam. The "bedouinization" reached its climax only in the nineteenth century when, for example, Pashtun nomadic tribes in Afghanistan obtained large summer pasture areas in the mountains and highlands of the country. Since the beginning of this century, nomadism has certainly declined everywhere. In some mountains and highlands of Southwest and Central Asia, however, important strongholds of nomadism persist.

Some parts of the old settled mountains show all the symptoms of *overpopulation*, i.e., their population numbers have exceeded the agrarian carrying capacity of their own habitable areas. It may appear almost paradoxical that high mountains as naturally disfavored regions tend to overpopulation. This fact has probably to be explained on historic grounds; high mountains for a long time were refuge areas for population groups which sought protection from conquerors, from aggressive nomads, and from the oppression and exploitation by regimes whose area of immediate authority ended at the margin of mountains. The role of mountains as "peasant resistance areas" against bedouinization (Planhol 1975: 41), as retreat areas, and as regions of continuity and tradition is most clearly expressed in Southwest and Central Asia. But mountains not only offered refuge. The small-scale segmentation of the living space into secluded valley regions, into basins and major and minor valleys, also favored separate linguistic, religious, and ethnic developments, as well as the formation of small political territories and "acephalous settlement areas" of free peasants or "kabyleien" (Kabyl-like areas) in the sense of Bobek (1962). These became integrated into the young national states only during the nineteenth century, and this only after fierce battles. An excellent example is the Caucasus where, after almost one and a half centuries of Russification, a variety of languages or ethnic groups is still distinguished (Geiger et al. 1959). A further example is found in Dardistan, the transition area between the Himalaya, the Karakorum and the Hindukush in northern Pakistan, which Jettmar (1979:vii) has called a "giant ethnographic museum."

The century-long seclusion of old-settled high mountain regions furthered their overpopulation. It could only be reduced by an out-migration or by the creation of new employment opportunities in the mountains themselves. A permanent out-migration is hardly a feasible solution in many developing countries as underemployment and unemployment prevail as well outside the mountain regions. Furthermore, the creation of new jobs in the mountains is a problem even in industrialized countries because of the locational disadvantage; and how much more is this the case for the poorly accessible high mountains in the developing countries.

It is, therefore, not surprising that in many high mountain regions of the type A1 the following *characteristics of overpopulation* can be observed. The agricultural potential of the different altitudinal zones is completely exploited; that is, in the form of a mixed agriculture of field cultivation and livestock operation, frequently also with additional horticulture. Agriculture is almost totally oriented towards self-sufficiency, but can cover only part of the need. Sometimes there is an over-use which can cause irreparable damage. The already mentioned soil erosion has to be listed in this context. It threatens to destroy the agrarian base of the mountain population wherever steep slopes have been cleared and transformed into fields, and where the remaining forests are used as pasture and as a source of firewood. Such irreversible ecological damages can be noted, for example, in parts of the Indian and Nepalese and Pakistan Himalayan foothills where population pressure on the available land has increased rapidly and in an uncontrolled fashion (Allan 1986; Eckholm 1975; Ives and Messerli 1981). These damages are also already a threat in large parts of the Peruvian Andes (Millones 1982).

Whenever the population exceeds the agricultural carrying capacity, and when permanent out-migration is only possible in a limited fashion, additional non-agricultural sources of income, often outside the mountain region, are the only alternative for a secure living. Until recently, the crafts provided additional non-agrarian income in many mountain villages, as for example, in the Hindukush of Afghanistan and in some valleys of the Himalaya. During the last decades, however, the crafts have largely succumbed to the competition from manufactured goods. In a similar way, this is true for the former transport trade and the migratory commerce. These types of employment have become victims in part to the closure of political boundaries as in the Himalaya, and in part to the competition from motorized traffic as in the Hindukush (Groetzbach 1969; Schweinfurth 1982).

Thus the gain of additional earnings outside the mountain regions, made possible by temporary short-term or seasonal labor migrations, remains an alternative. These migrations may be fairly common in the mountain regions of the type A1, though in varying intensities. They are particularly well developed in parts of the Pontic Mountains in northern Turkey (partially in the form of "guest worker" migration), in the Elburz Mountains, in parts of the Hindukush and Himalaya (Groetzbach 1969, 1982; Hourcade 1978; Staley 1969; Allan 1985). Employment as military soldiers and mercenaries, serving in armies, is still an employment opportunity which has become traditional. One may here recall the formerly famous Gurkha brigades of the British whose soldiers returned to their mountain villages after the completion of their service, where they lived off their pension. Military service is also very popular in the mountain communities of India and Pakistan. In this way, substantial funds can flow even into isolated mountain valleys. Thus, in the Garhwal Himalaya, for instance, a true "money order economy" has developed (Negi 1981).

The mountains of type A2 were in the past in a similar situation. During the middle of the nineteenth century the Alps represented a highly overpopulated region which—even if spatially rather differentiated— shared the same characteristics of overpopulation as described above: domestic trades, migratory commerce, migratory crafts and seasonal agricultural activity were wide-spread.

The situation in the Alps and in other high mountain regions of Europe has totally changed since the last century with their modernization at first by railways and later by individual motor car traffic. The temporary migrations were largely replaced by a permanent outmigration that frequently took the form of an "altitude or mountain flight" and led to "de-settlement" in unfavorable locations (Ulmer 1935). The pronounced retreat of agriculture on the one hand is contrasted on the other hand by a dynamic expansion of new, non-agrarian job opportunities. Along the major transportation lines in the large valleys, manufacturing plants and commercial enterprises sprang up, as was the case in the Tyrolean Inn Valley and in the Etsch (Adige) Valley. In the higher communities, mainly in the lateral valleys, tourism brought at least seasonal additional income. In this way, the carrying capacity of high mountains was in some parts considerably increased. Nevertheless, the supply of non-agrarian jobs is not everywhere sufficient. Therefore, today, a strong extra-regional employment activity still persists in some peripheral Alpine valleys supported by weekly and monthly commuter and temporal employees, as it is the case in the district of Lienz/East Tyrol (Figure 3.2; Groetzbach 1981).

Mainly as a result of *mass tourism*, the function of the European high mountain regions has undergone basic changes. Apart from the sea coasts, the high mountains are today the most attractive recreation areas, and thus the yearly destination of many million visitors. The seasonal increase of population numbers in the high mountains has indeed led to

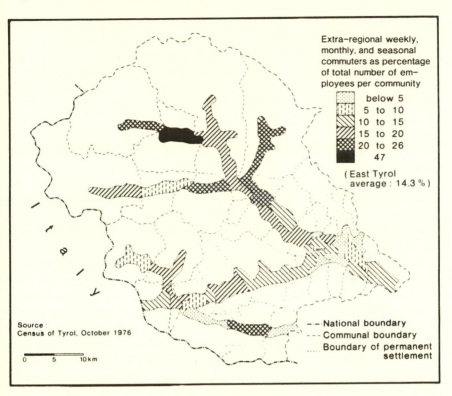

Figure 3.2 Extra-regional Commuters from the Communities of East Tyrol (District of Lienz, Austria), 1976. (From Groetzbach 1981: 81.)

economic prosperity, but also, at the same time, to new problems. For the modern forms of utilization also endanger the ecological balance even though in a different way from the former population pressure. Tourism, and here namely winter sports, hydroelectric power plants with their necessary diversion of entire river systems, the building of highways and roads—all of these activities result in substantial encroachments on high mountain landscapes. The protection and the conservation of the landscape, including the cultural landscape of the recreational space of high mountains shaped by man, has become an important new task which is in strong competition with economic interests. The alpine cultural landscape in particular is threatened by the invasion of the modern urban leisure society.

The third type of the old and relatively densely settled high mountain regions (A3) are those in Communist countries, namely in the Soviet Union and in the People's Republic of China. Their population of mountain peasants was, especially in Central Asia, predominantly overlaid by nomads; thus these mountain regions, until into the twentieth century, formed part of the mountain type A1b. However, the traditional economic and social forms of living were largely eliminated by the forced collectivization and by the establishment of large state farms. The mountain pastoral economy, frequently characterized by huge herds, is run by specialized personnel. It appears, though, that some remainders of the traditional economy have survived, because in the mountains the coercive measures could not be implemented and controlled with the same consistency as in the forelands. In spite of the decreed modernization, a significant out-migration, which has the characteristics of a "mountain flight," exists as well in the high mountains of the Soviet Union. Here also, a few resorts were created, as in the Caucasus (Radvanyi and Thorez 1976, 1980) and in the Tien Shan. But unlike the mountains of the type A2 (especially the Alps), this tourism has remained limited to island-like areas.

It remains to characterize type B high mountains, which are limited to North America, especially to the Rocky Mountains and the coastal ranges, as well as to New Zealand (New Zealand Alps). The specific aspects of the cultural geography of these mountains have their origin on a very different type of spatial development and different political and socio-economic conditions. Having been almost uninhabited and used only by migratory hunters before the penetration of Europeans, these mountains until today have remained sparsely settled and populated. Thus in large parts of the Rocky Mountains of Colorado (Dupuis 1975) and in the High Country of the South Island of New Zealand, barely one permanent inhabitant lives on one square kilometer. Extensive and specialized agricultural land use is the norm. It consists almost entirely of a market-oriented livestock pastoral economy carried out in modern large enterprises, whereas a mountain peasantry based on self-sufficiency is lacking. In this manner, the agriculture is similar to that of type A3, even though it has a completely different basis; it is, however, in sharp contrast to the traditional agriculture in the mountains of type A1. The tourist development of the high mountains in North America and New Zealand is much more advanced than in those of the Soviet Union. Nevertheless, the centers of tourism also exhibit a scattered distribution, and this mainly in the form of National Parks or winter resorts (Lutz 1981; Rinschede 1981).

The Future of High Mountain Human Habitat

Finally, an attempt will be made to answer some questions about the cultural-geographical trends of the recent past, the present, and the future, in the high mountain regions of the world. In this regard, this short review can be summarized in the following three points.

First, the high mountains have been increasingly integrated into the overall economy and society of their respective countries. Contributing primarily to this "opening up of mountains" (Groetzbach 1976:113) have been the modern transportation development, migrations of workers, and tourism; and also the proliferation of the hydroelectric projects has to be mentioned in this context.

Second, the formerly dominant traditional mountain agriculture is affected by a sharp decline in all those countries in which the modern socio-economic development shows a dynamic progression.

Third, the most spectacular new function of many high mountain regions is to serve as a recreation space. This functional change is most advanced in the high mountains of urbanized and industrialized countries. However, it is also already effective, although only weakly, and in initial stages, in developing countries. Examples for mountain tourism in these regions are found in the Indo-Pakistani Himalaya, in the Elburz Mountains of Iran, in the high mountains of Turkey, in the High Atlas, and in the South American Andes.

The future of high mountains as human habitat lies probably in their transformation from an isolated, traditional area of disfavor to an area of seasonal recreation for population groups predominantly from large cities outside the mountain realm.

4

Comparative Geography of the High Mountains of the World in the View of Landscape Ecology

A Development of Three and a Half Decades of Research and Organization

Carl Troll

Conceptual Framework

The title refers to two scientific terms which the author developed during the years 1938 to 1940. The term "landscape ecology" was coined in 1938 for scientific and practical purposes within the context of the goals and methods of air photo interpretation. For the 110th anniversary of the "Gesellschaft fuer Erdkunde" in Berlin, the author had suggested the general theme of "Geographische Forschung and Luftbildwesen" (Geographical research and air photographs). The publication "Luftbildplan und oekologische Bodenforschung" (Air photograph and ecological soil research) resulted from the major paper presented by the author at this conference (Troll 1939a, 1943d). In this paper the author summarized his experiences from a one year cooperation with the German-Colombian airline company, SCADTA, and the international results of a highly diversified air photo interpretation. He concluded that:

> air photographs represent the landscape and the spatial variations of land-scape images. These landscape images are produced by specific functions and ecological linkages which exist between the geological base and the structural formation of rocks, between landforms and soil types, and between water balance and vegetation. Therefore, vegetation is mostly in the center of observation. . . . Even air photo archaeology . . . is largely based on evidence of the soil and vegetation ecology of cultural ruins. . . . Air photo interpretation is to a large degree "landscape ecology." Only 28 years later, the author proposed the term "Geoökologie" (Geoecology) as a synonymous designation for international use. [Troll, 1968b, 1970b, 1971]

The problems of a comparative geography of the high mountains of the world, i.e., of high mountains in highly diversified climatic zones, were discussed by the author for the first time in 1940. Having been appointed to the University of Bonn in 1938 (after having been professor in Berlin) he was asked to report on the results of his high mountain research in four continents at the annual meeting of the "Gesellschaft der Freunde und Foerderer der Universitaet Bonn" (Society of Friends and Supporters of the University of Bonn). I had undertaken extensive journeys in the tropical Andes of South America in 1926–1929 and had worked specifically on vegetation geography, Pleistocene landscape history, and the ecological bases of Indian high cultures. A one year expedition with K. Wien through the highlands of eastern Africa from southern Nubia to Capeland followed in 1933–1934. In 1937, I participated in the Himalaya expedition to Nanga Parbat overshadowed by the alpinistic failure resulting from an avalanche disaster. This expedition resulted in a profile through the northwestern Himalaya as well as a vegetation map of the Nanga Parbat Massif at the scale of 1:50,000 (Troll 1939b). It was complemented by a hike through the Sikkim-Himalaya to the Tibetan boundary at the Natu La.

Of all the impressions and results of these journeys, two have proven to be particularly fruitful: in a biological sense, the convergence of vegetative forms between the tropical and subtropical regions of the New World and the Old World despite a very different floral equipment—a convergence which extends through correspondingly similar spectra of lifeforms into the formations of plants (Troll 1959b, 1969) (Fig. 4.1). Geographically, probably the greatest impression was the experience of the cool and cold high belts of the tropical mountains "cold tropics," which lack the familiar thermal contrast of summer and winter but which exhibit larger daily contrasts in temperature (Troll 1951, 1955a). This results in fundamental differences in pedological, geomorphological, hydrological, glaciological, and biological-ecological processes, as well as in agricultural conditions (Troll 1961). In the report entitled "Studien zur vergleichenden Geographie der Hochgebirge" (Studies to the comparative geography of the high mountains of the earth), presented in 1940 (Troll 1941), for the first time an attempt was made to determine the term "high mountain" and the lower limit of high mountain environments for the different climatic zones in the perspective of "landscape ecology" (Troll 1955b, 1973c). Furthermore, new insights were presented concerning temperature conditions; radiation and radiation exposure; glacier types in lower latitudes; snow cover and ablation forms (*Penitentes* snow); and soil frost, frost-patterned soils, and solifluction.

One fact became evident at that time: the widespread perception of a gradual climatic change in the high tropical mountains from the hot lowlands to perpetual snow at altitudes of 4,500 m to 6,000 m similar to

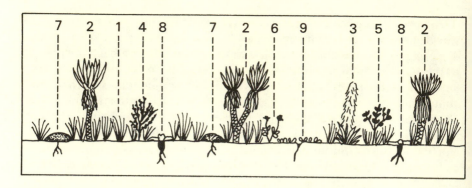

Figure 4.1   The Characteristic Life Forms of the *Paramo* Formation in Equatorial High Mountains. (1) Bunch grasses (tussocks). (2) Giant rosette plants with thick trunks and woolly leaves *(Espeletia* type). (3) Rosette plants scrubs with candle-like woolly inflorescences *(Lobelia* type). (4) Evergreen scrubs with a dense foliage of small squamous or rolled leaves *(Loricaria* type). (5) Evergreen broadleaved scrubs *(Befaria* type). (6) Scrubs with woolly leaves *(Helichrysum* type). (7) Hard cushion plants *(Azorella* type). (8) Acauluscent rosette plants with thick roots *Wernier* type). (9) Carpet-like halfwoody scrubs *(Acaina* type).

that in a horizontal direction from the equator to the poles—a notion which one tends to attribute to A. von Humboldt—is an error. Here is what I wrote at the time: "To each lowland climate belongs a graduation of mountain climates with different temperatures . . . Therefore, we have to supplement our existing climate classifications, e.g., the one by Koeppen . . . , by a third dimension, in general, we have to aspire to a three-dimensional analysis of climate, vegetation and landscapes, as a basis for comparative mountain studies" (cf. Troll 1961, 1962).

Analysis of Geofactors

This initial programmatic work was followed until about 1952 by systematic yet comparative studies of individual geofactors: (1) The seasonal or daily rhythm of temperature in the climatic belts of the earth by thermoisopleth-diagrams. This led to a representation of the contrast between the polar seasonal climates, tropical day climates (including those of the cold tropics), and the temperature seasonal climates (Troll 1943a, 1951). (2) The frequency of freeze-thaw action in the atmospheric and soil climates of the earth (Troll 1943b). (3) The climatic types at the snowlines (Troll 1955c). (4) The ablation forms of the snow cover and the *Penitentes* snow in the high mountains of the earth (Troll 1942, 1949). (5)

The frost-generated patterned soils and solifluction in the periglacial zones of the higher latitudes and high mountains (Troll 1944, 1947, 1948b). (6) The diurnal wind pattern of the tropical mountains and its influence on precipitation and vegetation (Troll 1952). (7) The three-dimensional synopsis of the climatological-ecological conditions in the lowlands and mountains between the poles and the equator, especially the influence of these conditions on patterned soils and on vegetative forms, soon led to the recognition of a basic asymmetry in the ecological arrangement of the northern and the southern hemisphere (Troll 1948a). (8) As the fluctuation between rainy periods and dry periods, i.e., between humid and arid seasons, is a determining factor for the climatic zonation of the tropical lowlands between rainforest and desert, it is similarly determining for the climatic zonation of the individual altitudinal belts (*tierra caliente, tierra templada, tierra fria, tierra helada, tierra nevada*). W. Lauer studied these conditions in a comparison between South America and Africa based on the average aridity and humidity of each month and drew ecologically significant "Isohygromene maps" for both continents (Lauer 1952). Thus, the tropical high mountain landscapes from the permanently humid *Paramos* to the seasonably humid *Puna* and to the permanently arid *Puna* de Atacama received their eco-climatological foundation (Figs. 4.2 and 4.3).

The eight mentioned studies of individual factors in the ecological characterization were carried out in the decade between 1942 and 1952 and were published—partially in condensed form. The interplay of the physical factors finds its best expression in the character of the vegetation cover. Therefore, vegetation studies, especially vegetation mapping in small regions, were undertaken during all previous travels, in order to record not only the general eco-climatological character of vegetation but also the local edaphic variations resulting from sil, topography, and soil water.

Comprehensive vegetation mapping for large areas was not possible, either in the Andes nor in the African mountains, because of the lack of topographic base material. I have compiled two topographic maps of the Cordillera Real of Bolivia during my travels in this region (Troll 1935). Only for the Nanga Parbat massif in the northwestern Himalaya could a vegetation map at the scale of 1:50,000 be compiled in 1937, as maps with contour-lines based on photogrammetric surveys were available, which R. Finsterwalder had recorded three years earlier.

Three-Dimensional Zonation of Mountains

Since 1952, several scholars have undertaken the task of representing entire mountain systems with the objective of ecological differentation of the landscape in three dimensions. During five years of work, Ulrich

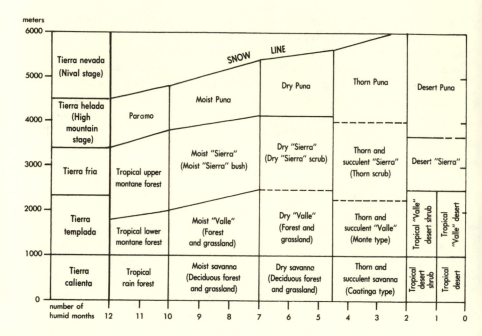

Figure 4.2   Horizontal and Vertical Arrangement of Climates and Climatic Vegetation Types in the Tropical Andes

Schweinfurth analyzed the distribution of vegetation types in the entire Himalaya system from the Yangtze Kiang to Kabul; he represented these types on a two folio map at the scale of 1:2,000,000 together with eight cross-profiles (Schweinfurth 1956). Based on this work, and on some of my older field investigatons, I was able to prepare for the research program. Nepal-Himalaya, a climato-ecological classification of the Himalaya based on vegetation zones and belts, as well as on small-scale topo-climatological features (radiation exposure, avalanche effects, valley winds) (Troll 1967). Based on the fieldwork of several summers, W. Haffner's (1965) recent work provides a highlight of ecological research in the Himalaya with a monograph on the vertical arrangement of the landscapes of central and eastern Nepal, from the lowlands of the Terai to the glaciers of Mount Everest. From his work in the Himalaya, U. Schweinfurth (1962) turned his research interests towards the southwest Pacific realm, and he analyzed the vegetation classification of Tasmania in a smaller ecological study. In a larger work, he studied New Zealand and portrayed the eco-climatological arrangement of the country's high mountains by a series of east-west profiles Schweinfurth (1966). H. V. Wissman (1960) represented the central Asiatic core region together with its transi-

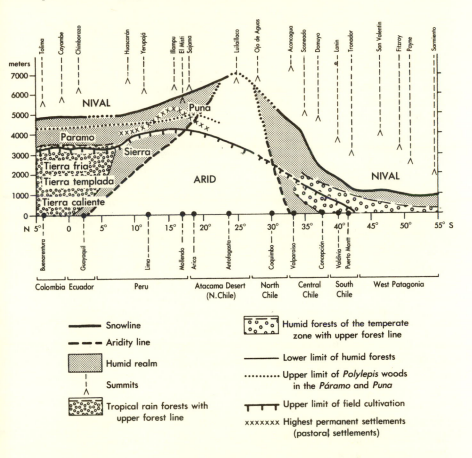

Figure 4.3   Ecological Limits and Evaluation of Living Zones in the Andes of South America

tion zones—the peripheral areas of Western China, Indochina, and the Himalaya—by a superbly reasoned study, magnificently illustrated by maps and profiles. Based on our geo-ecological perspectives, Henning (1972) using predominantly Russian sources, represented the three-dimensional arrangement of the entire Ural mountain system with its continuation into Novaya Zemlya. She portrays the ecological structure of the entire mountain system by a map and two separate longitudinal profiles for the western and the eastern slopes—ideal profiles through boreal Eurasia from the frost debris zone through the tundra, taiga, and deciduous forest zone to the Central Asiatic steppe zone. H. Ern (1966) studied the three-dimensional arrangement of the Iberian Peninsula in a broad profile from the coast of Cantabria and Galicia to the Sierra

Nevada. Most recently, Henning (1974) furnished a general geo-ecological representation of the Hawaiian Islands, which shows the extreme contrast within the zone of trade winds between the windward and the leeward sides of mountains and their transition towards the seashore. During the last decade, a large interdisciplinary research program has been carried out under the auspices of the "Deutsche Forschungsgemeinschaft" (German Research Association) in the highland of Mexico, specifically in the basin of Puebla-Tlaxcala and the surrounding volcanic high mountains. Under the direction of W. Lauer, the Bonn research team has recorded the various factors of the ecological balance of the landscape, especially climate, weather patterns, soils, geomorphology, and vegetative cover (refer to the series of articles by W. Lauer and research fellows 1973). Previously W. Lauer had established the link between the South American Andes and Mexico by his work in the mountains of Central America (Lauer 1959, 1968).

Research Organizations

The foundation of the "Akademie der Wissenschaften und der Literatur" (Academy of Sciences and Literature) in Mainz (West Germany) in 1949 offered the first possibility of providing a certain organizational framework for studies of comparative high mountain geography. The author, who was entrusted with the direction of the Academy's Commission for geographical research, recognized a welcome opportunity to include among the tasks supported by the Commission the rather general theme—High Mountain Geography—under the title: "The three-dimensional zonation of the climates, the vegetation, and the landscape ecology of the earth." His election to the Executive Committee of the International Geographical Union (IGU) in 1956 and to the position of President of the IGU in 1960 facilitated the task of advancing the ecological synoptic perspective at the international level (Troll 1958, 1966a, 1968a, 1970b). In 1965 he was invited by UNESCO to organize a symposium on the "Geooekologie der Gebirgslander der tropischen Amerikas" (Geo-Ecology of the Mountainous Regions of the Tropical Americas) in connection with the Latin America Regional Conference of the IGU in Mexico. (*Geoecology* 1968a; Troll 1968b). This again was an occasion for the Program Committee of the IGU to suggest to the author the foundation of an Ecological Commission at the time of the termination of his mandate in the Executive Committee of the IGU. This Commission was oriented towards the analysis of mountain regions and received the name "Commission on High-Altitude Geoecology." Within the framework of a comparative global program, three international geoecological symposia have been organized up to now: in 1969 in Mainz, about the High-Mountain Regions of Eurasia (*Geoecology* 1972); in 1972, about the High Mountains of North America and about the upper timberline in different climatic zones (*Geoecology* 1973a; Troll 1973b); and finally, in 1974, about the geoecological relations between the temperate zone of the southern hemisphere and the tropical mountains (Mainz Symposium in 1974).

Parallel with the foundation of the IGU Commission, the author was able to undertake, within the framework of monographs for the "Akademie der Wissenschaften und der Literatur" (Academy of Sciences and Literature), the editing of a series of publications entitled "Erdwissenschaftliche Forschung" (Geoscientific Research), which among other research areas is dedicated to the theme of Geoecology. Among the ten volumes which have appeared so far, four are devoted to the subject area of Geoecology: Volume III about the Kalahari (Leser 1971), Volume IV about the High-Mountain Regions of Eurasia (Troll 1972a), Volume VIII about the upper timberlines in the Alps and in Fennoscandia (Holtmeier 1974), and Volume IX about the Geoecology of the Hawaiian Islands (Henning 1974).

The Nature of High Mountains

In Central Europe, a distinction is made between the terms "High Mountain" and "Medium Mountain." But if we want to formulate the term globally and do not base it solely on elevation above sea-level or on relief energy (N. Krebs) but on geoecological considerations, we have to use the characteristics of geomorphology (the morphological forms of High Mountains), of climate, of soil formation (frost soils), and of plant and animal life (Troll 1973c). A High Mountain has to rise above the upper timber- and tree-line, e.g., in the Bavarian Alps above 1,500 m above sea-level, in Mexico above 4,000 m, and in eastern Tibet above 4,500 m. The geomorphology of High Mountains derived from the erosive effect of mountain glaciations during the Pleistocene, and finds its lower limit at the approximate altitude of the last Pleistocene snowline, which in our mid-latitudes does not deviate much from the present upper timberline. As a further criterion we can use the lower limit of the present periglacial dynamics of frost soils which results in very strong solifluction. Studies of the lower limit of patterned soils and of the slightly lower limit of solifluction have been done in different climatic zones, especially by the research teams under the direction of H. Poser (Gottingen) and G. Furrer (Zurich).

Soil Frost

Determining factors in the ecological characterization of High Mountains in different climatic zones of the earth are in general thermic conditions, especially frost conditions, and in the seasonally humid zones and in the arid zones of lower latitudes the hygric seasons as well. A noticeable expression of this is found in the vegetation and in the spectrum of animal life in High Mountains (Fig. 4.1). The largest contrasts in soil frost forms exist on the one hand in the Arctic region and in the Sub-Arctic High Mountains, and on the other hand in the High Mountains of the arid Tropical regions (Fig. 4.4). In the Polar seasonal climate of Spitsbergen, permafrost occurs already at a depth of one meter, above the permafrost, a thawed soil with a high water concentration exists in summer. In contrast, on the South Peruvian volcano El Misti at an elevation of 4,760 m above sea-level, the soil freezes every night (337 days with freeze-thaw action) to a depth of only a few centimeters which leads to the formation of needle ice. Consequently, the forms of the frost soil are very different: in Spitsbergen, soils are composed of stone nets and of stone stripes of large dimensions and strong solifluction is restricted to the summer months; in the tropical Andes of Southern Peru at an elevation of 4,500 to 5,000 m above sea-level, miniature stone nets and stone stripes exist to a depth of only a few centimeters. They are moved every day by superficial needle ice and as a result of this, are not covered by vegetation.

Humidity and Aridity

The tropical Andes of South America are most suitable for the study of the hygric conditions of tropical mountains. The tropical Andes are crossed by the "climatic equator" at approximately 4° North, and by the axis of the dry belt at the margin of the tropics between Antofagasta and La Rioja; between these two lines they reach the level of high mountains over almost the whole distance (Lauer 1952; Troll 1959a). As in the tropical lowlands with a decreasing number of humid months, the landscape belts exhibit a zonation from the equatorial rainforest, to the tropical moist savannas, to the dry savannas, to the thorn and succulent savanna, to the desert savanna, and to true desert. Thus the landscape belts in the high Andes show the transition from the permanently moist *Paramos* at the equator, to the moist *Puna*, to the dry *Puna*, to the thorn and succulent *Puna*, and to the semi-desert *Puna* de Atacama near the Tropic of Capricorn (see Fig. 4.2).

Glaciers and Snow

The glaciers of the tropics have the same morphological characteristics as those in temperate latitudes (*nevé* crest, *Bergschrund*, *nevé* trough glacier tongue), but they exhibit a totally different glacial budget according to the prevailing day climate. As a perennial snow cover is lacking in the high mountain belt of the *Puna* Andes, even in the glacier tongues, the

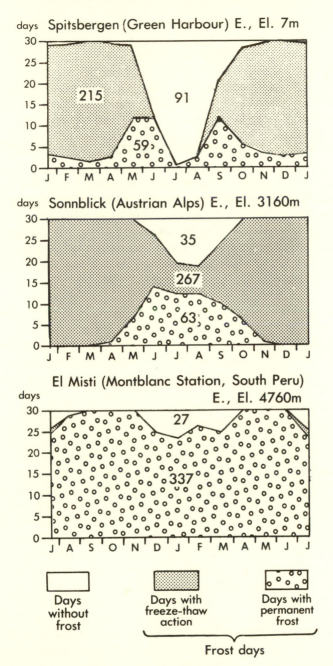

Figure 4.4   Seasonal Distribution of Frost-free, Freeze-Thaw, and Permanent Frost Days. *Top:* the Arctic region; *middle:* the High Alps; *bottom:* the arid tropical mountains.

lower melting zone of the glaciers is not affected by a seasonal summer ablation but by a daily ablation during the whole, or almost the entire, year. Wherever in the tropics long lasting snow covers occur below the snowline, they coincide with the zenithal rainy seasons (during the high sun positions). In this case, twice a year, longer lasting equinoctial snow covers can be observed in the equatorial *Paramos*. But the famous *Penitentes* snow (*Nieve de los Penitentes*) is not a characteristic element of the tropical high mountains. It is formed every year in summer from thick winter snow covers by very strong high mountain radiation, under conditions of clear skies and low air humidity. Thus the snow is not ablated through melting but through direct evaporation. These processes occur in high mountains of the so-called Mediterranean climatic zones with dry summers and moist winters. For a long time, these snow types were only known from the Argentinean and Chilean High Andes between 36° S and 27° S, at elevations between 3,000 and 5,000 m above sea-level. In the Old World, the conditions mentioned above exist in the same combination in one region only, namely in the high mountains of Southwest Asia, i.e., in the Hindukush (Afghanistan), and in a few high mountain regions of northern Iran: that is, between 32° N and 38° N, and at elevations between 4,300 m and 5,800 m above sea-level. The occurrence of these snow forms became much later than those in South America (Troll 1942; Schweizer 1969, 1972). It is true that in many tropical mountains the radiation conditions for the formation of *Penitentes* snow are present, but, as a substantial winter snow cover is lacking, the *Penitentes* snow can be formed only from local snow accumulations and under specific weather conditions, nowhere, however, in its genuine and widespread form as in the two mentioned mountain regions. In other subtropical regions the summer aridity at corresponding elevations is lacking.

Mountain Winds

A further characteristic of high mountains are the daily local mountain winds. At isolated mountains they are called "slope winds"; in the valley systems of mountains they are given the terms of "mountain" and "valley winds"; between plains and high plateaus they are called exchange winds. As they are the result of daily temperature differences, they are, of course, much more characteristic of the tropical mountains than of those in higher latitudes. They are most strongly developed in areas of high plateaus in lower latitudes. Where these conditions exist in the vicinity of coasts, the system of mountain winds may be linked to that of land and sea winds. The strongest effects of mountain winds can be observed in the deeply eroded valleys of the glacis of high plateaus. The author was able to observe these phenomena with all their modifications from 1926 to 1928 on his voyages across the Bolivian and North Chilean Andes. He could also study the effects of the mountain winds on the vegetation on the slopes of the Western Cordilleras towards the desert and foggy coast of Northern Chile, as well as in the different transection valleys which cut the eastern glacis of the highlands in the direction of Amazonia and the Gran Chaco (Troll 1952). The regular pattern of the winds observed in these regions was confirmed in other tropical mountains (Colombia, Venezuela, Mexico, Ethiopia, Natal-Lesotho) by Schweinfurth (1956, 1972), and also in the valleys of the Himalayas and western China.

Truly fascinating are the contrasts in the vegetation resulting from the daily wind pattern in the transection valleys of the Cordillera Real of Bolivia, where an altitudinal difference of 4,000 to 5,000 m exists between the valley floor of the Rio de la Paz and the snow-covered peaks of the mountains. During the day hours, a strong valley wind blows from the wooded eastern slopes of the mountains across the dissected divide of the Cordillera towards the dry Titicaca-highlands. The clouds, which are whipped across the crest of the mountains by this wind, form a daily *Foehn* cloud wall over the mountains, and are abruptly dissolved over the *Altiplano*. In the transection valleys, stormy winds set in during the late morning. They blow not only up the valley, but also as slope winds downhill on both sides of the valley. During the day, on both slopes at an altitude of 3,000 m–3,600 m above sea-level, they produce cloud banks and cloud forests, which are ramifications of the contiguous cool temperate mountain forests of the eastern slopes. Covered with characteristic *Polylepis*-trees (*Qenua*) they peter out in wedges towards the dry interior of the mountains (Fig. 4.5a). Very different conditions occur on the valley floors. Going upstream from the hot rainforest valleys of the east, one passes in rapid succession: moist rain forest, Quebracho dry forest, thorn and succulent shrubs, and finally, at about 1,500 m above sea-level at the deepest part of the valley entrenchment, even desert. These contrasts can be explained by the fact that descending air movement occurs above the valley floor as a compensating flow to the ascending slope winds. This descending air has a drying effect, which is strongest at the deepest entrenchment of the valley between the adjacent glacier covered mountains (Fig. 4.5b).

Radiation Exposure

A further aspect by which the mountains of higher and lower latitudes can be distinguished in an ecological sense is their exposure to solar radiation. In our latitudes, characterized by an oblique angle and seasonal change of radiation, the differences between the sunny and the shady sides are quite great. The wine-grower as well as the mountain farmer in medium mountains ("winter slopes" and "summer slopes" in the Black

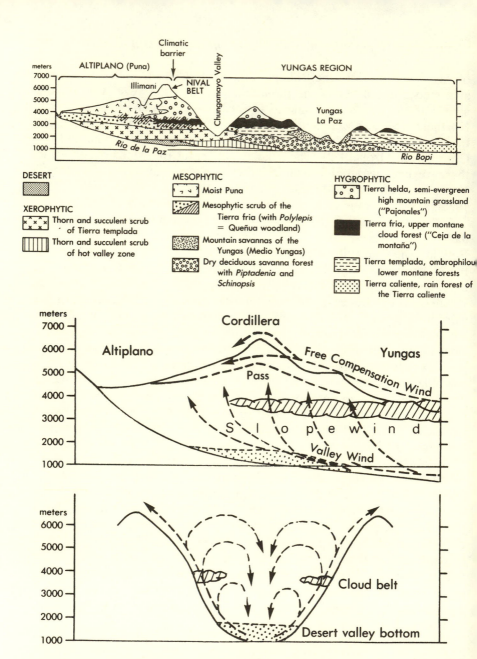

Figure 4.5 Distribution of Vegetation and the Daytime Wind System in the Valley of the Rio de la Paz in the Cordillera Real of Bolivia (the Eastern Andes). *Top:* Cross-section through the Cordillera Real and the valley of the La Paz River from Altiplano to the Yungas area, showing vegetation belts and the local landscape types. *Bottom:* Daytime wind system in the valley, with longitudinal section *(above)* and transverse section *(below)*.

Forest) are well aware of these differences. However, even larger is the contrast in the higher Alpine valleys (*adret* and *ubac* in the French Alps). Using the Paznaun Valley of West Tyrol, H. Boehm registered this contrast and also the effect of mountain shadows numerically and cartographically, and also studied its effect on the mountain agriculture (Boehm 1966). According to my experience, the most pronounced effects of radiation exposure are found in the mountains of the subtopics, approximately between the latitudes of 25° and 40° (Troll 1967, 1972c). It is evidence that these effects are not found in tropical regions where the exposure to the sun varies seasonally from north to south. In the high mountains of these regions a difference in radiation exposure sometimes occurs between east and west resulting from daily contrast in cloud cover.

The maximum effect of solar radiation exposure in subtropical latitudes, e.g., in the northwestern Himalaya with its long winter snow cover, has the following causes: (1) the high proportion of summer radiation in these latitudes, especially at higher elevations where the winter radiation on the soil is further reduced by the snow cover; (2) the particularly small amount of diffuse radiation as a proportion of total radiation in these subtropical latitudes, and this again is particularly so at higher elevations. In other words, the shadows, which contain only diffuse radiation, are particularly dark in the high mountains of these latitudes. According to E. Flach (1965), the proportion of diffuse radiation at Mt. Evans (Colorado) at an elevation of 4,355 m above sea-level amounts of only 0.05% of total radiation. The effect of the radiation exposure in the northwestern Himalaya, in eastern Tibet, and in the Tien Shan is often so pronounced that dark coniferous forests over a black humus soil on the shady sides face *Artemisia* steppes on the sunny sides or, in the high parts of the mountains, moist willow and rhododendron shrubs on the shady sides are found opposite dry dwarf *Juniper-Ephedra* heaths. H. V. Wissmann (1960–61) has cartographically represented those areas of the mountains at the southern and eastern peripheries of Tibet in which the forest is limited to the shady sides.

Agro-ecological Effects

The climatic peculiarity of tropical mountains must certainly also have its effect on agricultural land use, where it penetrates into high altitude zones. For instance, on the high plateaus of Ecuador, cultivation is no longer limited to specific seasons, under conditions of similar temperatures throughout the year and sufficient precipitation during all months. Here one can observe at the same time fields with young sprouting crops, those with more mature stands, and those ready to be harvested. Potatoes, as well, are growing in every season, which makes storage for months redundant. The situation is different in the *Puna* Andes of Peru and Bolivia with their contrast between rainy and dry seasons. But here the Indians of the pre-Hispanic time, foremost the Aymara and Quechua Indians, know how to adapt their land use in a particular way to the peculiarity of the tropical highland climate (Troll 1943c). Maize, the only cereal known in pre-Hispanic time, was the staple food in the warmer valleys up to an elevation of approximately 3,500 m above sea-level. Although frosts do in general already occur at 3,000 m above sea-level, the cultivation of maize was possible as it was cultivated during the rainy season when frost occurs less frequently (Fig. 4.6). The situation is again different in the higher settlement areas, especially on the Bolivian-Peruvian *Altiplano*, where the basin of Lake Titicaca at an altitude of 3,800 to 3,900 m above sea-level was, and still is, one of the most densely populated areas of the country. Before the introduction of the European cereals wheat and barley, the population was dependent on the cultivation of a single cereal, *Chenopodium Quinoa*, but mainly on different tuberous plants, potato, oca (*Oxalis tuberosa*), mashua (*Tropeaolum tuberosum*), and ullucu (*Ullucus tuberosa*); however, these crops cannot be preserved at altitudes where frosts occur regularly. It was, however, precisely the frost which the Indians knew to use for the processing of these crops, producing within a few weeks dry tubers with an unlimited durability from the freshly harvested tubers. In the process used, the tubers are for several weeks alternately exposed to frost during the nights and to running water during the days, which leads to dissolution of protein and cellulose and leaves a substance of pure starch tubers (*chunos*).

This invention, which made the settlement of these highlands possible, was one of the preconditions for the development of the Andean high

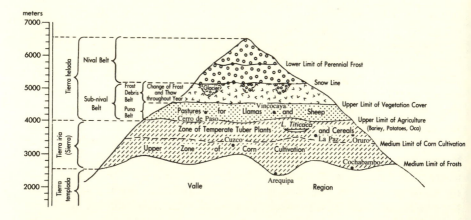

Figure 4.6   Climate-Ecological Gradation of the High Andes of Southern Peru and Northern Bolivia

civilizations, and finally for the superiority of the Quechua Indians and the expansion of their Inca Empire (Troll 1943c). Field cultivation, today based also on barley, reaches to an altitude of approximately 4,100 m above sea-level. Above this altitude follows the zone of pastures of the *Puna* region, in which—also as an important basis for cultivations—the wool-producing animals, the llama and the alpaca, have been bred since early times. The zone of high pastures reaches its upper limit in the more humid eastern parts of the *Puna* with the nightly occurrence of frost and with the upper limit of a contiguous vegetation cover. In the dry *Puna* of southwestern Peru, this limit extends even higher. In this region, Bowman (1916) found probably the highest permanent agrarian settlement in the world at an elevation of 5,210 m above sea-level—a region of permanent pastures in the winterless *Puna*.

Differentiation of the High Mountain Belt

So far, we have familiarized ourselves with the many effects of boreal, tropical, and subtropical climates on the ecological characteristics of high mountains. In comparing these characteristics in a systematic way, and in attempting to establish a terminological differentiation of high mountain types, three regular transitions should be observed:

1. In a global perspective, taking the meaning of H. Lautensach, from polar to equatorial high mountains. Here I would like to propose establishing the limit of polar characteristics where the lower limit of high mountain criteria reaches sea-level;
2. In temperate regions, from extreme maritime to extreme continental high mountains;
3. In certain latitudes, from permanently humid to arid high mountains.

The terms "subalpine," "alpine," "high alpine" (or "subnival"), and "nival," frequently used in the literature for the vertical gradiation (Lautensach's "hypsometrischer Formenwandel"), are quite suitable for the mountain regions of Western and Central Europe and for comparable climatic belts in other parts of the world. However, the term "alpine" is not appropriate for tropical and arid mountains, and it is hardly suitable for Northern Europe. A number of local designations exist which could be used in a general sense, similar to the term "alpine," for an ecological characterization of high mountain types; for example, *Field* (*Fjall, Fjell*) in Scandinavia, *Golez* (and accordingly *Podgolez*) in the Urals, *Paramo* for the humid high mountains, and *Puna* for the arid high mountains in tropical regions.

For a general designation of all high mountain types, their relative location with respect to the snowline provides a suitable criterion. As all climates beyond the snowline from polar to equatorial regions are designated as "nival," the term "subnival" is used for the altitudinal belts below the snowline. I have proposed (1972a) using the term in a wider sense for all altitudinal belts from the lower limit of permanent snow to the upper forest line onto the lower limit of the periglacial dynamic processes of the frost soil. The subnival belt could then be subdivided into a lower subnival zone (corresponding to the alpine zone in Central Europe) and an upper subnival zone (the hitherto used term "subnival" corresponding to the frost debris zone of periglacial morphology).

A particularly good understanding of the specific ecological nature of high mountains is gained by a study of the upper forest and timberlines and their transition into the high mountain zones. For these transitional belts, vegetation researchers have suggested the term "ecotones" (Tansley and Chipp 1926). Hustich (1953) has established the following zonation for the forest-tundra-ecotone (Fig. 4.7):

1. The limit of economic forests in which the cutting of timber can be carried out without jeopardizing the natural vegetation of forests;
2. The limit of biological forests or the limit of the contiguous forest;
3. The timberline or the line connecting pioneer individual trees or tree groups;
4. The species line to which timber-forming species can still grow under the protective cover of winter snow without, however, reaching the true height of trees.

In the *high mountains of the alpine type* (e.g., the Alps, the Carpathians, the Rocky Mountains, the Altai, northern Japan), the decisive ecological factors are the summer heat (according to duration and intensity) and the winter snow cover (according to duration and thickness), including the specific effect of snow avalanches (refer most recently to the work of Holtmeier 1974). The snow cover which accumulates more in the valleys and depressions, on the one hand protects the shrubs and the *Krummholz* from the winter cold, but it also shortens the vegetation period and, resulting from the accumulation of cold air above the snow surface, increases the frost danger (frost dryness) for the trees, which consequently reach higher altitudes on the open slopes than in the small valleys. The coniferous trees forming the frost limit are already mechanically eliminated in the avalanche furrows. Through the accumulation of avalanche snow farther down, a complete inversion of the vegetation profile may occur (Troll 1939b). On the ridges at the timberline, on which the winter snow is completely blown away, only high alpine dwarf shrubs (for example *Loiseleuria procumbens*) can still grow because of the strong frost dryness. Typical in the Central European mountains is the *Krummholz* belt which survives under the protection of the snow cover and from which individual weathered spruces emerge, fighting a hard battle against

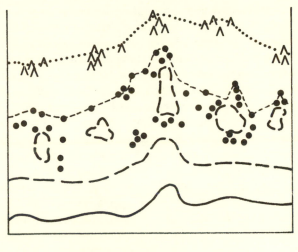

———— Economic forest line

— — — Limit of the contiguous forest
          (physiognomic forest line)

- - - - - Treeline or limit of pioneer individual
          trees or tree groups

    ●   Individual tree

·········· Species line (limit to which timber line
          forming species can still grow as
          dwarf or *Krummholz* woods)

   ⋀   Individual specimen

Figure 4.7   The Forest and Timberlines of "Forest-Tundra-Ecotone" at
the North Polar Limit of Forests

wind, frost and icy blasts. In the Rocky Mountains of North America, the
Krummholz and the weathered firs (*Picea Engelmanni* or *Abies la-
siocarpa*) are formed by the same species. The effects of the winter snow
protection and of the frost dryness can also be seen in summer from
growth forms of the trees and from the preservation condition of their
foliage. Completely different in every aspect, of course, is the *upper limit
of forests in the humid* tropical mountains. Here we find evergreen
deciduous trees, which frequently border sharply in dense stands on the
high mountain grasslands. One could perhaps designate as *Krummholz*
the shrubs of *Ericaceas*, or of *Helychrysum*, or the stem-forming ferns of

the family of *Lomaria*. But in an ecological sense they are not all the result of seasonal cooling or even snow cover. The stands of timber of *Polylepis* species at the forest limit, or even as islands high above the forest limit, in the tropical Andes of South America show particular relationships to the soil temperature and to the soil water. They grow predominantly on block fields. The *Polylepis tomentella*, a particularly frost-resistant species, reach in their stands almost 5,000 m above sea-level in the dry *Puna* of northern Chile, which represents the *highest growth of timber on earth*. But back to the humid tropical regions. Here, the contiguous mountain or cloud forest reaches its upper limit at 3,000 to 4,000 m above sea-level. These are highly mixed forests in a floristic sense with dozens of tree varieties from very different species which, however, show a surprising similarity in their appearance—a dense evergreen foliage cover which is limited to the exterior cover, with enough space below for epiphytes of all varieties (evergreen umbrella-canopy trees). Thus, this is certainly an adaptation to the specific temperature, radiation, and humidity conditions which, so far, however, are difficult to analyze because of lack of field experiments (Troll 1959a). The often very sharply marked limit of the forest towards the high mountain grassland could have been created in some places by natural or human induced forest fires, but certainly not in all instances. The designation of an *Ericaceas* belt, which von Humboldt has given to this highest zone of the tropical most forest in America, is also valid for the corresponding mountain forests in the tropical regions of the Old World (for example *Erica arborea, Philippia diff. spec., Rhododendron arboreum,* tree *vacciniae*). In a macro-climatic sense, the general temperature decrease, and in some cases also the decrease of precipitation and humidity of the air (belt forests) are precise factors for the upper limit of the forests in tropical regions. The particular location and course of this limit—the lack of forest on open ridges, the higher elevation of the forest in ravines—has topoclimatic and thermic, as well as hygric, causes.

Mountains of the Arid Core Areas and of the Mediterranean Climatic Zone

It is not possible to portray here all the eco-climatological variations of the nature of high mountains. A particular difficulty exists in the most arid core areas of the continents, in which a forest belt is no longer found, and in which even on the highest summits the snowline is barely, or not at all, reached (Troll 1972b). In the highlands of Asia, in northwestern Tibet, the limit of aridity climbs well over 5,000 m above sea-level and thus approaches the present snow-line (6,400 m) (von Wissman 1960–61). In the driest region of the earth, in the western Puna de Atacama of northern Chile, because of the extreme evaporation in the highland desert, even the highest summits Ojo del Salado (6,885 m) and Llullaillaco (6,723 m) have no true glaciers (Lliboutry 1958) (Fig. 4.3). In the core area of the Sahara desert belt, semi-desert conditions prevail even in the summit regions of the Ahaggar Massif (3,003 m) and of the Tibesti mountains (3,415 m). Here, clear-cut criteria for a numerical delimitation of the high mountain zone according to vegetation, morphology and soil dynamics are lacking (Messerli 1972).

Finally, a short overview of the Mediterranean climate zone between the Sahara and the Alps which extends from Spain and Morocco through the Middle East to the Hindukush and the western Pamirs will be given. In general, these mountains, located within a zone of summer-dry and winter-humid lowlands, can be divided from north to south into three sub-zones:

1. Within the *northern sub-Mediterranean zone*, the mountains still have precipitation during all seasons. Therefore, the forests are composed of central European coniferous trees or deciduous trees which are leafless in winter. Typical trees at the forest line are copper-beeches (*Fagus silvatica*, and *Fagus orientalis* in the eastern parts), partially mixed with *Abies alba*; and, in the drier mountains of Central Spain and Central Anatolia, forest pines (*Pinus silvestris*).

2. In the central, truly *Mediterranean sub-zone* these central European timber varieties are replaced by Mediterranean species: the winter leafless oak (*Quercus Fozza*) in Spain, the evergreen oak (*Quercus ilex*) in the western High Atlas, and the pine (*Pinus leucodermus*) at Mountain Olympus in Thessalia. H. Ern has portrayed this three-dimensional differentiation in Spain.

3. In the *southern Mediterranean sub-zone*, summer aridity also begins to penetrate into the high mountain zone, and thus gains an ecological significance for the upper timber and forest lines. Here different varieties of Juniper trees form the upper timberline: *Juniper thurifera* in the High Atlas at 3,100 m to 3,200 m, *Juniper excelsa foetidissima* and *drupacea* in the Anatolian Taurus at 2,200 to 2,300 m; *Juniper excelsa* in the southern Elburz at 2,500 to 2,700 m; and *Juniper polycarpa* in the southern Hindukush around 3,000 m above sea-level (v. Wissman 1972, Rathjens 1972).

For these southern Mediterranean-Middle Eastern high mountains with their summer-dry and radiation-intense climate, the transition into the true high mountain vegetation is also characteristic—one could call this a "Juniper-Tragacantha-Ecotone." Beyond the thin stands of Juniper, in parts already as their undergrowth, a very characteristic vegetation formation begins; namely one that is composed of woody, thorny, semi-spherical dwarf shrubs for which designations such as "hedgehog cushion-formation," "thorn cushion shrubs," and *Tragacantha*—hedgehog heaths were used (Gams 1956). Plants of very different families have taken this form, for example *Astragalus* and *Cytisus Papilionaccae, Alysum spinosum and Vella spinosa (Crucifers), Bupleurum spinosum (Umbillifers), Poterium spinosum (Rosaceae), Berberis (Berberideae), Acantholimon (Plumbaginaceae),* and *Ericacea pungens (Papilionaceae)*, among others. This information finds its upper limit in the Mediterranean high mountain steppes, in the High Atlas at 3,600 m, at Mt. Etna at 2,500 m, on the island of Crete at 2,400 m, and at Mt. Demavend only at 4,000 m above sea-level.

5

Mountain Agronomy in Ethiopia, Nepal and Pakistan

Peter T. S. Whiteman

Introduction

In spite of the general remoteness and isolation of mountains, centuries old human settlements are often to be found there. Conditions may actually be more conducive for living, as it is cooler and above the hot, humid lowlands infested with malaria and tsetse fly in the central African highlands, or mountains may have a more favored water supply, such as in the Jebel Mara in northwest Sudan, or be more fertile as with the volcanic soils on the slopes of Kilimanjaro. In other areas, conditions may be less congenial for living, but population pressure or refuge from former attacks and invasions have encouraged people to dwell in mountains. To live in mountains, people have had to adapt to the extremes imposed by the mountain environment and also have had to modify the environment to an extent that enables the crop growing potential to be harnessed. Success in doing this is reflected in the agricultural continuity over twenty centuries of stable systems of mountain land use that have evolved by trial and error to allow a balanced and sustained exploitation of resources.

Adaptation has been of three types. It has used the *natural* adaptations of indigenous species suited to the extremes of mountain climate; for example, yaks in the high mountains of Inner Asia, the annual tuber crops of potato, ullulucus and oxalis in the central Andes, and has optimized the ability of teff—the staple cereal in the Ethiopian highlands—to tolerate the seasonal surface waterlogging on the prevailing clay soils that are derived from basalt.

Several specific adaptations to mountain conditions have been selected from more widely occurring species, such as cold-tolerant sorghums for the Ethiopian highlands, hardy breeds of livestock, early maturing crops like buckwheat, barley to match the shorter growing season, and winter hardy varieties of wheat in the Himalayas.

A farming system has been developed with a mixture of complementary enterprises that fully uses the various resources available. It is the interaction between enterprises that increases the efficiency of overall resource use. There is an increasing reliance, through the mobility of livestock, on a vertically stratified land husbandry over a wide altitude range with a pattern of work requirement integrated with the seasonal movement of livestock and different sowing and harvesting dates for crops and fodder. Besides this local vertical stratification, there may be a more regional seasonal migration of pastoralists, for example the Gujars and Bakerwals in Kashmir, and by people searching for cash by labor or trading. The more climatically restricting the mountain environment, the more the farmer has to supplement his meager production by trading. The exchange rates in the Central Himalaya were such that before the border closure, the low yields of barley in the upper Central Himalayan hills were effectively doubled by first exchanging it with salt from Tibet in summer, and then bartering this salt with rice from the lowlands in winter (von Fuerer-Haimendorf 1975). Exactly the same trading pattern still occurs in northern Ethiopia. Grain from the highlands is exchanged for salt brought up to the highlands in Tigrai by camels from the Danakil desert, and then some of this salt is then traded again for grain from the irrigated lowlands of the Blue Nile plains.

Modification of the environment does the opposite. It adapts the environment to the crop, and this occurs at two levels. First, large scale transformation through conveying irrigation water to dry areas, e.g., the mountain oases in the trans-montane rainshadow areas of northern Nepal, India and Pakistan, the underground aqueducts, *karez*, in the western Hindukush, and attenuation of the natural slopes into terraces, either to create arable land from steep gradients or to control water distribution. This is possible through the retention of sparse rainfall by preventing run-off, thereby allowing uniform irrigation water application.

Second, there is a local in-field level of modification to ameliorate the growing conditions. Farmers are essentially applied plant physiologists, who alter such factors of the environment as they can manipulate to get the kind of production response that they want. Moisture and nutrient supply are those factors most obviously under his control. High technology control of temperature through protected greenhouses and heated beds are not feasible for developing countries' mountain farmers, but neverthless there is scope for influencing the ambient temperature, and most of this chapter will deal with traditional and new ways in which this can be done. It is the temporal and spatial variations in temperature that is such a marked feature of the mountain environment.

Before discussing specific examples from Ethiopia, Nepal, and Pakistan, it is necessary to consider the characteristics of agriculture in mountain environments.

The Mountain Environment

The problems confronting agriculture in mountain environments are intrinsically no different from those in other ecological situations. While there are many types of mountain environment (Price 1981), each with its own particular dominating feature, most exhibit the following physical environmental characteristics that impinge on agriculture and accentuate the basic problems resulting from the major effect of elevation and steep slopes.

Tropical mountains show a strong diurnal temperature variation, with excellent daytime growing conditions but with sharply falling night temperatures (partly because the nights are relatively longer than those in summer at higher latitudes), with, at altitude on clear nights, the risk of frost at any time of the year. This occurs at 3500 m on Mt. Kenya under the equator, compared with 4500 m in July in the Hindukush at 38 degrees North. Frost protracts the growth period so that "annual" cereals such as maize may take 13 months to mature above 3000 m in the equatorial Andes. Although it is the period of overhead sun, the Amharic word for the rainy season in Ethiopia, *Krempt,* means the cold season (10 degrees North). It also means that a different type of cold tolerance is needed throughout all stages of growth, compared with extra-tropical situations where it is only in the seedling stage in spring that resistance to low temperatures is required. In the mid-latitudes (25 to 30 degrees), both situations occur. At Jumla, 2300 m in northwest Nepal, there may be frost on the seedbed and at harvest on rice, plus the strong risk of cold-induced sterility through pollen damage at flowering in August if the night is cloudless. In the bimodal rainfall area of eastern Kenya, selected high yielding varieties of tropical sorghum will mature at 1500 m in the first rains that are caused by occasional convectional showers interspersed with long periods of sunshine, but the varieties fail to mature on the second rains, as they are susceptible to cold-induced diseases. A continuous cloud cover keeps the temperatures several degrees cooler.

Outside the equatorial region, not only does the seasonal variation in temperature become marked with increasing latitude and with its associated problems of frost and a long winter dormant period and a shorter growing season, but its interaction with topography produces a marked local variation. Superimposed on the general altitudinal temperature gradient is a mosaic of environmental differentiation imposed by the combined effect of slope and aspect, which is quite apart from the influence of relief on topographical shading and orographic cloud formation and rainfall. While the effect increases with higher latitudes, it is also exaggerated by altitude, so that in Nepal (27 to 29 degrees North), it is critical.

Several reasons explain this. The cultivated area extends through a higher range of altitude (up to 4000 m), where temperature contrasts are greater, as, at this altitude, cooling is rapid, and warmth is dependent on direct sunshine. For example, when sown in September, wheat takes 12 months to mature at 2800 m in northwest Nepal, on a steep north-facing slope, but only 9 months in the opposite aspect.

Steep slopes are cultivated up to 45 degrees, affecting not only the duration but also the intensity of incident radiation, and therefore the extent of soil warming and light transmisson through leaf canopy (see Figs. 5.1, 5.2).

Farmer's average field size is a small enough unit, about 0.05 ha, to be optimally managed to exploit the local variation in growing conditions. The mottled green/yellow appearance of a hillside of ripening barley "biologically" maps the small variations in aspect imposed by a range of spurs. This appearance results in a range of maturity of two weeks in fields only 50 m apart, and determines what, if any, the following crop might be to fit into the tight rotation before frosts terminate the growing season. Similarly, even on terraced land, the height of the terrace bank on the north-facing slope will be mirrored in the delayed maturity of the crop, reflecting the pattern of intercepted sunlight. Farmers in trans-Himalayan Nepal recognize this effect and even refine the crop pattern within the field, sowing the earlier maturing barley in a one metre strip in the shaded portion and the longer maturing and preferred wheat in the rest of the terrace.

Enough examples have been given to demonstrate the importance of understanding the physical basis for this variation. The fundamental cause of this habitat differentiation is the variation in radiation (Fig. 5.3) owing to the combined effect of slope, aspect, and season that results in a corresponding variation in thermal regime (length of growing season), potential evapo-transpiration (water balance), and photo-synthetic rate (dry weight increase). It should be emphasized that plants are highly sensitive biological thermometers and the pattern of their growth will closely reflect the temperature conditions prevailing during their growth and development. Even small differences of less than half a degree have a profound effect, because the response is accumulated over the duration of the growth period of the development phase. For crops growing near their lower temperature threshold, a small increase will have a marked effect compared with the same increase occurring when temperature conditions are near optimum. The interaction between the effect of latitude, altitude, topography, and cloud cover on the seasonal and local variation in temperature must be understood before useful interventions can be devised to modify and change the environment on a local scale. This can be effective as plants respond, not to the average condition over an area or in time, but to the immediate proximal and instantaneous situation that can be altered locally at a field level.

Further examples are now given to compare how farmers have tradi-

← Figure 5.1 Steep Slopes Being Cultivated in Northwest Nepal. Only south-facing slopes are cultivated at 300 m on recently cleared land. Note the attempt to attenuate slope through low stone wall on the contour.

Figure 5.2 Steep Slope in Nepal Being Prepared for Sowing. The summer monsoon rain will cause considerable soil loss; at 2200 m on a south-facing slope it is warm, but too dry to support a winter crop of barley. →

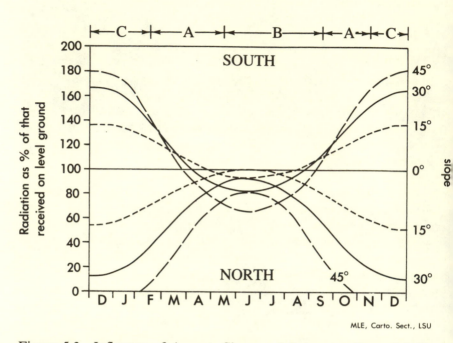

MLE, Carto. Sect., LSU

Figure 5.3   Influence of Aspect, Slope and Season on Potential Direct
Radiation in Jumla, Karnali, Nepal (29° N latitude)

Table 5.1   **Influence of Aspect, Slope and Season on Potential Direct Radiation in Jumla, Karnali, Nepal (29° latitude)**

	A	B	A	C	
Mean daily potential radiation (cal/cm²/day)	406 512 626 731 793	812 793 731 626 513		406 360	FLAT—0°
	370	761	370	47	N
	445	749	445	149	NW/NE
	582	744	582	330	E/W 30°
	679	699	679	513	SE/SW
	715	658	715	596	S

Period—A   Differences in insolation most effective on crop growth.
      —B   Differences in insolation minimal due to overhead sun and cloud cover.
      —C   Although large differences occur, their influence is small as winter cereal crops
              are dormant (above 2000m)

tionally done this in various mountain settings and on new ways to increase the efficiency of resource use.

Water Availability

In addition to the decreasing influence of monsoon in mainland Asia as one travels from east to west in the Himalaya range, there are also the attenuated rainshadow effects within and beyond the range. While the farmer cannot control this rainfed water supply, he does respond appropriately to the variations. Thus in the lower foothills cultivation is dominant on the north-facing slopes, where moisture rather than temperature is the overall limiting factor. At the upper limit (above 3000 m) the opposite situation prevails, with cultivation restricted to south-facing slopes. It is in the intervening partial rainshadow areas, however, where topography still exerts a strong local orographic influence, that cropping is still dependent on direct rainfall rather than irrigation. This situation occurs in northwest Nepal between 2000 to 2400 m, where there are enough heat units for double cropping on south-facing slopes, but there is inadequate moisture because evaporation rates are 20 percent higher and water stress is common with frequent crop failures. In contrast, the north-facing slopes have adequate moisture, but heat availability allows only one crop per year. The situation at this cross-over point between single and double cropping is very responsive to slight variations in temperature and moisture availability, because mean values of both are near the lower threshold of adequacy. Adjacent slopes that have contrasting aspects may possess quite different cropping patterns and intensities, and these variations are also reflected in the vegetation and forest types, especially in Nepal.

Superimposed on the increasing westward reduction of the summer monsoon is an opposite gradient of winter precipitation decreasing toward the east, thereby giving an unusual distribution of bimodal yearly rainfall in the Western Himalaya in Kashmir and in the eastern Hindukush mountains in Pakistan on the western side of the Indus River. The relative contribution of either summer or winter rainfall to the annual total varies both spatially and with season. Each peak is quite independent of the other. In some parts neither single peak is adequate for cropping, and water is stored in the soil from one season to supplement the following season's rainfall to provide enough for cropping. The choice of season for planting is according to the actual amounts that fall, in which winter is favored as the lower temperatures allow the crops to use the moisture more efficiently.

A similar situation occurs in Ethiopia where the inter-tropical convergent zone diminishes northwards, whereby 15 degrees N in Tigrai Province is the lower limit to rainfed cropping and vulnerable to slight variations below the norm. In addition, there are small incursions of *belg* rain in April on the east part of the central highlands that give a biomodal distribution. Farmers here sow a long maturing sorghum variety that is dependent on both rains and thereby is more vulnerable to failure.

Response in both Asia and Africa to the joint influence of both climate (imposed by latitude and altitude) and weather (synoptic events) in diminishing rainfall for cropping has been similar. Water conservation includes techniques for collecting run-off water into basins to supplement intermittent local rainfall that is inadequate for crop growth. These techniques that have been practiced extensively along the eastern edge of the Ethiopian Rift valley have been brought to a fine art in the highlands of Yemen. They are also common in the North-West Frontier Province districts in Pakistan. Flash flood water is diverted from wadis and then redistributed and impounded into basins in a communally agreed sequence.

Fallowing can be regarded as water conservation measured in time, but not in space. It stores a portion of a season's rainfall in the soil to supplement the next season's supply from rain. This technique is also practiced in Ethiopian and Pakistan mountains.

Where rainfall becomes too little for either of these techniques to work, the area becomes a desert, as is the case in northern Ethiopia. Here, there are no mountains high enough to have permanent snow, and if it were not for the glaciers in northern Pakistan, the area would also be an uninhabited desert. Indeed, even there, in catchments where there are no peaks above 5000 m to retain snow and allow ice accumulation, there is inadequate melt water for a full season's irrigation and the valleys have not been settled.

In these drier montane hinterland regions, irrigation is mandatory and therefore is dependent on both a source of meltwater and access to the meltwater across steep rugged terrain. Rather incongruously, glacier snouts with permanent ice may project as low as 2700 m into a surrounding barren rocky desert, yet barley is still cropped on adjacent south-facing slopes above at 3300 m. Unlike the wishful thinking of the Saudis who wanted to tow icebergs across the oceans to irrigate their deserts, the mountain dwellers of the Hindukush and Karakorum already have renewable "icebergs" sitting on top of towering peaks, and through courage and skill over the past two millenia, they harnessed this joint resource of gravity and water by intercepting the seasonal meltwater and directing it through remarkable channels to create oasis settlements in the valleys below.

Water availability varies from village to village for a combination of reasons. First there is the dependency on the relative contribution of glacier or snowmelt or spring water. Villages dependent upon snowmelt only are much more vulnerable to water shortage after winters with below average snowfall in the upper catchment. Second, the pattern in time and rate of melting is influenced by the amount and timing of snowfall and the prevailing temperature conditions in determining water availability. For example, if most of the snow comes late in winter, it does not pack down and melts rapidly. This is exacerbated if April and May are warmer than average, causing flooding and early depletion of water resources for late summer irrigation. Conversely, if little snow falls, or falls early in winter, giving it time to pack down, and it is followed by a cool spring, water shortage will occur in April and May due to slow melting, delaying the critical timeliness of sowing and spring regrowth of lucerne. This will necessitate strict water rationing (a necessary adaptive response that is covered by the villages). In the irrigated land-deficient district of Hunza, double cropping has been forced as high as 2500 m, partly by avoiding the possibility of such a spring delay in wheat establishment by sowing earlier, at the beginning of winter. The earlier harvest allows a second crop to barely mature. The other reason why Hunza is above the normal height zone range (Fig. 5.4) for double cropping is that it faces south, has few late spring, and early autumn frosts because it is the thermal zone of an inversion layer, being in the mid-slope portion, and it also experiences katabatic winds.

Third, the relative height of the village, together with its aspect orientation, will determine the rate of warming up in spring and the corresponding crop water demand. This may not always coincide with the rate of water release from glacier and snow melt. Thus a village in a valley as low as 1500 m and exposed to the south will have an early water demand that cannot be adequately met by a high altitude snowbed with a northerly aspect or topographic shading. Such villages may only be able to grow the later-sown maize crop rather than the preferred earlier-sown wheat. Villages where water resources are less reliable have a higher proportion of land under perennial tree and lucerne crops that can survive much longer periods of water stress than can annual crops.

In the similar agro-ecological zone of Mustang in Nepal, there are far fewer glaciers and much less snowfall with water availability limiting production and not land—the opposite situation to most valleys in the northern areas of the Pakistan Hindukush and Karakorum, where there is an immense reservoir capacity of water in the glaciers, but a great shortage of land level enough to be irrigated in the narrow valleys and safe from the summer river torrents. Unlike the isolated convectional showers of summer, the winter precipitation in Pakistan is general and widespread, and there is a strong correlation between the recorded rainfall in valley climate stations and snowfall in the upper catchments. One can then estimate the frequency of below average snowfall seasons, but it is then too late to apply management decisions to the crop. In Mustang, however, the villagers plant a mixture of a lower yielding, but earlier maturing

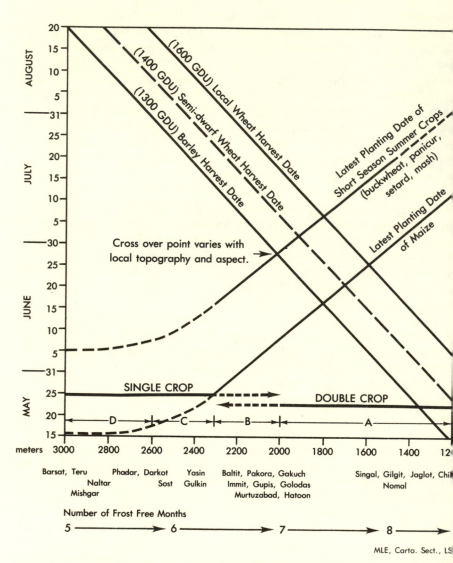

Figure 5.4 Cropping Pattern—Gilgit District (Pakistan). A = reliable double crop zone; B = marginal double crop zone; C = lower single crop zone; D = upper single crop zone. Barley and wheat harvest is retarded by 5 days per 100 m rise. Improved wheats harvest 10 days earlier than local with extreme double cropping by altitude.

variety of wheat, with a longer maturing, high-yielding variety, and so spread the risk of crop failure. Early drying up of water supply in July would allow the early variety to mature, but the later ripening component can exploit the yield potential of a longer duration of water supply. Because they plant in April after most of the snow has fallen, farmers can judge the likely duration of irrigation water supply and so alter the proportion of the two wheat components in the mixture to their advantage. This is a highly refined system, the farmers being able to "play the season by ear," not having to manage for a statistically average situation when potential would be lost if rainfall is above average and neither adapted to a below average situation. In practice, most *barani* rainfed farmers in Ethiopia and the Kashmir mid-hills play it safe with a lower seed rate of an earlier variety (i.e., reduce the duration and surface area of leaf for water loss) to ensure likelihood of yield if the season is below average. Moreover, unlike the irrigating farmers in the higher rainshadow areas, they are tied to planting when the rains come and not when they should plant to fully exploit the growing season. It may well be, however, that a correlation exists between the date of onset of rains and the total accumulated rainfall within the first few weeks. Or there may be an association with regional seasonal rain to give some kind of early warning in time for corrective action to be made, as Stewart has elegantly shown for the bimodal area of east Africa (Stewart and Hash 1982). Agroclimatologists could investigate this possibility for Asia.

The in-field traditional water application techniques are good, the length and width of the border irrigation strips being adjusted by centuries of trial and error to suit the gradient, infiltration rate and volume of water available (Whiteman 1985b). Of note are the fields of the villages on the north-facing slopes of Nagar, opposite Hunza, which have a considerable slope; their water supply is also greater and the evaporation less with no need to efficiently and carefully distribute and retain scarce irrigation water as compared to the measured supply to perfectly leveled fields in water-short Hunza, where even night storage tanks have been built.

In the marginally rainfed areas of northern Ethiopia, level terraces are needed not so much to create cultivated land from steep slopes, but to impound scarce rainfall, hence they not only have to be level but also have a retaining bund, neither of which have been widely adopted (with consequent massive soil loss). The easy expedient of simple low walls of stones on the contour to retain soil and allow the slope to naturally attenuate have not been adopted partly because of the lack of incentive from being former tenant share croppers to large landlords. In contrast, in the Yemen, steep mountain slopes have been most carefully terraced. Water is harvested from catchments and intricately distributed to each terrace on a rote system. The universal low level of management of communal resources of grazing and forest contrasts with the individual's intensively cropped land, and there has to be considerable communal discipline in irrigation channel maintenance and control of water application on such mountain sides with large vertical expanses of terraces. Neglect on a few individual terraces could cause instability of the whole slope.

Farther east from the Karakorum, in the Central Himalaya, with a higher monsoon rainfall, rice becomes an important staple crop. A vast amount of energy has been involved in modifying slopes into terraces designed either to retain water or to dispose of surplus water safely. The great advantage of rice over other crops in hilly terrain is that the paddies are level and they constitute an enormous surface storage reservoir to retain surplus rainfall that would other wise cause excessive splash erosion and enormous soil loss in run-off from forward-sloping terraces of upland crops. The preference to grow rice over alternative crops has a cultural basis—a survey in Kaski district of Nepal found that Brahmin and Chhetri villages were present up to about the 2000 m contour line, this corresponding with the upper limit at which rice can be successfully grown under full monsoon conditions. Above this height Thakuris and other ethnic groups predominated.

It is in the Ethiopian highlands that man has drastically modified the landscape in a retrogressive fashion by creating spectacular canyons and massive soil loss through centuries of erosion. To a large extent this has been encouraged by the heavy clay soils that are derived from the basalt-dominated mountains. These soils have a low infiltration rate and encourage a seasonal surface waterlogging of the soils. Although the total rainfall is still inadequate for supplying full water requirements, the rains come in a peak, limited amounts enter the soil for storage owing to low permeability, and unfavorable surface waterlogging occurs. Farmers encourage surface drainage by ploughing up and down the slope.

The erosion that this practice causes is aggravated by the tiny seed of the staple cereal crop *teff*, probably selected for its relative ability to tolerate this surface waterlogging compared with other cereals that require both a very fine seedbed and a late sowing after the rains have begun, exposing the fine tilth to the full erosive energy of the rain. Appropriate terrace designs and field management will help to reduce this loss. Changes are always more acceptable if they are based on simple modifications of existing practice. It was possible to demonstrate that by enlarging the two lateral supports (*dugris*) on the local plough, an enhanced ridge/furrow surface soil configuration effect could be achieved (see Fig. 5.5). For row crops such as maize and sorghum, these furrows could be cross-tied (blocked) at intervals that would allow complete retention of rainfall, thereby giving infiltration time at the beginning and end of the rains but opening these ties during the main period of the rains to allow a controlled graded drainage. All ties open or only those in

Figure 5.5 Simple Modification of the Local Ethiopian Plough. With handle and beam removed, the plough shows the large lateral supports that give a pronounced ridging effect.

alternate furrows would vary according to the nature of the rainy season. Not only does this give greater flexibility in management, but the water available to the crop is nearly doubled and erosion losses are greatly reduced. This technique is illustrated in Figure 5.6.

It was also possible to increase wheat yields by 50 percent on these same soils by ploughing the field after harvest and not at the time of sowing at the commencement of the next rains. The benefit did not arise from any difference in sowing date or extra moisture, but from the fact that the crop residues that were ploughed in after harvest were able to decompose using the residual moisture present in the profile. This moisture is eventually lost, and if ploughing is done later decomposition is dependent on the supply of new moisture from the next rains. Decomposition—which immobilizes soil nitrogen—then occurs simultaneously with

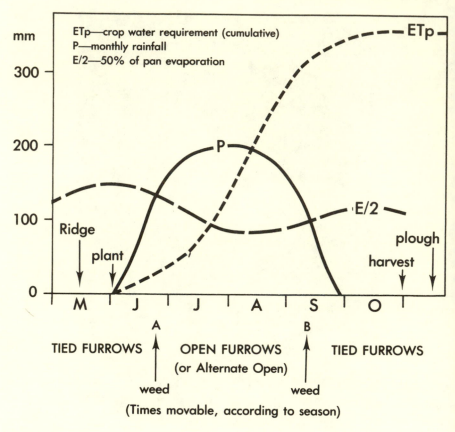

Figure 5.6. Soil Moisture Management. Before the rains, the land is ploughed, contour-furrowed, and cross-tied to retain all rain and soil during establishment of crop. Between time A and B (high rainfall) crop ties in every, or alternate, furrows are broken to allow controlled drainage. After peak rainfall, cross-ties are again established to retain water. The approximately 40 to 50 days growth is from stored moisture.

planting and the seedling is deprived of nitrogen, giving it a setback from which it never recovers.

Of northern Ethiopia, it has been authoritatively said that "in all of Africa no country has been more brutally ravaged by man." Leslie Brown (1965) goes on to relate the destruction of the countryside to the density of human population and length of time in the area—the bleak landscape has been so changed that it is hardly credible that the original condition was forest, parts of which still remain around churches and inaccessible slopes to provide living proof of what once flourished all over. It would be instructive to take a Nepalese delegation to Wollo district in Ethiopia to show them the end result of what population pressure is beginning to do in the hills of Nepal, where soil and land is being lost at increasing rates. Curiously enough, the opposite situation prevails at the dry western end of the Himalayas. The silt-laden rivers of the Hindukush and Karakorum mountains do not indicate massive erosion—what erosion exists is entirely of glacial origin and there is no surface run-off. Occasionally mud flows bring down the accumulated detritus of centuries, but these are geological events, usually triggered by rare localized rainfall. On the contrary the cultivated area is actually increasing, both by the addition of silt to land in the irrigation water and from new irrigation schemes reclaiming barren areas.

Throughout these high areas, whether the Ethiopian plateau or the valleys of the Asian mountains, anabatic and katabatic winds are a feature at certain times of the day and year. Everywhere one can notice response to the shelter of a wall or bank in terms of improved plant and crop growth. The oasis-like nature of settlements makes them susceptible to large increases in evaporation because of advective energy. Windbreaks, however, are a rare feature, as on the small and scattered holdings they would have to be communally managed and protected from browsing livestock.

Temperature Exploitation

The natural adaptation of the temperature gradient with altitude is reflected in crop zonation, and this imposes a similar sequence in the Ethiopian highlands, dry Hindukush, and monsoon Himalayas. Generally maize is the last of the sub-tropical crops (with a C-4 photosynthetic pathway) before coming into a belt of wheat and finally barley, often with peas and broad beans. The rate at which actual day (not mean) temperatures drop off with height will depend mainly on the cloud cover, but length of growing season also shortens, or becomes more protracted in equatorial mountains. Thus mean temperature is not a good indicator of season suitability or quality, particularly as the diurnal range increases with altitude. The case of rice illustrates this very well. The upper limit of rice on the monsoon-affected south side of the Nepal Himalaya is about 2000 m, but it is also found at much higher locations (2750 m) in the partial rainshadow areas, where, in the absence of prolonged cloud cover, the daytime temperatures are higher, allowing the crop to be grown. For the same reason of increased sunshine hours, rice is still grown at 2300 m in the Hindukush at 10 degrees farther north. Uhlig (1978) has commented on this phenomenon. Maize is not grown above 2000 m in Ethiopia at only 12 degrees N latitude, yet is found at 3000 m at 38 degrees N in the Hindukush. In Ethiopia the crop is tied to the rainy season, which, of course, is also the cloudy season that cuts off the sunshine. Provided there is irrigation, then the absence of cloud in the transmontane areas is an advantage, not only in terms of warmer temperature, but also because more radiant energy is available for photosynthetic dry matter production. These same conditions that give warm sunny days, at altitude, also give cool nights that reduce dry matter losses due to respiration. In fact, for this reason, the mountains of northern Pakistan are probably one of the best areas in the world for high yields of temperate crops, given adequate manuring and irrigation. Being in a rainshadow area there is an abundance of radiation with 70 percent of the maximum possible sunshine hours. The summer days are long at 37 degrees N and there is a 15-degree C diurnal range in temperature at 2500 m, giving rise to warm days and cool nights. As Figure 5.7 indicates, the area is excellent for potatoes. By planting as soon as the frost finishes in early April, tubers initiate at the beginning of June and then have a 100-day period of bulking at an average day temperature of 25 degrees C and night temperature of 10 degrees C, before frost terminates growth in mid-October. With healthy tubers, world record yields in excess of 90 t/ha have been achieved. In physiological terms the crops are "sink limited"—certainly the apricots are the

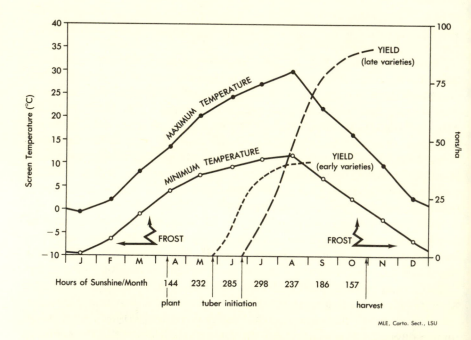

MLE, Carto. Sect., LSU

Figure 5.7   Potato Bulking Curve at 2500 m Altitude, Yasin, at Gilgit District, Pakistan

sweetest in the world with more than 20 percent sugar in the fresh fruit, and phenomenally high yields of wheat, fodder, and vegetables have also been recorded. The rapid cooling of night temperatures in late summer (a feature of the altitude at this latitude) develops the color in fruit and maintains sweetness.

Unlike irrigated areas, in rainfed situations clouds are inevitably present. In the central Rift Valley of Ethiopia, however, there is a marked tendency for the days to be clear, but cloud that has built up over the highlands drifts off the Rift scarp at night to give rain and then disperse by morning. At 1500 m altitude on the Rift Valley floor, a location that encourages a noticeable diurnal temperature regime, very high yields of beans and sweet potatoes have been achieved under these conditions that resemble those in the true irrigated rainshadow areas of the Hindukush.

In addition to the higher amount of sunshine in rainshadow areas, the quality of the radiation is more intense at higher altitude, where the atmosphere is both less dense with a higher transmissivity, and with less water vapor there is more ultraviolet radiation than at lower levels. Although the absolute values decrease, the relative values increase under cloud cover and when the sun is lower in the sky. Plants become adapted to these conditions, and Cooper (1970) gives an example of an ecocline of the grass *Lolium perenne* that has higher assimilation and light saturation levels with ecotypes from higher altitude, giving up to a 50 percent increase in photosynthetic rate that is specific adaption allowing exploitation of a shorter growing season.

The bimodal rainfall of the Western Himalayas encourages a remarkable coexistence of two separate floristic elements. A temperate flora develops in spring on the winter moisture and completes its life-cycle before the sub-tropical element grows up through it at the onset of the monsoon in mid-summer, giving a long season of grass availability. In Ethiopia, although the rainfall comes in summer (the period of longer days), the dominant element in the flora is Mediterranean (normally associated with a winter rainfall), because at those latitudes (10 to 14 degrees N) the cooling effect of summer cloud at altitude has a greater effect than the slightly shorter days of the dry "winter."

This cooling effect of shade at higher altitudes is very significant. In a series of investigations, Cooper (1979) discovered that the time of planting effect with maize on the East African highlands (the marked reduction in yield associated with delays in sowing after the commencement of the rains) could be reversed only by warming the soil (through plastic mulches) and was independent of effects of moisture, aeration, nutrients, or radiation. For the same reason, weeds proved more harmful through their shading and cooling effect on the soil than by the more expected forms of competition. Maize is especially sensitive as its meristem remains in the soil for the first 5-6 weeks of growth (Fig. 5.8).

← Figure 5.8 The Effect of Micro-aspect on Maize Seedling Emergence in Spring at 2300 m in Nepal. On the warm and sheltered southeast exposure, seedlings are 5 cm high. Seedlings on the cool north-facing side are 10 days later.

↑ Figure 5.9 Barley Being Cut at Various Stages of Maturity in Jumla, Northwest Nepal, at 2200 m. So tight is the rotation that after barley is cut, field is ploughed, flooded, and transplanted with rice the same day.

Similarly in Hunza in northern Pakistan, very strict rules regulate how close farmers can plant trees to their field border—at that altitude (2500 m) warmth is also very dependent on direct sunshine, and air temperatures can be as much as 10 degrees cooler in the shade of trees, thus protracting crop development, and delayed maturity would prevent the possibility of double cropping. Farmers can plant trees near their southern boundary, but not near their northern one as this will shade their neighbors' fields. Similarly, but on a larger scale, one village in a north-south-running valley can double crop, unlike several villages lower down, only because of a gap in the western side of the valley that breaks the topographical shading to give an extra hour of sunshine in the afternoon. The fields are being "fertilized" by heat units!

Unlike the large isolated East African mountains such as Mts. Kilimanjaro, Elgon and Kenya, in which there is a gross aspect difference because of prevailing wind and rain direction, the "mountain mass" effect of the large Asian ranges accentuates their continentality of climate. The rainshadow phenomenon causes aridity that enhances the heat burden as there is no insulating layer of vegetation, and also radiation is converted to sensible heat in the absence of moisture to evaporate on bare rocky mountain slopes. These slopes then function as storage heaters, giving rise to much higher temperatures than those found in free air at the same height. As at 37 degrees N where the days are long in summer and the nights correspondingly short, there is insufficient time for this heat load to be lost by terrestrial radiation, thereby causing considerable discomfiture to people below 1500 m, but enabling more heat units to be packed into a short growing season at 3000 m, where the effect is of definite agricultural benefit in hastening the maturity of crops. In fact there is a risk of crops failing to mature in 20 percent of the seasons owing to summers with more cloud than usual. In these instances the heat unit availability is reduced by only 10 percent.

Cool springs caused by above average cloud are also a problem in northwest Nepal at the upper limit of double cropping, where often the winter-sown barley has to be cut while still green (Fig. 5.9) so as not to delay the transplanting of rice which is the preferred crop and which has a cut-off date by frost at harvest in October. After a long winter in Gilgit in northern Pakistan when straw reserves for cattle feed have dwindled to nothing by end of March, a cool period brought on by above average cloud cover, rather than to the source of the wind and origin of the air mass, can seriously delay by two weeks the regrowth of *shaftal,* the first spring fodder for animals. The fodder shortage in these small irrigated mountain oases is so critical that it determines the whole cropping pattern. Farmers sacrifice wheat grain yield for the higher quantity and greater digestibility of the straw of local varieties, which they sow at high seed rates for extra straw. Barley may even be winter sown in a mixture with wheat and then later thinned out in spring as an early green feed. In Ethiopia, grain yield in sorghum is traded off with the need for long stalks for building and fuel purposes.

The latitude and altitude accentuate the very large seasonal variation in temperature. Figure 5.10 shows this relationship for Gilgit at 1500 m in the Hindukush. The shape of the curves are similar for all recording sites up to 3000 m (Fig. 5.11). The very rapid rate of change causes problems in crop adaptation as spring-sown crops inevitably mature under increasing heat stress, and summer-sown crops soon run into rapid cooling conditions of autumn, which in turn protract growth before finally cutting it off with frost. The optimum temperature for sub-tropical crops operating on a C-4 photosynthetic pathway is above 20 degrees C, and it can be seen that at 2200 m there are still 90 days for such growth available. The optimum temperature for temperate crops (operating on a C-3 photosynthetic pathway) is below 20 C. Above 2500 m there is a 5 to 7 month uninterrupted growing season. Below this height, however, the optimum season is split into two by the hot summer period of supra-optimum temperatures. For example, the temperate season in Gilgit is only 3.5 months in spring and 2 months in autumn, too short in either season for high yields of wheat. It is very apparent from examining the temperature changes depicted in Figure 5.10 that autumn-sown wheat would be hardy enough to withstand the winter cold that seldom drops below − 10 degrees C, yet farmers traditionally sow in early February when the soil thaws out. Sowing in October fits the plant's development stages into a well-adapted

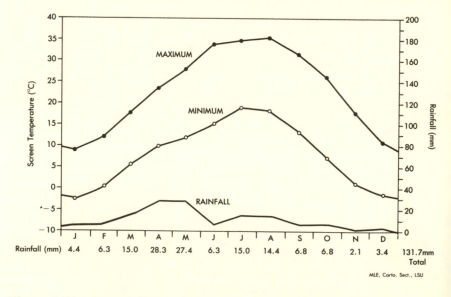

Figure 5.10   Annual Screen Temperature and Rainfall in Gilgit (1490 m)

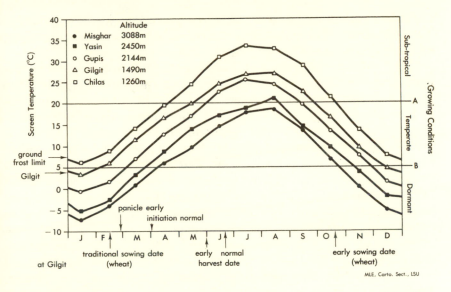

Figure 5.11 Monthly Mean of Average Daily Temperature, Northern Areas, Pakistan

temperature regime that allows both ear initiation and spikelet development to occur over a more optimum cooler period in early March, resulting in larger ears with more grain that completes its filling period at the end of May before excessive sub-tropical temperatures develop. This provides at least a 50 percent yield increase over the best normal planting dates. Early sowing also allows two other advantages: (1) harvest is 10 days earlier, increasing the chance of a good following crop, and (2) light grazing or cutting in late winter is possible to give a much needed green fodder supply or else a valuable cash fodder sale. Previous attempts to improve wheat yields were confined to changing the variety and applying more fertilizer. These helped, but the yield potential was then limited by an unsuitable temperature regime, which no amount of additional fertilizer could overcome. Temperature would be "modified" only by shifting the sowing date.

This approach, of purposeful crop sampling and analysis of climate elaborated elsewhere by the author (Whiteman 1985), has shown how it is possible to gain a rapid understanding of the most important factors limiting yield, and by the same token suggests ways to overcome them. In increasing the efficiency of resource use, it is the output per unit of the most limiting resource that must be maximized, and in mountains this is invariably temperature. While the farmers have generally clearly perceived the limiting effects of low temperature, have evolved, through trial and error over generations, strategies to minimize its harmful effect and exploit its variations, there is still scope for further increasing the efficiency of local variations in this resource use by modifying the micro-environment, as the following two examples demonstrate.

Stone walls are common, either to separate fields or to support terrace banks, but their value in extending season has not been widely used. In Nepal after observing the response of crops in the fields, the author was able to record a large temperature gradient building up in the morning, with the air temperature near a south-facing wall being 5 degrees C warmer than at 2 m away (Fig. 5.12). Regular afternoon wind disturbed this gradient, but when this had subsided in the evening, the gradient became most marked owing to the storage heater effect of the wall just before midnight, and then it slowly cooled until the morning before being recharged after sunrise. No doubt heat capture and storage could be considerably improved by wall design, thickness, and even color, but it represents an excellent ubiquitous micro-habitat for increasing the altitude range of sensitive species of fruit grown as cordons or espaliers and for extending the growing season of vegetables, or forcing an early crop. Simplistically, crops grow (increase in dry weight) in daytime, and develop (progress through stages of maturity) during night, and the wall "fertilizes" the crop with heat units at night, thereby advancing harvest date.

The final example concerns rice in northwest Nepal. It illustrates how the farmer has by trial and error over centuries developed a management system to extract the most growth from the local spatial and temporal variations of the resource of temperature, the greatest constraint to its growth at its upper limit of 2750 m. It was also possible to purposely increase this exploitation by a simple modification of existing practice.

At this altitude, rice frequently experiences frost on the seedbed and at harvest and is grown only on well-exposed south-facing slopes, with no topographical shading. The seed has to be sown at the end of March when frosts prevail, and the only way to get it to germinate, before sowing, is to put the soaked seed near the fire and even under the mattress at night to receive body heat. After sprouting, it is sown into a seedbed. After two months the seedlings are still only 10-12 cm high at the time of transplanting at the end of May. Unlike paddy fields at lower altitudes, the water is retained on the terrace to accumulate heat through the day and not allowed to continuously flow from one terrace to another. Paddies are topped up in the afternoon when the incoming water is several degrees warmer than in early morning. Paddy fields are less favored that receive water from the irrigation channel near its take-off point from the river—the water supplying those 2 km distant will be about 2 degrees C warmer and this rice will mature earlier. Progressive farmers even darken the submerged surface of the rice nursery with a carefully sifted mixture of compost and scorched dung, causing more heat to be absorbed (Fig.

Figure 5.12 The Storage Heater Effect at 2200 m in North-west Nepal. *a*: In February, seedlings have already respond-ed to the proximity of a south-facing wall. *b*: Five weeks later, the headshave has emerged more quickly nearer the wall. *c* and *d*: The effect of a terrace wall on a north-facing field, showing delay of germination and maturity of barley

5.13). Water warming basins are not used as the farmers are short of land, but an experiment by the author showed this technique to increase yields. Small windbreaks (of woven twigs) are put up to decrease the chilling of the water through the latent heat of evaporation. The local rice always flowers in mid-August, when on a clear night air temperatures could drop to below the minimum safe value of 15 degrees C, thereby greatly increasing the spikelet sterility from the average 20 percent. Anticipating a clear night in July, farmers raise the water level a few centimeters so that a higher proportion of the boots enclosing the developing pollen grains that are so sensitive to cold injury remain submerged and so reduce the incidence of sterility, as water does not cool off as much as air temperatures do overnight.

It was obvious that it was not day temperature of the water that was limiting seedling growth in the nursery, and that, simply by placing a rice straw mat over the seedbed from dusk to dawn, the rate at which water cooled off by releasing heat overnight was considerably reduced, resulting in seedlings three times bigger at transplanting time. The cover extended the time water was above 15 degrees C (the lower threshold for growth) by five hours during the night, the mean night temperature being

Figure 5.13   Preparing Black Humus for Greater Field Heat Absorption. Farmer scorches dung to spread on the rice seedbed *(behind)* to darken the submerged surface and increase heat absorption

3.8 degrees C warmer than the open plots (see Fig. 5.14). When a cold-tolerant non-photosensitive *japonica* rice was used, this enhanced seed-ing growth advanced flowering by one week, resulting in less cold induced sterility and a 40 percent increase in grain yields compared with the plots uncovered at night.

Conclusion

The scenarios in this chapter were chosen to illustrate that for continu-ity, traditional agricultural production must exhibit: (1) stability or resil-ience to environmental fluctuations, (2) sustainability or optimum level of renewable resource use and recycling, and 3) equitability, vested self-interest in non-overexploitation, and for shared resource maintenance with activities adjusted to the limitations of the environment. These concepts are elaborated by Conway (1985). Furthermore, the social structure and cultural habits are adapted to ensure the continued mainte-nance of the system.

Nevertheless, change is nowadays inevitable and is occurring along a number of lines. First, modernization has exposed formally closed, self-limiting agrarian systems of traditional societies and changed them to open systems. Consequently, rising expectations and an increasing re-sponse to, and dependence on, disruptive external resources and factors affect the environment directly, through modification of old customs and

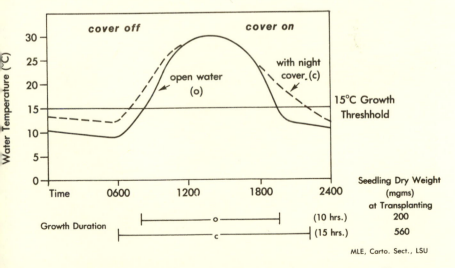

MLE, Carto. Sect., LSU

Figure 5.14   Effect of Night Cover on Diurnal Change in Water Tempera-ture of Rice Seedbed (10th April)

habits. There is even a demise on the range of available germplasm (Brush 1984), with increasing access to lowland areas.

Second, there is an inabilty to respond to the insidious "internal invasion" of people (for such is overpopulation) that like any invasion requires programs on a war-footing basis. In the past, populations responded to food shortage stress by either migrating or dying, but now with fixed borders, health and food aid, they remain sedentary. The tragic cumulative results of permanently exceeding the carrying capacity are seen now in Tigrai, Ethiopia, and inexorably in Kenya and Nepal later, where the demise of soil capital will reduce the annual interest of food income. All changes are for the worst.

Third, change, to be effective, must be widespread and not exclusive to favored community minorities, and therefore has to be small to be appropriate, based on simple modifications of present utilization practices of local resources, rather than dependent on imported resources. Simple changes, for example using a night mat cover for rice nurseries, advancing the sowing date of wheat, or enlarging the lateral wooden supports to the existing local plough, are non-disruptive and capable of widespread adoption. Discovering that there is scope for such beneficial changes depends on an appreciation of the physical nature of environmental differentiation at a local scale together with an awareness of the physiological basis of response in plants (Whiteman 1986).

6

Mountain People and Monastics in Kumaon Himalaya, India

Agehananda Bharati

The Himalayan region has only very recently been defined as a cultural area, at least by anthropologists. For reasons I cannot go into here, the predominant interest so far has been the Tibetan and Tibeto-Nepalese template. The Indian Himalayas so far have received somewhat step-motherly treatment, in spite of the fact that both in size and population, they equal all the remaining Himalayan regions. This chapter is an incipient attempt to remedy the situation, by introducing a very Indian and a very Himalayan scenario.

"Mountain peoples" has two meanings which overlap but which are by no means coextensive. The one is what anthropologists call the *emic* meaning, i.e., the term applied to themselves by people living in moun-tainous regions; the other is the *etic* term in anthropology, i.e., used by scientists who are not or only accidentally part of a mountain culture. Thus, the "worldly natives" I am going to talk about in this chapter are mountain people both emically and etically: they refer to themselves as *pahari*, which means "of the mountains" quite literally—they are the people G. D. Berreman (1963) talks about in his classic account, and their neighbors who share the same or at least a mutually intelligible linguistic idiom; and they are mountain people etically, since they live in an area that is geophysically alpine or in the *terai* that pre-Alpine land intermedi-ate between the mountains and the plains. But close to one hundred thousand Tibetans who now live as expatriates in Karnataka in South India, and in various parts of North America and Europe, are really no longer "mountain people," etically speaking—the generation born in the diaspora might not ever have seen a mountain; emically, however, they still are, since they perceive themselves as people from the mountains. In the vast plains of Hindu India, holy men, monks, and other paramonastic people often claim to be, and are regarded as "from the Himalayas," when most of them have sojourned only in such monastic centers as Hardvar or Hrishikesh, quite a distance from the Himalayas, with no mountains in sight—somewhat like a New Englander, who might think that everybody from Montana is from the mountains, when in fact there are no mountains at all in eastern Montana.

I lived in a Hindu monastery as a novice for over two years. While at that time, four decades ago, I never viewed my stay in terms of anthropological fieldwork, it proved to be just that, in addition, of course, to other things, by pragmatic hindsight as it were. With no qualms held and none expected, I have designated those as *bona fide* fieldwork ever since I was hired as an anthropologist at a major American university. The one thing that makes anthropologists boldly and self-consciously different from sociologists is that they do *fieldwork*, and a large portion of fieldwork consists in "participant observation," a phrase that never erodes from anthropologists' vocabulary.

At some two dozen locations in the Kumaon Region of the alpine sector of Uttar Pradesh, Northern India, there are Hindu monastic institutions of varying provenience, which I visited myself. There are many more, maybe ten times as many, since the lower chains of the Himalayan massive, an average altitude of 1,000 to 3,000 m, was always a highly touted, attractive region for Hindu and Buddhist monastic institutions. There is the pan-Hindu notion that the basic teachings of Hinduism were first propounded by sages who lived in the Himalayas, and that the quintessence of Hinduism diffused from that region into the most distant corners of the subcontinent. This is part of a pervasive mystique which I discussed elsewhere in some detail (Bharati 1978a). It is shared by the Tibetans: the highest mountains are sacred to the Tibetans as they are to the Hindus. To wit, the names of the highest peaks are diglossal—each of them has a Tibetan and an Indian name; and each of them has the name of a different deity, or a different myth depending on whether a Hindu or a Tibetan Buddhist speaks about them.

What Berreman (1963) showed in his magnum opus applies in a large measure to the area where I stayed: the agricultural landowners comprising the Khasa Brahmins of the priestly class and Rajputs from the royal or warrior castes of that whole region (Berreman's "Sirkanda" is no more than one hundred miles, as the crow flies, from my monastery) are Brahmins and Rajputs with a chip on their shoulders: they are aware of the fact that by plains Brahmin and Rajput standards, their ritualistic comportment does not measure up to Brahmin and Rajput norms. All Khasa Brahmins and Rajputs eat meat, all do agricultural work in the fields, and unlike the plains highcastes, the *paharis* did not object to widow marriage until quite recently. During the past three decades, however, some wealthy Kumaonis have begun to emulate plains standards. This is what M. N. Srinivas (1952) calls the process of "Sanskrit-

ation," and it appears to be strongly manifest in the area at this moment
time. It had well entered its incipient stage, though, when I spent my
novitiate years up there, and I will have more to report about it when
rther along.

Even for those Berreman calls "high altitude chauvinists" it seems all
it impossible to be accepted as a *pahari* among *paharis*.

Governments allow aliens to naturalize, and whether you call Henry
Kissinger or yours truly "hyphenated Americans" or not, naturalized
people are functioning Americans. But this is not the case in the Hima-
yas, and I suspect it isn't in other alpine areas. I recall I used to spend
ome lovely boyhood summers in the high Tirolian Alps in Austria—and
e Tirolians there called me *der Wiener* (the Viennese); that was not
irprising, but they also called a middle-aged farmer a *Wiener*. That man
id come from Vienna and settled in the mountains some thirty years
arlier, and he remembered nothing about Vienna, nor did he have a
iennese accent. Something similar happens in the Himalayas. Monks,
oly men, and other religious specialists who were not born in the region
e called *maidani log* or *maidani sadhu* i.e., people, or holy men from
e plains, regardless of how long they have been alpine residents; and so
re tourists, of course, more deservedly. Swami Anirvan, a very learned
engali monk whom I knew in Almora (the largest town in Kumaon), had
ined the order when he was about 15, and had left his native Calcutta to
ove to Almora, where he established his monastery, or *ashram* and
here he spent the rest of his life. When I met him, he spoke the Kumaoni
gional dialect like the *paharis* around, and he referred to himself as a
ahari sadhu (mountain-holy man). But not the indigenes around him: his
ook, his washerman, and his sweeper called him *maidani baba* (i.e., holy
an from the plains), and we were given understanding smiles when we
isisted Anirvan was a *pahari sadhu*.

This illustrates the difference between being a mountain man emically
r etically—only the Tirolian peasants and the Kumaoni-speaking,
uamoni-caste people are *paharis*, emically. Neither long-time resident
onks from elsewhere, nor tourists, nor mountain-born and mountain-
aised sons and grandsons or squatters who migrated from the plains
enerations ago are. Of the latter, there are two kinds. First, the rather
ortunate ones, who came as shopkeepers—and still come—who are of
iddle caste status, usually *banyas* or similar merchant castes. Since they
nported with them a small-shop economy which was nonexistent in this
rea prior to their arrival, they have greatly enhanced the economic
orizon of the *paharis*, so much so that an increasing number of *paharis*—
any of them trained by the merchant squatters—are now taking to the
hopping trade. Second, the unfortunate untouchables now referred to as
Harijans"—"people of God" in the official Gandhian terminology, who
ame from the plains as sweepers and for other menial jobs that are

regarded as low and defiling in all Hindu areas, plains and mountain.
Here in Kumaon, as well as in the adjacent Indian and Nepalese mountai
regions, there are indeed *pahari*—untouchables with the generic cast
designation *Dom*—cobblers, leatherworkers in general, tailors, and som
drummers and other musicians among them, as well as all people wh
remove carcasses from the village, the most defiling occupation by a
Hindu standards. The relation between the *pahari* untouchables and th
squatter untouchables and their descendants is quite clear—the latte
rank even beneath the *pahari Doms*. As is known to all students of India
society, there is hardly any group anywhere which does not look dow
upon an even lower group, with the exception perhaps of the *chamar*
the leatherworkers of Northern India.

The demarcation is quite clear in the Kumaon hills. It is purel
linguistic. People who speak the Kumaoni dialect natively are *pahari*
those who don't are not, regardless of their caste origin in the plains, an
of their knowledge or ignorance of the Kumaoni dialect. The sweeper i
our monastery was Pyarilal, a jovial, bright, helpful person, and
marvelous marksman. With his old pre-World War I rifle which looked a
though it might be more dangerous to its user than to its intended victim
he shot down whatever game got too near the monastery: the *kharod*, th
large tree-dwelling marsupial, as well as the *jarau*, the mountain-el
weighing about 500 kgs and standing nearly three meters from the groun
with its antlers—and the occasional Himalayan bear (*Ursus torquatu*
Himalayae), a beautiful black-furred animal with a T-like white strip
along his chest and forehead. Now Pyarilal shared the meat of his quarr
with the monastery's two cooks, one of them a *pahari* (Khasa) Brahmi
the other a Rajput, as well as with some highcaste friends in the village (
Lohaghat, the closest settlement. He was known to give a helping hand t
everyone, and cheerfully. Yet to everyone, he was not only an untouch
able, but he was a complete outsider, a *maidani admi*, a man from th
plains, in spite of the fact that he had never been to the plains even once
His father had migrated from Lucknow, the large capital city of the Stat
of Uttar Pradesh, then United Provinces. He spoke the Kumaoni dialec
well, but he didn't speak it natively. He spoke rather good standar
Hindi, or the sort highcaste mountain lads would learn in the newl
established school: a Brahmin father in Lohaghat, who sent his son to tha
school to learn the three R's, once remarked to me "It's all very good, bu
my son learns to speak like Pyarilal"!

There are close to a dozen monasteries in the Kumaon region of th
Indian Himalayas which I refer to as "modern" in contrast to conserva
tive or orthodox monasteries, of which there may be well over tw
hundred. I will talk about a "modern" monastery here, and for tw
reasons: first, it was at one of these that I spent my two years' novitiate
second, conservative monasteries in the mountains are not substantiall

ifferent in structure and organization from monastic institutions in the ndian plain (Miller, Wertz 1976; Tripathi 1978; Bharati 1980). The mod- -n monastery provides an impressive laboratory for the study of multi- vel adaptations. The monks and novices at these institutions located in he mountains do not belong to the local region—none of them is of .umaoni or other *pahari* provenience. Virtually all of them come from rban areas, and most of them have been exposed to some degree of ormal college education; some have been brought up in the orthodox lindu traditions of brahmanical learning with the emphasis on Sanskrit nd the Hindu scriptures. All the monastic personnel at my monastery new English, three of them very well indeed. Knowing English in South .sia catapults the knower into a separate social entity, and for such xonomic considerations it is not really important how well he knows it. iewed from below, from the folk level, "knowing English" means being modern" and hence different from the surrounding population.

At the pseudonymous Nirguna Ashram there were a dozen monks, ight of whom were fully ordained, i.e., carrying the title Swami; the rest ere *brahma-caris* (novices). Of the ordained swamis, five were Bengalis, iree were South Indians from Karnataka and Kerala respectively; two of ie novices were South Indians (Kanarese), one a Bengali, and one a luropean (i.e., the author of this essay). Although this was a somewhat nusual mix even for "modern" Kumaoni monasteries, it does not really ffect our study in the sense of reporting a typical situation. The interac- on between the *pahari* personnel, the proximate *pahari* populace and the ionks follow an identical pattern, because *all* these monastic denizens re, to the *paharis*, urban strangers from the Indian plains plus the ccasional foreigner, and to the monks all *paharis* appear alike, regardless f whether they (the monks) come from Bangalore in the South or from :alcutta in the East. The unwary foreigner (European or American, and heir number has multiplied since my days) who is not a social scientist uffers from the massive cognitive incongruities invading his perceptions rom all sides. He would tend to assume that since both the *pahari* opulation and the monks are Indians and Hindus, they must somehow ave more ideological kinship with one another than either of them with he foreign monk or novice. This, however, is a mistaken notion, and the oreign seeker establishing residence in such monasteries could save imself some anguish were he aware of the fact that such ideological onding between the *paharis* and the monks is simply not the case, and hat Indian urban monastics' view of things and people are likely to esemble his own much more than that of the *paharis*. This essay aims to ighlight this counter-intuitive situation.

Let me begin with the *pahari* views of and their interaction with the nonks (and novices) resident at the "modern" Nirguna Ashram. Four *aharis* lived on the grounds—one was the senior servant-cum-cook (an

Indo-English expression used along with "cook-cum-bearer" in this parlance), a Khas Brahmin man of about twenty-one from the large village of Lohaghat; two further cooks and servants were Khas Rajput lads "brothers" in their terminology, first cousins in American kinship terms they were about sixteen and eighteen respectively, and from the village of Champawat. Khas, Khasa, Khasiya are all similar Pahari terms for the local Brahmins and Rajputs, distinguishing them from all other, i.e., non-Pahari, upper castes (Berreman 1963). Lohaghat was located about five kilometers from the Ashram, Champawat about ten.

Then there was Ram Dulari, the resident *gwala* (cow-pen manager, as the English-speaking monks called him—and they did not mean it facetiously; the cowherd, in other words). He was a Khas Rajput from a small village near Champawat, and his age was undeterminable, between twenty-five and fifty-five. He had been in the Army and had probably travelled quite a bit, since he mentioned Aden and Tobruk. He also knew some Panjabi swear words, which he proudly used whenever I was near since he had found out that I knew Panjabi and had been a soldier myself. He didn't mean any harm, nor did he mean any insult to man or beast when he referred to them as *machod* (motherfucker) or *bahanchoa* (sisterfucker); such appellations were simply meant to document his philological prowess.

I did not include Pyarilal the untouchable sweeper in the list of four, since he was the son of a squatter from the plains, and not a *pahari*, as I explained earlier.

Hira, the Brahmin senior cook-cum-servant, Ucchu Singh and Lakshman Singh, the Rajput servants-cum-cooks, lived together in the servants quarters, which was a somewhat inappropriate eulogism for the lean-to-shack next to the smaller building which housed the monastery's post office and the office of the editor-monk of the monthly publication of the institution. The total living space for Hira, Lakshman and Ucchu was about fifteen square meters. Ram Dulari, the "cowpen manager," lived with the five cows of the monastery, rather spaciously, in the stable some five hundred feet downhill from the main monastery building. It took me close to a year to find out where Pyarilal the sweeper lived. The monks, including the abbot, claimed they did not know where he slept; Hira, Lakshman, and Ucchu did not agree with each other, each of them assigning a different habitat to Pyarilal; and he himself evaded the question, obviously because he was embarrassed about his lowly status and consequently about his off-duty whereabouts. In the villages nearby, there were sweeper families, however few, and other kinsmen; but up here at Nirguna Ashram, he was the only untouchable among four *pahari* highcastes and a large number of strange, highcaste and highlevel creatures from far afield. One day I followed him secretly to find out—and gave up after twenty minutes. He walked in the direction of Lohaghat, and since there is nothing but thick alpine forest between the Ashram and that village, I assume he walked back and forth every day; which would not be too tough except for the fact that he arrived, broom in hand, around six every morning, with no holidays, which meant that he must have left Lohaghat around four-thirty when it was still pitch dark during most parts of the year. He did own or borrow a kerosene lamp from the ashram—there was no electricity, of course, and all the non-daylight doings at the monastery were conducted with kerosene lamps. Yet, the walk from the village to the ashram at night was certainly not without hazards: bear, cheetah, and even leopards were reported to be seen at least once a week. He kept his rifle at the ashram, to my knowledge, and never carried it with him for his protection.

Pyarilal never complained. I often tried to engage him in quasi-political, ideological conversation, a fact not known to the monks, who would have resented and probably forbidden it. He was knowledgeable—he knew about his official rights, the abolition of untouchability by law, and all the claims he might have in theory. But he did not live within a corporate untouchable "Harijan" community where those rights might be lobbied and implemented as they are in the plains, where Harijan power is something that has to be, and is taken seriously on many levels (Lynch 1969). But here in the mountains Pyarilal lived as a lone untouchable, and he had resigned himself to this fact. The way the monks reacted to him was different from the way the highcaste *paharis* did. For the highcaste servants of the monastery, he was simply an untouchable to be physically avoided, and that was the end of it—there was nothing secret about such avoidance, it was ritualized, fully interiorized, and hence interpersonally inoffensive. They would not eat with him, but they often played cards or volleyball with him near the cowshed, at times when the monks and novices did not (we used to play about once a week for an hour or so). None of the monks would have dreamed of asking him or the *pahari* servants to join in the game. These were sophisticated urban people from the plains of India, and they were all highly cognizant of the political scene—they all talked a lot about the evils of untouchability. But it didn't seem to affect their attitude toward Pyarilal. The abbot himself said, "I wouldn't mind eating with an untouchable, but these people, like Pyarilal, have such filthy untouchable habits that I would not eat with them for reasons of hygiene and cleanliness." The man was a learned Brahmin from Kerala in the extreme southwest of India. He quoted Gandhi, he rejected caste, he decried the evils of untouchability. But in fact his argument about Pyarilal is quite typical for the vast majority of modern highcaste sophisticates: they have deritualized untouchabilty, and they reject it on paper and in discourse. But when it comes to charity which is

assumed to begin at home, it does no such thing. The only difference i
that rejection, once couched in terms of ritualistically conceived purit
and pollution, is now voiced in terms of "modern" rules of hygiene.

About two years into my sojourn as a novice, things came to .
showdown. The abbot called me into his cell and told me pointblank that
was not supposed to fraternize with the servants—neither with th
Brahmin and Rajput cooks, nor with the cowherd, nor, of course, witl
Pyarilal. "They are servants, you see, and your hobnobbing with them i
due to your muddled English thinking about these things. We believe in
democracy and socialism, but servants have to be kept in place." "En
glish," at least into the late forties, still meant "Western" in general.

About three times a year, visitors from the large cities of India came uj
to spend a week or so in meditation and religious discourse with th
monks. During my time, I recall about five such visitors—one wealthy
Sikh couple from Delhi, one retired Parsee civil servant from Bombay
and two medical practitioners from Calcutta. The tradition and th
personnel at Nirguna Ashram were such that they did not attract th
orthodox—and the fact that most of the monks spoke English in additio
to whatever their native Indian language was, accounted for the cosmo
politan character of such visits. These people are not the ones who
support Hindu religious institutions with large sums of money; those who
do belong to the *Marwari* and *banya* communities and usually do no
speak English—do not support the sort of doctrinally sophisticated
deritualized teaching current in these modern monasteries. Those who
did come combined religious and personal quest with a vacation in th
coolness of the central Himalayas. Orthodox, wealthy Hindus usually dc
not vacation in such fashion. They would rather go on a straight pilgrim
age to any number of holy places for their fulfillment of vows or the
seeking of *darshan* (Bharati 1970; Bhardwaj 1973). For these urbar
sophisticates who came to Nirguna Ashram, the idea of pilgrimage was nc
doubt there, but it was not paramount; discourse with the English-
speaking monks and alpine relaxation were.

The attitude of those visitors toward the *pahari* personnel was unequiv
ocal: they ignored them completely. That was to be expected, though
since servants are not really taken as partners in dialog anywhere in India
Yet I had the feeling that the urban guests' reaction or nonreaction to the
cooks and servants, who served them well during their stay, had to dc
with the "don't upset my idyll" syndrome. Tourists and pilgrims alike
view the Himalayas as the abode of gods and rishis (Bharati 1978). The
stark realities of *pahari* village life would frustrate them. If there is a
confrontation between plains and *pahari* values, the plains score in a one
upmanship relation, as Berreman has shown so convincingly (Berreman
1963). I tried to probe some of these guests' ideas about the few *paharis*
they had actually encountered on the way up to Nirguna Ashram—

villagers, teastall owners, and coolies carrying their luggage—and then, of course, the cooks here at the ashram. "These are simple people, they are one with nature, we from the cities should not try to change their ways, to make them choosey, to spoil their natural manner" etc. On the other hand, when the more inquisitive guests who stayed for a whole summer came to know—the more perceptive and curious among them at least—about the ways of the *paharis*, their religious ideas and practices, their comparative laxity in sexual mores, their medical "superstitions," the guests put a distance between themselves and these de-idealized, actual people. There was no opportunity for strife, since the situation was so construed that no potential for friction arose. There was just a total ignoring of the actual people around. I got the impression that our guests from the plains viewed the *paharis* as though they were actors on a stage, not connected to them in a real give-and-take situation.

As to our *paharis*' reaction to the guests, they were far more positive and defined. Here were wealthy people who might tip the cooks or who might provide some jobs in the plains, as cooks, bearers, servants. The *paharis* psyched them out as potential employers or as mediators to potential employers in the plains. It did work in one case. The younger of the two Rajput cooks was asked to join the wealthy Parsee gentleman's household in Bombay where, apart from seeing the big world outside, he would earn a multiple of what the Nirguna Ashram paid for his services, which were more numerous and more arduous than the tasks in the Parsee household in the great city 1200 miles away.

Pahari ritual has been studied by a number of anthropologists, again headed by Berreman (1963); its style is shared in large sections of neighboring Nepal, where research is accessible and intensive at this very time. But the interface between *pahari* religion and ritual and a highly Sanskritic form of monastic Hinduism has not been presented, to my knowledge, and this may well be a first report. It so happened that a tiny local shrine, built by *paharis* for *paharis* only, was situated smack within the Ashram compound, and had been there long, long before the monastery. The boundary line of the monastic property was overgrown with thicket and dense forest, the outlying sections of the property were indeed subalpine forest with fur, cedar, and pine, in no way different from the unpopulated forest land between the monastery and the next village five kilometers away. Just why the monastery had been built so close to the shrine, I don't know, since no one remembered—the *paharis* said "it has always been here" and the monks knew that it had been there before the ashram was built in the late sixties of the last century. I will guess, however, that the presence of the simple shrine might have served as a kind of psychological marker for the founder of the ashram, who was a fairly learned monk from Calcutta. Hindu monks from the cities have little sympathy for local cults—like all urbanites, they refer to them as

"superstitions" (Bharati 1970) or by some other unflattering epithet, and
if I project myself into the mind of the founding monk over a century ago
some such thoughts might have occurred: here is a simple shrine made by
simple people in a simple manner, just some piece of stone under a tree
but the stone represents the mountain goddess, the villagers tell me, and
we worship *Parvati* the mountain-girl, the spouse of Siva—so why don't
we plan on this site, amidst the realm of Siva and Parvati, where other
people have been worshipping them for a long time. Or thoughts of that
kind. Still, this kind of religious solidarity is somewhat academic; just as
there is no social contact beyond the daily service situations, there is no
religious contact of any sort. Twice every month, on full moon and new
moon nights, the monks conducted the *Ramanamasankirtanam*, the great
Hindu epic of the hero Rama, incarnation of Lord Vishnu, telling the
whole story of the Ramayana in 108 chanted verses. The only *pahari*
participant was an old highcaste man from the village four miles away,
who had been a close friend of one of the abbots long since deceased,
given a standing invitation to come to the ashram, play carromboard with
the monks, eat with them and play the finger drum, *tabla*, to accompany
the chant. He kept doing this for close to thirty years, when he finally
became too old to walk up the four miles. Thereafter, one of the novices
took over the *tabla*, and no other *pahari* was ever asked again to
participate. The summer guests from the plains, the affluent lay devotees I
already talked about, did sit in and look on as the litany was in progress. I
asked the abbot and some of the monks on several occasions why the
paharis weren't asked to share the event. They are servants, was the
reply, and that was it. I asked each of the *pahari* crew separately over two
years whether he would like to participate—they all said they would, but
it was unthinkable for them to suggest or ask for such participation. But it
was quite clear that they did appreciate the religious deeds of the monks,
although of course they, the *paharis*, did not know much about the
theological content of the monastic life in this ashram. That was hardly to
be expected. The swamis were all followers of the monistic school of
Vedanta, a highly scholastic segment of the Hindu tradition. In it, there
was no room for ritual, no room for communal or congregational worship—the *Ramananamasankirtanam* on full and new moon days was
decorative rather than instrumental to the pursuit of the monastic routine,
and there was no room for any icons. It was this last fact that was pointed
out with some bewilderment by the *pahari* staff: other swamis they knew
always worshipped a particular deity and had their little shrine with an
icon, or else they lived near places of pilgrimage where there were shrines
and icons for formal worship. Still—and this is the genius of Hinduism on
all levels—the two cooks understood me quite well, when I explained the
basic ideas of monistic Vedanta to them on a long and dark winter night.

Both Hiramani and Ucchu Singh nodded interested consent, and Hira—I remember distinctly because it struck me as rather marvelous—said, "this is also one of the paths [*marg*, a highly sophisticated, Sanskritic term he used] whereby the divine is attained [*yah bhi bhagavan ki prapti ke liye ek marg hai*]." This is elite Hindu talk. There is a possibility that Hiramani had picked it up from either the monks or the visitors, but I doubt it for the simple reason that not a single one among the monks and the novices spoke Hindi very well—they all came either from Bengal or from South India, and their Hindi was kitchen and servant talk only. Also, I never witnessed a situation where the monks talked religion with the *pahari* staff, never. They simply did not regard them as their spiritual clientele. I think Hiramani's pensive expression reflected a general highcaste *pahari* tendency to utilize the sort of pan-Hindu parlance which has become quite marked in rural areas where some people read, some go to school, and where some sort of religious pamphlet is available, as is the case in most monasteries and certainly at the larger centers of pilgrimage, all of them *pahari* shrines (Bharati 1970; Bhardwaj 1973), and it is almost inevitable that they picked up "great tradition" talk on several levels.

Yet when I asked Hiramani and Ucchu Singh whether they ever worshipped at the little shrine under the tree in the ashram compound, they denied it. Then who did? Who was it that deposited some coins there which I saw along with red powder (*kunkum*) spread over the central stone? Both of them suggested it might have been some villagers from Lohaghat who had been around either to hunt deer or to collect firewood. Whether this was the case, or whether it had actually been one of the *pahari* staff, the fact was that they did not want to be associated with this rather lowly ritual—at least not in the eyes of the monks. There is a lay way to explain this, and there is an anthropological way. The former belongs to the tourist impression-box: the natives don't want to show their rustic, primitive ways to us, hence they dissemble such actions or conceal them from outsiders. The anthropologist specializing in India, however, has a far more complex (not necessarily more correct) etiology for denials of this type: all Hindus except the brahmins on top constantly emulate purer, more literate, more authentic ways of ritual practice—the ideal is the Sanskritic ritual of the learned brahmins, again an instance of the aforementioned process of Sanskritization. Local cults are "improved" to conform more to the official brahmanical cults; local deities are "upcasted" so as to be identifiable as aspects or forms of the Sanskritic gods of the brahmanical pantheon. McKim Mariott calls this process "universalization" and its involute "parochialization," i.e., when Sanskritic gods and rituals are explained in local terms by a local, non-Sanskritic clientele (Marriot 1955). There is a ubiquitous pecking order in the Hindu system of mutual assessment; there is always a group to look down upon, right to the bottom where there are such group leatherwork ers as the *chamars* who, of course, cannot look down upon anyone else since they rank as the lowest and most defiled: our Pyarilal belonged to that group. But why should the cook Hiramani, a brahmin himself, aspire to brahmanical talk as he did in commenting on the ideas of the monks in the ashram—and why should he deny having anything to do with the little local shrine under the tree in the cloister compound? Because *pahari* brahmins are looked down upon by plains brahmins, and *pahari* brahmin and rajputs know this too well, resent it, and react against it not by denying the validity of such hierarchical claims and assumptions, but by "Sanskritizing" their speech, positively by using plains brahmins religious commentary style, which they may have witnessed at places of pilgrimage where holy men and brahmins from the plains mingle with the locals, and negatively by denying any involvement with local, blatantly non-brahmanical, non-Sanskritic religious expression. The goddess repre sented by those simple stones under a tree can be and is no doubt explained as the local form of Parvati, the Daughter of the Mountain, Spouse of Shiva, Lord of Mount Kailasa (the highly sacred Tibetan mountain), when *paharis* sit together and smoke their locally made cigarettes. Yet to the outside world, particularly to the higher ranked plains people with their ritualistically more complex and "purer" ways, it may be felt safe by the *paharis* to simply deny any such involvement. Suppose the Gran' Old Opry of Nashville were located within three blocks from the Metropolitan Opera in the Lincoln Center of the Performing Arts, and suppose that there was a totally separate, non-overlapping audience in both institutions. Then one might assume that the ticketholders for the Gran' Old Opry might feel slightly off base when confronted, in a putative mutual encounter, with ticketholders for *Tristan und Isolde* at the Metropolitan Opera. I think that, if it did not represent what modern philosophers call a "counterfactual conditional," some such hierarchical feelings toward themselves and the other group might arise, and that would be quite analogous to the self—and the mutual assessment of *pahari* highcaste and plain highcaste Hindus.

What does the future hold for Himalayan parcels like the Nirguna Ashram? I think it holds lots, lots of tourists and it engenders the changes tourism brings about in previously unexplored regions. The Himalayas from this vantage point, hold three attractions which market themselves: first, it is the air conditioned part of the Indian summer—most Indians who can afford to get away from the sweltering plains go to the Hima layas. Second, it is the inner core of the alpinist dream—since Tenzing Norgai made it to the top with his patron from New Zealand, Himalayan life hasn't been the same. In parts, it has begun to center upon the alpinist professional. Third, and this is the most direct sequel to what was presented in this report, the Himalayas are the cynosure of the quest for the sacred, the mystical, the holy, to Hindus, and to westerners in search of the mysterious East. Now the mysterious East is also being cleverly marketed by Indians (Mehta 1980), but there is scope for the genuine seeker, and they can and will find sites similar to Nirguna Ashram. And then, pardon the pun, the sky is the limit.

7

Transhumance in European and American Mountains

Gisbert Rinschede

As a result of extreme climatic conditions in many regions of the world, the livestock industry represents the only possible kind of land use. It appears in various economic forms as sedentary livestock industry, as migratory livestock industry, and as stall-feeding, which includes keeping livestock in feedlots.

Transhumance—a Part of the Migratory Livestock Industry

Forms of Migratory Livestock Industry

The migratory livestock industry is that part of the industry in which livestock is driven from range to seasonal range throughout the year. The ranges cannot be used during the whole year and are situated too far away from a fixed station to allow direct management. Nomadism, semi-nomadism, transhumance, and "livestock industry based on alpine pastures" belong to these traditional forms of the migratory livestock industry. Transitional forms exist not only between the migratory and sedentary livestock industry but also between the various forms of migratory livestock industry.

Nomadism is a form of migratory livestock industry in which the livestock is herded by a whole social group (e.g., a family) as owners on their permanent and periodic movement from range to range. Nomads live all year round in mobile tents, yurts, or huts, and rarely in permanent settlements. They almost exclusively live on livestock raising (great livestock: camels, bovines, horses; small livestock: sheep, goats) and regularly practice no cultivation (farming). Therefore non-animal food is often purchased by exchange of goods or by collecting fees.

Semi-nomadism is a transitional form verging toward a more sedentary economy. It regularly combines the seasonal movement of livestock with seasonal cultivation. On their seasonal migrations—largely with small livestock—the social group lives in mobile camps but also in permanent settlements. Mountain nomadism is a special form of nomadism and semi-nomadism, through which the seasonal movement proceeds vertically, often corresponding to the orographic conditions, between valley or foreland and mountain.

The "migratory livestock industry based on alpine pastures" (*almwirtschaft*) is a special form of mountain pasture farming in which farmers drive their livestock from their base ranch situated in the mountain valley or foreland partly over *mayen* (intermediate pasture) stages to the highest mountain pastures. The livestock industry based on alpine pastures is generally characterized by stabling animals and feeding them hay during winter and using of mountain pastures (*alps*) during summer.

Transhumance is a form of the migratory livestock industry in which the livestock is generally accompanied by hired men but also by owners and their relatives, but rarely by a whole family, on a long migration or transit between at least two seasonal ranges. This seasonal movement is caused by the different characteristics of the ranges in terms of altitude, thermic, hygric or agro-economical conditions. Like nomadism, traditional transhumance is combined with year-round grazing. Stabling or supplemental feeding is practiced only during the cold season if absolutely necessary. The settlements are permanent at the location of the base ranch, while at the other location the herdsmen can live in permanent settlements as well as in tents, mobile huts, or carts. At the base ranch cultivation can be practiced; at the other locations the settlements are only seasonally used. Rarely are both settlements occupied at the same season.

Farmers, ranchers, or even non-agrarian groups can be the owners of transhumant herds. Transhumance is practiced with small livestock (sheep and goats) as well as with large livestock, especially with cattle. There is some agreement among etymologists about the origin of the term "transhumance." It is derived from the Latin "transhumer," from the terms "trans" and "humus," meaning land that—from the viewpoint of the sedentary groups—is situated across (and beyond) the cultivated land, vineyard, and olive groves.

The modern term "transhumance" derives from the colloquial language of the Mediterranean regions (France, Spain, Italy) and was adopted into the scientific literature (Vidal de la Blache 1892) at the end of the nineteenth century. In the Romance languages it refers even today to migration and is only to some extent applied to the transport of transhumant livestock. Geography has broadened the term so that today it characterizes an economic form of the migratory livestock industry other

than nomadism, semi-nomadism, and migratory livestock industry based
on alpine pastures.

In English-speaking countries the term "transhumance" is mistakenly
used to mean the "migration of ethnic groups or seasonal workers." In
the English geographical literature the term—for want of a better English
term—is also used for the economic form of "migratory livestock industry based on alpine pastures." The French literature often uses the term
wrongly in the meaning of nomadism and semi-nomadism.

Forms of Transhumance

One can distinguish between uni-stationed and a dual-stationed transhumance according to the number of permanent operation stations (Fig.
7.1).

From the viewpoint of the beginning area and the location of the base
ranch we distinguish among the uni-stationed form with only one permanent operation in the plains, in the foothills, or in the mountains. Ascending transhumance (transhumance of the lowland settlement) has its base
ranch and winter ranges in the plains or foothills and uses summer ranges
in the mountains. Descending transhumance (transhumance of the mountain settlement), on the other hand sends out the livestock from the high
elevated private summer ranges close to the base ranch to spend the
winter in temperate lowlands. Intermediate stationed transhumance has a
base ranch in the region of the transitional ranges in the foothills and has
to partly cover equally long distances to the summer ranges in the
mountains and the winter ranges in the lowlands.

In contrast to the so-called uni-stationed form with only one permanent
operation station (fixed station), dual-stationed transhumance has two
equivalent permanent stations (base ranches) in the mountains and in the

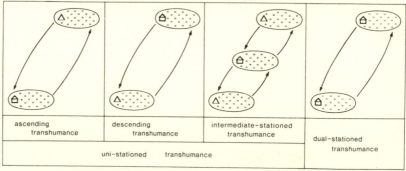

G. Rinschede

Figure 7.1   Forms of Transhumance

lowlands, i.e., one livestock station at each end of the seasonal movements. This form derives mostly from ascending and descending transhumance by using and buying a second, mostly abandoned, ranch close to the seasonal range.

General Environmental Conditions and Distribution of Transhumance

The existence of transhumance is connected with special natural and economic environmental conditions. Of course the most important factor is the natural contrast of climate and vegetation between lowland and mountain regions. This applies to transhumance in all climatic zones, for transhumance is a global phenomenon and is to be found in all continents between the equator and the fiftieth parallel north and south. Accordingly, we distinguish between extra-tropical (mainly Mediterranean) transhumance and tropical transhumance.

In extra-tropical transhumance (i.e., in subtropical and temperate zones) the seasonal movements occur primarily according to the thermal rhythm of the year. Low and high temperatures and a different distribution of precipitation give a push to the movements of livestock. The lowlands are mostly winter humid, nearly snow-free, and mostly summer dry. The mountain regions are winter cold and snow-covered as well as humid and snow-free in summer. Because of summer droughts, especially in the subtropics, ascending transhumance moves from the lowlands to the mountains and returns from the mountain ranges before the first snowfall. Descending transhumance especially is connected to climatic and orographic conditions, as it keeps more livestock than it is able to feed during winter in the mountains.

Besides these natural factors transhumance of the extra-tropics owes its existence to a number of agroeconomic factors. These are especially important for ascending transhumance, for the intensive cultivation on the base ranch allows no grazing during the main vegetation period. Owners of herds, therefore, give the livestock to hired men to herd on the mountain range, while they themselves and their relations bring in the harvest. In addition, one can recognize that grazing on mountain ranges for several months favors the health and meat quality of livestock.

This extra-tropic transhumance is to be found in nearly all regions of the young fold mountain belt of Eurasia and North Africa: the Atlas, Pyrenees, all mountains of Spain and Portugal (Cordillera Cantabrica, Sierra Nevada, etc.) Cevennes, French, Italian and Swiss Alps, Dinara Planina, Carpathians, Balkan Mountains, Pindhos Oros, Pontic and Tauros, Zagros, Hindukush, Baluchistan, Kashmir, Himalaya, and Tien Shan. In the Asian mountains the transhumant types are closely associated with, or have developed from semi-nomadism.

On the North American continent transhumance is found in nearly all mountains of the West, especially in the Rocky Mountains, in the Sierra Nevada, on the Colorado Plateau, in the Cascade Range and in the Great Basin Ranges. In the South American Andes it is widespread in the Argentinian province of Neuquen and in the Chilean province of Cautin. Transhumance-related forms of migratory livestock industry are also to be found in South Africa (Drakensberg), in Australia (Great Dividing Range), and in New Zealand (Alps).

In the tropics, the wet seasons are important for the change of seasonal ranges. With nearly constant temperatures the droughts and the rains determine the start of the cattle movement. There are regions where the cattle stay in the savanna during the rains and ascend in winter to the humid mountain regions. In other regions the cattle, forced by heavy rainfall and flooding, leave the lowlands for higher and dryer regions until they descend again when the flooding recedes in winter. Tropical transhumance is found in Colombia, in the Andes below 27°, southern Ethiopia, Kenya, and Ruanda.

Transhumance with Examples from Europe and North America

Although the transhumance of livestock in the mountains of the New World surely originated in the patterns of the classic Mediterranean regions of southern Europe, transhumance in the American West developed quite differently during its 100-year-old history, mainly because of the different natural conditions.

Natural Regions and Seasonal Ranges

The mountain regions of the Alps and Pyrenees are surrounded by temperate and Mediterranean lowlands. On its western slope, the Western Cordillera (Coast Range, Cascade Range, and Sierra Nevada) rises above warm temperate and Mediterranean coastlands. The Rocky Mountains, the Colorado Plateau, and the ranges of the Great Basin, however, are surrounded by high elevated semi-arid steppes and semi-deserts.

The summer ranges in the French Alps and the Pyrenees are mostly situated on artificial clearings (i.e., deforested grasslands) but also on alpine tundra above the timberline. In the mountains of the American West, however, the mountain ranges are forest ranges and natural grasslands. The following are prominent on an altitudinal profile of Intermountain West.

At the lower elevations bunchgrass-covered Ponderosa pine forests predominate, with clear-cuttings and openings of earlier fires in Douglas fir aspen forests higher up. So-called mountain parks—broad semi-arid mountain valleys—have, because of their rich vegetation, an extremely high concentration of grazing livestock at the next level. Mountain

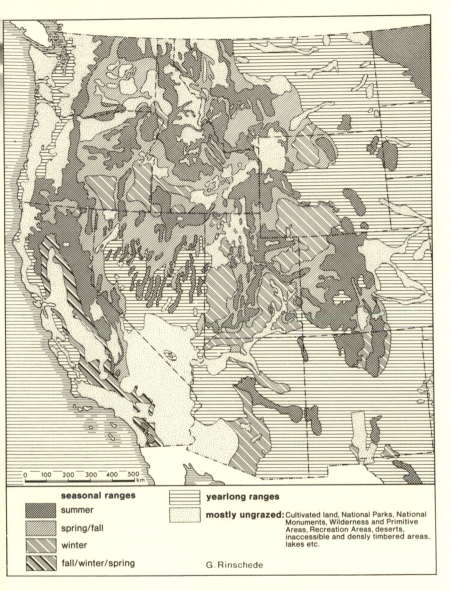

seasonal ranges

summer

spring/fall

winter

fall/winter/spring

yearlong ranges

mostly ungrazed: Cultivated land, National Parks, National Monuments, Wilderness and Primitive Areas, Recreation Areas, deserts, inaccessible and densly timbered areas, lakes etc.

G. Rinschede

Figure 7.2   Seasonal Ranges in the Western United States

meadows, much preferred by cattle, are followed by open, sub-alpine grasslands grazed by both kinds of livestock. Finally, alpine tundra, if at all grazed, is the domain of sheep.

On both continents, Europe and North America, the use of the alpine tundra by livestock is decreasing. Whereas in the United States it is

nearly completely given up in favor of tourism or environmental protection, this development of the alpine tundra is not advanced so far as in the
Alps and Pyrenees.

The spring and fall ranges are often situated in the foothills or on
mountain valley bottoms. They are mostly covered with grass, shrub, and
pigmy-forest formations. On the lower slopes of the Sierra Nevada and
Cascade Range under oak woodland, so-called fall-winter-spring ranges
with annual cool-season grasses occur.

Patterns of Land Ownership

The seasonal ranges in the Alps and Pyrenees are predominantly in
private and communal ownership but seldom in state ownership, so we do
not have a distinct pattern of landownership. In the Rocky Mountains and
the Intermountain West, the patterns of seasonal grazing correspond in
broad outlines to the patterns of landownership. The winter ranges are
mostly federally owned land, which is administered by the United States
Bureau of Land Management. The irrigated pastures along river courses
and the foothill ranges are mostly in private hands. The spring and fall
ranges—situated in middle altitude between ranch and mountain range—
are important lambing grounds, and therefore mostly in private hands,
too, but also partly on federal lands. The National Forests, administered
by the United States Department of Agriculture Forest Service, represent
the most important mountain summer ranges of the migratory livestock
industry. But there are also mountain ranges on more elevated federal
land and on private land of abandoned ranches close to the National
Forests.

Forms of Transhumance

On both continents the different forms of transhumance depend on the
natural conditions but also on the historically caused man-land ratio, on
intensity of land use, as well as on the common stage of development in
adjacent lowlands and mountain regions.

In the French Alps ascending transhumance accounts for about 88
percent of transhumance. In the Pyrenees, however, descending transhumance dominates with 65 to 100 percent, according to different parts of
the mountains. This situation is caused by the general decline of the
mountain economy. Descending transhumance is diminishing, too, but
partly in favor of the ascending transhumance of the lowlands. In the Alps
and Pyrenees dual-stationed transhumance, derived from descending
transhumance, is characterized by a second station in the plains, which
secures the important winter range. Because it is not easy to define, it is
included with descending transhumance. Intermediate-stationed trans-

humance does not appear in the Alps and Pyrenees because, in contrast to the western United States, there are no foothill ranges that serve as transitional ranges (Fig. 7.3).

In contrast to the European mountains, the mountains of the American West are only sparsely populated, therefore ascending and intermediate-stationed transhumance predominate. Both are traditional forms, which had already developed in the first decades of settlement. Descending and dual-stationed transhumance developed later, when rural exodus and change of land use began in the high mountain valleys.

Patterns of Movement

Essentially, the differences in altitude between the seasonal ranges determine the patterns of movement, thus ascending sheep transhumance of the western Alps goes to the plains and hills of Provence from the Côte d'Azur and eastern Languedoc. It covers long distances—up to 450 km into the northern Alps and the inner high valleys close to the Italian border. In the Pyrenees the herds of ascending transhumance cover in general distances between only 30 to 75 km. Their base ranches are mostly situated directly at the base of the mountain at the valley mouths (Fig. 7.4).

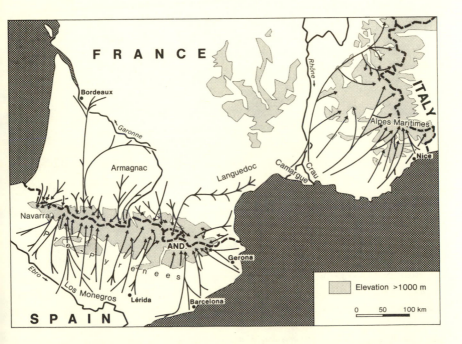

Figure 7.3   Seasonal Movements of Sheep in the Alps and the Pyrenees

Figure 7.4   Seasonal Movements of Sheep in the Western United States

Descending sheep transhumance is not widespread in the western Alps. It mostly comes out of the valleys of the Alps Maritimes. Out of the high Pyrenees it partly reaches remote leased ranges in the pre-plains, such as Garonne-lowland, Languedoc, and Ebro-basin. Descending cattle transhumance is to be found only sparsely in the Alps and Pyrenees, covering distances up to only 100 km down into the winter temperate lowlands and pre-Pyrenees.

In the western United States, altitude as well as the latitude is important for the patterns of seasonal movements, because the area extends more than 2000 km from north to south and includes several climatic zones. Therefore, in some regions we also have movements from north to south in addition to the vertical movements. They cover longer distances to mild winter ranges in regions of lower latitude.

The movements of cattle in general are shorter than those of sheep. In the temperate American Southwest the herders start from the winter ranges, and in the colder northern states from the irrigated pastures close to the ranch, where the cattle have been fed during the winter in a form of "Almwirtschaft." If the ranch operations are not situated directly at the base of the mountains, they have to cover distances up to 150 km, as in the Snake River plains of Idaho. Modern truck transportation permits them to cover distances up to 550 km, such as between southern Oregon and California.

The distances covered by transhumant sheep bands are—because of the use of transportation—sometimes longer than they were 80 to 100 years ago. In Nevada and Utah bands cover distances of up to 450 km between summer and winter ranges. Sheep bands from Idaho are even transported over a distance of 1500 km to winter ranges in southern California.

Moving and Transportation of Livestock

Among the various kinds of livestock movement (migration, transportation by truck and rail), hoof migration has lost in importance during the past decades. In the Alps and Pyrenees migration is only a small percentage of transhumance. In Southern Europe, only the Spanish Pyrenees and the French Western Pyrenees have higher proportions, as shorter distances between the seasonal ranges exist here. In the Spanish Pyrenees and in the United States special migratory routes are still existent; in the French Alps and Pyrenees, however, they disappeared long ago by being taken over as public roads or private land.

In the western United States during 1975, 45 percent of the migratory sheep used special drove roads to reach the seasonal ranges, and 30 percent were transported by truck. The high percentage of hoof movements in the United States may be caused by the low population density, the large portion of public land, and the adjacent seasonal ranges through which transportation, in many cases, is not necessary.

The transportation of transhumant herds by rail decreased in France and Spain during the past two decades, primarily because the access to loading stations in the plains and mountains was through dense road traffic.

In the United States transportation by rail began between 1930 and 1950, but it was never so important as in the Eastern Pyrenees and the French Alps, where in 1970–71 20 to 40 percent of all transhumant sheep were still transported by rail. The relatively high transportation tariffs, the thin rail network, and the fact that most important migratory directions do not run parallel to the railway routes account for the nearly total discontinuation of transportation by rail in the United States.   Transportation by trucks in the United States, just as in Southern Europe, started in the 1950s, because of increased traffic circulation, restrictions on the use of traditional migratory routes, and lack of shepherds to accompany the bands. High transportation costs sometimes allow the herds to be transported only a part of the whole distance, such as in the densely populated Salt Lake region. Rising transportation costs will also have their influence on the distance between the seasonal ranges, because livestock movements over 500 to 1500 km are not cost-efficient.

Because of high traffic concentration and long distances in the Alps the cattle are basically transported to the seasonal ranges, whereas because of high transportation costs and shorter distances in the Pyrenees and in the western United States they are still driven on migratory routes. But the 70,000 cattle of the Klamath Valley/Cascade Range in southern Oregon have been transported every year by truck over a distance of 500 km down to the Sacramento Valley.

Shepherds

In general, the employment of hired workers is considered to be an important characteristic of transhumance and often distinguishes it from the other forms of migratory livestock industry (for instance, nomadism). Research in the classic regions of transhumance, however, showed that in reality, hired shepherds, and herders, and their relatives are in the same way involved in herding bands. Even whole families sometimes accompany their bands on summer and winter ranges (dual-stationed transhumance).

In southern France (Provence) only a small part of the shepherds originate from the native region of transhumance. Usually they are recruited from other regions of the same country, from other southern European countries, and from the northern continent. A distribution of shepherds by nationality in the Provence from the early 1970s is Italian 57 percent, Frenchmen 35 percent, Spaniards 3 percent, Portuguese 2 percent, Moroccan 2 percent. In the French Pyrenees and in Andorra the shepherds are predominately of Spanish nationality. In the Spanish Pyrenees many are partly from the interior provinces of Spain.

For more than a century in the American West, shepherds of Basque origin were the backbone of the sheep industry. With their knowledge of Spanish transhumance and the experiences they had gathered in the South American Pampa, they were especially qualified to practice transhumance between the summer ranges in the mountains and the winter ranges in the adjacent steppes and deserts.

In the 1950s new rules for the recruitment of Basque shepherds were enacted. The contracts were restricted to three years and were renewed only if the shepherd left the country for a short time so that he could not assert a claim to American citizenship.

Between 1957 and 1970, 5495 shepherds were placed by the "Western Range Association." Until 1965 about 95 percent of all applicants were of Basque nationality. Later young men from other parts of Spain, from Peru (1971) and from Mexico (1973) were also recruited. On December 31, 1976, a total of 742 shepherds were under contract. Of these, 58 percent (433) came from Latin America (271 Peruvians, 161 Mexicans, 1 Colombian); out of the remaining 309 shepherds, only 106 were Basques.

In the last decade not only did the ethnic origin of the shepherds in the West shift, but the total number of contracted shepherds was reduced by half. Many owners gave up their bands so that the number of sheep was diminished greatly in the whole West.

Importance and Decline of Transhumance

In the mid-1970s the number of transhumant livestock in the Alps and Pyrenees amounted to about 800,000 sheep and 8,000 cattle. At the same time in the western United States about 1.3 million sheep and 1.3 million cattle took part in migratory livestock movements; nearly all sheep belonged to transhumance, whereas with strong regional differences most of the cattle belonged to the migratory livestock industry based on alpine pastures.

The strong preponderance of the transhumant sheep industry in the Alps and the Pyrenees is remarkable. With a general decline of all mountain range use by transhumant animal units we have to distinguish clearly several key features.

For six decades the sheep industry has been declining steadily, whereas since the middle of the 1960s the cattle industry has increased. This is true not only for the United States but also for the Alps and Pyrenees.

The reasons for this are quite different in the European and American mountains. Among reasons for the downward trend of the migratory sheep industry in the United States are the following. General reduction measures have been promulgated by the Forest Service and the Bureau of Land Management which administer the range land. Furthermore, there are increasing grazing restrictions, especially in the alpine tundra, that are caused by the strong influences of environmental protection and conservation agencies. There are also fewer shepherds as a result of poor working conditions. Sheep herding has large expenditures of labor and effort and receives little prestige as compared to the cattle industry. Finally, costs have increased from rent increases and predator losses, primarily from coyotes. In the Alps and Pyrenees there was a loss of classic winter ranges by alternative land use such as agriculture, industry, and urbanization—for example, Los Monegros, Los Bardenas, Garrigue on the coast of Catalonia, Camargue, Crau, and Plateau de Haute Provence. Costs for wintering increased along with higher transportation costs by trucks instead of migration or transportation by rail. Many young people moved to the cities thereby causing a shortage of good shepherds. The decline of the transhumant sheep industry in the United States is based largely on changed land use demands on the mountains. In the Alps and Pyrenees the reasons are to be found only slightly in the mountains themselves, although many conflicts between tourism and migratory livestock industry occur there, as well.

Whereas the dairy cattle industry in the form of transhumance and "Almwirtschaft" in the United States ceased to exist at the turn of the century, in the Alps and Pyrenees transhumant dairy cattle operations are still to be found in addition to the migratory dairy cattle industry based on alpine pasture, as in the Départements Alpes de Haute Provence and Savoie. The transhumant dairy sheep industry is still existent in the Alps Maritimes and in the Western Pyrenees.

8

The Importance, Status and Structure of Almwirtschaft in the Alps

Hugo Penz

The low temperatures associated with the highest areas of mountains are the most important factors in the agrarian exploitation of mountainous regions. Alps farmers developed *almwirtschaft*—a special agro-pastoral system adapted to the mountain environment—to allow for low temperatures in cultivating particular altitudinal zones.

In the Alps there are a few permanent rural settlements extending higher than the limit of grain cultivation. Because of the predominance of subsistence economy, until World War II it was difficult for the mountain farms to survive without grain cultivation. Mountain farmers were interested in using *almen*—the grass pastures above the limit of grain cultivation and the tree line to increase the basis of their marginal existence. The mountain farmers therefore built small secondary farmsteads at high altitudes to be used seasonally. Harald Uhlig (1976) called this model of agrarian organization with branches in several altitudinal zones a "staggered system" (German, *staffelsystem*). These *staffelsysteme* were markedly different in particular valleys and have changed very much during the modern impact on *almwirtschaft*.

Typical features of the staggered system in the Tirol are shown in Figure 8.1. The valley zone is the center of the agrarian production, but since the decline of self-sufficiency the fields have been converted for use as meadows. The fields as such have disappeared and the high common pasturelands for the most part have been ceded to individual landowners. The bosky meadows of larch became marginal land and many have been reforested. In the forest zone itself, agrarian production has almost ceased and now forestry predominates. The forest-glades have been reduced and grass mowing has ceased. Formerly, when the hay was harvested, the farmer's entire family moved into the mountain huts, which were called *maiensaess* in Switzerland, *asten* in the Tirol, and *baite*

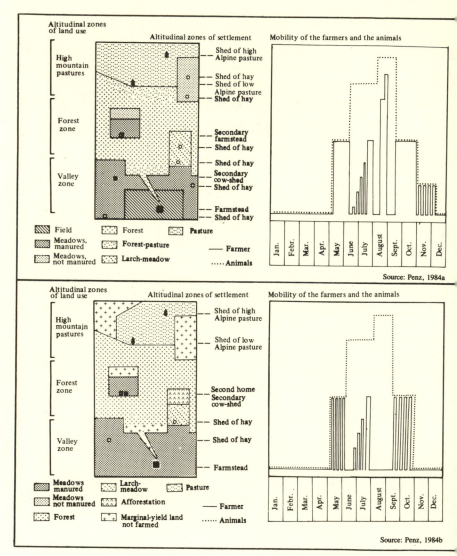

Figure 8.1 *Almwirtschaft* in Tyrol. *Top:* Traditional staggered system; *bottom:* actual staggered system.

or *casolarie* in Italy (Werthemann, Imboden 1982). Today many of those mountain huts are connected by paths and vehicle tracks so that meadows can be managed from the farm. But most of the high-sited communal meadows which were not manured, German *bergmaehder,* have been reapportioned to individual farmers (Ruppert 1982).

In the Italian, Swiss, Austrian, German, and Slovene Alps, cattle grazing predominates, but in the French Alps sheep pasturing is important. Pasturing is organized in a staggered system. Alpine pasture, in German called *alm* or *alpe,* represents an ecological niche of Alpine agriculture that operates only during the summer time and is involved mainly with cattle rearing. In France, sheep *transhumance* is more common.

Functions of Alpine Pastures for the Mountain Farming Agriculture

Within *almwirtschaft* the Alpine pasture fulfills three main functions. First, it supplies and enlarges the production of fodder; second, it relieves the summer (working) schedule; and third, it promotes the rearing of healthy cattle (Hartke, Ruppert 1964).

In the Alpine valleys, cattle-farms require large amounts of winter fodder because the vegetation growing season is short, hence, farms need larger areas for fodder growing. At the upper limit of the winter rye (about 1300–1500m), cattle can be provided with fresh feed for about 150 days of the year and at the limit of grain growing (about 1600–1800m) only for 120 days of the year. The rest of the year cattle have to stay in the cow-sheds. These Alpine farms are especially interested in exploiting Alpine pastures to substitute for cultivated fodder. When an Alpine farm sends all its cattle to mountain pasture for 100 days, it can keep 27 percent more cattle. When two thirds of the cattle are kept on Alpine pastures for 100 days 18 percent more cattle can be kept in winter.

The steep slopes of the mountains strongly restrict the number of meadows in the valleys. As the mountain farmers have relinquished subsistence farming, they have restricted plow agriculture. Consequently, valley land also became vacant because of the abandonment of farms, but the profits increased owing to the introduction of chemical fertilizers. Nevertheless, winter fodder still plays a central role for the contemporary mountain farmers, as agrarian income of most farmers depends exclusively on dairy farming.

Because industrialization and urbanization have continually attracted labor from agriculture, farm labor has been reduced to a minimum in the management of farms. The conditions for cultivation have also changed, and farmers have tried to relieve their schedules during the summer by supplementing their income. Farms have adopted cash cropping. Fieldwork is now concentrated on two peak-periods, namely the first and the second mowing of valley meadows. Higher farms are more labor intensive at the first cutting, because the profits of the second cutting are so small that it remains undone. At the upper limit of grain growing, farms that rent rooms to tourists face additional loads because the first mowing coincides with the peak of the summer tourism at the beginning of July.

Most mountain farms of the Alps are so small that any greater mechanization of cow-shed work would be unprofitable. Several calculations show that the same working time that is needed for one cow can be used for the harvesting of a hectare of meadow. Thus the farmers are able to cultivate far greater areas with the same staff. They get more fodder, and they can keep more cattle in winter.

Several studies show that cattle which have been kept on Alpine pastures in summer achieve higher prices when they are sold. Thus Alpine pastures have become an important location for cattle rearing in the Alps.

Regional Differences of the Alpine Pastures

Traditional *almwirtschaft* is an agrarian system synchronized with altitudinally determined ecological niches, which are well adapted to the mountain environment and to the former economic system of the mountains. The differences of the natural and social resources that are typical of the Alps have led to strong regional contrasts in the structure of Alpine pastures.

The structure of *almwirtschaft* is closely connected with the relations between property and ownership, and these arrangements influence the relationship between the main farmsteading and the Alpine pastures. The closest relationship exists between the private Alpine pastures that are a secondary outlying farm to one single main farm. Consequently, the possessor can decide the type of cultivation of the Alpine pasture without consulting other farmers. Alpine pastures that belong to a community of farmers, however, are different, as each farmer owns only a mountain hut. Agrarian communities' Alpine pastures that are communally owned and grazed by a communal herd are subject to established Alpine pasture rules that are the basis for cultivation and grazing and regulated by farmers meeting with their elected functionaries. In addition, there are also Alpine pastures in possession of public corporations (municipality, district, province, and state), which decide the land usage. Farmers whose cattle graze such pasturelands have no direct influence on land use policies governing this pasture.

These publically owned Alpine pastures are mostly remnants of medieval common pasturing. These have traditional forms and are often large pasturelands on which big herds can graze. Most of these Alpine pastures, however, are located at high, unfavorable places. Nevertheless, farmers are modernizing them by concentrating the land use on the most promising areas and by abandoning marginal-yield pasture lands. Previously, privately owned Alpine pastures were grazed only by cattle of each owner, and therefore the pastured area was much smaller than the extensive pasturelands held by tenured public corporations or agrarian communities. Because of the minute size of some private Alpine pasture, it is difficult to consolidate them or improve their quality. Hence, many of them have been sold or deeded in recent years, despite the fact that many are well situated in the forest zone and provide superior ecological growing conditions to the high Alpine pastures owned by public corporations or agrarian communities, many of whose pastures are still manured and mowed.

The regional distribution of the different *almen* types exhibits two significant regularities, apart from many minor differences in space. First, the private Alpine pastures that are more recent and are situated in the forest zone are generally nearer to the farm than Alpine pastures in common possession. They are very important in the well-wooded Lower Alps (France, Italy, Austria, Bavaria), where the arable land of the farms, the forest, and the Alpine pastureland intermingle (Brugger, Wohlfarter 1983; Lichtenberger 1975). Second, Alpine pastures in possession of public corporations and agrarian communities are more important in Romance-speaking regions (France; Italy; French, Italian and Rhaeto-Romance-parts of Switzerland) than in the German-speaking regions of the Alps (Zwittkovits 1974). This differentiation is not an ethnic division but a correlation of different traditions of economic and social and religious organization. For example, Alpine pastures owned by an agrarian community are dominant in those German-speaking regions (Switzerland, western Austria, Allgau in Bavaria), in which common functions have been developed in the course of the common pastureland (German, *allmende*).

Whereas Alpine pastures in the possession of communities have normally existed since the Middle Ages, many private Alpine pastures are very recent (Loehr 1971). In eastern Austria, for example, many permanently settled farms have been transformed into Alpine pastures only since the beginning of the industrial age (Penz 1978, 1984). In other parts of the Alps the social and economic change has also had consequences for the *almen*. Sheep transhumance in the French and Italian Alps declined and lowland winter pasturelands receded as field enclosures, agricultural intensification, and urbanization occurred. The municipalities leased the areas that had become available to farmers from the Alpine foreland. Leasing of Alpine pastures is therefore very important in the French and Italian Alps; in the remaining Alps, however, the Alpine pastures are farmed mainly by the owner-occupier.

The farming of the Alpine pastures has changed dramatically in the past three decades. At the beginning of the industrial age farms were well adapted to the natural environment. In the lower zone there were manured pastures for grazing cattle where milk was processed into cheese. Above these pastures the young cattle grazed, and the highest zone was used for rough grazing by sheep and occasionally goats. During the industrial era strong regional differentiation occurred. Alpine pastures for sheep are important only in France and some Italian mountain areas. In all other Alpine regions sheep herding has declined to the extent that many high pastures formerly grazed by sheep have been abandoned. Pastures for cattle reflect regional priorities. In the Italian Alps, foreland farms of dairy cattle now predominate. Although yearling cattle rearing and dairy-farming coexist in Switzerland, Bavaria and western Austria, the number of Alpine pastures for cows has markedly decreased in these regions since World War II. As cow herding in the Alpine pasturelands is labor intensive, this facet of *almwirtschaft* has been greatly reduced by an increasing shortage of rural workers. In eastern Austria and in the Slovenian Alps, small Alpine pastures predominate, on which milk processing is economically unfeasible. Dairy cattle *almwirtschaft* has become insignificant in those regions (Vojvoda 1969; Senegachnik 1984).

The change of the farming structure of *almwirtschaft* is directly related to changes of national and global economy. The "economic miracle" after World War II caused an immediate and fundamental structural change. Since the 1974 oil crisis the impact of new industry and increasing tourism on mountain farming economy has decreased, and the stability of *almwirtschaft* is ensured. A further contribution to the increasing stability has been the provision of supplementary government grants which have been much more prevalent since 1970.

Alpine Pastures and Regional Planning

Since the beginning of the industrial age the principal location of agrarian production has shifted from the Alps to the forelands. *Almwirtschaft* has lost significance in conjunction with the all-mountain farming. Foreland industrialization has induced the development of conurbations and has attracted rural labor. Therefore the available labor for *almwirtschaft* is reduced, causing a structural transformation of the pastoral economy. Herding has been made more efficient, and unproductive *almen* have been abandoned. The amount of decline is only partly connected with the economic and social changes encountered in various regions. The improvement of the road network has increased the marketing areas of the dairy farming products that have expanded into the forelands. This is valid for France as well as Switzerland, Germany, and Italy.

The lowland oriented transition in mountain farming products contrasts with the enormous upward transition of many mountain farming settlements. This upward transition is caused by tourism, especially winter sports tourism. The mountain landscape that is cultivated by the pasturing of cattle and sheep is an important basis for these recreational activities. This situation has induced the governments of the Alpine countries and provinces to maintain and improve the high pastures with farm subsidies. Besides providing subsidies for modernizing mountain farming in general, they afford direct subsidies to farmers. Farmers get a fixed amount for each animal grazing on the Alpine pasture. These subsidies have allowed the traditional economy *almwirtschaft* to coexist with the space preferences of a leisure society. The ominous prognostications of many experts about mountain pasture economy were not realized. The number of cattle on the Alpine pastures in most regions of the Alps was stabilized by expanding the milk product markets into the forelands and by providing government subsidies. The future development of *almwirtschaft* will be strongly dependent on regional national and European political integration, which should benefit this traditional, highly valued aspect of mountain farming.

9

Traditional Agricultural Strategies in the Hill Lands of Tropical America

Stephen B. Brush

This chapter discusses agricultural strategies of traditional farm folk in the mountainous regions of tropical America. Its focus is on land use patterns and agricultural technologies of small, subsistence-oriented farmers. These farmers are often representatives of native cultural traditions such as the Maya, Quechua, or Aymara, and their agriculture reflects pre-Hispanic as well as European influences. Three major sections deal with (1) a delineation of the particular farm population and farming systems to be discussed, (2) a summary of traditional land management and farm technology in those systems, and (3) a concluding discussion on problems and development options confronting this population.

The data base of the first two sections is derived from micro-economic studies of farm communities in the hill lands of Central and South America. Relatively few detailed studies of traditional hill land agriculture in tropical America are available, but useful contributions come from work done in southern Mexico and Guatemala (Kirkby 1973; Collier 1975; Nigh 1976; Wilken 1976, 1977, 1979) and in the central Andes of Peru and Bolivia (Brush 1977; Gade 1975; Carter 1965; LaBaron et al. 1979; Mayer 1979; Mayer and Fonseca 1979; and Orlove 1977).

Defining Traditional Farm Systems

What defines "traditional" farm systems in highland Latin America? Two primary dimensions stand out: (1) the ancestry of agricultural practices and (2) the socio-economic and cultural status of the community in the regional and national context. "Traditional" farm systems are often imagined to be direct descendants of pre-Hispanic cultures. This view is erroneous in that it overlooks the vast changes in farming cultures in the

Americas during the past four hundred years. Many social and technological elements of pre-Hispanic times have been lost or fundamentally altered. A few elements have been retained, however, by a process of cultural selection of adaptive strategies. In this sense, "traditional" farm systems are as "modern" as any other in that they are products of contemporary processes. What is important is the reason why certain pre-Hispanic elements have consistently endured since the sixteenth century.

Two major native and extensive farm systems existed at the time of the Spanish Conquest, in the tropical highlands of Middle and South America. In the north, the *milpa* system of maize, bean, and squash cultivation dominated Middle America, extending into the northern periphery of the southern continent. To the south, root crop agriculture combined with limited grain production and extensive grazing dominated. Each system had both simple and complex variants characterized by differing degrees of land and labor intensity and centralized control. Both were capable of supporting dense populations combined with centralized agricultural planning, irrigation and terracing, and each left a clear imprint on existing farm systems.

Contemporary agriculture in the region includes elements derived directly from these aboriginal systems, including (1) highly diverse collections of native crops and animals, (2) multiple cropping within single fields, (3) indigenous tools and tillage practices, (4) the reliance on shifting cultivation, (5) the use of several agroclimatic zones, (6) systems of reciprocal and nonmarket distribution of goods and services, and (7) varying mixes of individual and communal control. These seven types of elements provide the core of "traditional" farm systems, and relative emphasis on them determines whether we should consider a particular farmer or farm community as traditional.

Traditional farm systems are also defined by a type of socio-economic and cultural response to the post-Conquest society dominated by European and national elites. This response is characterized by the creation of "regions of refuge" of "Indian" culture and subsistence economies (Aguirre Beltran 1967). These ethnic and economically autonomous regions may also be understood as adaptations by native and subservient populations to colonial domination. What looks like an anachronism may be explained as part of a dynamic response to a changing set of political, economic, and cultural factors with national and international origins. Similarities among farm populations in the highlands of Middle and South America suggest that different native societies have adapted to similar socio-economic conditions. Conversely, the differences between these populations appear to derive from pre-Hispanic culture and from agroclimatic differences.

The post-Conquest environment was defined largely by the domination of areas of optimal agricultural resources by a small elite tied to national and international economic, political, and cultural elites. Examples are the Valley of Mexico, the Quito Basin, and the *altiplano* of southern Peru and Bolivia. Capital investment, market production, and infrastructure development characterized the use of these optimal resource regions. Typically, a small percentage of the population controlled the largest portion of the productive resources, while the majority existed on marginal and highly fragmented resources. Unequal access to productive resources was accompanied by debt peonage and racism. One common response by the native population to this situation was the retreat to marginal areas. This process was abetted by the Spanish colonial policy of recognizing native territorial rights. The marginal areas were regions where resources were poor and markets limited or nonexistent, without infrastructure development. In the highlands, these marginal areas were places of steepest terrain, poorest soils, and frequent hazards to agriculture. The local economies established here were oriented toward subsistence and marginal to national and international interests dominating the more optimal resource areas.

The regions of refuge attracted large populations, accentuating the imbalance in resource distribution between prime and marginal areas. Part of the defense of these refuges seems to have been the assertion of "Indian" culture with emphasis on such things as language, dress, and ritual. Native agricultural traditions, crops, and land use patterns were likewise reinforced. Particularly important in this regard were traditions that emphasized local autonomy and self-sufficiency: communal control over strategic resources, reciprocal economic mechanisms, egalitarianism, subsistence orientation, and local self-sufficiency in energy, nutrients, and pest control. These traditions, to the extent that they exist today, suggest an adaptive value during post-Conquest times.

To summarize this section, the traditional farm systems of highland tropical America are defined by two major attributes: (1) emphasis on indigenous agricultural patterns and (2) the organization of regions of refuge in marginal areas where native cultural patterns, including indigenous agricultural practices, are stressed. These farm systems are the results of selection and adaptation to an elite-dominated economy as well as to natural environmental conditions in the highlands.

Traditional Farm Technology

This section surveys traditional land use patterns and adaptive strategies, focusing on land and water management and on adaptations involving slope modification and crop resource allocations.

Land Control

Throughout the area, land rights are held by individuals, families, and public institutions. Among the latter are municipalities, parishes, communities, cooperatives, and peasant corporations whose rights derive from pre-Hispanic and Spanish Colonial patterns renewed in more recent times. Indeed, the defense of territorial rights is the *raison d'etre* of many local institutions. In many places, individual land rights originate in community membership defined by birth or marriage.

Most frequently, public institutions exercise only loose control over land, under a vague principal of eminent domain. Unused land, such as that on slopes too steep to farm or in wooded ravines, is held in common, and unused farm land reverts to the community. Under this tenure, most land is owned and managed by individuals and families. Decisions concerning the use and disposition of the land are made privately. Apparently, individual tenure and use rights under a communal umbrella have both pre-Hispanic and European roots (Fonseca 1972). This system effectively decentralizes land management and confines the role of the community to the general defense of lands against encroachment from the outside.

A virtually universal characteristic of traditional land holding in these hill lands is the ownership of numerous small parcels or *minifundia* by single individuals or families. These are generally scattered throughout the territory of the village. In Oaxaca, for instance, Downing was reported to have found a mean holding of five parcels per household (Kirkby 1973:28). In Bolivia, Carter's (1974) detailed study of Irpa Chico (504 households) estimates that less than half of the community's land base is divided into 11,000 separate parcels. Carter records that "one five hectare *aynuqa* section is divided into 42 different plots, i.e., the average holding is only about ¼ acre" (Carter 1974:17). Some families in Irpa Chico have 90 or more plots scattered in four or five different agroclimatic zones, and the mean number of plots per family is 21 (Carter 1974:18).

This fragmentation may be traced in part to the inheritance system in which all sons, at least, are entitled to a portion of their father's land (Kirkby 1973; Collier 1975). Fragmentation also serves a positive adaptive function by spreading a particular family's investments of labor and seed over a wide area, thereby reducing the risk of crop loss from natural hazard. Moreover, the small scale is conducive to intensive cultivation and field maintenance procedures, which may limit land degradation.

Despite emphases upon individual tenure, communal organizations in some areas exercise a high degree of control over land rights and use. Two types of communal control can be identified. First, specific zones are designated communal—most commonly pastures and non-cultivable areas such as steep slopes. Activities of importance to individual household economies are conducted in these zones, such as grazing and firewood collection. As commons, these lands are subject to abuse by over-exploitation, although the extent of abuse is disputed. Orlove's (1974) study of communal pastures in southern Peru argues that herd size is communally controlled to limit over-grazing and to maintain pasture quality. On the other hand, a Utah State University project in Bolivia reports serious over-grazing and subsequent land degradation because of unrestricted use of communal pastures (LaBaron et al. 1980).

The second type of communal control is exercised over the use of farmland. This varies from loose controls, such as restrictions on the sale of land to outsiders and the division of *ejido* lands in Mexico, to elaborate controls on field rotations in Peru and Bolivia. In the central Andes, a system of fallowing and crop rotation is managed communally. Village farmlands are divided into a minimum of five to seven sectors that are again divided into family plots. Communal control determines what crop will be planted, the work schedule of the farm cycle, and the length of cropping and fallow periods. All work except the harvest is often done cooperatively. A typical rotation pattern consists of three years of cropping followed by four to five years of fallow. The key to the system seems to lie in allowing at least seven years between potato cultivation in the same parcel. Possibly, this rotation system was worked out by pre-Hispanic Andean potato farmers to combat nematodes. Seven years appears sufficient to render nematode cysts unvi b'e. Obviously, this system of communal control depends on ample land resources and public institutions and authority to manage the system. Perhaps the most common variant of the system is a three crop, eight sector system that requires cultivation to be confined to 38 percent of farm land (Mayer and Fonseca 1979). My work in the Andes (Brush 1977) indicates that an average family of five depends on roughly 1.5 hectares under cultivation for subsistence. To maintain this average by rotation, an average family would need roughly four hectares of cultivable land.

Fallowing remains widely practiced in the Andes, although it is under mounting pressure from increasing populaton. This pressure is manifested in increased fragmentation of parcels and especially in the breakdown of the rotations and shortening of the fallow period. Extended fallow periods must be counted among the primary strategies for maintaining land quality in traditional agriculture.

In contrast to the Andes, a more primitive form of shifting cultivation is practiced by the Maya of southern Mexico and Guatemala (Collier 1975; Nigh 1976). This system emphasizes individual control of rotations. In its simplest form, this horticulture abandons plots to forest fallow without subsequent community control. In virtually all areas, however, population pressure has shortened the fallow to bush fallow of six years or less. In higher elevations of the Mayan highlands, fallow periods have been reduced to the point that permanent grass cover has taken hold in many years, converting crop land to pasture. As in the Andes, population pressure on the land has also led to increased fragmentation (Collier 1975).

Water Management

Like land control, water management involves various mixtures of communal and individual levels of activity. Water is generally considered a common resource, although its management is usually decentralized into the hands of individuals. By far the most common approach to water management in the hill lands of Latin America is the control of surface runoff, beginning at the field level (Wilken 1977, 1979). Runoff is retarded by a variety of check strips and embankments. Beyond the field, series of check dams or *trincheras* are often built across stream beds to slow runoff, spread floodwater, and catch valuable alluvium (Kirkby 1973). At their most advanced stage, these check dams resemble terraces.

Besides the control of runoff, the other principal objective of water management is irrigation. A hierarchy of water control techniques is available to traditional farmers. Depending on water volume and velocity, these systems may involve substantial construction of dams, gates, and canals. Unlike runoff management, irrigation depends on cooperative labor, decision-making, and management. These systems are controlled by one village or by cooperation between villages (Mitchell 1976). Canal maintenance and water division involve the most sophisticated organizational structure found in traditional agriculture, and they are often ritualized. Large scale irrigation systems are relatively limited compared to individually managed techniques. The difficulty of sustaining a sufficient level of organization and cooperative labor, added to the increased labor and management costs, explains this.

Slope Modification

Closely related to water management, especially runoff control, is slope modification, which alters surface geometry in order to manage soil and water conditions. Again, the level of effort and complexity varies from simple, individual field preparation techniques to complex landscape architecture and permanent terracing (Donkin 1979; Wilken 1976). Slope modification is the result of the evolution of tools and tillage practices, demography, and political and economic variables.

Traditional tillage practices with digging sticks, footplows, and numerous variations on the shorthandled hoe alter surface geometry. Seedbeds, ridges, hoe terraces, and plant mounds are common and account for a substantial portion of labor investment. At the field level, the most basic modification is accomplished by such practices as the orientation of crop rows, the construction of simple check dams or embankments across the slope, and the construction of fences and hedgerows. These impediments to runoff allow material to accumulate and result in low sloping terraces, lynchets, or ridged fields. In steep terrain, slope or bench terrace construction is widespread. Both sloped and flat terraces are designed to retard runoff, build and retain soil, raise soil temperature, and manage soil moisture.

Slope modification demands continuous labor investment. Unlike canal irrigation, however, large scale terrace systems do not require central planning and management. There are few areas where the construction and maintenance of large terrace systems are communal, which contrasts sharply with evidence of massive, state-sponsored terracing in pre-Hispanic times.

Crop Resources

The final element of traditional farm technology to be discussed here is the management of crop resources. Two features stand out: (1) the maintenance of great genetic diversity in a few staple crops, and (2) the maintenance of a great interspecies diversity.

The highlands of both Central and South America were major centers of crop domestication and development, and the result is a high diversity of crop germ plasm in the plants domesticated in the region. This is most evident in the primary staples, maize in Central America and potatoes in the Andes, but it is also found in numerous secondary crops. The importance of this genetic diversity has been noted by botanists and others. Recent research (Brush et al. 1981) revealed that the large collections of native potato varieties in the Andes are carefully maintained and selected. Different varieties are adapted to local environments and the distribution of native seed potatoes is an important part of traditional production. Throughout tropical America, these genetic resources are vital to both traditional and modern agriculture.

Traditional agriculture in the highlands is also characterized by the cultivation of numerous crops within a single field (multiple cropping) and the use of many different crops in diverse microenvironments. Diversity within fields is typified by door-yard gardens and by the intercropping of maize, beans, and squash in Central Amerca. In the Andes, bitter lupine *tarwi* is often planted as a border, both for its valuable oil seeds and as deterrent against foraging animals. Diversity between fields is typified by the existence of different crop zones at different altitudes controlled by a single village and used by single households within the village. The diversity within fields helps protect soil by layering and provides a continuous plant cover that shields the soil from rain. Crop diversity between fields makes optimum use of a highly complex and diverse environment. The control of different environmental zones and the fragmentation of land into numerous parcels encourage this manipulation. Crop and field diversity is clearly a major risk management strategy by traditional farmers. The diverse and widely scattered collections of indigenous crops and varieties replicate natural plant diversity and are an important means of compensating for the danger of perceived hazards and the predation of the many pests and pathogens that have evolved along with crops.

Conclusion: Development Issues and Options

Summary

Traditional farm systems have evolved a complex set of strategies to cope with perceived hazards that place agriculture at risk. These strategies rely on reducing the human disruption of hill land environments by such techniques as long fallows, and by using very wide varieties of crop genetic resources adapted to different microenvironments. These strategies succeed by replicating mature plant communities. External subsidies of energy and nutrients are minimized, energy is evenly distributed throughout the human population, and net energy yields are positive. Socio-economic stresses have also been met by the evolution of adaptive mechanisms, especially the reliance on local resources, communal land control, and social and economic organization that emphasizes reciprocity. The result of this adaptive proces is an agriculture characterized by low productivity, high labor intensity, low energy use, and great crop and animal diversity.

The durability of these traditional farm systems over wide areas is evidence of their adaptive success. The late twentieth century, however, is fundamentally different from the environment that generated these systems. Three interrelated changes are identified that call into question the suitability of traditional adaptations: (1) population increase, (2) expansion of roads, markets, and other links to national and international economies, and (3) rising expectations concerning living standards.

Traditional farm systems have responded to rising populations by exporting population, by shortening fallow and subdividing parcels, by raising levels of labor intensity, and by applying external subsidies, especially fertilizers and pesticides. New land is rarely available. Although pre-Hispanic populations in parts of the highlands may have equaled or surpassed current levels, it seems doubtful that traditional land use patterns will remain viable under mounting population pressure. This already bears clear responsibility for serious land degradation in the highlands.

The expansion of roads and markets is followed by urban demand that pressures traditional farm systems to raise production above local subsistence needs. Most of these systems have succeeded in providing adequate nutrition for the local population (Ferroni 1980; Fleuret, Fleuret 1980). The commercialization of traditional agriculture depends on higher productivity per unit of land and labor than under subsistence conditions. Higher productivity is customarily achieved by intensifying labor, shortening fallows, applying imported subsidies of energy, nutrients, and pest control, and by using new crops and crop varieties. These methods, however, raise the same problems as increasing population.

Increase of farm income as an important objective in the household economies of marginal areas accompanies population increase and commercialization, providing a means to purchase farm and food supplies. Beyond this, however, income is desired to meet rising expectations of the purchase of services and manufactured goods. Hill land agriculture is disadvantaged for income earning by limited arable space, thin soils, liability of erosion, low temperatures, and higher transportation costs. Moreover, the status of Meso America and the Andes as centers of crop domestication may disadvantage them for profitable production of their most important staples (Jennings, Cook 1977). A solution to this disadvantaged position is to seek income from activities specifically tied to hill lands or from wages. Wage income usually implies a migration from the highlands. Marginal advantage in hill land production lies in several widespread activities: (1) livestock production, (2) special cash crops such as coffee and cocoa, (3) forestry and forest products, and (4) tourism. The optimal strategy among small farmers is to continue subsistence agriculture and to add income earning activities that do not compete for the essential resources of land and labor. Special production zones, such as high pastures in the Andes, make this possible. Reliance on subsistence production, however, usually drains land and labor away from income generating activities. As a result, farm populations in hill lands are adequately fed but have low incomes.

Development Issues and Options

Development of hillside agriculture must take into account four sets of facts. First, the advantages of traditional hill land agriculture suggested in this essay can be summarized as follows.

There is an emphasis on equitable distribution of energy, resources, and food throughout the community and on ecosystem maintenance by techniques that replicate stable plant communities and minimize disruption of natural ecosystems. Another advantage is the reliance on local energy, nutrients, and pest control; and net energy production in agriculture.

Second, the traditional agro-ecosystems have deficiencies. These include the need to export population to maintain low densities, and the inability to generate surplus and/or farm income to meet rising populations, urban demand, and income expectations. Third, the intensification of traditional agriculture is usually achieved by familiar means, for example, shortening fallows, manipulating labor schedules, soil and water resources, and adding external subsidies of energy, nutrients, and pest controls. Traditional cultigens are substituted by improved crops and crop varieties that are selected for productivity, resistance to pests, and responsiveness to fertilizers.

A fourth point is the limit to these technological options. Shortened fallow may accelerate the rate of erosion and soil loss and raise the level of pathogens in the soil. Increased labor intensity in one area may require decreased intensity in another activity and lead to resource depletion or degradation. Substitution of improved crop varieties, besides leading to genetic erosion, may make agriculture more susceptible to highly evolved pests and pathogens and may result in greater dependency on expensive external subsidies of seed and pest controls. Another feature of externalization is the increased vulnerability of local farmers to world inflation, especially in the case of petroleum-derived products. Furthermore, relative disadvantages of hill land agriculture may preclude significant income generation and force long-term debts, and the demands for capital in marginal areas may be met only by increasing population to pay for investment through low wages.

The search for development options must reconcile these four sets of factors. The ability of traditional agriculture to produce subsistence for low population densities has obvious advantages, but it cannot be readily transformed into intensive production for large populations and income generation. On the one hand, the success of traditional agriculture in creating genetic material, in preserving mountain landscapes and resources, and in producing adequate and well-distributed nutrition cannot be overlooked. The growing stresses on traditional agriculture are, however, a reality, and the problems associated with applying customary development techniques to hill areas are also apparent and probably explain the slow pace of agricultural change in many marginal areas.

An ideal solution would produce adequate food and income to increasingly dense populatons without degrading hill environments and avoiding dangerous dependency on external subsidies. Unfortunately, no single or simple set of development options will accomplish these goals on a regional basis. The effort to reach a solution for local development options should stress the following priorities. First, the long-term viability of an agricultural system is as important as short-term productivity. Permanence in the agro-ecosystem should be sought by maintaining crop genetic diversity, soils, and local fauna and flora such as tropical rain

forests. Second, most indigenous farm technology can be intensified t
produce adequate nutrition for the local population. Farm income, how
ever, is more difficult to attain and should, therefore, be the objective c
development efforts. Because of the disadvantages of hill and commodit
production, non-farm activities should receive priority. Third, greate
diversity in household economies is advantageous, and developmer
should simplify these. Fourth, it appears that decentralized planning an
decision-making is preferable to centralized planning, and finally, loca
control of strategic resources is desirable as is local self-sufficiency i
energy, nutrients, and pest control.

Under this set of priorities, the intensification of agriculture is tempere
by the sustainability of the activity and the successful adaptation of th
system.

PART II
Methodologies for Examining Mountain Life

10

Introduction

Gregory W. Knapp

The chapters in this section illustrate some of the ways that human-mountain interactions have been studied. Although chapters in other sections of this volume are also pertinent to the consideration of methodological issues, here our concern is primarily with method and only secondarily with the specific topics.

Mountains clearly affect people and people clearly affect mountains. The challenge has been to isolate those elements of mountain environments which are most closely and forcefully related to human coping behavior itself. Each chapter in this section has a distinctive conceptualization of the significant environment and a distinctive view of human behavior in the face of challenge.

In general, the study of human-environment relationships has been historically the prerogative of human geographers and, more recently, cultural ecologists drawn from the fields of geography, anthropology (ecological anthropology), history (environmental history), biology, sociology (human ecology) and geology (economic geology). Readers interested in the evolution of ideas in cultural ecology may be referred to a number of recent texts (Moran 1979; Bennett 1976; Netting 1977; Butzer 1982; Jochim 1981; Ellen 1982; Carlstein 1982; Goudie 1982); most of these refer in passing to mountain problems. A book produced from papers presented at a recent symposium (Moran 1984) provides perhaps the best critical assessment of key ideas in cultural ecology.

During the course of the nineteenth century, relationships between various components of the environment were discovered and studied. Alexander von Humboldt traveled to the tropical mountains of the Americas and founded the subdiscipline of biogeography by carefully relating altitude to temperature, air pressure, and species of plants and animals (Humboldt and Bonpland 1955, original edition 1805). V. V. Dokuchaiev performed a similar revolution later in the century by relating soil formation to factors of climate, slope, plants and animals, and

geology. Albrecht Penck, early in the twentieth century, explored relationships between climate and landforms and coined the word "geomorphology." Thus the foundations had been laid for a "landscape science"
which would study the interrelationships of climate, slope, soil, water,
and life on the earth surface, including mountain areas. The principal
advocate of this "school" of mountain geography was Carl Troll (see
Troll, this volume).

The earliest and most pervasive idea of the geoecologists and landscape
ecologists has been that of altitudinal zonation. As Uhlig (this section)
observes, models of altitudinal zones "remain a useful orientation . . .
including important integrations of ecological and socio-economic geofactors." He also observes that altitudinal zonation schemes have been
attacked as layer-cake oversimplifications (Uhlig 1984).

Uhlig's work provides an example of the application of altitudinal
zoned typologies to the study of land use and settlement in mountains all
over the world. Much of this work has a distinct practical orientation,
concerned with recent changes and policy options.

Another chapter reflecting the altitudinal zonation tradition is that by
Forman. In this case, she is particularly concerned with traditional
ecological control over multiple complementary vertical zones, or "verticality" in the jargon of Andeanists (Murra 1975a; Brush 1976; 1977;
Webster 1971; Camino 1982; Mayer and Fonseca Martel 1979; Masuda,
Shimada and Morris 1985). She stresses that traditional interzonal relationships may be efficient solutions to problems of subsistence and that
development efforts should act to further rather than restrict village use of
diverse altitudinal zones.

Allan (1986) has suggested that land use patterns shift to motor vehicle
accessibility under conditions of modernization. Sanchez (1976) has
criticized schemes of altitudinal zonation and verticality by pointing out
that use of complementary zones is simply one of a number of options
available to peasants, and that it is unwise to assume that villagers have
any a priori commitment to a particular subsistence strategy in their
pursuit of well-being.

Knapp (1984) has also argued that altitude may be over-rated as an
environmental factor (in comparison with rainfall, soil, or slope), that
there are numerous technical and crop options for each altitudinal zone,
and that the supposed efficiencies of using multiple zones have never been
rigorously demonstrated.

Altitudinal zonation schemes are based on empirical observation of
existing land use and the assumption that land use is primarily altitudinally determined. Relatively few efforts have focused on determining
actual relationships between crop success and elevation. Thus general
altitudinal-zonation treatments of mountain-human relationships (Guillet

1983; Dollfus 1981) still have a rather tentative and typological (rather than analytic) character.

Altitude is of course only one aspect of mountain environments. Landscape ecologists have also focused on such specific problems as frost risk, drought, landslides, and erosion in mountain environments, and these problems have also attracted studies of their human consequences. Ives (in this section) describes an approach to mapping hazards in mountains to provide a basis for planning (see also Stadel 1985; Knapp and Canadas 1986).

In general, hazards approaches have appealed to environmental planners but have been criticized for insensitivity to social and political structural problems which limit ability to avert or respond to disaster (see also Hewitt 1983 and this volume).

Cultural ecologists have frequently used the concept of ecosystem to cope with the large number of interrelationships in the environment. Reality is of course not a system (reality is reality); rather, we "model" reality as a set of boxes with flows between them (a system), with the assumption that by so doing we can better explain or predict events. As Thomas (this section) says, human "responses sometimes influence each other both positively and negatively . . . these considerations limit the usefulness of analyzing variables one at a time and suggest that a more integrated systemic approach . . . could better approximate reality."

Many of the efforts to study mountain adaptations from a systemic perspective have been sponsored by the United Nations Man and the Biosphere program (Thomas et al. this section; Baker, Little 1976). In general, these studies have assumed that villager communities prior to recent times can be studied as homeostatic (balanced, self-regulating) ecosystems. Diagrams and computer models track the flow of energy from sun through crops and livestock to community members.

Full-scale systems studies of mountain communities have proven, however, to be expensive and cumbersome. Some have found the results disappointing in terms of the effort expended. Others have questioned the presuppositions of the systems approach. The approach usually cannot account for change, while the historical record tends to indicate continuous change even for traditional societies (Netting 1981). Systems approaches tend to divert attention from human actors as agents of choice. Use of energy as the currency of systems flows may divert attention from other important flows (nitrogen, water), or from the importance of specific non-quantifiable events, hazards, or catastrophes such as drought. It is often difficult to determine appropriate boundaries for systems in the real world, since relationships tend to be regional as well as local. Finally, the systems approach may lend a spurious air of scientific knowledge or expertise to what are in fact often quite tentative or speculative studies (see Moran 1984). Thus at least for the present the systems approach may be most valuable simply as a reminder of the complexity of the real world and a tool for suggesting further investigations of the relationships.

A final set of approaches to the study of mountain adaptation involves a focus on human technology and human choice. Rather than treating mountain environments or ecology as given, these approaches stress the ability of humans to modify their environment in novel and sometimes unpredictable ways. Studies of crop plants and tools (Gade 1972, 1975), terracing (Donkin 1979), mountain irrigation (Mitchell 1976; Sherbondy 1982; Mothes 1986), mountain soil fertility management (Winterhalder, Larsen, and Thomas 1974), and other traditional technologies such as raised fields (Knapp and Denevan 1985; Denevan 1980), have indicated the enormous flexibility of traditional societies to adjust to changing demographic pressures (Boserup 1965) and changing levels of demand. Such studies, corresponding to what Bennett called "adaptive dynamics" or the study of adaptation over time, may prove to be one of the most fruitful approaches to the understanding of mountain worlds.

11

The Future Value of the "Verticality" Concept
Implications and Possible Applications in the Andes

Sylvia Helen Forman

In confronting the complex and urgent issues of social and economic development, the Andean nations must grapple with particular versions of development problems—versions that are shaped by cultural and environmental features unique to the Andean region. Some special aspects of their development problems derive from the mountainous terrain of these countries and from the traditions and importance of agriculture in their highland areas. In this chapter I want to explore some implications which the concept of "verticality" (German: *staffelsysteme*) and related ethnographic data on the economic and ecologic integration of Andean social groups have for treating the specifically Andean problems of peasant agricultural development now and in the future.

In examining this topic I will first briefly review the general framework of Andean ecology and the model of vertical adaptation. Then I will outline one perspective on the problems of economic development in the Andean nations. Finally, I will discuss some of the implications and possible applications of "verticality" and related ethnographic information in treating highland development problems, primarily in Ecuador, Peru, and Bolivia.

Andean Ecology and Verticality

It has long been recognized that high mountains present difficult environments for human societies and for plant and animal life (Peattie 1936; Tosi 1960; Troll 1968). Nonetheless, humans have found it worthwhile to exploit mountain environments, and have developed cultural mechanisms that permit and facilitate such exploitation. Today about 10 percent of the world's population lives in highlands (Eckholm 1975:764). In Ecuador, Peru and Bolivia, about half of the population lives in the *sierra* highlands.

In a general way the Andes, like other high mountain systems, present a picture of ecological zones that vary with increasing elevation above sea level. But the vertical ecozones of the Andes are not simply strata which duplicate, with rising elevation, the global bands of latitudinal variation (Tosi 1960; Troll 1968). Rather, there is immense variation among and within the ecozones of the Andes (Basile 1974; Brunnschweiler 1971; Cuatrecasas 1968; Heath et al. 1969; MAB 1974; Pulgar 1946; Tosi 1960; Troll 1968; Webster 1973). This extreme degree of local and regional variation is a function of the interplay of such factors as elevation, latitude, geologic and edaphic conditions, steepness and orientation of slope, wind and precipitation patterns, mountain mass and relief of terrain (Peattie 1936; Tosi 1960). To exist in the highlands, people must cope with the manifestations of these variables as local patterns of climate, terrain, soils and biotic distribution. In a given locale these patterns occur in an approximation of vertical strata. Both the specific local variations of climate, soils and biota and the vertical structuring of them have great impact on the life-ways of humans living in the Andes.

The original Troll-Uhlig *staffelsysteme* model (Troll 1943c; Uhlig 1984) represents an effort to understand cultural responses to the vertical zonation and extreme environmental variability of the Andean region. As modified much later by Murra in his ethnohistorical studies, the model treats both cognitive and behavioral levels. The perceptions, knowledge and values of highland inhabitants *and* their behavior in economic and political activities and institutions are viewed in the context of their ecological situations (Murra 1975a, 1975b). Murra states his main thesis this way:

> The Andean world was conceived by its inhabitants as a totality of levels arranged "vertically," one on top of another, forming a macro-adaptation, a system of ecological relations purely Andean. As settlements moved higher and higher on the slopes, the inhabitants had to cope with continuous changes in climate, fauna, and flora.
>
> Throughout the Andes, the village and ethnic communities had always attempted to control as many micro-climates as possible. Those regions not reached by a day of walking, or by seasonal migration, were settled by groups of permanent colonists, who herded, collected salt, or cultivated coca leaf, maize, or tropical peppers.
>
> When the scale of political control shifted from that of a small ethnic group to kingdoms as large as that of the Lupaqa, the perception of what was ecologically obtainable expanded enormously. Where the rural village or small ethnic enclave thought of the micro-climates as arranged vertically in a quite literal sense, large-scale political units could expand this notion of

"verticality" to include desirable areas as far away from Lake Titicaca as the Pacific Coast or the hot valleys of Larecaja or Capinota, beyond Cochabamba (1975b: 204–5, my translation, with reference to Murra 1968:121).

In a later article, Murra refers to "archipiélagos verticales" (Troll and Uhlig's *staffelsysteme*) and examines five ethnohistorical cases of "simultaneous control of ecological levels, or 'islands,' under quite distinctive conditions" (1975a:60, 61). His examples illustrate the nature and operation of indigenous control of multiple vertical zones in small communities, larger regional ethnic groups, and states (*reinos*) of large scale. He points out that vertical control of a maximum possible number of ecological zones "was an Andean ideal shared by ethnic groups which were geographically distant from each other and which were quite distinctive from each other in terms of their economic and political organization," and goes on to note that these differences among Andean social groups inevitably implied other differences in the institutional forms of their verticality (1975a:60). Recent ethnographic studies illustrate that significant variations in the organization of verticality still exist among peasant communities and ethnic groups in the Andes (see for example Basile 1974; Brush 1973; Burke 1971; Carter 1965; Custred 1973; Dorsey 1975; Flores 1968; Mayer 1974; Mitchell 1976; Orlove 1974; Webster 1971).

Drawing on a range of ethnographic examples, as well as on Murra's model, Brush (1974) has distinguished three types of ecologic integration of peasant groups in the Andes. His first type, "compact," is found where a set of very different vertical ecological zones occur in close proximity to each other and are accessible to the members of a community directly, without requiring major travel or extensive exchange with other communities (Brush 1974:292–93). "The archipelago type," the second, is basically that delineated by Murra (1975a), in which the ecological zones utilized by a social group are more or less distant from each other and separated by unused areas (Brush 1974:293–94). Access to the different zones requires extended travel (several or more days) and often involves placing permanent colonies, from the home community, in diverse sites. Because the colonists are still members of their home community, the modes of exchange that characterize the archipelago type of vertical control are reciprocity and redistribution. In the third type, "extended," each social group exploits directly only one or a few of the ecological zones in a region, specializing in certain products, and access to the needed products of other ecological zones comes through exchange among communities based in different ecozones (Brush, 1974:294–95). Such exchange may take a variety of forms, including barter and marketing (ibid.; Burchard 1974; Custred 1974; Flores 1975; Mayer 1971; Orlove 1974; Webster 1973).

In a comparative discussion of cultural-ecological patterns in mountain environments, Rhoades and Thompson (1975) suggest that two broadly defined types of adaptive strategies may be distinguished. Their "generalized" type "involves a single population which, through agro-pastoral transhumance, directly exploits a series of microniches or ecozones at several altitudinal levels," while in their "specialized" type

> a population locks into a single zone and specializes in the agricultural or pastoral activities suitable to that altitude, developing elaborate trade relationships with populations in other zones which are also involved in specialized production [Roades, Thompson 1975:547].

My own impression, from the ethnographic literature and from my research in the central highlands of Ecuador (Forman 1972), is that, at least under contemporary economic conditions, a mixed form of verticality is prevalent in many parts of the Andes. This mixed form involves direct access to two or more vertical ecozones, by members of a peasant community, combined with indirect access to other ecozones through exchange with comunities based in different ecozones or through commercial marketing.

Custred (1973:50) has pointed out that we need to take two approaches to the study of human life-ways in the highlands: One is to investigate adaptations to specific vertical life zones, the other to examine the uses made of the entire range of such zones and the role this has played in shaping the social and economic patterns of mountain populations.

The verticality model, as elaborated by the authors cited above, represents the general principles of adaptive strategies of social groups in the highlands. Ethnographic data provide a complementary set of descriptions of how specific local groups exploit the ecozones available to them. I will return to these two levels of study in my discussion of possible applications of the verticality model to agricultural development.

Andean Problems of Development

In addition to exhibiting a great degree of local variability, the Andes, like other high mountain regions, are a most fragile ecosystem (MAB 1974:21 ff.). "When the environment starts to deteriorate on steep mountain slopes, it deteriorates quickly—far more so than on gentler slopes and on plains. The damage is far more likely to be irreversible" (Eckholm 1975:765).

In mountains, such phenomena as deforestation, poor agricultural practices, burning and over-grazing of grasslands and improper irrigation very rapidly lead to decline in soil fertility and to erosion. Highland erosion has the direct effect of leaving the eroded land partially or entirely unusable for agriculture, forestry, animal husbandry or recreation. It further has secondary effects of major importance. It leads to greater damage from earthquakes and landslides, local loss of water for agricultural and domestic use (due to increased surface run-off), periodic flooding of down-stream lowland areas, and reduction of hydroelectric and irrigation capacities through silting of lower river courses and of lakes and reservoirs (Eckholm 1975; Hewitt 1976; MAB 1974:21, 119; 1975:9–10, 17–18).

Irreversible and dangerous damage to the Andean ecosystem is not an abstract or distant matter. A great deal of erosion and soil deterioration has taken place already, and current practices of agriculture, pastoralism and forest use continue to reduce the life-support capacity of the highlands and to threaten the usefulness of adjacent lowlands (Eckholm 1975; MAB 1975; Tosi 1960).

The fragile nature of the highland environment and the ramifications of continuing damage to it constitute serious problems themselves. They also stand as the necessary background for understanding some of the other development problems of the Andean countries. I will outline certain aspects of these problems below. But first I must note that the view to be presented is not a complete picture. Indeed, our knowledge does not encompass even nearly all of the social and environmental problems of development. My view does not attempt to express all of the complexities and local variations of the difficulties of development in the Andean agricultural sector. Nor, being a linear written expression, does it adequately represent the systemic nature of these problems (i.e., the feedbacks among the components and levels of the problems). My discussion is based on an assumption that economic development is a real, and feasible, goal of the Andean nations and, moreover, that one major aspect of Andean economic development must be improvement in the quality of life of the entire population, including the peasantry.

One crucially important issue in Andean development is population. While it probably cannot reasonably be said that the Andean countries are presently over-populated, it can be noted that they are likely to be over-populated within the next couple of decades, since their population growth rates are very high (about 3 percent per year for Ecuador, Peru, and Bolivia). The pressure of increasing populations, now and in the future, creates increasing demands for food, housing, fuel, clothing, and jobs and also for social services. There are also pressures for improving the living standards of this increasing population—so demands for increases in goods and services rise at higher rates than the rate of population growth itself.

Food production, in particular, is not increasing sufficiently rapidly in the Andean countries (Anderson 1975; Coutu and King 1969; Jorgenson 1971; Mitchell and Schatan 1967; Santa Cruz 1967). Efforts to expand production of food (and of fibers and wood), in the context of inadequate inputs and infrastructure, are causing over-use and mis-use of the highland ecosystem.

As noted above, damage to the sierra environment is already marked and is continuing to be aggravated. Because much of this damage is either irreversible or reversible only over long time periods, the environmental deterioration not only undercuts contemporary efforts to raise the level of agricultural production and to improve the quality of life of the poorer portion of the population, but also bodes very badly for the long-term capacity of the highland ecosystem to contribute to the support of increasing populations in the Andean nations. Damage to the highland environment will inevitably exacerbate existing problems of poor nutrition and poor health, low levels of education, migration to urban areas and under-and unemployment.

It appears that the Andean countries are caught in a vicious circle, in which increasing population and demand for food mean more pressure on the land, with resultant environmental deterioration and lowered agricultural output, yet more pressure on remaining arable land, and so on around. One possible effect of this cycle is relatively rapid depopulation of the Andean highlands. Clearly that outcome is not desirable; it not only means that crucially needed land and labor are removed from production, but it also creates a new problem of the resettlement and employment of the displaced peasants. Since the Andean countries do not have, and in the next couple of decades are not likely to have, a large industrial base that can employ a significant percentage of the peasantry, it seems both desirable and necessary to have a large proportion of their populations remain in primary agricultural activity.

One possible way to break this positive feedback system is to have the death rate increase—another undesirable, and humanely untenable, approach. Another possible way to break the vicious circle is to decrease the rate of population growth by lowering the birthrate. This is probably the most desirable approach, and is certainly a component of any eventual solution. But there is good evidence that people do not voluntarily control their fertility until their standard of living reaches a certain minimum level, commonly represented by a per capita income of about 700 dollars a year (Rich 1973). The living standard necessary for reduction of population growth through voluntarily controlled fertility is well above that of most of the rural population of the Andean countries. It is probable that the peasants' standard of living will have to rise before their birthrate declines.

Yet another possible way to break the circle is to make massive inputs of technology (of industrial and green revolution sorts) into the highland agricultural sector. However, this tactic also presents problems: the costs of importing the technology, the feasibility of employing such technology in the highlands, the dangerous effects of such technology in terms of pollution and further environmental deterioration (Alexander 1974; IUCN 1968; Johnson 1972; Jorgenson 1971; Schumacher 1975; Sternberg 1973), and the potential conflicts between the technological inputs and existing social organization and social reform (Coutu, King 1969; Thiesenhusen 1974). More moderate inputs of agricultural technology are not likely to lead, by themselves, to sufficiently increased levels of production, and would still present many of the same problems as massive inputs (Flores 1965:130; Wetering 1973:9).

From the perspective of this discussion, the general problem might be phrased: How, without doing irreparable damage to the highland ecosystem, can the quality of life of the highland population be improved to such a level that the rate of population growth substantially declines? Stabilizing the population would alleviate the increasing pressure on the sierra environment and permit maintaining it in such condition that it could continue indefinitely to provide needed resources for human use (MAB 1974:20).

While the more obvious and urgent problems of development in the Andean nations can be expressed in terms of factors as poor nutrition, lagging agricultural production, underemployment, erosion, etc., less obvious problems arise from the very efforts to deal with these primary issues. These secondary problems derive from the development process itself when, due to lack of relevant information or to personal misunderstanding, bias, or poorly elaborated policy, development programs ignore problem areas or take actions that create new sources of difficulty or exacerbate existing ones. Certain aspects of the ideas, attitudes, and behaviors of planners and political leaders in the Andean countries stand out as past and future sources of these secondary development problems.

There is a general tendency among the development agencies in the Andean countries to use the industrialized Western countries as direct models for development, rather than creating their own models, which might be better adapted to local features of resources, ecology and culture (Sternberg 1973). Yet while pollution and environmental degradation have come to be recognized as major problems in the industrialized countries, many planners and political leaders in the Andean nations are not urgently concerned with conservation and anti-pollution issues (IUCN 1968; MAB 1975:22; Sternberg 1973). While there is some increased interest recently in indigenous agricultural methods and in intermediate technology, there still is continuation of the tendency among Andean developers to prefer hard to soft technology, commercial to subsistence crops, larger-scale capital-intensive to smaller-scale labor-intensive productive institutions, novel to traditional agricultural methodologies (Gade 1969:49; Sternberg 1973; Tendler 1975; Thiesenhusen 1974). The development agents are more impressed by and concerned with encouraging agricultural development in the "easier" coastal regions than in the highlands (Tendler 1975:313–337; Wetering 1973:5, 8). This fact may be related to the negative image that most Andean developers seem to have of highland peasants in general and of Quechua- and Aymara-speaking Indian peasants in particular (Forman 1972; Tendler 1975:282–283). In addition, it may well be the case that for the most part development planners are and think like "flat-landers," that they conceive the problems of agricultural (and other economic) development in the Andes as though the environment were horizontally rather than vertically arranged and homogeneous rather than immensely varied (Rhoades and Thompson 1975:548–549).

These attitudes on the parts of development agents can lead to the creation of many sorts of new problems, including poor foreign balance-of-payments (for imported food and technology) (Aquino 1967:4), severe and sudden disruptions of traditional cultures, and loss of genetic variability of plants and animals (as species are decimated or traditional crops are dropped from production) (IUCN 1968:83; Reitz, Craddock 1969). In particular, as Eckholm (1975) points out, a failure to devote adequate attention and resources to agricultural development in the highlands is short-sighted and potentially extremely dangerous for the agricultural base of both lowland and highland areas.

Given the fragility of the Andean environment and the human costs of creating new problems or aggravating old ones, it is clear that research to improve our knowledge of the highland ecosystem and the human place in it should precede or at least accompany development activities. A number of anthropologists, geographers, and ecologists have underlined the current limitation of our understanding both of the natural conditions of the Andes and of the human ways of dealing with those conditions (Custred 1973:49–50; Dickinson 1971; Heath et al. 1969:388–389; Jorgenson 1971; MAB 1974, 1975; Momsen 1971). But at the same time, much valuable information, about the ecological and cultural complexities of the highlands, already is available for use in development planning. This information could and should be utilized by development planners to help them achieve a thorough-going recognition of the special problems of the highlands and an understanding that these problems may be enlarged rather than reduced by programs designed for other ecological and social situations.

Murra makes a relevant point when he says that in the Viceroy Toledo's *reducciones* "the patterns of vertical ecologic control were ignored, thus reducing the resources available and permanently improverishing the Andean economy" (1970:9). It seems that current efforts at economic development in the Andean countries similarly ignore verticality, and other pertinent data and concepts, and hence are on the threshold of even more thoroughly damaging the economic underpinnings of the sierra.

Implications and Applications of the Verticality Model and Ethnographic Data

There are both general and specific ways in which anthropological concepts and data may be applied in Andean rural development. The most general application is probably a precondition to the effective implementation of any others; it concerns the expectations and ethnocentrism of those managing the development process. Some of the attitudes of development planners have been mentioned above; the first step here is to present some general responses to them.

Preference for Western industrial models has been, and in many cases still is, strong among Andean developers. But the "modern, industrial, scientific" ways—the hard technology, capital-intensive ways—of doing things are not the only ways and, indeed, may not be the most desirable or appropriate ways in many circumstances (Aquino 1967:6; Schumacher 1975). Moreover, economically rational development does not necessarily mean the same thing in all times and all places (Skinner 1976:5, 19; Schumacher 1975). The subsistence orientation of peasants can be preferable to a commercial orientation under some conditions (Nietschmann 1971; Sternberg 1973). Family-size farms are often more productive (per land unit) than larger operations (Santa Cruz 1967:152; Thiesenhusen 1974).

Peasants, particularly Quechua- and Aymara-speaking peasants, are usually viewed by development agents as ignorant and irrationally conservative. Peasants do tend to be conservative, but their resistance to change is not automatic and, especially in such matters as agricultural practices, must often be seen as rational and even wise given their knowledge of the resources available to them (Rhoades, Thompson 1975:548–549). Indeed, their understanding of their environment and its limitations is usually far more profound than that of development workers, who often are neither farmers nor agronomists. Moreover, peasant conservatism should not be viewed as complete reluctance to innovate and experiment. The evidence is conclusive that they are creative and open to change when economic and cultural conditions are appropriate (Johnson 1972; Thiesenhusen 1974).

The starting points, then, for the application of ethnographic data and the verticality concept to Andean development must be: 1) an appreciation for the adaptations already made by highland agriculturalists to their unusual environment, and 2) a willingness to consider seriously routes to rural development that are non-ethnocentric and non-industrial, in terms of values and models of rationality as well as in terms of scale and type of technology.

The verticality model, in its most general form, tells us that access to and exploitation of multiple vertical ecozones—either directly or indirectly through exchanges—is the Andean cultural method for achieving a tolerable subsistence level in a limited, fragile, and vertically diverse environment. The inherent limitations on agricultural production and resource exploitation in any one ecozone are made up for by the utilization of more than one vertical zone. Although Murra (1975a) has shown that verticality has operated as an integrating principle on levels as great as the indigenous Andean kingdoms, I think that in application to modern

problems of rural development, the verticality model will be most useful
on the levels of the local community and region.

Ethnographic information on the ways that verticality actually operates
indicates that specific adaptations (in the forms of productive emphases,
types of livestock, or systems of exchange) enable the exploitation of a
wide range of ecozones, with some kind of optimal usage pattern for each
ecozone being exploited (Brush 1973; Burchard 1974; Carter 1965; Custred 1973; Dorsey 1975; Flores 1968, 1975; Heyduk 1974; Mayer 1971,
1974; Mitchell 1976; Orlove 1973, 1974; Vallee 1971; Webster 1971, 1973).
The nature and extent of verticality in a given community or region in the
Andes is, then, a function not only of the vertical ecozones available, but
also of the human manipulation of plants and animals, tools, and productive techniques in interaction with the environment.

There is no question about the need for increased agricultural production in the Andean countries. And improvement in the quality of life of
most small agriculturalists in the highlands depends on increasing their
crop and livestock yields. There seems to be general agreement that
increased production should come about primarily through more intensive use of existing farm land, rather than through the opening of new land
(Coutu and King 1969; Jorgenson 1971; Mitchell and Schatan 1967:99–
102; Santa Cruz 1967; Sternberg 1973; Thiesenhusen 1974). Achieving
more intensive farming and increased yields in the sierra requires some
changes in productive methods. Among the requirements are: improved
crop and livestock varieties, better combinations of crops, maintenance
of soil fertility, control of crop pests, and conservation of arable land and
water resources. But these requirements must be fulfilled within the
bounds of the Andean peasants' economic and ecologic circumstances.
Ethnographic information on specific adaptative features of highland
agriculture and pastoralism can be used as a foundation for approaching
the needed changes, and I will draw on it in the discussion below. The
suggestions to be made in this discussion are not exhaustive of the
possibilities. Rather, in addition to any intrinsic merits they may have,
they are meant primarily to indicate the types of development approaches
that could contribute to raising the standard of living of Andean small
agriculturalists and to increasing highland agricultural production without
great cost and without further damaging the highland ecosystem.

Animal Husbandry

The camelids, especially the llama and alpaca, have long been an
important component of multiple ecozone exploitation in a large area of
the central Andes. Camelids are adapted to life at elevations up to almost
5,000 meters. Because they can eat the coarse grasses available as pasture
at high elevations, camelids are the crucial intermediaries in human

exploitation of ecozones—the *páramo* (high steppe) (3,200–4,700 m), humid *puna* (3,400–5,200 m) and humid *ceja* (up to 5300 m)—that cannot be used effectively for crop production (Custred 1973:19–20; Flores 1975:300–301; Webster 1971:177). While some other livestock, particularly sheep, can be raised at high elevation, "the llama is the most efficient converter of altiplano vegetation to live animal weight" (Stouse 1970:138).

The llama and alpaca provide Andean peasants with transportation, wool, bone and hides, meat and fat, and, very important, dung for use as fuel and fertilizer (Custred 1973; Flores 1975:306–307; Stouse 1970; Webster 1971; Winterhalder et al. 1974). Improved yields from camelid herds—in terms of greater reproductive efficiency, higher quality wool, and greater meat production—could contribute significantly to improving the diet and increasing the cash income of many peasant families. There is some research on improving the breeding and husbandry of camelids underway (Instituto Veterinario 1972), but there is undoubtedly a need for much more. Further, there is a strong need for means of disseminating the results of camelid research to small-scale pastoralists. To allow camelid herding to decline is to forfeit the option of exploiting certain of the available ecozones.

To benefit fully from increased yields of wool and meat, peasant pastoralists must be able to exchange camelid products for other goods. Such exchange requires more effective marketing mechanisms and infrastructure than now exist. Both producers and consumers would gain from legal means, with appropriate sanitary measures, for marketing camelid meat. Improvement of wool quality and yield needs to be backed up by marketing mechanisms that encourage peasants to market partially and completely finished wool products as well as raw wool, control the quality of marketed wool and insure prices which reflect an adequate return for peasant labor. In some regions marketing camelid products might involve some exchange among communities in different vertical ecozones as a first stage (e.g., exchange of raw wool for agricultural produce) and commercial marketing as a later stage (e.g., finished wool products for cash). In regions where pastoralists do not traditionally engage in any agriculture, camelid (and sheep and cattle) dung is sometimes sold or bartered to agricultural communities. Increases in herd size and/or improvements in transportation or marketing means in these regions might lead to increased distribution of dung for fertilizer and fuel. This would not only profit the pastoralists, but would be important in communities in which people cannot afford to purchase other fuels or chemical fertilizers.

In conjunction with efforts to improve yields from camelids, several steps are necessary to insure that peasant pastoralists will receive benefits from increased production without endangering the delicate *puna* and *páramo* environments. Already in some areas increasing population has

led to increased herd sizes and to overgrazing (Tosi 1960:130, 135, 142)
Overgrazing lowers the productive capacity of pastures, makes wate
control more difficult and leaves pasture lands vulnerable to erosion
Improving the quality of pasturage, by seeding it and using irrigatio
where possible, is an integral aspect of increasing livestock yields an
would alleviate some of the danger of overgrazing.

Despite their efficiency in using *puna* and *páramo* ecozones and th
value of their products, camelids are not today distributed throughout th
Andes. Improved breeding and more effective husbandry methods migh
make camelids attractive introductions to regions where they are not no
raised, opening to the peasants of those areas the opportunity to exploi
ecozones that are presently of marginal utility.

Crop Production

While some Andean peasant groups specialize in pastoralism, a fa
greater proportion engages in a combination of livestock and crop produc
tion and some rely almost entirely on crops. Successful agriculture in th
highlands requires a diversity of crops (to match the diversity of vertica
ecozones) and certain types of crops that are suitable for cultivation a
higher elevations and under specific ecological conditions (Heath et al
1969:388).

A number of tubers, legumes, and grains are native Andean domesti
cants and are well adapted to specific highland ecological conditions
Important among these native cultigens are: tarwi *(Lupinus mutabilis),*
legume; oca *(Oxalis tuberosa),* melloco *(Ollucus tuberosus),* mashu
(Tropaeolum tuberosum), and many varieties of potatoes *(Solanum* spp.)
all tubers; maize *(Zea mays),* quinoa *(Chenopodium quinoa)* and cañihu
(Chenopodium pallidicaule), grains (see Milstead 1928; Pulgar 1946:110-
120). While some crops have been introduced (historically) into Andea
agriculture with success—particularly barley, wheat, and broad bean
(Vicia fava)—and while it may be that some other crops might still b
introduced (e.g., soy beans), there is much to be said in favor of heav
reliance on the indigenous highland cultigens.

The native Andean cultigens represent a fund of plant genetic variabil
ity and of indigenous agricultural knowledge that it is important to
preserve for the future (Gade 1969; Reitz and Craddock 1969; Rowe 1969
Sternberg 1973). They also hold great potential for improving diet an
nutrition, and they enable the exploitation of ecozones that are no
suitable for the production of introduced species. In addition, some o
these traditional Andean crops have significant potential for commercia
export. With appropriate research and improvement in stock and produc
tion techniques, some of the native cultigens, which are already adapte

o local environments, could contribute greatly to the effort to increase gricultural production in the highlands.

Unfortunately, most of the native crops have not been the subjects of gricultural research efforts (Gade 1969:49; Thiesenhusen 1974; Santa Cruz 1967:155). Some of these crops have been or are being dropped from :ultivation (Gade 1969, 1970). They are being displaced, in some cases, by ntroduced cultigens which have higher yields under ideal conditions (but ften have lower or no yield when conditions are not optimal), or which ire in more demand in the market. In other instances, difficulties of reparation of the native crops lead to reduction in their cultivation.

Cañihua, for example, is one of the traditional crops whose production s limited and declining. Yet it is of great potential value in highland igriculture. "Perhaps no other crop is so resistent to the combination of rosts, drought, salty soil, and pests, or requires such little care in its :ultivation. At the same time, few grains have such a high protein content is does cañihua (13.8%), surpassing quinoa (12.3%), wheat (12.0%), parley (9.7%), and maize (9.4%)" (Gade 1970:55).

Cañihua grows at very high elevations—in protected sites as high as 4 500 m (Gade 1969, 1970). Its resistance to frost, drought, and pests makes it an excellent form of crop insurance in higher ecozones. Because t has different nutrient requirements from potatoes and other tuber crops, t can successfully be planted the year after a field is used for tubers. Cañihua can be eaten as a whole grain or can be made into flour. Its only drawback is that the pericarp of the seeds is very bitter and must be removed, by soaking in water and rubbing, before the grain can be consumed. Quinoa, a close relative of cañihua, is almost as hardy and as nutritionally valuable as cañihua, but shares this problem of a bitter seed coating (Gade 1969, 1970).

Both these chenopoids could be improved by selective breeding for non-bitter varieties and for increased yields (IUCN 1968:83). The availability of improved varieties would probably lead to increased production of these crops by small farmers. Increased production of quinoa and cañihua could be used within the Andean countries to improve nutrition, and also might lead to the development of an export market—they would be a great hit in U.S. health food stores at least.

Tarwi is another native crop which is disappearing from cultivation despite significant potential. Tarwi can be grown up to elevations of about 3600 m. Like cañihua, it serves as an insurance crop, as it is more resistant to cold and insects than maize or broad beans. Like many other legumes, tarwi fixes nitrogen in nodules on its roots and releases nitrogen to the soil. Thus it fits as a form of fertilizer into a rotation pattern in which it is planted the year before tubers, maize, or broad beans. Tarwi is a good source of protein, but like the chenopoids, its seeds have a bitter (and mildly toxic) component that must be extracted by removing the skin and soaking for several days. Again, improved varieties, bred for greater yields and a non-bitter seed, could be developed and would lead to increased cultivation. The nitrogen-fixing capability of tarwi gives it important potential as part of an efficient mixed-cropping system. In addition to its use for human consumption it might also be used as a green manure and for livestock fodder.

Tarwi, quinoa and cañihua serve as examples of the potential value of native highland cultigens. Other Andean crops, particularly the tubers, should also be the subjects of research and selective breeding to enhance the adaptations they already have (Rowe 1969). These crops can provide the continuing diversity needed and could form the bases for more intensive high elevation agriculture. That they are primarily subsistence rather than commercial export crops, or that they are associated with Indians (Gade 1969:49), are not reasonable grounds for agricultural research and development agencies to ignore them.

Fertilizers and Pest Control

Increased and improved use of fertilizers is another important step in the effort to intensify highland agriculture. Andean peasants are well aware of the importance of fertilizer application, but few of them can afford to purchase chemical fertilizers. Traditionally they use the dung of camelids, sheep, and cattle on their fields. However, the use of dung (from llama, alpacas, and cattle) for domestic fuel reduces the amount available for manuring fields.

Under appropriate conditions, swine are another potential major source of dung for fertilizer (Champeau 1975). Currently swine production does not seem to be very great in the Andean region (Mitchell, Schatan 1967:130). Further, I am not aware of any examples of swine dung being employed by highland peasants for fertilizer. Research on varieties of hogs that produce well at higher elevations and education on proper swine husbandry methods could lead to much greater use of swine dung for manure. Increasing swine production and using swine dung for fertilizer could have valuable side-effects: it would mean that more camelid and bovine dung could be spared for use as fuel, and it would increase the supplies of pig meat, fat, and hides for producers and for the market.

Composting of animal dung and vegetable matter, for use as fertilizer, does not seem to be a common or fully developed practice among Andean agriculturalists. This probably is due in part to the fact that at high elevations the rate of organic decay is very slow (Cabrera 1968). But even if decomposition is slow and incomplete, composting would improve the quality of organic fertilizers and make more efficient use of potential fertilizer materials. The techniques of composting are relatively simple and straightforward and could easily be learned and used by peasant farmers. Research might indicate some methods for improving rates of decomposition even in the colder areas and point to mixtures of compost materials which would provide the organic and mineral elements needed in specific local soils.

I would guess that a major reason for the apparent lack of attention to composting is the emphasis placed on the value of chemical fertilizers by many agricultural specialists, who share some of the pro-industrial, anti-traditional biases mentioned above. Yet both Chinese and U.S. agricultural experience—as well as that of the Andean peasants—illustrates the value of organic fertilizers (Champeau 1975; National Academy 1975; Wade 1975). Moreover, organic fertilizers are less likely than chemical ones to contribute to water pollution, and they are far less expensive. Dung and compost not only supply nutrients for crops, as do chemical fertilizers, but they also provide organic matter, which is the basis of biological activity, to soils. Organic matter improves soil aeration and water retention and also helps bind the soil, lessening erosion (Winterhalder et al. 1974).

Careful and thorough composting should significantly increase the amount of organic fertilizer available to highland peasants. Increased application of composted material would contribute directly to increasing crop yields and would facilitate more intensive cultivation by reducing the fallow periods of fields. As a side-effect, composting could lead to some improvement of sanitary conditions in rural households and communities by giving the peasants a good reason to dispose of waste more carefully.

Reduction in the amount of crop loss due to insect pests and plant diseases would also help increase highland agricultural yields. One possible partial solution to the problem of insect and disease damage is the development and dissemination of pest-resistant varieties of crops. Another possible tactic is the use of naturally occuring controls, such as predator insects. Both of these approaches require much more intensive research on highland crops than has been undertaken so far. Chemical pesticides, of course, are yet another possible approach to reducing crop damage. But chemical pesticides are expensive—especially by the standards of Andean peasants—and most of them are dangerous to use and are ecologically harmful and polluting. If pesticides are to be used, even in limited quantities, the safest and least expensive ones should be chosen. One of the safest pesticides known is pyrethrum. It is made from the flowers of the pyrethrum plant *(Pyrethrum aureum)*, which grows at elevations up to at least 3,000 m. It is already cultivated in limited amounts in the Andes. If local processing facilities were available pyrethrum production could be increased. This would be of direct economic benefit to pyrethrum growers and would make a safe pesticide available to small agriculturalists at much lower prices than imported chemical ones (C. S. Koeler, personal communication).

Terracing and Reforestation

Intensification of highland agriculture is predicated on adequate land and water resources. Maintenance of land and water resources in the Andes requires prevention of erosion and of surface run-off of water. The best means for controlling erosion on steep slopes is to terrace fields. Terracing of arable slopes was extensively practiced by the pre-Conquest societies of the highlands, but has largely disappeared from the Andean peasants' repertory of agricultural practices (Eckholm 1975:766). The re-introduction of terracing, in those regions where steepness of slope and local ecological conditions call for it, is urgently needed to prevent further erosion. Terracing also facilitates better control of water for agricultural purposes, and in some places might encourage the use of small-scale farming machinery.

As the lack of forests in the Andes is known to be a primary cause of soil erosion, reforestation is seen already as a necessity. All the Andean countries have initiated reforesting efforts in the highlands. However, a number of problems are involved in reforestation. One of these is the issue of which land should be reforested and under what sorts of arrangements with rural communities (Budowski 1968:161). In this regard, there is a need for greater integration into forestry planning of information about the existing land use and ownership patterns—including verticality practices—of local peasant communities. Possible peasant use of forest products also needs consideration in planning reforestation.

The use for reforestation of already eroded land and of zones too dry or too steep for farming is an obvious option. But forest development cannot be planned in isolation. The possibilities, in some areas, of interspersing or combining pasturage and forests deserves greater attention. In many parts of the Andes, population pressure has led already to the use of marginal ecozones for agriculture. If reforestation efforts were joined with efforts to improve and intensify farming in optimal areas, the marginal zones could be used for tree production, to the benefit both of the peasantry and the environment.

Another issue in highland reforestation is the types of trees to be used. The current emphasis is on the use of eucalyptus and secondarily of certain pines (Budowski 1968:159–160). Apparently little attention or research is being devoted to the possibilities of using native highland trees and shrubs or new varieties developed from them for reforestation, despite the fact that they are adapted to local ecological conditions and ould be improved to suit specific ecological and cultural needs (Sharp 970).

The principles of drawing on local traditions and resources and developing culturally integrated technology which is low-cost and ecologically afe can be extended to a number of areas that relate directly to enhancing he living standards of Andean small agriculturalists. For example, improved stoves for burning dung, wood, and straw could be developed. ligh efficiency wood-burning stoves already exist, but they are of castron and are very expensive. The point for the rural Andes is to design ocal variants of such stoves, drawing on the ideas of advanced models, ut relying primarily or entirely on local materials and technological apacities for making them. This same approach might be used in many ther ways: to improve means of storing foods for better preservation and ess loss to rodents, or to design a cheap, simple grain milling machine hat could be powered by streams or in integration with irrigation works. ven manufacture and introduction of small-scale mechanized agriultural tools, such as simple corn-huskers or small garden tractors or 'roto-tillers," might also be feasible in the near future. The main determiants of success for these kinds of efforts to develop the rural highland conomy will be the devotion of sensitive attention to the productive raditions, needs and limitations of peasant agriculture and the integration f planned changes with each other as well as with the existing culture and cology.

Ethnographic information on the patterns of peasant exploitation of pecific ecozones is particularly valuable as a basis for planning certain inds of changes in agricultural practices, crops, and technology. When thnographic data of this kind are subsumed in the more general model of verticality, a new range of rather broader possible applications becomes visible. The verticality model (informed by information on contemporary peasant life-ways) has significant implications for the programs of land reform, agrarian law reform, agricultural extension, and infrastructure building that are so fundamental to increased agricultural production and mproved standard of living in the highlands.

The training of agriculturalists and extension personnel should incorporate verticality and foster an appreciation for appropriate utilization of local vertical ecozones (Coutu, King 1969:142; Mitchell, Schattan 1967:53, 83–85). At a minimum, agricultural extension work should include attention to understanding local operation of verticality and the ramifications of verticality in terms of local diversity of crops and productive techniques. Calendrical agricultural patterns (e.g., transhumance movements) which are linked to verticality should also be taken into consideration by extension agents. The labor demands of exploiting several ecozones dictate rural patterns of geographic movement and daily and seasonal use of time and work force. To make effective contributions to the development of peasant groups, extension agencies must be flexible and adapt their activities to the places and time made available in the highland agricultural routine—not vice versa.

One of the most immediate and general possible applications of the verticality model is in land reform. There is evidence that land reform actions in the Andean countries, during the last two decades, sometimes have been carried out in such a manner that verticality has been maintained in communities where it already existed (Burke 1971; Dorsey 1975; Forman 1972). But I have not encountered any information that indicates that maintenance or enhancement of verticality is an explicit goal in the land reform planning of the Andean countries (Heath et al. 1969). Further, it seems likely that, at least where land reform includes efforts to reduce the degree of minifundia, some land reform actions have reduced the access of some people to multiple vertical ecozones (Scott 1974:342).

It seems to me to be highly desirable to incorporate considerations of verticality into all phases of land reform planning and implementation in the sierra. In general, such application of the verticality model should mean examination of the possibilities for direct exploitation of contiguous vertical ecozones in a given locale, whether or not such a pattern of exploitation is the existing practice. Then, as appropriate, land distribution should be compatible with optimal productive use of the ecozones available. In instances where vertical patterns of land use already exist, examination of these patterns and of their significance to a community should precede redistribution of land and help dictate the form the redistribution will take.

Incorporation of verticality into land reform programs must also include attention to local patterns of residence, communal land holding, cooperative labor, and economic exchange beyond the community (Scott 1974:342–343). Highland peasant communities range in settlement patterns from completely nucleated to extremely dispersed. Where members of a community are directly exploiting a large set of vertical ecozones, they may have residences in more than one area (Brush 1973; Flores 1975; Webster 1973). Sometimes settlement and residence patterns may be artifacts of hacienda organization, but in many instances they are products of the local verticality practices. Where residence and settlement forms are closely linked to verticality, land reform actions should not disrupt them.

It is not uncommon in the Andes for peasant communities to possess communal lands (Basile 1974:71; Forman 1972; Mayer 1974:302–304; Webster 1973). However, the nature and scale of communal land holdings is highly variable, ranging from small areas of pasture or *páramo* to some or all of the arable land of a community. The type of communal holding in a given community will be integral in most cases with the practices of verticality. Land reform agencies need to determine the existing patterns of communal land holding and use before either reducing its type and extent or attempting to augment the degree of communal land use. Generalized theories that highland Indians are all communally oriented are belied by the actual diversity of cultural traditions and peasant behavior, and ought not to be blindly applied.

Similar injunctions apply in the case of cooperative labor practices. Cooperative labor practices are also highly variable both in organization and degree of importance (Carter 1965; Fonseca 1974; Forman 1972; Isbell 1974; Mitchell 1976; Orlove 1974). Such cooperative work forms as *minga* and *ayni* (Fonseca 1974; Orlove 1974) have different bases in different regions of the highlands; they are often related to some aspect of verticality as well as to the kinship and political organization of a community. They should not be mistaken for a general propensity for cooperative organization, but rather their role in local production and community organization should be examined carefully before efforts are made to modify or elaborate them. The frequent failures of cooperative organizations established in connection with land reform illustrate the problems that can arise from ill-founded efforts to create collective labor institutions where they do not fit with local cultural and ecological patterns (Alberti, Mayer 1974:32–33; Brush 1973:13; Heath et al. 1969:393; Orlove 1974:320; Tendler 1975; Webster 1971:179).

In areas where verticality has operated through exchange mechanisms (of market or non-market types), land reform and changes in transportation networks or commercial opportunities may either enhance or reduce access to the products of multiple ecozones (Burchard 1974; Custred 1973; Flores 1975:309-311; Mayer 1971). Exchange of labor for goods outside a community may be an important avenue of access to the resources of other ecozones (Burchard 1974; Custred 1974:282-284), and ought not to be restricted by agrarian legislation (Alberti, Mayer 1974:3-33; Scott 1974:343).

In terms of raising the standard of living of highland peasants, direct exchanges among communities in different vertical ecozones may be preferable to shunting the flow of products from different zones through a commercial market in which a significant portion of the value of those products is diverted to the profits of largescale entrepreneurs. Wherever appropriate, traditional forms of exchange should be supported by the development of rural infrastructure (in terms of transportation networks, credit facilities, small markets, agricultural extension). The fact that some peasant production is aimed at commercial markets should not mean that other forms of exchange (especially of subsistence products) are ignored or undercut (Alberti, Mayer 1974:30–33).

Summary and Conclusions

The ethnographic and geographic information we possess makes it clear that in the Andes we are dealing with complex and unusual ecological and agricultural conditions. Variations in the mix of topography, elevation, soils, climate, and biota make the Andean highlands a mosaic of ecological settings. Variations in social, political, economic, cultural, and demographic conditions create a superimposed mosaic of human use of the diverse Andean ecozones. In the context of this complex situation there are the linked needs of improving the quality of life of an increasing population while preventing further, eventually disastrous, deterioration of the fragile highland environment.

Given my view of the nature of the problems being faced by the Andean countries in their efforts to achieve greater economic and social development, it is clear that verticality is a useful, perhaps a crucial, concept with many possible applications to the direction and the content of development programs. Ethnographic and ethnohistoric information demonstrates that it is possible to support a relatively large population in the Andean highlands—as long as people are willing and able to adapt their productive practices and patterns of exchange to the vertical organization and local ecological variation of the sierra.

Application of the model of verticality in such components of development as land reform and agricultural extension should lead to programs that are less disruptive to the people and the environment than has often been the case to date. The elaboration and improvement of local crops, livestock, technologies, and exchange systems hold a promise of raising the standard of living of the peasants, without driving them into the cities and without irreparably damaging the fragile ecosystem of the mountains.

While in purely environmental terms it might be preferable to reduce the human population in the highlands, in social and economic terms it is to utilize fully—but not over-use—as many of the ecozones of the Andes as possible. Full use will require diversification and intensification of small-scale agriculture and pastoralism, as well as improvement of infrastructure. I have argued in this essay that optimal development of the highland agricultural sector can most effectively be carried out by drawing on ethnographic information about past and present adaptation of Andean cultures, especially their traditional use of multiple vertical ecozones. I have also stressed the desirability of relying on local resources and small-scale technology to enhance and develop the traditional agricultural practices of the peasants.

It is true that our understanding of the Andean ecosystem and the human ways of exploiting it is still incomplete. Yet the verticality model and related ethnographic data on specific adaptations to local ecozones provide us with some sound guidelines for proceeding with rural development in the Andes.

Acknowledgments

A number of friends and colleagues have helped me with one aspect or another of this essay. I would like to thank Glen Custred, George Miller, Benjamin Orlove, J. J. Parsons and Judith Tendler for helpful conversations and loans of materials, and Stephen Beckerman and Lisa Falkenthal for editorial aid. I particularly am grateful to John H. Rowe and Patricia Lyon for helping me find reasonable working conditions, and to Karen O. Bruhns for more kinds of aid than I can mention here.

I acknowledge with appreciation the grant-in-aid for travel that I have received from the Massachusetts Chapter of Society of the Sigma Xi.

12

Mapping of Mountain Hazards in Nepal

Jack D. Ives

Post–1950 Land Use Changes in the Environment

The popular image of high mountains embraces ice and snow, great rock faces, raging torrents, inclement weather, and, at lower elevations, precariously placed village and farmhouses, with fields clinging to steep slopes or overhanging deep gorges. To this could be added snow and ice avalanches, rock-falls, mud-flows, landslides and floods, amongst other catastrophic processes acting under the influence of gravity. Traditionally the world's mountain areas have been occupied by small groups of subsistence agriculturalists and pastoralists who, through generations of accumulated wisdom, have learned to minimize the catastrophic potential of their special environment. Through this process the relatively safe sites have become well recognized and occupied.

This view of high mountains is biased towards the Alps. With some modification it will fit the Caucasus, the Pyrenees, the Carpathians, the Rocky Mountains and the North American coastal ranges. With further modification it can be applied to the Japanese Alps, the Southern Alps of New Zealand, and the southern Andes. In essence it encompasses the high mountains of mid-latitudes prior to about 1950. Since 1950 the traditional mid-latitude mountain areas have had to absorb a massive influx of new activities, and large transient populations. This has been associated principally with the unprecedented development of two-season tourism and recreation, especially skiing, for the growing urban populations of the neighboring lowlands. The enormous pressures generated by such growth in demand for recreation have all but submerged traditional land-use intelligence. Once hitherto marginal land has soared in value because of the demands for hotels, ski-resort infrastructure and roads. In another mode of post–1950 land-use intensification, the construction of hydro-electric or irrigation reservoirs emerges as a new form of inexperienced mountain entrepreneuring. Construction occurs under such circumstances on sites previously avoided by the traditional subsistence mountain farmer. Control passes from the mountain village to large financial interests located far away from the development sites. The motif is one of short-term cash profit rather than long-term balance between subsistence livelihood and environment. While the Alps were the first mountains to experience these tremendous economic and social forces that in turn led to severe environmental impacts, the other mid-latitude mountain areas are now also being similarly threatened. One observer has commented on these disturbing changes as follows:

> An unmistakable increase in the number of disasters (floods, torrents, landslips, landslides and avalanches) occurring in the Alpine territories raises the question: What are the causes of this dangerous development? In former times, a balance existed between the vegetation, the water regime, and erosion, and man had no power to make drastic changes. With no modern techniques to help him, man had to trust to his instinct when siting his settlements and choosing his working methods. Our century, and especially the last decade, has seen the multiplication of anthropogenic components until they became practically dominant [Aulitzky 1974].

The tropical mountain regions are also incurring progressive destabilization, but the processes involved are, for the most part, very different. Here the pressures are also generated by large increases in population, but in this case the increases are mainly due to the natural growth of local populations rather than the influx of transient recreation seekers. Again 1950 is a convenient benchmark date, although in many tropical mountain areas pressures were building up during the preceding decades. Nevertheless, following the Second World War, the great expansion of health care and provision of medical facilities produced worldwide reduction in infant mortality and extended life-spans. The mountain kingdom of Nepal serves as an effective example. Nepal first opened its borders to the outside world in 1950 and began its transformation from a closed feudal kingdom to a small mountain state increasingly tied to the world market and progressively dependent upon it. In this case a rapidly growing rural subsistence population covered its immediate needs by felling trees, both for cooking fuel and to make way for new agricultural terraces on steeper and steeper slopes. As the nearest trees were cut the villager had to spend progressively more time carrying fuel from increasingly more distant sources.

When a family finds itself devoting more than two man-days per week to cutting and fetching wood-fuel, a critical limit is reached whereby animal manure, the principal, and often the only, form of fertilizer, is used more and more for fuel. This is the current condition of almost half the rural population of Nepal. As the agricultural terraced lands are deprived of manure two additional developments become progressively more severe. First, crop yields are lowered, necessitating additional terracing of more marginal terrain on steeper slopes. Second, reduced soil fertility leads to a weakened soil structure and increased incidence of landsliding during the monsoon season.

A Serious Threat to World Stability

The somewhat simplified scenario outlined above represents a series of vicious circles one within another. Torrential rains during the monsoon induce mud-flows and debris flows (locally referred to collectively as landslides). Such geomorphic processes are characteristic of steep mountain slopes, with or without human modification. However, the type of modification occurring in Nepal and many other tropical and subtropical mountain areas has led to a rapid acceleration in the incidence of landsliding. Basically, as deforestation continues soil erosion accelerates. This is a chronic rather than a catastrophic situation since it can best be compared to a slowly spreading infection or disease. Nevertheless, the consequences of this process, while severe in the longer term for the mountain area itself, may have effects downstream of even greater magnitude. Thus significant changes in the mountain hydrological regime, with more rapid run-off during the rainy season and reduced flow during the dry season, lead to floods and siltation and to dry-season water shortage in the neighboring lowlands.

Nepal has lost half its forest cover in the last thirty years. This situation characteristizes much of the Himalaya. As a direct consequence the Ganges delta is rapidly advancing into the Bay of Bengal and silt in suspension can be seen 500 kilometres south of the present coastline. The problem of the Himalaya/Indo-Gangetic Plain is of sufficient magnitude, with major international ramifications, that it can be described as one of the more serious threats to world stability over the next two decades. Yet this situation is not unique to the Himalaya. It embraces much of the Andes, the East African highlands, the mountains of Burma, Yunnan, Laos, and northern Thailand, the high country of Papua New Guinea and Indonesia, amongst many other areas. Concern for this international problem has been expressed by many agencies and governments.

The United Nations University Mountain Hazards Mapping Project

The involvement of the United Nations University is by no means unique or original. What is new, however, is the approach that is being taken to mountain-hazard problem-solving in tropical mountain countries. This approach stems from the realization that the overall problem of increasing economic, social, and environmental instability in mountain lands would be unmanageably large even if enormous financial resources and manpower were available. With the very modest resources of UNU's

Programme on the Use and Management of Natural Resources, it was decided that the best approach was to develop, and apply on an experimental scale, the recently emerging methodology of natural hazards mapping.

As implied in the opening paragraphs, steep mountain slopes, by definition, are subject to downhill movement of material (snow, water, and rock, soil, and vegetation, in various mixtures) under gravity. Mountain geomorphologists with an academic bent, and engineers with a practical interest, have involved themselves in the study of the effects of geomorphic processes and snow mechanics on mountain-slope stability for several decades. Furthermore, there have evolved numerous methods of identifying areas especially subject to mass movement. Perhaps the best known is the work of the Swiss Avalanche Zoning Plan (Frutiger 1980). In Austria, H. Aulitzky has recommended and implemented combined mapping of avalanche paths and mountain torrents and has developed a traffic-light color system (red, amber, and green) to designate areas subject to hazardous processes (Aulitsky 1973). Many individuals and agencies throughout the world have tackled specific problems, whether they be landslides, mud-flows, floods, the dramatic interaction of volcanic eruption and mud-flow, coastal erosion, and so on.

Within mountain areas many forms of natural processes overlap both in time and space. An avalanche path may be a threat to life and property from flowing snow in winter and spring, while in summer and autumn the dominant processes could be mud-flow, mountain torrent, landslide, or rock-fall, and the flooding of the valley-bottom run-out area. This concern with multiple hazards has recently led to a geographic or regional approach to the delineation of areas subject to mass movement. Amongst others, two projects, one in the Bernese Oberland, the other in the Colorado Rockies, led to experimentation with the cartographic representation of all natural hazards within a single area. The Swiss approach resulted in the production of a very detailed and highly accurate series of multicolored maps for the area around Grindelwald on a scale of 1:10,000 (Kienholz 1977). In the Colorado Rockies the area to be covered was significantly greater and the available topographical base maps were at the reconnaissance scale of 1:24,000 (Ives et al. 1976). This resulted in the production of two series of maps in black and white (avalanches treated separately as one series). From these beginnings the two groups joined forces and developed a combined natural hazards map at 1:24,000 for a test area of the Colorado Front Range (Kienholz 1979; Dow et al. 1981).

Nepal Selected for Experiment

The brief foregoing description provides the setting for the United Nations University involvement in mountain-hazard mapping. Within the UNU program on natural resources, concern over the use and manage-

ment of these resources in mountain lands led to creation of a subprojec
to study highland-lowland interactive systems. One component of thi
became mountain-hazard mapping, with Nepal selected as a test area
This development depended upon the natural-hazard mapping collabora
tion between Berne University and the University of Colorado. It wa
deemed timely to attempt an adaptation of the natural-hazard mapping i
the two mid-latitude high-mountain areas to a tropical or subtropica
mountain area. Following an invitation from the Nepalese Governmen
Nepal was selected for the experiment in 1978. And it was quickl
realized during a field reconnaissance in March–April 1979 that the ter
"natural hazard" should be replaced by "mountain hazard" to tak
cognizance of the overwhelming human modification of the Himalaya
landscape.

The reconnaissance in the spring of 1979 led to the outline of a mediun
term research project. The major component was the production c
prototype mountain-hazard maps for three representative areas of Nepa
a high-altitude area extending above and below the upper timberline i
Sagarmatha National Park of the Khumbu-Himal; a section of the Middl
Mountains, extending along the Trisuli Highway between Kathmandu an
Kakani; and a low-altitude transect across the Siwalik Range and out o
to the Terai. This selection of three areas was also appropriate in provid
ing a field base for possible future in-depth analysis of highland-lowlan
interactions. In addition, realization that human activities had almos
totally modified some of these areas led to the incorporation of ethn
graphic studies as a means of determining the responses of the loc
people to landslide and other catastrophic processes as well as assessin
their possible reaction to future land-use policy making.

For a variety of reasons the Middle Mountain area (Kathmandu
Kakani) was given first priority (see Fig. 12.1). The fieldwork wa
initiated in September 1979 and completed in April 1981. Much dat
analysis and report writing has been completed, two multicoloured map
have been printed (land use and geomorphology), and several technica
papers are already in print (Caine, Mool 1981). The final mountain-hazar
prototype map, on a scale of 1:10,000, is scheduled for publication in mid
1982. Fieldwork will begin in the Khumbu-Himal for the second phase c
the project after the 1982 monsoon, and for this area the mapping scal
will be 1:50,000.

Mountain Research Benefits Development

Multiple-hazards mapping is still so recent an approach that effort t
justify it is needed even in developed countries:

> Mountain hazards mapping is far from being a widely recognized component
> of either regional or site specific land-use planning. This may seem surprising

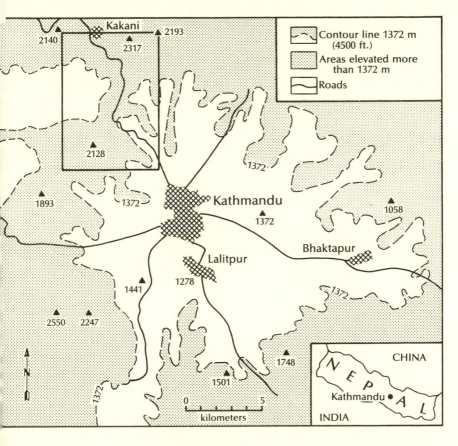

Figure 12.1   Kathmandu-Kakani Survey Area

in view of the series of spectacular disasters that have occurred in mountain areas in recent years. This may be because many of the large-scale mountain developments are very recent and because of the relatively new awareness that manipulation of one or a few components of a landscape affects all other components. This applies particularly to the mountains of the "Western World" where a major proportion of human impact is due to large-scale technological modification. It can also be applied to the mountains of the "Developing World" where population growth and deforestation resulting from the expansion of subsistence agriculture is the main driving force, although large-scale engineering works are by no means rare [Dow et al. 1981].

Justification for mountain-hazard mapping in Nepal rests upon a number of assumptions. First, any land-use decision-making, whether it relates to the relatively simple process of locating and designing a new

highway or to the more complex process of design of an integrate
regional plan, will depend for its effectiveness in large part on the type
and reliabilty of available information. Thus a mountain-hazard map
should be regarded as one component of the overall data bank to be use
as a basis for decision-making. In the case of the UNU project in Nepal,
some additional and very useful components are being added: studies of
dynamic geomorphic processes and of human responses and perceptions.
A second consideration is that the very attempt to produce a series of
experimental prototype maps should lead to a much fuller understanding
of landscape dynamics, including the human-natural interrelations, so
that prediction of the possible effects of implementing a given policy
should be that much more reliable. Additionally, the project, through its
incorporation of young Nepalese scientists, is seeking to reduce Nepal's
dependence on the contribution of "outside" scientists. Finally, should
the experiment lead to production of a practice applied-mapping methodology, with minimal modification it will be available for immediate transfer to other tropical mountain areas around the world.

Rate of Land Loss Alarming

But in terms of results gained from fieldwork in the Kathmandu-Kakani
area some provisional conclusions can be drawn (Fig. 12.2). First, the
studies of geomorphic processes have led to the realization that land is
being lost much faster than the local people with their existing resources
can reclaim. It was calculated that the areal density of landslides is in
excess of $2/km^2$, with an average expansion rate of 60 m^2/year. From this it
can be estimated that the mean rate of land loss due to landsliding alone is
120 m^2/km^2/year. Furthermore, this figure should be doubled to take into
account the inception of new landslides (estimated at 1 in 6 km^2). With a
mean depth for landslides of 4 meters, an annual loss of 1,000 m^3km^2 will
result. This is an extremely high rate of loss for agricultural land, to which
must be added losses from other forms of mass movement, soil erosion
and loss of soil fertility, which may appreciably exceed the losses due to
landslides.

Even if the population of the Kathmandu-Kakani field area had already
achieved a zero growth rate, the figures for the rate of land loss have
serious implications for the near future. Given a continuation of the
existing high population growth rate the predictable outcome is mountain
desertification, mass migration, and increased pressure on other lands. I
can be argued, therefore, that a study such as the one described here, i
given adequate publicity, could influence the decision-making proces
before the drift to mountain desertification gets out of control.

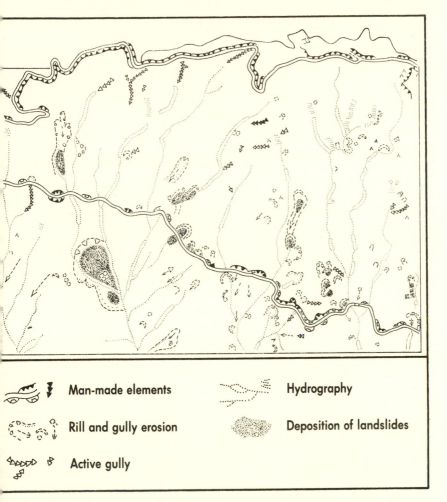

Man-made elements

Rill and gully erosion

Active gully

Hydrography

Deposition of landslides

Figure 12.2   Geomorphic Damage in Kathmandu-Kakani Area

Local Practices on Land Use

The ethnographic studies also lead to some interesting conclusions. First, there is extensive local knowledge about mountain hazards and their control, and mitigation derived from close, long-term observation and experience. This knowledge is interwoven with local occupancy and land-use practices. There are two local practices that at first glance appear to be contradictory, but in fact complement each other in face of the increasing pressures of slope instability and population growth. The first practice is to reclaim landslide areas by reterracing during subsequent dry seasons as labor becomes available. The second is to reduce the intensity of land use when hazard potential cannot be controlled. Thus wet terrace slopes, the most productive and intensively utilized, are allowed to revert to dry terraces, dry terraces to rough pasture, and so on. Up-grading and recovery is then attempted when labor is available. Finally reforestation is regarded as impractical because it limits essential crop production. This is the key indicator in terms of a mountain system moving from a stable to an unstable mode. Nevertheless a general confidence, even if qualified, is in order. Land-use planning, and technical measures developed in mid-latitudes and modified for local use, can facilitate conversion from the unstable to the stable mode based upon available knowledge, or relatively easily acquired knowledge, provided the political will can be generated. At least it is well known what types of information are needed and how they should be collected. But such an optimistic view becomes impaired when it moves from immediate focus on one, or a few, specific areas to the worldwide span. The situation in the Nepal Middle Mountains is not unique. Proof of this can be obtained from a quite casual inspection of the Himalaya westward and eastward from Kathmandu.

The Darjeeling floods of 1968 provide an example of the magnitude of problems associated with population growth, deforestation and landsliding in the eastern Himalaya. Towards the end of the 1968 monsoon, heavy rains deluged Sikkim and West Bengal, and over a three-day period precipitation amounts varying between about 500 and 1,000 mm fell on the Himalaya foothills in the vicinity of Darjeeling. While this may have been a rare event (for instance a 100-year event) and while such heavy rain would likely damage mountain slopes untouched by human activity, extensive deforestation, and the presence of innumerable roads, jeep trails and foot trails, set the stage for a disaster. Some 20,000 landslides released during the third day of the rain-storm; approximately 20,000 people lost their lives or were displaced; the 60-kilometer mountain highway to Darjeeling was cut in ninety-two places. Many of the losses were incurred by the villages and farms on the plain where the mountain streams debouch from the Siwaliks. But the hard lesson to be learned is that unplanned use of mountain lands can lead to disaster. This disaster may occur suddenly and spectacularly as in the Darjeeling foothills in 1968, or as a creeping disease with a little more land lost per unit area per year than can be reclaimed. And the two are by no means mutually exclusive.

The Need for an International System of Mountain Hazards Mapping

One of the very real needs facing the mountain world at large is a substantial increase in accurate data on process both human and natural. In addition much of the large volume of existing data is scattered, relatively inaccessible, or not available in suitable format. Synthesis of available data is urgently needed, as well as identification of gaps in knowledge. The dangers of mountain deforestation, overgrazing and soil erosion have been highlighted for a decade or more. Much of this has been based upon qualitative inspection of critical areas, hypothetical consideration, and emotion, all necessary as a vital first step. But precise calculations of soil losses under different cropping systems and on different slopes are a rarity. It is common to sound the alarm about the silting of reservoirs due to soil erosion in the neighboring hills, but accurate measurements are required under a range of different natural and human-use systems, and a time perspective must be developed.

Mountain hazards individually, such as a single winter avalanche in the Alps, or the initiation of a landslide in the Middle Mountains of the Himalaya, are insignificant compared with other struggles between humanity and nature. Also, individually these chronic disorders can be controlled or checked. Nineteenth-century deforestation and, after 1950, uncontrolled land use in the Alps led to the insertion of people and property in places subject to the ravages of mountain hazards. The Alpine countries have gone a long way towards controlling the situation. While the countries concerned had a much stronger economic base from which to respond than have developing countries in the tropics, it can be argued that the prime needs are development of awareness and creation of political will, as much within international aid agencies as within the countries themselves. In this sense the concept of highland-lowland interactions is potentially very important simply because the need to avert mountain instability is crucial for the wellbeing of the neighboring lowlands. However, the efforts to control and check specific sites will be much more effective if the location and size, date of initiation and rate of growth are known. Governments as well as international and bilateral agencies have expended enormous sums of money on disaster relief, repair, succor to the destitute. Some proportion of such funds should be devoted to prediction and prevention, and establishment of an international system of mountain-hazard mapping would seem one useful step.

Postscript

The fieldwork in Nepal, referred to above, was completed in 1983. Since then a larger, concerted investigation of the Himalaya–Ganges Problem has been initiated. While this larger study substantiates the need for a more vigorous response to the problems facing the region, it has also led to the realization that the situation is much more complex than hitherto assumed. Many facets have been dealt with individually in various issues of *Mountain Development and Research*. In particular, it has been shown for many areas that deforestation has had a long and complicated history, dating back several hundred years, and that it has been influenced more by government policy than population pressure. It is also now realized that the assumed linkage between deforestation in the mountains and increased flooding and siltation on the plains is either not valid, or at the least unsubstantiated. This leads to the reaffirmation of the critical gaps in the knowledge and the absolute unreliability of many of the available "data." Without an improvement in this dangerous situation of excessive uncertainty, rational resource development policy will remain seriously restricted.

13

Simulation Models of Andean Adaptability and Change

R. Brooke Thomas

Anticipating Change

As change in human-environmental systems in mountains proceeds at an unprecedented rate and scale and frequently bears unanticipated and disruptive consequences to human well-being, social organization and environmental quality, scientists and planners alike are confronted with an urgent need to uncover regularities about this process.

In attempting to understand processes of change it has become abundantly clear that our traditional analytical approaches are overly restrictive. The information base needed extends far beyond any one area of expertise. Conditions we are asked to assess have no historical precedents to guide our expectations. Information once collected is outdated by the time of publication. Experimentation with human-environmental systems is frequently unfeasible or unethical. Briefly, information we are able to bring to understand change has often lacked realism or relevance because it does not adequately take into account the too many variables interacting in dynamic systems that are too complex to track.

If solutions indeed can be found they will have to rely upon analytical procedures that incorporate a broader information base drawn from human biology and the social and environmental sciences; emphasize interconnectivity between multiple variables operating in complex systems; and yet reduce the complexity to a consideration of critical variables in order that the problem become analytically tractable. As our capabilities for predicting most forms of change remain rather rudimentary, it seems that analytical techniques that could anticipate alternative consequences of a change might contribute significantly. In this respect modeling of complex systems serves as one such technique.

Models

Models are partial representations of perceived reality, which depend heavily upon a visual component to demonstrate interactions between essential features of a system: interactions not easily comprehended by other means.

Thus mannequins and road maps are a type of model representing aspects of reality important to a particular objective. If effective, these and other models represent degrees of generality, reality, and precision appropriate to their purpose, and ignore irrelevant features. Models are therefore based on a series of assumptions concerning what are important components of a system and how these relate to each other. As the assumptions and relationships between components reflect the state of the art, models should be regarded simply as a heuristic tool whereby complex phenomena can be assessed, and from which testable hypotheses generated.

When system variables and rates of flow between them are quantifiable, a model can function with the following components (Shantzis, Behrens 1972:259).

1. The theory of complex feedback loop systems can aid in understanding and organizing the important causal relationships in the observed system.
2. Analysis of a model's sensitivity to changes in its parameters can indicate where precise observation or measurements are important and where large observation errors are relatively unimportant in understanding overall societal functions.
3. The model provides a framework within which one can raise new questions and perceive missing information to design further studies more efficiently.
4. Analysis of the model can provide information on the behavioral implications of observed relationships outside the range of parameter values historically observed. Thus it is useful for testing the probable effects on the society of new technologies or social policies.

Simulation modeling can therefore be used as a device to gain insights into a system's operation. In addition, it is a useful technique when for ethical, financial, or time considerations experimental manipulation and observation of the system are not possible (McRae 1979).

In constructing a model, several considerations, reviewed by Levins (1966), are noteworthy. First, it is difficult to simultaneously emphasize generality, reality, and precision. Like other analytical techniques, models are constructed to address specific problems. By design they must leave out a lot in order to concentrate on essential features; hence they are bound to be inaccurate and incomplete when judged from a perspective different from that for which they were designed.

Second, a model is neither hypothesis nor theory. It is built from relationships between variables represented in reality. What is important, however, is not that such relationships exist, but how important they are in influencing systematic functioning. Validation of a model in an ultimate sense, therefore, depends on its capacity to generate testable hypotheses about the interconnectedness of multiple variables interacting in complex systems. In this sense the model is a transitory phenomena. Once it has served its purpose it is usually discarded or altered in order to more precisely address a problem.

Selection of a Currency

In modeling a system that quantifies variables and shows rates of change between them, selection of an appropriate flow currency needs to be considered. In human systems important flows track monetary exchange, energy, limiting nutrients, materials, and information.

As Thomas and collaborators (1979) have noted, while no single factor can adequately explain the complexity of ecological and human systems, energy perhaps comes the closest. It is required by and underlies life processes whether biological or social. At the very least it serves as a common denominator in quantifying dynamic relationships within them and providing a basis for their comparison. Rather than an analytical end in itself, energy is a convenient starting point in the study of human-environment relationships. It is quantifiable, making testing of hypotheses possible—hypotheses that can be based on an extensive literature in energetics.

The study of energy flows in human groups is a one-variable approach, thus it lends itself to considerable criticism (Vayda, McCay 1975; Burnham 1982). The approach is valuable, however, as it serves as a broad organizing concept within a limited range of reference. Its utility lies in the wide variety of phenomena—behavioral, ecological and biological—that influence or are influenced by the flow pattern. Energy values can be assigned to most biobehavioral phenomena, and their influence quantitatively assessed.

Andean Models

The first effort to model an Andean human population was an energy flow analysis of adaptation to limited energy availability. Thomas (1973) worked in the highland district of Nuñoa (Department of Puno) in southern Peru. The study made use of extensive data collected by Paul

Baker and colleagues from the Pennsylvania State University (Baker, Little 1976) who worked in the area from 1964 into the early 1970s.

Building upon energetic relationships established in this diagrammatic model, three simulation models were independently created. Each simulated the effects of introducing some form of change anticipated to impact the area in the near future. These were: (1) the consequences of improved health services, (2) changes in land use strategies, and (3) erosion of cooperative networks. Discussion of the contributions and limitations of these models follows a brief description of the Nuñoan environment and human responses to it.

The Study Area

The District of Nuñoa lies at the northern extreme of the Lake Titicaca drainage basin. Minimum elevation is 4000 m, and the food-production zone extends up to the frost desert at 5000 m (see Figure 13.1). The population of the district in recent times appears to be remaining stable at approximately 8000 to 9000 people. Quechua is the predominant language. Most residents make their living through agriculture and pastoralism. Only a small number of *mestizos* were present in Nuñoa during the 1960s when it was intensively studied. These individuals generally owned

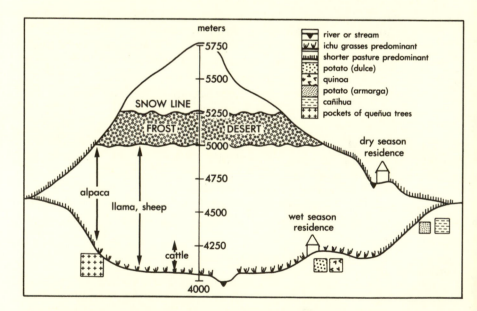

Figure 13.1   Altitude Limits of Cultigens, Herd Animals, and Natural Vegetation, Nuñoa, Peru

or managed haciendas which controlled much of the land and hence productivity of the area.

Significant environmental conditions of Nuñoa have been reviewed by Winterhalder and Thomas (1978). The following have a primary influence on food production: (1) environmental heterogeneity in time space and pattern, resulting from rugged topography; (2) poorly developed soils susceptible to erosion and marginal availability of certain nutrients; (3) low temperatures with pronounced diurnal variation; frequent and intense frosts that can occur in any season; (4) reduced oxygen and carbon dioxide tension, low absolute vapor pressure and high background radiation; (5) a lengthy dry season and irregular monthly distribution of precipitation; unpredictable droughts that may last several years; (6) a biotic community with limited productivity spread over wide regions.

While the lengthy dry season, soil conditions, and diurnal temperature variations impose fairly constant limits on biota, it is the irregular stressors such as frosts and droughts that are primarily responsible for fluctuations in productivity from year to year. The success of the human adaptive pattern is largely explained by the wide range of biobehavioral responses employed to decrease environmental perturbation and to increase the quantity and variety of resources available.

These resources include a number of frost-resistant Andean cereals and tubers and herds of alpaca, llama, and sheep. In terms of shared characteristics, they are capable of adjusting to and producing well in a variety of microzones and are generally amenable to storage, transport, and exchange with products of other regions. When possible, a multiple resource base consisting of items having different environmental tolerances and recovery rates is used. These often have nonconflicting schedules, and are spatially accessible to localized groups. Production techniques generally call for a dispersion of resources in time and space in order to avoid a simultaneous loss. This requires high mobility on the part of the productive unit and dispersion of settlement pattern.

Finally, exchange between productive units of the same group serves to buffer the effects of localized resource loss and provides access to labor for tasks that the unit could not perform alone. Exchange between groups residing in different zones has the same function in addition to providing essential resources not produced on the altiplano (Thomas 1978).

Diagrammatic Model: Human Energy Flow

Limited capacity to channel food energy into the human population suggested that a number of energetically efficient biobehavioral responses might be found upon examining subsistence activities of rural families. Goals of the investigation were therefore to determine levels of energy production, consumption and expenditure for families in order to describe their energy flow patterns. Second, to assess the adequacy of their caloric intake, and, finally, to identify adaptive responses that facilitated adequate procurement and efficient utilization of food energy.

Analysis focused on productive and food processing activities of families during an annual cycle, when harvests were considered "normal." Detailed attention was not given to exchange patterns outside the area or to the economic role of the hacienda.

The energy flow pattern for an average nuclear family of four children is presented in Figure 13.2. Many of the results of the author's (1973) study support observations long noted by ethnographers of altiplano groups. Quantification of these data and their organization into a systemic model which focuses upon a single problem, however, provides a basis of comparison and experimentation with alternatives, not possible in more descriptive accounts.

Baker (1979:161–63) has summarized contributions of this work as follows. Beginning with the human input, it will be noticed that the energy expended in crop production was influenced by a number of decision-making and structural characteristics of the family. As indicated by energy (Joules) expenditure, the vast majority of human energy expended in the productive process went into animal production, rather than agriculture. Agricultural inputs were, in fact, only about 1:7 as great as those in herding. The energy input for agriculture was expended in the

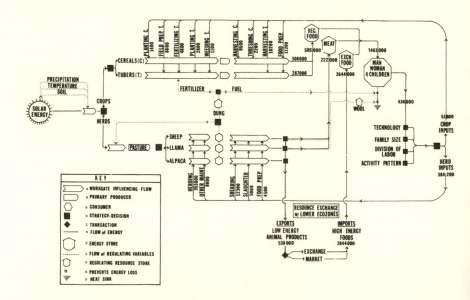

Figure 13.2 Energy Flow Pattern for an Average Nuclear Family of Four Children

various activities of planting and harvesting. This activity yielded, at the end of a cycle, a total of 24.9 GJ compared to an input of only .21 GJ. The division of production by input gives an output/input energetic efficiency of 11.3.

The energy flow analysis in relation to herding is more complex. Herding behavior requires the major input, while the input into other animal-related activities is rather minimal. As shown in Figure 13.2, the output of herding was energetically returned to the individual nuclear unit in two forms. First was the meat itself where caloric yield was quite low, providing many less calories than are actually expended. However, 2.25 GJ of herding production was traded or sold. Thus, if the amount of food energy directly used in the meat and the amount of Joules exported are combined, the yield is about 2 Joules for every Joule of input. However, the export and sale of the animal products, including meat, wool, and skins, modified this relation substantially. From the exchange of the herding products for foods produced elsewhere, the actual energy yield rose to about 6 units derived from every input unit. Even this value does not provide a complete measure of the energetic efficiency, as some of the animal products were not exchanged directly for food but were sold for cash, which purchased salt, coca, tools, and other goods. If all of the money obtained by selling animal products is converted into purchased food energy, the energetic efficiency is very similar to agriculture. That is, if all animal products had been sold and exchanged for foods from sources outside of Nuñoa at the prices current during the study, herding would have yielded between 11 and 12 Joules for every one expended.

Many generalizations may be derived from this analysis. First, this population obviously has a tight energy budget, with a very limited excess. In addition, the system probably could not have supported the population unless the animal products from herding could be traded so that they yielded a great energy benefit. Without this benefit, the family could obtain only 2 Joules for every one put in, and would probably not survive with this very low yield in relation to energy input. By trading, the yield went from 2 Joules for each one expended to a yield of 11–12 Joules.

A second generalization is that the herding is an important regulator of the agricultural output of the community. The center of the diagram indicates that dung is critical for providing the fuel and fertilizer for this society. Indeed, Winterhalder, Larsen, and Thomas (1974), in a more detailed analysis, showed dung to be the prime regulator for the amount of agriculture that can be carried out in the district. Unless other low energy cost sources of fertilizer or fuel could be found, agricultural yield could not be increased without increasing the size of the herds. As the sizes of the herds are regulated by the geographical area and quality of pasturage, this appears to have been a system whose yield could not be very substantially increased within its present technology.

In response to these restrictions on energy capture, it seems that the population size had adjusted itself by a series of precise adaptations that allowed production of sufficient energy surplus to support the present population size. Among the adaptations that allowed the balance were the ways in which the productive labor was distributed by age and sex. Thus, the activities that could be accomplished by small individuals were assigned to children. If the same labor had been performed by adults, the energetic efficiency would have decreased significantly because the energy costs would have been higher. By the same token, certain productive activities are assigned to women. The use of women in the herding and agricultural activities also increased the energy efficiency compared to the use of male labor. Thus, any alteration in the age and sex distribution of the tasks within the system would reduce its efficiency, perhaps critically. In order to keep this labor system functioning, it was also necessary to export children as they became adults. Indeed, the population had a very high out-migration rate of about 2.5 percent per year in terms of permanent migration and an even higher rate of seasonal migration which reduced the caloric needs. This migration consisted primarily of young adults, and thus did not reduce the child labor force required to keep the system functioning.

Finally, it is argued that the heavy reliance on pastoralism was critical for this population to maintain itself, not only because it provided the necessary dung, but also because the herds represented an on-the-hoof storage of energy. The need for this reserve was important because of the year-to-year fluctuation in the potential productivity of agriculture. Long-term climatic records indicated that total crop failures must have been rather common occurrences in Nuñoa. Thus, although additional land for agriculture was available, the results of heavy reliance on agriculture would have been disastrous in those years when the yield was nonexistent or very low. With the herd maintained, however, a buffer existed for food, allowing the population to survive in years when agricultural productivity provided a low energy yield.

In summary the diagrammatic model of energy flow through a modal Nuñoa family, however simplistic and adaptively oriented, has raised numerous questions about the nature of this and other altiplano human-environmental systems. It has drawn attention to the indispensable nature of herd size in providing dung and exchanging products that are critical for the support of the population. In addition it has emphasized the importance of different types of exchange and the inadequacy of the Nuñoan data in this area. Quantification of levels and flows has in turn permitted experimentation with the efficacy of alternative solutions and comparisons between biological and behavioral responses.

The analysis indicated that, for whatever reasons, a number of important biological and behavioral responses fit expectations of what would be adaptive in an energetic sense. Obviously not all behavior conforms to this pattern. When high energy inputs results in no energy output, such as fiestas, it signals that other goals are important enough to counteract this pattern and deserve attention.

The principal problem with the diagrammatic model lies in a one-variable-at-a-time mode of analysis. While feedback is assumed, it does not become analytically tractable. Adaptiveness is therefore assessed at strategy decision points in the system. It is difficult, however, to comprehend how an energetically efficient alternative will affect a number of other responses in a precise manner.

As McRae (1979) has noted, interconnected adaptive responses have two characteristics. First, they are engaged in a hierarchical fashion, meaning priorities exist for activating a series of responses. In time of drought, for instance, people are likely to slaughter or sell some animals before moving out of the area. Second, responses sometimes influence each other both positively and negatively. Hence their cross-adaptive properties become important considerations in evaluating a response's effectiveness. These considerations limit the usefulness of analyzing variables one at a time and suggest that a more integrated systemic approach, such as that provided by simulation modeling, could better approximate reality.

Simulation Models

Although simulation modeling of human-environmental systems is clearly no substitute for careful empirical research, the analysis combines concepts of systems dynamics, known relationships between system components, and a set of tools designed to translate system descriptions into formal models. These models, in turn, can explore the probable behavior of the entire modeled system to a variety of conditions, rather than to simply specific points in that system as the diagrammatic model is capable of doing (Shantzis, Behrens 1972).

THE BLANKENSHIP MODEL: EFFECTS OF IMPROVED HEALTH.

The first attempt at simulation modeling was carried out by James Blankenship (Blankenship, Thomas 1977). It addressed a type of change affecting many peasant groups throughout the world as they become integrated into national economies and modern health care. In the integration there are normally three basic changes. First, modern medicine is introduced, drastically reducing mortality, particularly among children. Second, either fertility control is introduced intentionally or the population goes through a voluntary birth restriction process. As a third or sometimes contemporaneous event, attempts are made to increase the economic productivity of the population often by improved agricultural methods.

As rather complete data on the energy flow and the demographic structure of Nuñoa were available, it was possible to develop a mathematical model that simulated the demographic consequences of these changes within this small population. In designing the model, productive capacity of the Nuñoa region (represented in the diagrammatic model) was linked with demographic characteristics of the population. This permitted an analysis of the probable effects of introducing various degrees of modern health care and its systemic consequences, particularly the negative feedback loops influencing the region's carrying capacity and the population's quality of life (see Fig. 13.3).

The model was intended to be simple, exploratory, and general, applying to a wide range of peasant groups who employ mixed agricultural

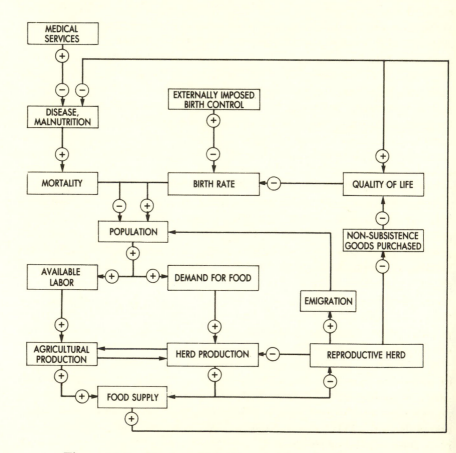

Figure 13.3   Blankenship's Energy Flow Analysis Model

strategies and are exposed to the aforementioned changes. As such, a number of simplifying assumptions were introduced that do not reflect reality in altiplano groups. The important factor of out-migration among Andean populations was not considered in the response repertoire. Thus the model pertains to groups who have a fixed land base, whose members do not have or select the option of leaving. Although the authors were well aware of problems of assuming a carrying capacity, they have employed this concept as one such simplification. These assumptions, however, do not seem to distort Blankenship's model for general use in generating a set of testable hypotheses that are testable for specific human-environmental systems.

Results suggest that improved health conditions could reduce mortality among infants and young children to the level found in industrial countries, and that Nuñoa's population could double in 40 years. A second analysis considered how much and how fast fertility would have to be reduced in order for the population to stabilize its numbers. Even with an immediate and drastic reduction of completed fertility from seven to two children, this would take 60 years and result in a stabilized population approximately 50 percent greater than at present. Such a population could be sustained only by increasing an emphasis on pastoralism and using all cash obtained from the sale of herd products for food. This, of course, would depend on production and prices remaining stable, which is hardly the case in the Andes because of unpredictable environment and economy conditions. Indeed, even if fertility dropped as low as three children per woman, the present productive capacities of the area would be exceeded in less than 20 years.

Let us reiterate that these models are not predictions of what is going to happen, but only predictions of what could happen if only the variables that have been included are modified. Thus, in the real world, it is clear that first, modern medicine introduced to Nuñoa would be unlikely to produce the response predicted. Second, the economic value of the herding products is not constant over time. If this were to increase in relation to carbohydrate food costs, the carrying capacity of the system in terms of numbers of people would certainly increase. A final point is that the area is already experiencing a very high out-migration and that, if the population continued to grow at a more rapid pace than at present, the out-migration would undoubtedly increase proportionately.

If we evaluate the model's contributions, at one level it confirms a set of processes that seems intuitively obvious. That is, increasing health services should reduce infant and child mortality and thereby increase population size. Furthermore, if fertility decline or out-migration does not compensate for lower death rates and no economic growth were to take place, the quality of life in a material sense would also be expected to decline. Beyond this point intuition does not help much, for it is very difficult to imagine how the changes in levels of the variables mentioned would affect others in a precise manner. Quantification allows one to perform this kind of experimentation with the system and arrive at much more concrete observations about its operation.

These observations are useful in generating new research questions that modified forms of the model can address, or for which better empirical data can be gathered. For instance, the order in which government services such as public health, family planning, education (expected to increase out-migration), road building, and agricultural improvement are introduced would very much influence population pressure on essential resources. Similarly, focusing on morbidity, one might identify those pathologies most disruptive to the productive capacity of the population and target these for priority attention.

THE MᶜRAE MODEL: LAND USE ALTERNATIVES

The model developed by Stephen McRae (1979, 1982) addresses another aspect of change prevalent in the Andean region, where agrarian reform and attempts at agricultural specialization are expected to bring profound alterations in human systems. McRae compares the productivity and resiliency of three common land use alternatives to assess their adaptability to the heterogeneous and unpredictable conditions of the altiplano.

Land use alternatives considered include the following: the "traditional system" consists of households engaged in farming and herding on their own or community land, the "hacienda system" that adds labor and herding obligations to the family's responsibilities of farming and herding its own animals, and the "alpaca based system" specializing in alpaca herding without hacienda obligations.

Each version of the model is simulated under conditions representing both drought (stress) and non-drought (non-stress) situations. The non-stress simulation is examined over ten years under what might be considered optimal conditions. The environmental stress mimics the effects of a three-year drought, with heavy crop losses and high herd mortality. In this situation, the simulation begins with a three-year stress period in which the human population is provisioned with a session's worth of resources. A variant on this theme is considered with the initial resource buffer amounting to a five-year accumulation of resources. For both of the simulations involving a stress period, the initial stress period is followed by a seven-year recovery period.

In contrast to the Blankenship model, McRae's emphasizes a considerably greater degree of realism about rural altiplano groups. An impressive number of variables not derived from the energy flow analysis have been entered into the model. These include not only the human demographic ariables, but also the herd animal vital rates, factors controlling crop roduction, other income sources (handicrafts), and financial data. The najor model components are given in Figure 13.4. The simulation is argely based on two types of submodels: population projections and esource allocation routines. The human and herd population models rovide the prime driving force for the overall model. Linked closely to he human population model are submodels for crop and craft production. animal product production is linked with the herd population. These nodels are seen as both supplying and demanding resources to and from a esource stock. The arrows in Figure 13.4 indicate the types of resource tocks and flows involved. The process is mediated through resource llocation models that take into account the buying price of resources eeded from the outside and the selling price of resources traded out. The

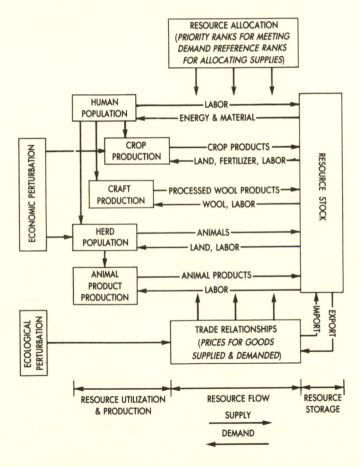

Figure 13.4   McRae Model of Three Common Land Use Alternatives

resource allocation models operate on a system of priorities to determine which resource demands are satisfied first and a system of preferences that determine the order in which different sources of supplies are used to fill those demands. While the model is general in the way it is constructed it can be calibrated quite precisely to represent a specific situation.

Whereas results from this model indicate that the herd population drops (sales or mortality) for each land alternative system during drought conditions, losses are relatively small compared to crop yield. For this reason, as well as the increased marketability of alpaca versus sheep wool, the alpaca-based system could be considered superior. Its vulnerability becomes evident, however, in further analysis. As sale of animal products is a major component of the production system, the role of prices is a significant factor in the relative support capacity of the simulated production systems. An experiment was performed to examine how significant price changes by lowering the price of alpaca wool and raising the price of wheat flour. Both events were programmed to occur during a stress period. Price modified curves resulted from decreasing the price of alpaca wool by 38 percent and raising the price of wheat flour 50 percent. In the model, wheat flour represented the primary source of energy coming from the lower areas. A change in key prices had the effect of increasing the amount of wool that must be sold for a kilogram of wheat flour. As a consequence, the human population was reduced to less than half by the fourth year, and recovery was insignificant to the end of the decade both for herd size and the number of humans supported.

This scenario demonstrates the heightened effect of combining an economic with an environmental stressor and suggests that the human support system provided by specialization in herding is very vulnerable to such perturbation. It also underlines the importance of storage in a variety of forms as an adaptive strategy. Entering a prolonged drought with a five year storage build-up results in relatively few people being forced out of the system, as opposed to only one year's storage.

With the exception of impact on pasture, the alpaca specialized system seems to be superior to the others for most measures examined. However, this conclusion may be modified by the facts that the alpaca is productive only in the upper *puna* zone, and that the effect of interspecies variability in terms of impact on pasture was not considered. Only when the extent of accessible dry-season pasture in the upper *puna* of the Nuñoan region and the impact of different species on the pasture are known, will it be possible to reach more definitive conclusions by entering these variables in the model. Similarly, no consideration was given to the incidence and severity of herd pathologies which might increase the risk of relying upon a single species.

The results represented above are seen as preliminary, serving primarily as a focus to further research and discussion. Further testing with the present model as well as further model development are needed and anticipated. Data upon which the model is based were collected primarily in the middle and late 1960s. Since that time agrarian reform has eliminated the hacienda system, replacing it with the two other alternatives. This provides an excellent opportunity to validate predictions of the model. Slaughter and sale of hacienda herds, for instance, significantly reduced the Nuñoa herd population, suggesting that dung for fuel and fertilizer may have been scarce in the region. Conversely, removal of hacienda obligations has freed labor. This could be used for building up a family's storage capacity, well beyond that possible under the hacienda system. As we have seen, this might considerably buffer the effects of drought and unpredictable market prices.

THE OAK RIDGE MODEL: SHARING BEHAVIOR ALTERNATIVES

The unpredictable nature of environmental problems on the altiplano presents conditions in which a single family cannot rely solely upon its own efforts or stored resources, and thus must depend upon other individuals within and beyond the group.

While such dependency can take a variety of forms, reciprocal relationships based on kind and fictive kin are emphasized in rural areas (Alberti and Mayer 1974). One advantage of forming cooperative units with relatively strong and long lasting bonds, such as kin cooperation, is the extent to which generalized reciprocity can operate. Repayment in kind or within a particular time period is not emphasized as it would under a more formal arrangement. Such reciprocity, therefore, provides considerable flexibility for a household encountering a sequence of bad luck, as it demands only that the household contribute to the cooperative unit what it can afford.

In evaluating generalized reciprocity as an adaptive strategy, David Weinstein, Hank Shugart, and Craig Brandt (1983) from Oak Ridge National Laboratories have developed a detailed and versatile, stochastic model that considered each individual in a hypothetical altiplano group separately. This differs from the Blankenship and McRae models, which are deterministic in nature, establishing key relationships in a fixed rather than a probabilistic manner.

The goal of the Oak Ridge effort was to track individuals within the population in order to investigate adaptive phenomena at the individual, family, and kin group level of organization. This was not possible with the other two models, which were designed to consider adaptive phenomena at the population level.

The Oak Ridge model is composed of three submodels: the family, agriculture, and herds (Fig. 13.5). The family submodel calculates food energy requirements for each family based on the sex and age of its

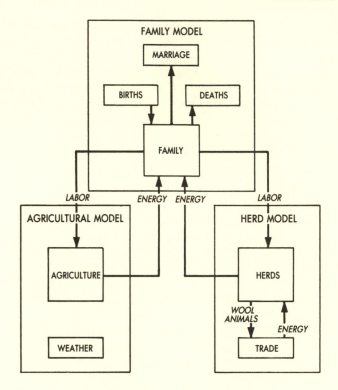

Figure 13.5   Oak Ridge Model

members and keeps track of their births, deaths and marriages as they change over time. The agricultural submodel calculates energy expended and produced per year for seven crops. The effects of temperature, precipitation, potential evapotranspiration, and occurrences of frost and hail, which effect productivity, are stochastically introduced. The herd submodel maintains an inventory of three herd species owned by the family and simulates herd demographic behavior including slaughter and sale of animal products. Sharing of surplus food among extended family members is also handled by this submodel (Weinstein et al. 1979:517).

In examining resource sharing, the simulation commences with a population of 100 nuclear families equally divided into 20 extended families (designated as clans). The model then is run for 250 years, or approximately 12–15 generations, with clan size inventories taken every 50 years.

Results suggest that extended families, which expand rapidly, do so by accumulating a large resource base available for sharing. This, in turn, leaves fewer resources available for other extended families, blocking their expansion, and in some cases affecting their persistence. In spite of a significantly restructured distribution of families in the course of the simulated period, the number of families and the total population size remain fairly constant, indicating a stable population.

To examine the role of sharing more directly, three cases of resource sharing are compared: no sharing between families, sharing within extended families or clans, and sharing among all families. As models with stochastic components must be repeatedly run to determine the mean and variance of the resulting variables, ten 250-year simulations were made for each case, starting with the same initial population and weather conditions. The random number sequence for the stochastic models was changed for each repetition.

Based on the probabilistic occurrence of hail or frost, the population is subjected to stress through an energy deficit resulting from crop loss. With restrictions on the amount of energy that can be imported through trading animals and animal products owing to, among other reasons, a finite herd size, energy deficits also result on a probabilistic basis.

There is a negative feedback loop linking population with energy deficits. Thus, births are reduced and deaths increased because of energy deficits. The effects on families are shown in Figure 13.6. The results suggest that families cannot survive alone, isolated from other families. This result is corroborated by results from the McRae model, which assumes sharing of all resources (including labor) within the community.

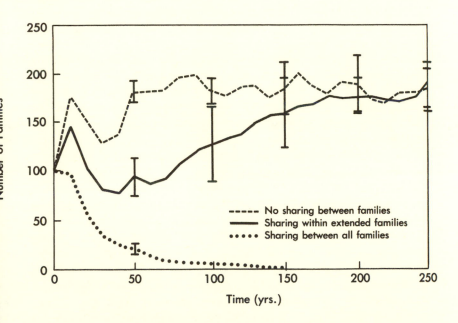

Figure 13.6   Three Cases of Resource Sharing

While the long time span over which the Oak Ridge simulation runs brings into doubt the realism of assumptions that future production relationships will remain the same, the model nevertheless provides an opportunity for anthropological experimentation not possible in the real world. For instance, it would be of interest to compare sharing potential among a group having a bilateral kinship system, where relatives are claimed on both sides of the family, as opposed to one with a matrilineal or patrilineal system. Likewise, one could trace the spread through the population of advantageous genes, such as those effecting increased working capacity, using different mating systems. The culmination of deleterious genes, effecting susceptibility to respiratory disorders and their reduction in working capacity, could be followed as well.

Summary

In assessing the role modeling can play in anticipating change in the Andes, three simulation models have been considered. All of these share a data base taken from the diagrammatic, human energy flow model, yet each has added information relevant to a specific type of change. As a result they differ substantially in the number of relationships, the nature of these relationships between variables, and time periods considered.

It should be kept in mind that these represent three independent attempts to assess the utility of this approach, hence, they should be regarded together as a first-generation of altiplano models. The Blankenship model, for instance, emphasizes generality, or a set of feedback relationships between health, population growth, and limited resources assumed to apply to human groups residing on and beyond the altiplano. Many simplifying assumptions such as the absence of out-migration, however, make the model unrealistic in terms of what we know to exist among highland populations.

McRae's model on land use alternatives approaches a much closer reality of the altiplano. It incorporates considerable information from the region. Likewise, it assumes that observed relationships between variables are transitory, and that the analysis would lose validity after ten or fifteen years. In spite of this attention to realism, however, its design is general enough that it can be applied to a wide variety of groups who are reliant upon crops and animals under different conditions.

The Oak Ridge model, which was designed to consider stochastic or probabilistic relationships between some of its variables, introduces an added dimension of reality mimicking the unpredictable environment. While its long time stage makes the analysis somewhat unrealistic in times of rapid change, it becomes an excellent tool for exploring consequences of long term genetic or social change that could not be tracked by other means.

In summary, the three models address various degrees of generality, reality, and precision. By necessity all have simplified reality of altiplano human environmental systems to some extent and have introduced biases derived from the Nuñoa data base. What is apparent, however, is the analytical diversity of these first generation simulation approaches and their potential for incorporation into a much more sophisticated modeling effort.

Together they have provided insights into the operation of altiplano systems, identified areas sensitive to change where more precise data are needed, and analyzed effects of alternative strategies upon system operation. The extent to which alternatives judged as better by simulation modeling are generally acceptable by other scientists, planners, and people residing in the system is open to debate. This, in fact, is one form of validation of the model.

Modeling techniques seem particularly appropriate in the Andes, whose rapid change is coupled with a diversity of human-environmental systems and a limited data base. Clearly the time frame within which most changes will impact these systems is not sufficient to collect detailed data on each set of conditions. We do, however, have information on a general set of relationships operating in the Andes and detailed data from selected areas. Combining these within a modeling approach whereby it is possible to change conditions and responses to fit specific situations may make most efficient use of these data. The model under these circumstances cannot be used so much as a predictive device, but one of self-instruction in some potential consequences of alternative responses and policies to change.

The author and associates at the University of Massachusetts are currently engaged in an investigation in Nuñoa that draws upon these models. The research focuses on the consequences of different patterns of human illness on productive activities and cooperative responses in buffering their effects. Results are expected to identify illness patterns that most disrupt household and agricultural activities. In turn, this is dependent upon identifying segments of the population, times of the year, and agricultural practices most impacted by illness.

Whereas such results will have obvious relevance to local health care, modeling techniques permit their extrapolation both to conditions not encounted during the research as well as to other altiplano populations. For instance, respiratory disease is one of the most prevalent and incapacitating forms of illness among small scale farmers in this region. Adults are frequently affected, and others must therefore assist them not only in health care, but taking over strenuous tasks. By simulating a progressive increase in the frequency of tuberculosis or some other chronic debilitating disease, one could better assess disruptive limits beyond which further assistance from relatives or friends would not be possible. This could be modeled at the household level for families of differing size and composition (single, female headed households) or at the community level.

In the course of the past twenty years, Nuñoa has experienced several major epidemics and droughts. In 1956–57 these two significant disruptions occurred together. While only stories and some aggregate mortality data remain from this event, simulation modeling might reconstruct some of the systemic consequences. This, in turn, could reinforce the need for better preventive health care at the onset of a drought.

Finally, it would be possible to simulate the consequences of increasing rates of out-migration by men seeking labor opportunities. Here the effect would be to increase labor demands on remaining family members, especially women, and to reduce the effectiveness of the cooperative network. By coupling this with the aforementioned consequences of illness, the seriousness of this labor drain can be better ascertained across the altiplano.

In conclusion, simulation modeling offers considerable hope in glimpsing beyond the typical community or regional survey analyses, which are restricted by what is observed at a given location and time. Whereas small-scale farmers are found throughout the Andes, there is great diversity in their social organization, political-economic ties, and environments. Likewise, change processes are impacting their lives in significant ways. Analytical techniques that can alert these people, as well as policy makers, to the deleterious consequences of some of the more pervasive changes, and the relative advantages of alternative paths of action are, indeed needed. We will need to identify relevant problems, those subgroups at greatest risk, and key variables or relationships that pose limiting conditions to these highly stressed groups. Given the urgency of the situation and the limited resources available to forge solutions, decisions need to be made as to areas where precise measurement is necessary, and where approximations will serve just as well. Simulation modeling can be helpful here.

Acknowledgments

This chapter has drawn upon reviews of Andean modeling efforts in Baker (1979), McRae (1982), Thomas, Winterhalder and McRae (1979) and Thomas (1976). Portions of the chapter were originally presented at a Human Biology Conference in London (Harrison 1982) and published as "The Use of Models in Anticipating Effects of Change on Human Populations." The contributions of Stephen D. McRae and Paul T. Baker are gratefully appreciated.

14

Problems of Land Use and Recent Settlement

Thailand's Highland–Lowland Transition Zone

Harald Uhlig

Several attempts have been made to classify land use, settlements, ethnic groups, and rural development in northern Thailand into three geoecologically and culturally distinct altitudinal zones. In the modern world, this basic tripartite structure is being changed rapidly by the dynamic processes of higher mobility and by planned and spontaneous development.

The three zones may be characterized roughly by (1) predominantly sedentary (wet) rice cultures and a relatively well-developed infrastructure in the valleys and intra-montane basins; (2) a zone of intermediate elevation with a mixture of land rotation and permanent agriculture, occupied by "tribal" as well as by Thai (Khon Muang) populations; and (3) the upper mountain zone with shifting cultivation (swidden) by hill peoples.

This chapter is concerned mainly with the second, or intermediate zone, which may be regarded as the Highland-Lowland Transition Zone. It has been changed by extensive construction of new roads and by lumbering, followed by extensive forest clearings for spontaneous settlement.

While the attention of most observers is focused on the hill peoples (the opium problem!), the pressure initiated by "land hunger" and speculative exploitation of the forest and land resources in this transition zone has become equally alarming. Notwithstanding the relatively well-balanced land use practices by some longer established groups (e.g., the Karen), heavy inroads of pioneer settlers during recent years have converted and endangered large areas of this zone. Landless Thai settlers and agricultural entrepreneurs have pushed in with a crude swidden cultivation of maize, cassava, dry-upland rice, and other crops, attracted either by the export boom of maize and cassava or by more modest hopes for self-supply with rice. Additionally, smaller movements by hill peoples, who are normally residents of the upper zone, have increased this pressure.

Introduction

More than 50 years ago Wilhelm Credner undertook fieldwork in Thailand (1927 to 1929) and focused on the topic of the present symposium on highland-lowland interactive systems. He developed a model of three different cultures occupying three altitudinal zones:

a. "Pflugbauern der Ebenen (Überschwemmungsreisbau)"—plough culture of the plains (wet-rice cultivation);

b. "Waldhackbauvölker"—swidden cultures of the forests;

c. "Berghackbauvölker"—shifting cultivation of the hill peoples.

He demonstrated these by references to a series of landscape profiles (Credner 1935a). Wissmann (1943) extended this presentation to Yunnan, China, adding data on the natural conditions. The present author gave a more detailed profile for northern Thailand (Uhlig 1969), which aimed at an integrated graphic expression of the relief, geo-ecology, settlement, and land-use pattern of the various socio-economic and ethnic groups, including certain extensions of the traditional setting (Credner 1935b; Uhlig 1969).

Adapted to the recent development of research methods as well as to the changes by the modernization of this region, several authors arrived at a somewhat similar division into three zones—be it in terms of infrastructural development (Hinton 1967), of the differentiation of rice cultivation (Matzat 1973, 1976) or in a spatial model of the inter-ethnic relations (Bruneau 1974).

Growing mobility, contacts, and exchange between highland and lowland populations, and socio-economic and political impacts caused by the recent rapid rate of development have resulted in many changes and have disturbed the traditional structure to such a degree that many authors doubt the validity of the concept. Kunstadter (1980) expresses this by opposing the "stereotype" in which the distribution of ecological zones, ethnic groups, and local economies were arranged in the form of a "layer cake."

Apart from later over-simplifications of Credner's abbreviated terms, it is obvious that the dynamic processes of the last two or three decades (and the much more detailed knowledge due to the expansion of research) have brought about a rapid increase in exchange, interaction, and acculturation, thus overriding many distinctions between the three zones. This essay is concerned with these changes and with the dynamic development within the "Highland-Lowland Transition Zone." To appreciate fully the recent social altitudinal zones remains a useful orientation, a nomothetic typology of the original structure, including important integrations of ecological and socio-economic geofactors.

In traditional northern Thailand the Khon Muang (Bruneau 1974) have been predominantly attached to the wet-rice fields of the valleys and intra-montane plains—the true *Lan-na* ("land of the million rice fields"). However, one group of mountain dwellers of Thai stock penetrated that Highland-Lowland Transition Zone very early, possibly centuries ago— the so-called "Hill Thai," collectors of wild (and later propagated) tea in the mountain forests. Their villages, scattered in the forests between 400 and 800 m. with only a few wet-rice terraces and some dry-upland rice, specialize in the picking and fermenting of tea-leaves into *miang* pickled tea for chewing, which used to be in strong demand on the market. Van Roy (1966), Le Bar (1967), and Bruneau (1974) gave descriptions of the origin and distribution of these early Thai pioneers in the mountain forests. It should be noted that their estimated number of 75,000 to 100,000 represents one of the largest single ethnic groups of mountain population in Thailand, apart from the Karen. In addition, because of the most recent development of the dramatic last decade, the Hmong in the higher hills have grown rapidly by influx from Laos and Burma (McKinnon, Bhruksasri 1983).

This study will now turn from those early mountain Thai, whose villages are affected by fast development following the opening of their remote valleys by road-construction and a growing infrastructure, to the present migration from the valleys and plains into the hills. But even earlier certain marginal extensions of the Thai rice farmers occurred which have affected the terraces and foothills, i.e., the lowest parts of the Highland-Lowland Transition Zone, as a result of population pressure.

Expansion of Lowland Agriculture into the Foothills

The constantly growing subdivision of the irrigated rice fields on the main valley floors enforced the extension of cultivation towards the middle and upper terraces, not reached by the irrigation systems. An initial phase was the establishment of marginal wet-rice farming, based on impounded rainfall only, and to compensate its uncertain yields by more intensive cattle-raising (grazing in the degraded dipterocarp forests). Additional shifting cultivation by Thai rice farmers in this bushland *(lao)* followed, *ray des Thai du Nord* according to Bruneau (1972), comprising rotations of dry upland-rice (by dibble) with intercropping of various other plants, followed by hoe-cultivation of mixed crops in the second and by bush-fallow in the next two to three years before the next swidden cycle (Fig. 14.1). A Thai hill and pioneer settlement, pushing up into the smaller tributary valleys, cultivating the narrow valley floor with wet-

Figure 14.1   Swidden Fields of the Lisu Tribe, near Doy Chiang
Dao. A large karst doline at approximately 1200 m.

rice, accompanied by an additional shifting cultivation (dry-rice) on the
slopes, has been described by Uhlig (1969:12, Fig. 14.2). Credner
(1935a:203). Troger (1960:183), as well as Young (1962), noticed similar
small extensions. Thai swiddening of dry-rice was reported by Judd
(1964) from parts of northeastern Thailand, which had extremely poor
irrigation possibilities, if any. Weber (1968/69) also stressed the existence
of widespread shifting cultivation practised by Thai farmers as soon as
wet-rice land was no longer available.

In the Nan valley, Chapman's research (1967, 1970, 1973) into the
swidden extensions of the wet-rice farmers, restricted to extremely small
properties of irrigated land, was followed up by an Australian agricultural
project. Deep-ploughing with heavy tractor-driven disc-ploughs, uproot-
ing all stumps, roots, *Imperata* grasses, and associated vegetation, and
working the soil deeply, proved to allow continuous dry-rice cultivation,
or rotations such as with soya beans, instead of shifting cultivation. This
is a contradiction to the "textbook" rule of only one or two swidden crops
in tropical dry cultivation, which should be followed by several years of
bushfallow to avoid degradation of the soil nutrients. It seems that the
existence of a regular and pronounced dry season of at least four months
is a prerequisite for any attempt at permanent dry-rice cultivation. This
allows for evaporation of the soil moisture and re-accumulation of soil
nutrients near the surface. This might be as beneficial as crop rotations, or

Figure 14.2 Recent Clearing by Thai Pioneer Farmers for Maize and Other Crops. Steep forest slopes near the Lomsaka-Campson Road at approximately 500 m to 900 m.

intercropping with soya beans, peanuts, and other legumes. Several heavily populated karst regions of Indonesia with similar climatic conditions, on Java, Madura, or Sulawesi (Uhlig 1976), show comparable well-developed examples.

Recent Uphill Extensions into the Intermediate Zone

All these extensions towards shifting cultivation and permanent dry-rice cultivation in the lowlands of northern Thailand (Chapman 1970), however, were only earlier phases of a process which is now carried farther from the terraces and foothills into the intermediate elevations of the mountain forests, the true Highland-Lowland Transition Zone (Fig. 14.3). This process is to a high degree responsible for the rapid decline of Thailand's forest areas from over 50 percent of the country's surface around 1963 to an estimated 30 percent in 1978, as Dr. Sanga Sabhasri has pointed out. The easy access to large stretches of mountain forests, opened by timber exploitation and the rapid construction of new roads, combined with the boom of maize exports, especially during 1971 to 1974, and of tapioca (manioc) in more recent years, caused a new phase of radical clearing and squatting. "Squatting" as seen by the legal position of the state authorities, as in contrast to most of the extensions of the

Figure 14.3 Permanently Consolidated Upland Market Gardening by Thai Pioneers. Campson plateau, west of Lomsak, at
approximately 800 m.

cultivated land mentioned above, relates to recent clearings usually
pushed into "Reserved Forests." According to the rural traditions of the
Thai as well as of the hill peoples, the clearing of new land from the forest,
if it is needed, however, is regarded as common law, practiced since
ancient times. This caused several land conflicts, which resulted even in
armed clashes and casualties between forest officers and "squatters,"
readily labeled as communist insurgents, and in land conflicts between
various social groups. It is tragic, but almost a rule, that areas of
spontaneous land clearing are likely to become politically sensitive areas;
a more flexible land policy and effective aid by the authorities to genuine
settlers, instead of attempts to prevent cultivation, would be more in the
public interest of the country. Obviously, the forest authorities are aware
of this and frequently are quite tolerant to prevent deprived settlers from
being driven into the arms of communist insurgent groups. At the same
time, the rapid extension of the world market for maize and tapioca
(manioc) was very favorable for Thailand's agricultural exports. The
official land policy, opening up various project areas by the Land Settlement Division, Department of Public Welfare (Klempin 1978) was not
sufficient to satisfy the growing "land hunger." Uncontrolled clearing,
especially of broad strips parallel to the new road alignments or to timber
tracks, pushed rapidly into the forests.

Initially, swiddening started with a first crop of upland rice for subsistence (Fig. 14.4). Fairly soon, however, the cash crops, maize and tapioca, became dominant. The fields are usually irregular and dotted with stumps and remaining trees. In most cases it was an initial or incipient shifting cultivation, aimed at opening up the land, with permanent cultivation intended to follow (Fig. 14.5). Very often, however, the nutrient content of the soil collapsed after two or three years. New clearings were felled and burnt and the former were left to *Imperata* grasses. Thus, in practice, a new shifting cultivation of a very crude and unregulated nature emerged, much more harmful to the environment than the old-established "integrated" swidden systems of some of the tribes, notably of the Karen and Lua.

One of the most outstanding examples evolved along the road from Phitsanoluke to Lomsak across the mountain ranges of Tung Saleng Luang National Park (Fig. 14.6). Constructed in the early 1970s, the new road attracted a large influx of settlers from the northern parts of the Central Lowlands and from the poor northeast. Within a few months they felled and burned the forests in a most destructive way. Today a belt of several kilometers' width parallels the main road and several side roads, situated at an elevation between 500 m and 1,000 m. It is dotted with irregular plots of maize and tapioca under the skeletons of dead trees. Nearly two-thirds of the clearings have been overgrown already by *Imperata* and *Saccharum* grasses or bushes. Scattered huts form the settlement pattern, partly for temporary, partly for permanent use. The authorities refuse to grant deeds to the land and the foresters try to defend the National Park, but the local administration is forced to accept the facts and to try to arrange for registration, basic rural organization, schooling, and so on.

The limited success of these attempts can be judged by comparison with enquiries in a similar "village" of spontaneous forest clearing and squatting near Sakaraet Research Station of the National Research Council along the new highway across the forest mountains of the Khorat escarpment. In 1978 it consisted of some 150 registered households plus nearly 80 more still unregistered!

Four types of settlers may be distinguished. Some are rice farmers from nearby villages who came to the forest for additional shifting cultivation. Accordingly, their housing facilities consist of temporary huts only. Second, a similar cultivation is practiced by people coming from long distances. Peasants with limited wet-rice land, sometimes from more than 100 km away, migrate temporarily (usually by public transport) to the swidden sites after transplanting their rice fields in their native villages. After harvesting the maize crop in the forest clearings (with temporarily inhabited huts only), they return home to harvest the wet-rice there. Frequently their land in the clearings is held on tenancy from better

Upland Rice of a Karen Settlement. Near Bo
Luang at approximately 900 m.

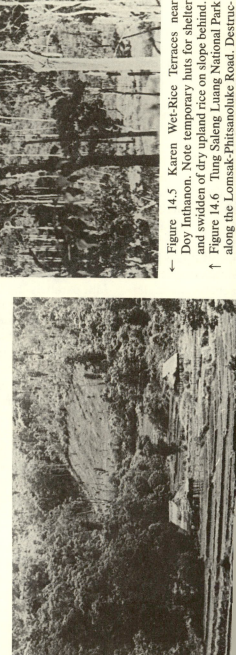

← Figure 14.5 Karen Wet-Rice Terraces near
Doy Inthanon. Note temporary huts for shelter
and swidden of dry upland rice on slope behind.

↑ Figure 14.6 Tung Saleng Luang National Park
along the Lomsak-Phitsanoluke Road. Destruc-

established, permanent settlers (who may have been squatters themselves).

Of greater importance is the third type of peasants, who are landless or in debt and who attempt to gain a permanent new settlement. They originate both from villages of the nearby valleys and from distant regions. Usually their first shelters are simple bamboo huts again, but the establishment of gardens with fruit trees, spices, and vegetables, and the gradual improvement of the houses, distinguish them from the temporary types. If the settlers lack the capital to hire tractor-ploughing and have to restrict the cultivation to traditional tools (hoes, dibble), after two or three years *Imperata* grasses invade the fields which were originally planned for permanent use. Then, they have to be abandoned and replaced by fresh swiddening elsewhere. Only a small percentage of the settlers establish themselves successfully; many of them will soon be in debt from purchasing seeds, fertilizers, pesticides, additional food, and goods on credit at high interest rates and from mortgaging crops before the harvest. Their clearings are taken over by middlemen and come into the hands of a "second generation" of usually more well-to-do farmers, while the first settlers have to pioneer fresh clearings. A distinction can be made between poor subsistence colonists and others, who, although smallholders, are cash-crop oriented from the very beginning; they may even buy rice for their own consumption.

Legally, all reserved forest land is regarded as property of the Crown. There are land conflicts arising, however, because many of the settlers find themselves confronted with people claiming property rights to the land the settlers had intended to clear. These may be farmers from the nearest, previously established village, claiming rights of usufruct forest use; road and timber workers, for instance, who claim "stakes" during the first inroads into the forest. After purchasing their new land from such claimants, the new settlers may think they have acquired property rights, although in reality the former claimant also had little right or none at all to land which the authorities still regard as Crown property. It may be equally complicated if traditional claims to swidden-rotation land by some hill peoples are touched upon.

The fourth group, making up a considerable share of the colonization, are those engaged directly (with hired labour) or indirectly (via dependent settlers who are indebted to or otherwise financed by them) as agricultural entrepreneurs. Traders from regional centres and smaller market towns, partly ethnic Chinese, but also officials, professionals, and so on, are similarly engaged, as well as progressive farmers, some of them holding degrees in agriculture. There is a wide range of land-management. It comprises examples of very advanced farming, contributing considerably to land development, the growth of the national agricultural production, and to the provision of jobs for quite a number of wage-earners. Unfortunately, however, there is also a strong involvement of speculative entrepreneurs who ruthlessly exploit the forest and soil resources, and who may be involved in corruption and illegal logging.

Quite distinct from these pioneer types is a more permanent and intense form of upland colonization: high-altitude market gardening. This type has only recently emerged in Thailand, while it has been long established in Indonesia, Malaysia, the Philippines, and the Himalayas. After opening up quick transport routes to the lowland markets, the utilization of the cooler upland climate for the cultivation of vegetables and fruits of temperate latitudes became profitable and has been taken up by various groups. These include entrepreneurs acting as pioneers for this agricultural innovation, Thai settlers, and also hill peoples. The most extensive area of upland gardening, to my knowledge, occurs on the Campson Plateau, a few kilometers east of the above-mentioned pioneer clearings along the Phitsanoluke-Lomsak road. The steep and winding road connection down to the latter rural center (and from there via the new Petchabun Valley Highway to Bangkok) was already under construction around 1962, in a phase of more liberal land policy, which allowed strips up to 2 km alongside new roads to be cleared for settlers. Replacing the original spontaneous colonization, some entrepreneurs consolidated land for fruit and vegetable plantations and gradually also became the innovators, advisors, and marketing organizers for greater numbers of smallholders who followed them into this permanent cultivation of intensely worked vegetable fields (with some wet-rice terraces in suitable valleys for home consumption). By now, some six villages have come into existence, with approximately 7,000 people, including a fast-growing central place for marketing and storing of supplies. The farmers, who enjoy title deeds, are partly pioneers and partly "second generation" settlers. The favourable soils are derived from basaltic tuffs and, towards the higher mountains at the southern edge, from limestone. The area is an undulating plateau between 700 and 900 m elevation and is deeply ploughed (by hired tractors, crushing local pans in the soil) and worked intensely in holdings of 2 to 20 rai on the average. Terracing is still generally lacking and the ploughing of steep slopes in vertical strips may cause soil erosion, but apparently the consistency of the soils, usually well covered by two or three crops per year, is quite satisfactory.

Smaller development of a similar type has sprung up since 1971 on both sides of the pass of the Bo Luang-Mae Sariang road. One is worked by a Thai entrepreneur, employing Karen labour from nearby villages (two crops of cabbage per annum, use of fertilizers, transport by own mini-trucks to Chiang Mai) and, to the west of the pass, by a number of Hmong families who settled down permanently and do extremely well with such crops as cabbage, bananas, oranges, onions, beans, maize, and dry rice.

Kunstadter and Chapman (1970:153) have reported similar innovations by Hmong, cultivating potatoes and vegetables around Mae Tho, Mae Chaem District.

Extensions Downhill from the Upper Mountain Zone

In the foregoing section we have already touched upon a second, gradually growing influx into the Highland-Lowland Transition Zone, downhill from the traditional areas of the hill peoples, which is dealt with further below. The development of permanent hill peoples' villages based on the cultivation of vegetables, such as carrots, various other tree and field crops, and even of ornamental flowers for sale to distant markets (instead of former shifting cultivation) as demonstrated by Dr. Pisit Voraurai and his team at the Huai Thung Chao experimental station, is another step in this direction.

An extension of market gardening, an acceleration of population growth, and an increase in ethnic variety are exemplified by seven villages with about 6,700 inhabitants (Mote 1967) of Chinese immigrants from Yunnan. Market gardening is also increasing in some of the settlements adjacent to camps originally established by remnants of the Kuomintang army. However, the latter are more characteristic of the zone of higher mountains along the Burmese border.

As an expansion of the typical "middleman" function of the older established Chinese traders, some of them have settled down permanently in tribal villages. Their activities cover a wide range, from opium trade to the presently increasing transport and sale of vegetables to the markets. The majority, however, has settled after immigrating from Yunnan via Burma (since 1951/52) in true Chinese villages, manifested by enclosed courtyards and dwellings on flat ground, distinct from Thai habitations. Otherwise, they try to integrate themselves into the Thai state, with agricultural practices of high intensity and permanent rotations of dry-upland rice or maize in the rainy season and vegetables in the dry season, supplemented by fruit growing and pig raising. Utilizing the advantages of the altitude zonation, additional cultivation of potatoes at higher elevations is included. At Ban Yang (Fang Province), a small fruit-tinning factory is a first step towards an agricultural industry, supported by a King's Project.

Local Population of the Highland-Lowland Transition Zone

In addition to the many influences pushing uphill from the valleys and plains, we still have to consider the local population of the Highland-Lowland Transition Zone and other groups pouring down from the higher mountains. Kunstadter (1967:70) focused the attention on the formerly underestimated, but recently fast-growing economic, social, and cultural links between the Thai and the minorities in the forests and mountains.

The earlier established inhabitants of the Highland-Lowland Transition Zone, such as Karen and Lua', are usually concentrated in specific regions of the zone. The settlement density is considerable and they practice an agricultural system which combines swidden and permanent cultivation and preserves carefully the ecological reserves (Fig. 14.7). In contrast to exhaustive practices by the recent colonists, after felling and burning, the Karen have only a single rice harvest, with intercropping of cotton, maize, sorghum, etc., from their swiddens. Afterwards, the land is allowed to rest again under bush-fallow for another seven to ten years. Strips of remaining forest are kept along the watersheds and the courses of streams, protecting them from erosion and serving as reservoirs for reseeding the forest plants. Fairly large tracts of a well-regulated field-forest system, with permanent traditional right to the soil for the individual families, are characteristic of this land-use type. A forest-botanical research project by Kunstadter et al. (1978) proved that the establishment of a stable forest/cultural vegetation system seems to safeguard the ecological balance. In almost every Karen village, these land rotation plots are supplemented by some irrigated terraces, or valley floors, for

Figure 14.7   Karen Village with Permanent Wet-Rice Terraces and Swidden in Land Rotation. First year of regrowth of bush fallow, near Bo Luang.

permanent wet-rice. They are sited near the village if water is available; otherwise they may be situated at some distance and equipped with temporary huts for shelter. Consequently, the Karen, like the Lua', have become sedentary to a fairly high degree.

The relative stability of this agricultural system does not exclude the Karen areas from the influence of fast population growth, modernization, improved communications and, as a result, growing acculturation into the mainstream of Thai society. The advantages of new road access and of labor during their construction may be counterbalanced by the loss of former wages as porters or horse and oxen drovers in the old caravan trade. The same may be said for the introduction of trucks and jeeps, partly replacing the income from the Karen's traditional working elephants. Deriving additional income from livestock (buffaloes, pigs) is facilitated by easier transport to the valleys but hampered by the replacement of many *kwei* (buffaloes) by tractors and *kwei lek* (motor hand-ploughs) in a quickly modernizing agriculture. More examples could be quoted; none of them exceed, however, the impact of modernization and change caused by downhill as well as by uphill migration, moving Karen into the towns and non-agricultural jobs, and bringing up more and more Thai into the hills. The tribal broadcasting system, schooling, health services, improved administrative control, and growing motorization are quickly transforming hitherto remote mountain districts.

This introduces further land conflicts, for instance, by the expansion of valley dwellers into potential reserves for the Karen's land rotation. Even worse is direct interference between different shifting cultivators intruding into the other's protected bush-fallow. This has occurred (Kunstadter 1970; Marlowe 1967) as groups of the Hmong, in search of new swidden for dry-upland rice when their older swiddens higher up-slope had been overworked by intensive opium/maize cultivation, pushed into the Karen's carefully preserved bush-fallow. Usually the conflicts were solved by the authorities in favor of the more vigorous and wealthy Hmong who take advantage of the lack of precise knowledge of some officials about the traditional property rights in remote mountain areas. Another conflict has arisen from the downhill movement of some Lisu groups, allegedly encouraged by missionaries to participate in the swiddening-inroads into protected forests alongside new roads for commercial maize production and illegal timber extraction (Fig. 14.8). Smaller and more isolated groups, Hmong again, also started to acquire wet-rice plots on lower sites (with additional land rotation) and thus to change to permanent habitation. The more promising high-altitude market gardening has already been mentioned.

Moreover, the various *Nikhom* settlement schemes of the Hill Tribe Welfare Division contribute to the stabilization, development, and infrastructural incorporation of larger parts of the Highland-Lowland Transition

Figure 14.8   Young Lisu Preparing Their Swidden for a Second
Crop of Maize by Hoe. Near Doy Chiang Dao, at approximately
1400 m.

Zone into the intensely occupied parts of the country. Examples of a
successful development may be found around Mae Chan Nikhom, with
the establishment of permanent arable rotations (rice, maize, soya beans,
sorghum, and sunflowers) for Yao villages. The Mae Salap Scheme has
also opened up effective irrigation and terracing systems in quite remote
valleys for several Akha villages, which consequently changed from
shifting to permanently established villages.

The change from the former philosophy of placing development officers
in the valleys and trying to persuade the hill peoples to move down, to the
policy of sending mobile teams of development workers (teachers, agricultural instructors, nurses, etc.) up into the hills has proved to be more
effective.

Despite all the benefits of such development, land pressures increase
because of continued population growth. The same is true for another,
short-term highly beneficial action: the success of malaria eradication,
especially in the foothill regions which had been infected frequently,
sometimes preventing a more widespread habitation in this zone. In the
past, the Highland-Lowland Transition Zone may thus have acted as a
buffer zone between hill-people areas and the valleys, as Kunstadter still
observed in 1969. But the recent rapid development has upset this buffer
function over a wide area of this region, and many factors are contributing

towards a critical pressure on this intermediate altitudinal zone. Thus the viability of this sensitive ecological "valve" between the highlands and the lowlands is being progressively reduced.

Discussion

One cannot deny a strong and genuine need for land by landless or underlanded Thai as well as by the rapidly growing hill populations. The hill populations are increasing both by natural growth and through refugee immigration from Laos and Burma. There is, in addition, the need to make up for the restricted opium cultivation in the higher mountains (above 1,100 m). Finally, these pressures themselves are accelerated by equally justified commercial interests in new land for economic cultivation of export crops. All this requires an adequate opening of new agricultural land, which would be mainly available in the forests of the Highland-Lowland Transition Zone. Its colonization will be successful only if the best land, rather than marginal land, in terms of soils, accessibility, is provided. The need for land cannot be controlled by restrictive means; this will only cause new problems and produce socially and politically sensitive issues. A recognition and balance of the different legal positions of the rights to land is urgent, especially between valuable forest reserves and the people's traditional rights of land accession. Therefore, the Highland-Lowland Transition Zone, as the most important reserve for both demands, requires especially careful consideration and planning. It is climatically favorable; it is usually situated within easy reach of the fully established regions; and, in many cases, it is also the area which is most affected by the construction of new road connections between various lowland districts.

Shifting cultivation—be it "integral," "additional," or only "incipient"—is still the prevailing means of extending agriculture and settlement into this zone. Many scientists, foresters, and authorities are aware that it is unwise to pass an over-simplified verdict on this old established form of agriculture; that it is unrealistic to declare it illegal without providing alternatives, which not only offer a narrow edge for mere survival, but for a real share in development and growth by earning a satisfactory existence. Grandstaff (unpublished) has given a very thorough and well-documented plea in favour of a well-managed and fully integrated shifting cultivation, or rather, land rotation. As most research workers with a high respect for the values of the native cultures, I would subscribe to many of his theses. Still, the problem needs further consideration. Will the pressure of growing population and standards of living and the awareness for the need of preservation of the daily dwindling forest reserves to guarantee an ecological balance really allow the continuation even of a highly controlled and well-managed shifting cultivation? Will it be feasible to continue the maintenance of the amount of land a family of shifting cultivators needs for its existence, even though it is roughly tenfold that needed by a family practicing intensive permanent cultivation? Even in well-organized swidden communities shouldn't attempts be made to transform the practice carefully, for instance, by replanting the swiddens with a cultivated, instead of a natural, secondary forest of commercial tree and bush plantations, or fast-growing timber species? Some old established practices in parts of Europe, incorporating the peasants or the rural communities into a certain degree of forest-economy, might be considered as long-term alternatives, although of course, it should be different from the *taungya* and similar forest-village systems, which are criticized by Chapman. He thinks rightly that agro-forestry would mean also that farmers should have fields as well as forestry plots, or various forms of community forests, which could provide for those vital firewood and lumbering needs that so easily produce uncontrolled forest destruction if they are not adequately met.

There should be no objections against the urgent need to stop those widespread swidden practices which are integrated neither into the culture of hill peoples nor into the ecological balance of the mountain forests. The scientist can only encourage the authorities not to hesitate to spend public money in attempts to prevent further extension of these destructive forms of clearing. Such an input would include recognition of the loss of those forests, which *de facto* have been occupied already by spontaneous colonization and will be, most likely, irreversible. Instead of restrictive measures, any possible help to improve the infrastructure, to provide better agricultural values by extension work, fertilizers, better tools, credit, and marketing systems, should be offered. This should ultimately reap greater benefits for the nation than would any struggling over legal positions or allowing the decay of exhausted clearings into *Imperata* savannahs! In return for all concerted attempts to help and establish the settlers, a more effective protection of the remaining forests might be gained. Thus efforts should be made to stabilize the pioneers on the very areas already cleared and which would possibly be abandoned again for new inroads into the forests if they are not preserved from decay through loss of fertility.

15

Limits to Obergurgl's Growth

An Alpine Experience in Environmental Management

Walter Moser and
Jeannie Peterson

The village of Obergurgl lies up in a valley of the Tyrolean Alps of Austria not too far from Untergurgl, and just down from Hochgurgl (Fig. 15.1). Together, the three Gurgls boast a permanent population of about 330.

Obergurgl has been transformed over the past 15 to 30 years from a bucolic pastoral village into a highly successful resort. The same ski-boom tourism that has affected other Alpine resorts has undoubtedly brought Obergurgl prosperity. The environmental price of this prosperity, however, began to escalate some years ago, as threats to the ecological integrity and long-run socio-economic stability of the area started to appear (Krippendorf 1975; Wichmann 1972; Wolkinger 1977; Hardin 1968). For tourism began to erode the environmental resource base on which Obergurgl's future would have to depend.

Hundreds of Alpine villages have found themselves in similar situations. What makes Obergurgl unique is neither its prosperity nor its problems, but the explicit identification of those problems, an intensive scientific study of the components contributing to them, the formulation and application of potential solutions, and the participation and support of the local population in the entire process.

The Obergurgl experiment, which is a MAB project, now stands as a model for other Alpine resorts, attracting observation teams of experts from the region and serving as a focus for international attention. The Obergurgl experience, from which others are anxious to learn, gave its citizens the prerogative of mapping out their own future, aware in advance of many of the consequences of their choices and actions.

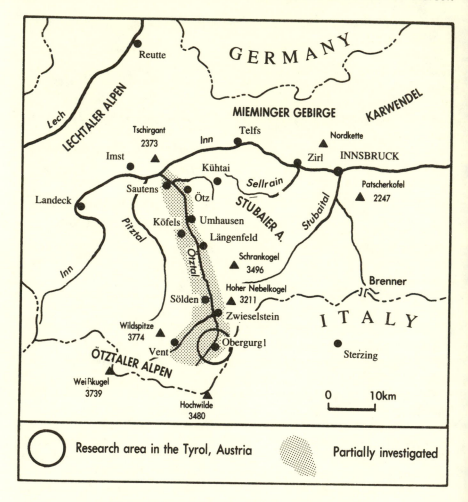

Figure 15.1   Site of the Obergurgl Project

This article will present the setting, participants, plan of study, and some of the results of the Obergurgl project.

The Setting and the People

Obergurgl is located at the head of the Oetztal (Valley of the River Oetz), about 100 km southwest of Innsbruck, at an altitude of about 2000 meters. The upper Oetztal is an area of steep and rocky slopes, where 90 percent of the land is unusable the year around.

The Valley has been settled since the 12th century. The early inhabitants based their economy on livestock, using meadows, forest and Alpine grasslands in a closed, self-sufficient system, where nothing was imported from the outside.

Theirs was a life of continual challenge. Little could be done to achieve short-term gains in the fragile Alpine environment, for it was the long-term effects that proved decisive for both the individual and the community. There were countless attempts to force a richer yield during the short mountain growing season, or to tip the crucial balance between harvesting and protecting the forest, or to "develop" land for new uses. Even slight errors could produce catastrophic results, and wild waters, avalanches or rockslides could destroy what had taken decades of labor to establish (Aulitzky 1974). Throughout the Alpine region, the inhabitants gradually developed great skill in dealing with natural forces (Kyselak 1829; Lewald 1835; Noe 1869).

The relatively stable balance between humans and their environment which developed early in the upper Oetztal supported a population of about 120. By 1830, however, the pressures of population growth resulted in a communal ban on marriages; it lasted until 1850.

The grandiose beauty that surrounded the Obergurglers was not so important to them as the landscape's productivity, upon which their lives depended. Despite the impassibility of the mountains, the first tourists arrived about 100 years ago, and their enthusiasm over the glories of the Alpine landscape was great. The villagers, however, assessed the mountains in their own way: "If the visitors had to work here for only three weeks, they would lose their delight in the mountain world and they, too, would say 'You damned nature' " (Schoepf 1855).

The grandfathers of today's Obergurglers led a life that was self-sufficient and independent, in reasonable harmony with the hostile environment, and little influenced by the outside world (Senn 1969). No one expected great changes (Gorfer 1975). Only a few privileged tourists made their way to the Gurgls. The village chronicle records that on the occasion of an official visit in 1903, ". . . a cannon blast and two modest flags . . . were the total outdoor greeting. What else could be done in this region of ice and snow, even if the Pope or the Emperor should come?" (Sinner 1978).

Although those two eminences have still not arrived, the Obergurgl region is now host to about 40,000 visitors annually, and the age-old equilibrium between humans and the Alpine environment has been disturbed.

Starting in the early 1950s when winter sports gained in popularity, the village drew increasing numbers of tourists, and this brought economic prosperity. Construction of hotels, ski lifts and roads was part of this development, as was an increase in the amount of traffic in the village, and obvious wear-and-tear on the fragile Alpine environment in the different altitudinal ecozones. Thus the "problem of Obergurgl" began to be evident, and the specter raised by the slogan "tourism kills tourism" suggested that something should be done (Moser 1975).

Obergurgl as a MAB Project

Obergurgl was chosen for intensive study within the framework of MAB project 6 (Impact of Human Activities on Mountain and Tundra Ecosystems), and the Obergurgl experiment in environmental assessment and management was launched in 1971. The instigators of the Obergurgl experiment had previously, as collaborators in the International Biological Program (IBP), had the opportunity during the 1960s of learning the methods of systems analysis in detail (Larcher 1977; Moser et al. 1975), and as a consequence this experience was expanded into a MAB project. Eighty scientists eventually participated in the study, and the University of Innsbruck and its Alpine Research Station in Obergurgl played important roles.

Mobilization of support among the villagers was of crucial importance in the first stage of the project. However, as the local people already enjoyed a state of great prosperity, with incomes far above the average in the Austrian Alps, and as investigation of this situation did not promise economic improvement in the short run, there was intensive discussion and vigorous controversy when the residents were informed about the problems, the research methods and objectives, and the possible positive and negative consequences.

A Systems Approach to Obergurgl

In 1974 the International Institute of Applied Systems Analysis (IIASA) near Vienna joined the study and a simulation model was prepared (Holling 1974). The model was designed to forecast different possibilities for Obergurgl's future, and about 30 50-year scenarios were developed (Bunnell 1974). Four major components were included: recreational demand, population and economic development, farming and ecological change, land use and development control (Fig. 15.2). The predictions of the model depended largely on a few key relationships, which can be summarized as follows (ibid.):

- In the face of essentially infinite potential demand, growth of the recreation industry had been limited by the rate of local population growth.
- The amount of safe (not prone to avalanche) land was disappearing rapidly, while the local demand for building sites was continuing to grow.
- As land was developed, prime agricultural land was lost and environmental quality decreased.

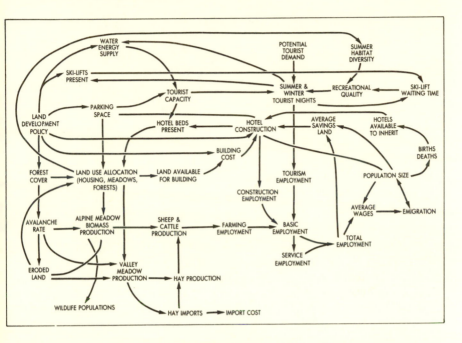

Figure 15.2   The Obergurgl Model with Four Major Components: recreational demand, population and economic development, farming and ecological change, and land use and development.

- Recreational demand could begin to decrease if environmental quality were to deteriorate further.
- The conclusion was that the village could soon be caught in a painful trap, when its growing population collided with declining resources and demand. Overinvestment in hotels appeared likely to occur, until a state would be reached where no hotel owners would do very well.

The model served to evaluate newly gained information for a better understanding of the system, but it also served as a means of keeping the dialogue between the scientists and the population active. Three representatives of the Obergurgl population participated in the model-building and evaluation, and brought their expertise and experience directly into play.

From the scenarios, which were presented, displayed and then were actively discussed by the villagers, agreement was reached on the following points:

- There would be wide-ranging negative consequences for the area if the development then in progress (e.g., increased building of hotels,

increased tourism, increased degradation of the environment) were to
continue.

- Control measures, if introduced into different parts of the system,
  could help to slow or prevent further degradation.
- Critical information gaps existed in many areas, calling for reseach in
  a number of fields.

Organization of the Study

Two main project groups were organized. The biological studies group
focuses on the effects of summer tourists and skiiers on the Alpine
grasslands, and on the carrying capacity of the area. The other group
concentrates on the economic and sociological elements of the system
(Tables 15.1 and 15.2).

In addition, there is a coordination group (W. Moser, G. Patzelt and six
collaborators) which is responsible for administration and logistics, integration and distribution of information flows (data bank, modeling), and
cooperation with the inhabitants.

MAB-6 Obergurgl is led by a commission whose membership includes
the project leaders and representatives from the Obergurgl population and
the Tyrol Provincial Government (chairman: H. Janetschek). The progress of the research program is checked at five meetings a year of the
MAB-6 Obergurgl Commission. This results in the allocation of means to
the individual projects according to the prevailing critical points of
research.

The financial means are provided by the Federal Ministry of Science
and Research, the Federal Ministry of Health and Environmental Protection and the Province of Tyrol. MAB-6 Obergurgl is part of the Austrian
MAB-6 program (Cernusca 1977, 1978).

Local Participation

The involvement of the population right at the beginning of the investigations was necessary and advantageous, although difficulties of several
kinds naturally had to be expected.

The villagers showed great patience and willingness to cooperate, and
this proved to be essential for the success of the project. From the
villagers' point of view it was a new experience. One might lead the
ethnologist through every room of the house in the morning and account
for old customs and practices, spend the afternoon with the zoologist in
the stall, and in the evening explain to guests the geographer's questionnaire while the economist was already discussing the date of the enterprise analysis. Furthermore, a researcher might then appear to take blood
samples and measure the size of one's ears, while botanists, geodesists,

Table 15.1 Biological Projects in Obergurgl

Project	Objectives

Meteorology
  M Kuhn
  6 collaborators
	Four meteorological stations in year-round operation. Intensive study of radiation and heat budget in two experimental fields. Preparation of meteorological reference values for questions of erosion, land use etc.

Vegetation analysis
  H Reisigl
  14 collaborators
	Phytocoenotic samples at various dates. Measurement of primary production in the Curvuletum (trodden and untrodden) by means of field methods and calorimetry, growth rhythmics, phenology and trampling effect.

Alage
  H Pitschmann
  1 collaborator
	Isolation and culture of soil algae (trodden and untrodden)–indicator organisms.

Ecology
  A Cernusca
  4 collaborators
	Growth analysis; energy-flows.

Invertebrates
  H Janetschek
  8 collaborators
	Determinatino of species endowments and their population dynamics in meadows and on ski runs as well as of alpine grass heaths (trodden and untrodden).

Vertebrates
  H Janetschek
  4 collaborators
	Survey of animal husbandry and land use as well as their changes. Hunting.

Microbiology
  W Moser
  5 collaborators
	Quantitative expression of aerobic and anaerobic bacteria in trodden and untrodden soils (meadows, alpine grass heaths). Measurements of enzymatic activities of microorganisms in soil.

Soil Science
  1 Neuwinger
  2 collaborators
	Soil mapping. Hydrology of soils.

meteorologists and soil scientists stood in the middle of a meadow with their equipment, surrounded by a herd of curious tourists. The Obergurglers were always ready to provide such special service. They also provided all experimental areas and land transport free of charge, and did not reduce their willingness to help, even on those occasions when they were of a different opinion than the researchers.

Results

The results of MAB-6 Obergurgl fell into three categories: scientific knowledge, effects of the investigation on the area, and wider-ranging aspects. Some of the results from selected parts of the project will be presented here.

Table 15.2   Anthropological Projects in Obergurgl

Project	Objectives
Ethnology K Ilg 1 collaborator	Survey of changes of custom in Obergurgl and Damuls (Vorarlberg) for comparison.
Anthropology H Janetschek 1 collaborator	Anthropometric and somatologic studies in Otz and Pitz valleys, blood group determinations.
Geography H Heuberger 6 collaborators	Building mapping according to age and function. Population structure and occupational status in community of Soelden. Population development in Upper Otztal since beginning of relevant records. Quantitative expression of land use by summer and winter tourists. Ecological and economic evaluation of tourist behavior. Analysis of trail network.
Sociology F Geiger, J Morel 4 collaborators	Comparative study of value systems and of process of opinion formation in Obergurgl and Vent.
Regional planning F Heigl	Evaluation of village character, photo assembly for possible developments.
Economy theory F Munnich 3 collaborators	Analysis of enterprise structure. Motivation research on producers and consumers.

Modeling

The first Obergurgl model was simplified and served in the course of the program as a convenient vehicle for summarizing and interpreting practical conclusions and for formulating new objectives. A comprehensive presentation of the totality of the results remains to be finished.

Impact on the Landscape

In Obergurgl, as in other Alpine areas, tourism gobbles up the landscape (Moser 1972). Skiers, in particular, leave behind heavy damage (Grabherr 1978). When ski runs are first established, the closed vegetation is removed, leaving raw soil which is subject to erosion (Grabherr n.d.) and to colonization by pioneer plants. The establishment of ski lifts leaves a succession of bare scars on the mountain slopes. In the preparation of the ski runs, caterpillars and other heavy machines are used which impact the snow cover, and as a result the snow cover remains longer, leaving a shorter vegetation period. Ski edges shave off the vegetation on elevated areas and ridges, and the turf is damaged during periods of little snow.

The dominant species of the alpine grass heath, *Carex curvula*, needs decades to revegetate ski runs (Janetschek 1976). Attempts with some other grasses which have been introduced experimentally show that they are able to form only 1/3 of the root mass formed by *Carex curvula*, the original vegetation. Thus the stabilization of the ground and the dense plant cover provided by the natural vegetation cannot be matched by other species. "Prevention rather than cure" is an important consideration in dealing with Alpine areas.

Other vegetation, such as Rhododendron and Vaccinium, can regenerate so long as the soil has not been abraded down to bedrock. Many areas, however, need to have an occasional period of rest from skiers, a "closed season," in order to regenerate.

When ski runs are constructed and the terrain graded, the natural cover of *Carex curvula* can be maintained if the sod is cut away and stored, before the grading work begins, and restored to the slopes afterwards. Although the method is both labor-consuming and expensive, it has been shown to be successful.

Don't Tread on Me!

Summer tourists, too, do their share of damage, but it is neither as extensive nor as serious as that caused by winter tourism. The "stamping effect" of hikers and mass summer tourists causes various degrees of injury to different species. Some types of plants cannot even tolerate being stepped on once before succumbing: others show great resistance because of their tough leaves. An investigation of the ground cover made at the Hohe Mut experimental area (Grabherr 1982) showed the range of "stamping resistance" among the plants found there. Table 15.3 shows how many tourists per day cause a decrease of 50 percent of the coverage by a given plant because of "stamping" damages. As more plants die off,

Table 15.3 Number of Tourists per Day who Cause a Decrease of 50 percent of the Coverage by a Given Plant because of "Stamping Damage"

Lichens	Less than 30 tourists a day
Mosses	20–25 tourists a day
Tanacetum alpinum	50 tourists a day
Phyteuma, Geum, Homogyne and other species	70–80 tourists a day
Some grass species	100–150 tourists a day
Ligusticum mutellina	200 tourists a day
Carex curvula	More than 200 tourists a day

the amount of phytomass is reduced, and there is less available for soil organisms.

Studies of soil organisms were carried out in natural meadows and grasslands, and on ski runs, and in hiker-trampled areas (Janetschek et al. 1976). Insects and bugs were found on natural meadows in quantities of 2.3 $g/m^2/yr$, and in natural grasslands in quantities of 0.42 $g/m^2/yr$, while lesser quantities were found in skied on or trampled areas. On a grass-covered ski run that had been in use for ten years, only one earthworm was found per square meter, compared to 160 earthworms per square meter found in natural meadows. The beetle and harvester count showed 2121 individuals per square meter in natural areas, and 1015 on ski slopes. On summer grasslands, 100 insects per square meter were found in trampled sections in July and October, while the undisturbed areas yielded 1000. Perhaps it should not be surprising that the decomposition rate is lower on ski runs, whether measured as decomposition of straw or presence of enzymes.

Tourism from Various Perspectives

Although winter tourism is the main environmental destructive element, there are three or four times as many winter tourists as summer tourists, and winter tourism brings in about five or six times the summer tourist income (Tappeiner 1979). Summer tourists are concerned with the esthetics of their touristic experience; erosion and long raw scars on the mountain slopes do not amuse them.

Winter tourists, on the other hand, cannot see the ugly patches under the snow cover. The skiers are more loyal visitors than the summer tourists, and 50 percent of them return to Obergurgl the following winter.

In 1977, both tourists and villagers were interviewed, personally and by questionnaire, to find their opinion on the future development of Obergurgl. Eighty-five percent of the tourists (summer and winter) indicated they did not favor further development, and opposed further expansion of tourist facilities.

The results of the project investigations (Degenhardt 1980) had a great influence on opinion–formation in the village. In addition to the above studies there were findings from a traffic study, a study of the use of hiking trails, and the behavior of one-day visitors and long-term visitors.

When the surveys made it clear that the hitherto successful policy of expansion would have negative consequences and that especially the building of new hotels to provide beds for more tourists should be reconsidered, the situation became difficult for the project coordinator. The farmers, in particular, were not pleased by the idea of halting construction. As landowners, the farmers traditionally provided a livelihood for their children by providing the land and building a hotel, and they were not eager to see this way of life changed.

The results of the program also showed that with the retention of the prevailing income structure, agriculture would no longer be economically attractive for the younger generation. Hitherto, farmers had invested most of the money earned from tourism into the running of the farms.

Hotel owners, on the other hand, were positive toward the concept of an eventual restriction on building activity. However, they declared that the scientists were merely upsetting the farmers and disturbing the peace of the village.

It took many discussions with representatives of both groups, with emphasis on a long-term perspective, including the past, present and future possibilities for the village, to make it clear that there were local problems which could not be surmounted by confrontation, but which required cooperative actions for their solution.

Actions Taken by the Villagers

As a result, a series of actions were undertaken by the local population to stabilize the system:

- The area allocation plan reduces further growth and prevents subdivision of still-open areas.
- Some hotels have reduced the number of guest beds, as a quality improvement measure.
- The use of the land for summer tourism is being managed in ways which keep the damaging effect low but do not impair the recreational effects (*e.g.*, circular tours, separation of activities of day visitors from those of long-term guests).
- Natural history tours guided by specially trained residents.
- Establishment of quiet zones and nature protection areas.
- Reduction of water pollution by the newly built biological sewage plant.
- Exclusion of lifts and cable railways from the west side of the valley.
- Assignment of considerable funds to the revegetation of ski runs.
- Restrictions on traffic in the village.
- Premium payments to farmers by participants in the tourism sector for the stabilization of local agriculture.
- Foundation of choral society.
- Foundation of music group.
- Expanded youth education program.

Many of these actions involve a renunciation of monetary gain in favor of long-term stabilization.

Wider-Ranging Aspects

The results to date of the MAB-6 Obergurgl project have stimulated similar projects (Messerli, Messerli 1979) and have produced materials for the Province's regional planning. Parties of professional visitors visit the site for on-the-spot information, and a number of international conventions have been organized by MAB-6 in cooperation with the local population. Students participating in the program have been given special ecological training. It has been obvious even to the tourists that a whole village is collaborating with scientists in order to achieve long-term stability.

Thus in this Alpine area where the quality of the natural surroundings was deteriorating, a UNESCO program brought about 80 scientists together with the inhabitants, to assess the consequences of future development, and to probe for solutions to the problems. Years of work led to increased understanding of the system and to a consequent change in the attitude of the Obergurglers. They decided to forego relatively quick and easy profits in favor of a stabilized future.

PART III
Modernization of Mountain Regions

16

Introduction

Nigel J. R. Allan

Modernization is sweeping over mountains all around the world. Despite efforts by groups favoring "cultural survival" or "cultural preservation" in remote locations, the inexorable process of acculturation and integration into national and world systems of order is underway. To cite just one example of this process one need only note the recent completion of a 1,000 bed 4-star hotel in Lhasa, Tibet, and the completion of the world's highest paved road to bring tourists to the hotel.

With modernization has come a reorientation of the people's daily lives in mountains and a drastic change in the perception of the world at large towards the physical environment. I have documented these changes elsewhere (Allan 1986a, b), and the prime cause of the modernization has been the rapid accessibility of lowlanders into the mountains. The principal feature of mountains, slope, has been overcome by motive power.

The five chapters in Part Three document the rapid transition in the Old World, the New World and in the northern and southern hemispheres. Perhaps no mountain landscape is so firmly etched in the minds of the urban population as that of the Alps. Lichtenberger charts the process of integrating the Alps into the urban leisure society of Europe. Soelden in the Oetztaler Alps of Austria exemplifies how urban residents dominate mountains. Year-round skiing is available to residents of large cities like Munich, who drive to the ski slopes on limited access high-speed highways in a few hours. A key feature of Lichtenberger's work is that the ideal mountain landscape is not being defined from the viewpoint of the inhabitants but is an artifice formed by the taxes paid by urban dwellers, subsidies to mountain farmers, and by print and visual media that constantly bombard us with material about travel and tourism.

Recreating in the outdoors invariably moves from a casual personal experience to a highly institutional form with geo-political overtones. Kariel, who lives in the foreland of the Rocky Mountains, examines the surge of human interest in tourism and recreation developments, many of which have been brought on by the forthcoming Calgary Winter Olympics in 1988. Much of the turmoil that Calgary is now facing was experienced earlier in Denver when the opportunistic commercial developers of sites to be used for the 1976 Winter Olympics were defeated by local groups and the venue moved to Innsbruck where there was a long tradition of holding formalized, rationally planned winter competitions.

As this introduction is being written, large numbers of tourists are flocking into a formerly remote valley that is the reputed "Shangri La" of writer James Hilton. The Hunza valley nestles below the majestic pinnacle of Rakaposhi and has long been recognized as a place where people lived to a great age on an ideal, almost vegetarian diet. This is, of course, absolute nonsense, as most of the weak and infirm died very early in the annual spring starvation which afflicted most traditional mountain societies. Kreutzmann explains the use of water in this almost desert environment and the ceaseless toil by the mountaineers to wrest a living from such a marginal environment. With the opening of the Karakorum Highway to China in 1986, the Hunza valley will undergo a rapid change as the adventurous tourist will gain access to the Marco Polo Silk Route in adjacent China.

Most mountains have been occupied for millenia, but New Guinea mountains have had a relatively brief period of human impact. Allen's chapter traces the introduction of a key food item into the mountains that permitted a rapid migration upward. Other places in the mountain world are now experiencing a similar surge only in commercial activity as temperate crops are grown in the mountains and marketed in a more sophisticated urban population living in a tropical or subtropical lowland. Vegetables and fruits dominate these cropping innovations. As mountaineers become economically integrated into the greater society, they also become more dependent on lowland governments, and in the process their self-sufficiency and resilience to adversity are reduced. Bryant Allen's contribution is a sober reminder of the erosion of the traditional mountaineer's integrity and independence.

The last chapter concerns Afghanistan, a nation state brought into being by external powers one hundred years ago and now being demolished by superpowers. Its mountaineers, fierce and independent, really relinquished their independence in 1880 when they were subjugated by a new urban based political power put in place by external authorities. As Daniel Balland shows, complementarity existed between traditional groups who exploited the physical environment. With the establishment of urban based political elites and the formation of nonsensical political boundaries, the fate of Afghanistan was sealed many years ago. Balland documents the strife among competing groups that must have led to the dissolution of Afghanistan as a political entity and the consequent usurping of power by an external state anxious to protect its border. The fate of Afghanistan is symbolic of the contemporary human impact on mountains. Mountains and mountaineers are being dominated by lowland urban people, but the paradox is that at no time in history have mountains been viewed with such concern, and even affection.

17

The Succession of an Agricultural Society to a Leisure Society
The High Mountains of Europe

Elisabeth Lichtenberger

The Bipolar Socio-Ecological Model of the High Mountain Areas of Europe

The general public in European countries shows little interest in problems concerning life in rural areas, mainly because an ever larger proportion of the population is being molded by the socialization with urban norms and value systems. Growing demands of the urban leisure society on high mountain areas have, however, directed its attention to the problems created by them, especially in the Alps.

The request for a "conservation of the natural landscape" doubtless is informed by worries concerning the commercial value of the "good" landscape in the tourism market fairly often, thus, somehow, mirroring a resources ideology that tends to consider a good valuable only when it is no longer ubiquitous. Who would, otherwise, display any interest in the devastation of settlements or arable land that has been characteristic of vast areas in European high mountain regions? While rapid suburbanization burdens parts of the Alps with all the problems of densely populated areas, the regression of settlements and arable land continues everywhere else. Therefore, the question ought to be raised concerning what the future of the high mountain areas of Europe will be like when there is an exogenous polarization between increasing depopulation on the one hand and pronounced urbanization on the other hand.

An attempt will be made to present a general solution for this problem by means of an extended socio-ecological approach. For two different social systems, namely the traditional agricultural society and the modern urban leisure society, the natural surroundings are being defined as the ecological potential of the high mountain areas, as opposed to the viewpoint of the social ecology derived from the circumstances of large North American cities, for which the physical surroundings are described by economic parameters, such as land rent. Ecological aspects pertaining to agriculture and to leisure activities are, however, only partly identical (Fig. 17.1), as the often cited recent "re-evaluation of the high mountain areas" for the recreation of the urban population is based on different locational demands than those of rural settlement and agriculture. The spatial basis for two societies, one with a negative and one with a positive developmental trend, is thus formed by different natural potentials. With respect to the location in space there is a partial superposition of the regression model concerning the agricultural society by the growth model depicting the leisure society.

The following statements pertaining to the agricultural situation can be derived from the regression model:

1. A devastation of settlements and agricultural land is inevitable and unstoppable wherever economic marginality is not accompanied by ecological attraction appealing to the expanding urban leisure society.

2. On the other hand, there is a modernization, intensification, and, partly, a restructuring of properties in agriculture in areas with favorable ecological conditions, such as the forelands.

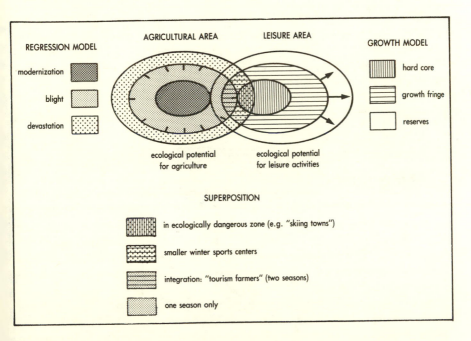

Figure 17.1   The Bipolar Socio-economic Model of the Succession in the Agricultural and Leisure Areas in the High Mountains of Europe

3. A wider or narrower belt with an extensification of rural settlement and agriculture ("mountain blight") that might, at least partly, become devastated in the near future is situated between a stabilized core area and the blighted peripheral regions.

The following aspects of the leisure area are clearly depicted in the growth model:

1. Leisure's "hard core" is situated outside the core region of re-generating agriculture described above.

2. Its expansion tends to reach into agricultural areas. On the one hand, rural settlements are integrated, with new "lebensforms" coming into existence, such as the "tourism farmer" or the "second homes farmer"; on the other hand tourism, especially skiing, also invades the devastated agricultural regions and, thus, the ecologically dangerous zone of the high mountain areas.

3. The ecological potential of the high mountain areas with respect to leisure activities is by no means exhausted yet (Fig. 17.2). Future developments will largely be informed by whether public measures will continue to further a partial occupation of these regions by the urban leisure society, which has followed capitalistic rules so far. There is a surplus of developers' plans for an ever-increasing number of still more and even larger "leisure society ghettos," and of investors ready to finance them.

As can be seen from the statements made above, the model implicitly contains the following assumptions: (1) economic rationality of, and free choice of location for, the individual; (2) high mobility of productive factors and especially of the population.

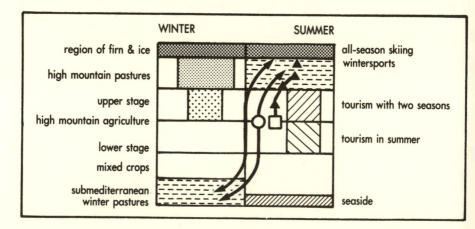

Figure 17.2   Seasonal Shift in the Third Dimension of Segments of the Ecological Dimension

According to geographical reality, the following external variables herefore must be used for explanation: (1) variables pertaining to the political systems, such as political models, restrictions in the real estate market, investment measures, mortgage control; (2) the socio-economic and technological development stage of the individual states; (3) influences of economic competition between high mountain areas and forelands; (4) a transfer of urban capital and of members of the leisure society according to the respective location of the high mountain areas and the densely populated regions.

Within each system the variables given below are to be considered:

- social organization (groups of *lebensforms*) and enterprise structures in agriculture and tourism,
- their economic targets,
- the internal transport systems of high mountain areas,
- technological aspects, and
- cultural influences, such as the behavior of minorities.

Historical and present influences of the society on the landscape as well as an analysis of the potential for specific social activities cannot be discussed here.

The Vertical Structure of the Agricultural and Leisure Areas

Spatial models like the regression model of the agricultural area and the growth model of the leisure area are adaptations of the von Thuenen model and always exclude the third dimension. For a wider discussion it must, however, be introduced (Fig. 17.3). Below a very simplified description of the three ecological storeys of the Alps is presented, neglecting the variations from east to west and north to south as well as the differences between the more humid outer flanks and dry inner regions of the continually settled Alpine areas.

Above a lowest story of mixed crops extending into the Alps from the forelands, there are two storeys of high mountain agriculture not easily separable from each other, with a predominance of arable land in the lower one and of forms of ley farming in the upper one. Both of them had links with the storey of high mountain pastures above, with a complicated system of a series of stages.

With respect to the regression model mentioned above there are entirely different developments to be observed in these storeys. Surprisingly enough, consolidated and modernized vineyards and orchards are to be found in some areas of the *lowest* storey, with considerable and increasing exports, organized cooperatively in the South Tyrol and with large enterprises in the French-speaking Valais. On the other hand there is a zone of marked devastation in the Italian and French Southern Alps,

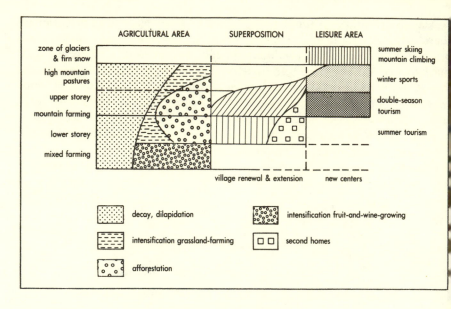

Figure 17.3   Vertical Structure of the Agricultural and Leisure Areas in the Alps

affecting the former storey of vineyard terraces and the stands of sweet chestnuts above in a belt round the lower mountain flanks. Because of the competition of the forelands, there are hardly any measures on the part of the state to encourage a replanting.

For the lower *storey of high mountain farming* the ecological variation in the Alps can be reduced to a simple dichotomy of areas dry in summer or humid in summer. Arable land plus irrigated pastures and ley-farming were the characteristic basic forms of land use. With traditional agriculture, the former areas had the advantage of a higher carrying capacity, whereas the opposite is true now because of the decline of arable farming. It has practically vanished completely in large parts of the Alps since World War II. A conversion of arable land into pastures is, however, impossible there without irrigation.

The importance of this climate-ecological factor cannot be overrated, therefore, with respect to the present devastation process. A zone of formerly intensive arable farming, especially in the Southern Alps and the dry inner-Alpine valleys, the Valois in Switzerland and the Valtellino in Italy, has become a vast region of seemingly irreversible blight, covering almost all of the storey between the low-lying wine-growing areas and the former area of the lower Alpine pastures that were stocked in spring and in autumn. Tourism centers have replaced them in favorable locations (see below), although dairy-farming, an economic activity that had always been predominant in the high mountain areas, has gained even greater importance in large parts of the Austrian and Bavarian Alps, owing to an intensified grassland economy. In the eastern section of the Alps there is another observable change in the "montagne moyenne." For more than one hundred years forestry has benefited from the crisis of high mountain agriculture.

While there is some favorable development in the lower storey of high mountain agriculture, there is none in the upper one. The complicated forms of ley-farming have vanished without being replaced by an intensified grassland economy, and this storey has generally become one of blight. Where tourism has come in, the upper boundary of settlement has been stabilized, the population and number of buildings increased, but there is even more social fallow in these areas, as can be seen in the surroundings of wintersports resorts in the Austrian Alps.

With respect to transport cost, risks, and hardships in working conditions, the traditional high mountain pastures economy is even further removed from the standards of prosperity and consumption of the urban leisure society than high mountain farming. A lowering of the upper boundary of permanent settlement brought about blight in the alps' settlements, most of all in the French Alps. Transhumance of sheep has replaced cattle pasturing in many places.

With creeping extensification, lack of maintenance, increasing number of rocks and abandonment above, and natural expansion of woodland below, the tree-line cannot be quantified or even estimated easily. Where alps are still kept up, there are trends towards simplifying formerly complicated systems, such as having a smaller number of intermediate stages between the lowest and the highest alps, reduction of alps personnel by restricting dairy farming and leaving cattle to themselves for long periods, increasing the number of cooperative alps, especially for producing cheese, with highly specialized personnel. As a measure for the economic value of the alps for a country like Austria it should be considered that an additional 100,000 head of cattle can be fed in this way. As about 140,000 cattle are exported each year (1982), the alps, indirectly, have an important function for exports. To explain the variations to be found in the Alps one point ought to be mentioned: The number of cattle reared in all of the French Alps is down to fewer than 80,000!

The sequence of storeys from mixed crops via the "moyenne montagne" and the "haute montagne" to the alps corresponds to a von Thuenen model based on accessibility and a time-cost-effort relation. It cannot be applied to the third dimension with respect to the leisure area in which there is an inversion—both of capital input and of the strata of society involved. A first step was made by the Alpine Clubs around the turn of the century when mountain cabins were built and paths laid out in the actually uninhabited top storey, only in places reaching down into the storey of alps. Wintersports resorts were built in a second step, above the permanently settled agricultural villages, which, in many cases, depend on an interregional labor market for their staff. In these cases, such as in large parts of the Italian and French Alps, there is an almost complete segregation of the agricultural and the leisure societies, both spatially and functionally.

No doubt wintersports are the growth industry proper in this upper storey of the Alps. They came into existence in the area of former high alpine pasture economy, but they do not share profits to any considerable extent. There is hardly any, and if so, only local and in rare cases regional dual use of objects and the technical infrastructure (Tyrol).

Climatic conditions are favorable for double-season tourism in the higher storey of high mountain farming. As opposed to winter tourism, summer tourism calls for attractions both as to settlements and the cultural landscape to a much higher degree. Blight in settlements and disuse of arable land tend to stop its expansion completely, though there seem to be differences as to the perception of, and the reaction to, such blight phenomena between members of different nations, a field little studied so far.

Whether there is any economic integration of agriculture and tourism strongly depends on a number of variables such as agricultural-social organization, public subsidies, and structure of buildings. It is strongest in the Tyrol where more than two-thirds of the farms might be considered as "tourism farmers."

Generally speaking, double-season tourism has succeeded in stopping rural exodus and even bringing about a population increase owing to its rapid growth, but it is predominant in a very few sections of the Alps, namely, in the west of Austria, the Southern Tyrol, Graubuenden, Valais, and Berner Oberland in Switzerland, and a few places in the French Northern Alps. In any case there is further exodus from agriculture and extensification of land use.

Only summer tourism is feasible in the lower storey of mountain farming, therefore mountain blight is of extremely high importance there. Dependent upon its accessibility and distance from densely populated areas in the forelands, it might, however, get another chance because an increasing number of second homes are appearing in abandoned agricultural areas, especially all along the Alpine fringe in Italy in a height over about 700 to 800 meters, and also in the French Southern Alps and in the easternmost parts of the Alps influenced by the Austrian capital.

The lowest storey, that of mixed crops, shows very little influence of the leisure society. Only in those areas in which large lakes mark the former extent of Alpine glaciation and in which there is historical villegiatura, second homes of an urban population are of some significance.

The most serious problems and conflicts with regard to valuable arable land result from the space required by improved road and railway systems and industrial settlements. The latter not only attract labor from agriculture, but they bring about disastrous pollution and devastation of the natural surroundings. Examples for this could be presented that had been hailed "important progress" at first, e.g., in the Valais or in the even earlier industrialized valleys in the northern French Alps.

Because of a marked vertical increase in infrastructure cost there is an inversion of the socio-ecological variation in the leisure area of the Alps if compared with the farming area. Thus luxury tourism caters to the jet set and upper and middle income strata only in many of the wintersports resorts above the settlements and tree lines; dual-season resorts still offer accommodation with all conveniences, whereas modest inns and boarding houses are predominant in the summer resorts. This inversion tends to increase as winter holidays gain importance and skiing facilities are improved.

The Autochthonous Population and the Leisure-time Population Coming from Outside

So far, mainly the relationship between landscape and spatial differentiation of the agricultural society and the leisure society has been discussed. In reality, societal relationships in the Alps are, however, much more complex, as the agricultural population forms only a part of the residents and workforce of the villages.

The autochthonous population is made up of a number of groups:

1. On an average, the agricultural population amounts to about 25 percent. In the Austrian Alps, even of this group only about 40 percent are engaged in agriculture full time.

2. The rest are an increasing number of part-time farmers who often are "three-job people" in Austria, holding jobs in the secondary or tertiary sector and letting rooms to tourists.

3. There is a fairly high deficit of jobs in the Alpine areas, even in Austria. It amounts to approximately 50 percent and forces about 50 percent of the autochthonous population to commute to larger central places or other centers offering jobs.

4. Building and other local trades as well as services provide a number of workplaces in the villages.

5. There is the local elite such as tradespeople, owners of hotels, and catering establishments for tourists and professional people in private practice.

As can be deduced from Figure 17.4, a specific feature of the Austrian Alps is a group of two-job people, namely "tourism farmers" ("second

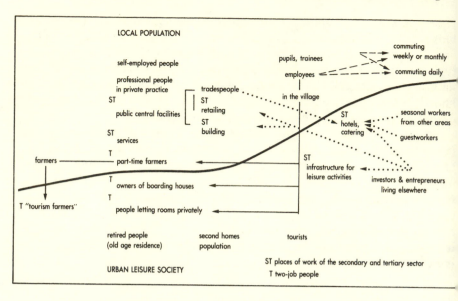

Figure 17.4   Local Population and Urban Leisure Society in the High Mountain Area of the Alps

homes farmers'') and people letting rooms privately, who come in between the autochthonous population and the leisure population. They are of enormous ecological and social importance for the Austrian Alps, therefore utmost efforts must be made to secure their existence and further economic development.

A highly diversified situation exists in the local labor-markets with respect to the function of the leisure population in accordance with the conditions on the national labor-market. A marked segmentation oriented toward specific types of demand is found in Switzerland, with very little interchange: Resident men hold the full-year jobs in the technical infrastructure (cable-cars, etc.) as well as in trades and industry. Moreover, there is a strong connection between tourism and building activities, with up to 40 percent of the male employees working in building trades. Resident women hold jobs in retailing and with local authorities.

These conditions in the tourism sector of the labor market still force many young residents to leave the village if they want to be trained for a specific vocation or business and go on to work in that line. Therefore qualified seasonal positions in hotels and restaurants are mainly held by young, mostly single Swiss citizens who come from outside the village, whereas mainly guestworkers are employed in unskilled jobs.

The overall ratio of foreign labor in catering is 45 percent in Switzerland. Guestworker politics with a reduction of their number has brought about serious problems and practically prevented the development of a hotel business in the mountains, but furthered both a boom of other forms of commercialized accommodation and of second homes, thus bringing about a ratio of about 1:4 between these two basic forms of tourist accommodation. The latter needs only one tenth of the labor required by hotels, in which, in Switzerland, 37 to 53 all-year jobs plus 28 to 30 seasonal jobs for every 100 beds are considered necessary.

There are push-factors for a rural exodus outside the labor market, too, especially for those persons who do not own houses or real estate and have hardly any chance to have a house built because of the forbidding cost of real estate. Owing to the competition of the urban leisure population, the housing shortage for this "subproletariate" is even more pressing than in large cities. A lack of reasonably priced lodgings constitutes a severe problem in the Austrian Alpine area, too, being a shadow-effect that came into existence in the wake of visible prosperity. There is, however, considerably more pressure on the rural communities to provide acceptable housing for the autochthonous population by means of active land politics and housebuilding.

18
Tourism and Recreation Developments in the Rocky Mountains of Canada

Herbert G. Kariel

Introduction

Over the past 120 years, a slow, steady, and continual increase in tourism and recreational developments has occurred in Canada's Rocky Mountains and the neighboring Columbia Mountains. The accompanying landscape changes, almost imperceptible at first, became increasingly noticeable as development accelerated. They lead one to wonder how much more development will take place under the ever increasing pressures from the tourism industry, the private sector, and political decision makers.

Other related questions come to mind: How long will it be before the public begins to notice and becomes concerned about the changes? How do developers justify the economic viability of their projects? How do developers and political decision makers perceive the natural scene? What overall planning is being done? What type of a future society and environments are being designed and, most important, for whom?

This essay presents, within the historical context, current issues and proposed tourism and recreational development projects in the region, along with governmental positions regarding them. In conclusion, some implications for regional planning and an outlook regarding the future course of development are considered.

Characteristics and History of the Region

The region, an area approximately 100,000 km² (40,000 mi²) consists of the southern portion of the Canadian Rocky Mountains and the Columbia Mountains (the Purcell, Monashee, Selkirk, and Cariboo ranges) to the west, together with the adjacent lowlands. It is divided politically between Alberta and British Columbia, with the national parks being administered by the federal government. It is relatively remote from population agglomerations and the centers of political and economic power: Victoria and Vancouver to the West, Edmonton and Calgary to the east, and Ottawa and Toronto in Canada's heartland. In spite of being separated by political boundaries, it exhibits a unity in that all parts of it are characterized by a resource-based economy, relative isolation, distance from the centers of political and economic power, and the attitudes of its inhabitants, most of whom prefer living in relatively remote and primitive natural surroundings.

The major tourist attraction is the awe-inspiring natural scene: numerous impressive peaks over 3,350 m (11,000 ft) in elevation, topped by snowfields and glaciers and drained by swift rivers. Lower elevations are covered with vast expanses of virtually impenetrable forest. The region provides a home for many species of animals, including both black and grizzly bears, moose, elk, and mountain sheep and goat. It contains seven national parks, numerous provincial parks and preserves, rivers for fishing, canoeing, and kayaking, public and private campgrounds, ski areas, guest ranches, hot springs, and mining districts, both active and defunct.

The population of the region is 223,864 (1981), and all the communities are quite small; of the 120 settlements, only one (Cranbrook) is over 10,000 population; five are between 5,000 and 10,000, and most are a few hundred. Over time, centers have grown or declined in size with the vagaries of the economic base—primarily mining, forestry, dam construction, and tourism.

From the earliest contact of Europeans with the indigenous people less than 200 years ago, the history of this region has been one of exploitation of its natural resources, primarily for the benefit of persons outside it. First came the fur trade, then mining, forestry, ranching, and hydroelectric development. Tourism began as early as 1862, when two Englishmen, Dr. W. Cheadle and Viscount Milton, undertook the first journey across Canada "for pleasure only." Today, the focus is turning increasingly to tourism, still for the benefit of outsiders (Kariel, Kariel 1984).

With the completion of the trans-continental Canadian Pacific Railway (CPR) in 1885, the company was eager to promote business. It constructed several hotels in the mountains and hired Swiss guides to conduct trips for hikers and mountaineers. In 1883 a Canadian Alpine Club (now the Alpine Club of Canada) held its inaugural meeting at Rogers Pass in the Selkirk Mountains. By 1890 visitors from the Swiss and English Alpine Clubs were comparing the Selkirks very favorably to the Swiss Alps. Tourism developments now include downhill, cross-country, and heli-skiing areas; developed hot springs; second homes; campgrounds and recreational vehicle parks; and other tourist attractions such as waterslides and small theme parks. Although they are dispersed throughout the region, most are located near settlements.

Current Tourism Development Proposals

The awarding of the 1988 Winter Olympic Games to Calgary is exerting new pressures for development on the entire region, especially the Eastern Slopes of the Rocky Mountains and Banff National Park. Many proposals related to tourism have been made; some are little more substantial than dreams, while others have good chances of becoming reality in the near future. Some proponents, either the government or private developers, perceive that the Games will make their projects financially feasible. Developments which have been selected for discussion are either associated with the 1988 Winter Olympic Games or give a general idea of the size and types of proposals which have been made. Most of the major ones are included; the list of smaller ones, some of which could expand, is very extensive.

Although most of the Olympic events will be held in Calgary, Kananaskis Country is the venue for the downhill and cross country and biathlon ski races; facilities for them should, therefore, be viewed within the context of other developments there and in the Canmore Corridor. Kananaskis Country, a provincially owned and managed year round, multiple use recreational area, which encompasses Peter Lougheed Provincial Park, was established in 1977 on the Eastern Slopes of the Rocky Mountains, adjacent to Banff National Park and about 90 km west of Calgary. Its 4,200 km² contain a variety of vegetation and many species of wildlife, and encompass a diversity of terrain which lends itself to many activities. The Alberta government has constructed three information centers, a spacious, comfortable, and impressive visitor center, a lodge for disabled persons, a world-class 36-hole golf course, a service center with gas station and store, a small store and fast-food restaurant, a privately operated recreational vehicle park, about 3,000 units at developed campgrounds, 75 day-use and picnic areas, an extensive network of bicycle, equestrian, and hiking trails, some of which are trackset for cross-country skiing, and designated areas for off-road vehicles in summer and winter (Kananskis Country n.d.) (Figure 18.1). Roughly $200 million will have been invested by the end of 1985, not counting $120 million for road upgrading and paving or services provided by other governmental agencies. Annual operating cost is the neighborhood of $10 million (Marshall 1985).

Before the current development, the area was accessible via a gravel and dirt road, and contained small-scale, low-key developments such as a modest downhill ski area, a youth hostel, a cabin subdivision, several relatively primitive campgrounds, and unimproved hiking trails. The

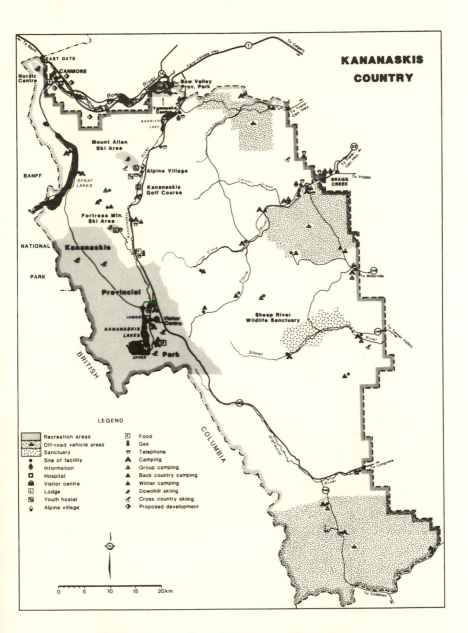

Figure 18.1   Alberta's Kananaskis Country

rather impressive and generally aesthetically pleasing developments have transformed a quiet, relatively undisturbed backwater to a more modern, busy, and urbanized recreation area.

There is a major concentration of facility-oriented recreation in and around the Ribbon Creek area. The Nakiska Ski Resort on Mount Allan is under construction, infrastructure for the Ribbon Creek Alpine Village, where construction of a large hotel is to begin soon, is largely in place, and the Kananaskis Golf Course has been in operation since 1984.

After a long, complex, and highly secret process, Mount Allan was selected by government decree as the most suitable of the sites considered for the downhill ski events, in spite of opposition by interests as diverse as downhill skiers, who claimed the course was inadequate and the snow conditions generally unfavorable, and environmentalists, who expressed concern about potential impacts on wildlife, especially a healthy herd of Rocky Mountain bighorn sheep. The government is now developing the resort, at an estimated cost of $25 million. The ski facilities, which will occupy 44% of the total area, include two triple and one double chair lift serving 30 major trails for all levels of skiers; snow making equipment for the entire area; two warming facilities, an emergency shelter, and a mid-mountain lodge serving food and beverages. At the base, there are access roads, parking, a day lodge with meeting rooms and storage space, employee housing, and cross-country trails connecting with the existing Kananaskis Country network. Temporary facilities for the Games will include additional toilets, bleachers for 30,000 spectators along the course, trailers for officials, extensive media facilities, and an additional lift for the start of the men's downhill races higher up on the mountain (Beck 1983; Geist 1983; Ski Action Alberta 1983; Landplan Group 1984).

Ribbon Creek Alpine village, adjacent to the Nakiska Ski Resort, will be a new development on a bench overlooking the Kananaskis River Valley. The focus is a large hotel with retail facilities, complemented by two smaller ones. When completed, the complex built around a "village green" will provide 250 units of rental accommodation, with a total of 1,000 pillows; 150 units of retail space; a conference center; underground parking; staff housing; and recreational facilities, including six tennis courts, an ice skating rink, a day lodge, and hiking and cross-country ski trails.

Although the province claims that a favorable market exists for both Nakiska Ski Resort and Ribbon Creek Alpine Village, private investors have yet to commit any money. The province had hoped that private developers would build the large hotel, to cost an estimated $30 million, but when no firm commitments had been made by mid-1985, decided to go ahead in order to have it completed by 1988. The government has made a major commitment to assist the private sector: infrastructure and surface parking costs will be borne by the province, while the underground parking will be cost-shared. Some environmental hazards, such as unstable slopes, poor snow conditions for cross-country skiing, hazardous winter driving conditions, flooding on the flood plain, danger from wildfire, and avalanche hazards, have been identified, but the province claims that they can be disregarded because they are not right at the proposed development site, and are the same as those in other mountainous areas such as Banff National Park (Alberta Tourism & Small Business 1981).

Developments In and Around Canmore

Canmore, with a population of about 4,000, is a former coal mining community located on the Trans-Canada Highway in the Bow Corridor, 105 km west of Calgary and 23 km east of Banff. Because of its attractive natural setting and the limitation on and cost of homes in Banff, it is serving increasingly as a home site for persons employed in Banff. It has been designated as the major service center for Kananaskis Country, and is looking increasingly to tourism as the major generator of income and employment. Since the closing of the mine in 1979 and major cutbacks in the nearby rock wool and cement plants, employment opportunities are limited. The overall plan for the area emphasizes growth and commercial development, especially through tourism. There is pressure to build an airport to bring tourists to Banff and Kananaskis Country. In addition to promoting the Nordic Center, Canmore backs tourism through a brochure and slide show, a new information center, and support of numerous development proposals.

The Cross Country Ski Center has been built at Georgetown, a former mining community on the west side of the Bow Valley just north of Canmore, in the shadow of Mount Rundle. Planned are a $3 million day lodge, a road to cost $15.4 million, and other facilities costing $12.9 million, all needed to meet Olympic technical requirements (Olympic Secretariat 1984). It is intended that these facilities will also provide long-term training, competition, and recreational opportunities, but some cross-country skiers feel that the course is too difficult and not scenically interesting enough to appeal to recreational skiers, and too far from major population centers for training racers.

The residential Cougar Creek subdivision on the northeast benchland, across the Trans-Canada Highway from Canmore, benefits from the scenic mountain setting without being affected by mountain shadow. Phase 1 (277 units) is currently under construction; judging from the information brochure, an additional half dozen phases may be possible. If all units were constructed, there would eventually be around 1,500 homes (Alberta Housing Corporation 1983).

The Echo proposal of the Patrician Land Corporation calls for the construction of five "amenity villages" on former Canmore Mines property along the Trans-Canada Highway, extending from the east boundary of Canmore for 11 km west towards the Pigeon Mountain area south into the Wind Valley. Containing a mix of year around homes, vacation condominiums, and associated retail and recreational facilities, it is presently on hold, but may well proceed if and when the economic climate improves (Inntrec 1981, 1982).

Several other proposals, such as Village in the Pines, a condominium-style vacation home development, have also been put forward, but perhaps the most grandiose is the Mount Star Resort, a $1 billion international-class resort complex, which has been proposed for the northeast benches. It would contain three luxury hotels with a total of 1,500 beds, restaurants, bars, and a European-style casino. Subsidiary facilities include a 100-store shopping mall and entertainment complex, a historical park, and a railway station and bus depot for tour operators, as well as a cluster of "small alpine villages" with boutiques, inns, bed-and-breakfast accommodations, and apartments (Dobbin-Cochrane Group 1985).

Other Developments

The Columbia and Kootenay river valleys south of Radium Hot Springs contain numerous provincial parks and private campgrounds. Natural attractions include Radium and Fairmont Hot Springs and Columbia and Windermere lakes. Arterial highways provide good access from urban centers in Alberta, British Columbia, and Washington; the regional airport serves both Kimberly and Cranbrook. A number of resorts and communities are planning major expansion, and some new developments are proposed.

Panorama, located up Toby Creek, is primarily a ski resort, with condominiums and second homes; it also serves as a base for a heli-skiing operation. Further development proposals envision a year-round destination resort with a convention center for 250–300 persons in a 100-room hotel, and facilities for sports such as tennis and trail riding. A $3 million expansion of the snow-making equipment will extend the ski season. Three phases are envisioned, with a final total of 11,000 beds. The first will see the building of commercial and retail attractions, along with additional condominiums, hotel rooms, and single-family units. The second will be primarily residential, while the third will involve expansion of all types of facilities. This expansion offers a promise of jobs for valley residents, in spite of constraints such as limited space on the valley floor and shortage of water. Other environmental impacts have not been fully determined (Mayfair Place 1980).

Fairmont Hot Springs Resort is a year-round family recreation area with a 132-room lodge and cabins, a serviced campground, single-family residential lots, and cluster condominiums. Recreational attractions include four outdoor hot pools, tennis courts, riding stables, an 18-hole golf course, a ski hill with a day lodge, hiking and cross-country ski trails, and hang gliding. Future expansion plans will help the local economy by increasing employment opportunities and improving the tax base. The first phase includes an upgraded sewage disposal system and an expanded commercial area with community services, residential housing, including a mobile home park and villas, a small artificial lake, and expansion of the lodge. The second will add a 27-hole golf course, tennis courts, two clubhouses, and low- and medium-density housing for about 4,000 people. The third will have a low-density subdivision, another clubhouse and an 18-hole golf course, a marina and beach, an additional chair lift, and a new day lodge (Mercon 1980).

The proposed Jumbo Glacier Ski Area would provide for year-round glacier skiing as well as offering seasonal facilities in a bowl below it. It includes a staging area, with an access lift to the 2,840 m level, from which other lifts would lead to the ski trails. A summit house, consisting of a restaurant, viewing platform, ski shop, and gift shop, would be constructed. Natural hazards which have been identified include crevasses, a bergschrund, and rockfall. The proponents suggest that these can be mitigated by filling in the crevasses with snow (!) and erecting netting and fences to keep skiers away from other hazards. Avalanche control and clearing of the access road may pose some problems. The access road is used by heavy trucks much of the year (Ecosign 1983).

Second home developments are scattered throughout the region. There were very few before 1949, and about half have been constructed since 1973. Over the years there has been a change from single-family dwellings to resort condominium complexes, some of which are time-sharing. The greatest concentration is in the Windermere-Columbia Lakes area. In 1979 there were 1,066 lots around Windermere Lake, 788 of which were fully developed. Ninety-three percent of the owners were Calgary and district residents (Mackintosh 1979). Since then, more of the lots have been built on, and there appears to be pressure for at least a fivefold increase.

Other areas of second home development in British Columbia include Christina Lake, Moyie Lake and Lake Koocanusa, the area around Golden, as well as the Arrow, Slocan, Shuswap, and Kootenay lakes. In Alberta, the Ghost River, Kananaskis Lakes, and Canmore corridor contain some second homes; there is little land available for additional developments unless the government decides to sell or lease additional Crown land.

Also in Alberta, the Westcastle ski hill, a small but challenging ski area about 50 km southwest of Pincher Creek, used primarily by local residents, may become a major four-season resort if proposed expansion plans materialize. These envision an alpine village, condominium units, nine new ski lifts, and extensive snowmaking equipment. Summer facilities include an 18-hole golf course. This expansion is advocated despite the conclusions of a 1975 Alberta Business Development and Tourism Department evaluation: "It is highly improbable that any amount of additional capital investment will allow the ski area to operate at a profit." The possible sale of 648 hectares (1,600 acres) and lease of an adjacent 2,833 hectares (7,000 acres) of Crown land is expected to buoy up the project's viability. In addition, the province is willing to provide technical assistance and some infrastructure improvements (Lamb 1984; Pharis 1985).

The Odyssey Resort proposal, dating from the late 1960s, envisaged a four-season resort located 193 km west of Red Deer on the David Thompson Highway, near the Kootenay Plains. The plan called for a luxury hotel complex, complete with an 18-hole golf course and clubhouse, recreation building for tennis courts, swimming pool, racquetball and squash courts, cinema, dancing and exercise areas and the like, as well as staff housing and utility buildings. VIP suites would help to provide an overall market appeal. The long history of criticism and controversy revolved around such issues as siting of the resort adjacent to, and the possibility of expansion into, the Prime Protection Zone of the Eastern Slopes, where such a development is not allowed; outstanding native land claims, since the Kootenay Plains is a traditional sacred spot; the accuracy and thoroughness of the draft Environmental Impact Assessment; the failure of the government to hold public hearings in spite of the insistence of local residents and environmental groups; and the generally supportive position taken by the provincial government (Chomyn 1985). On 11 March 1986, the Provincial Government precipitately and without explanation canceled the development lease.

Political Context

In order to place this region's resource and land-use planning and management within the appropriate context, it is helpful to understand how the decision-making process works within the Canadian political framework (Dickerson, Flanagan 1982; Young, Morley 1983).

First and foremost is the centralization of power associated with the "responsible" government of the British parliamentary system. This is derived from the monarchy, which developed gradually from absolutism to democracy, while retaining many of the earlier characteristics. Essentially, the virtually absolute power of the king was delegated to the group of ministers called the Cabinet. While in power, the government is expected to formulate policy and to make decisions; at election time the people are given the opportunity to pass on these decisions, either renewing the government's mandate or electing a new government. Within this governmental structure there is no formal provision for public participation other than this periodic "yes" or "no." The role of the federal parliament or provincial legislature is to endorse decisions already made by the government; because of the tradition of party solidarity, Members of Parliament or representatives to provincial legislative bodies belonging to the party in power simply endorse decisions already made by Cabinet, while members of the opposition usually vote against whatever legislation the government has proposed. Thus, as long as the party in power has majority, legislation will automatically pass.

In addition, many Cabinet decisions are formalized by an Order-in-Council. Such important matters as establishing a new provincial park or drastically reducing the size of an existing one may be settled in this way, virtually overnight, without prior notice to anyone outside the inner Cabinet. The public often does not know what is taking place or why until after the event. This system, in turn, leads the public to feel powerless; there is a public deference to authority, and most complaining is done privately rather than by taking action such as writing letters to members of the government.

Second, it must be emphasized that laws relating to planning and management are generally permissive rather than mandatory; thus, even when a law is in place, the minister responsible for the department to which it pertains is not required to follow it. Most laws read something like "The Minister may, at his discretion . . ." This discretionary power is an essential characteristic of the parliamentary system.

In contrast, the United States Constitution was carefully designed to avoid some of the excesses of the British absolute monarchy. The government was based on the concept of separation of powers, and a system of checks and balances was included so that no one arm of the government—executive, legislative, or judicial—could function alone. The executive has only indirect power to influence legislation, and the judiciary has the power to review both legislation and its implementation by the executive.

Another major difference between the Canadian and United States systems of government is the role of policy and the way in which, once established, it is carried out. Cullingworth (1984) explains that in Canada,

> Policy is not "applied"; it is "interpreted" in the light of the circumstances of particular cases (and in the context of time.) In interpreting policy and the situation to which it relates, policy is given meaning. Indeed it has no reality other than this.

An important factor affecting land use planning is the more powerful role of the Canadian provinces in relation to the federal government, as compared with the United States. The provinces have virtually complete control over their own natural resources, including public (Crown) lands and forests. The province takes the lead role in land use planning, delegating certain powers, under very controlled conditions, to local municipalities and planning districts. When provincial government policy changes, the government in power (meaning essentially the premier and inner Cabinet) can take such actions as taking direct control of planning, abolishing existing regional plans, and depriving planning districts of virtually all their power. Thus it can authorize a new development anywhere at any time, with no public input regardless of the wishes of the local governments or populace, and without having to consider environmental impacts.

Governmental Policies Regarding Tourism

The move towards environmental protection of the late 1960s and 1970s gave way in the 1980s to a strong pro-development stance on the part of all three governments responsible for the region's land. When recession quickly quelled the booming economy, tourism was looked upon as a quick cure. The federal government has cooperated with both provinces to develop new tourism strategies, expanding programs already in place and creating new ones. A government-industry development strategy has been proposed to ". . . identify profit opportunities in the marketplace and assist the private sector to develop facilities to take advantage of those opportunities—again, with one goal in mind—profit" (Lowey 1985).

Planning for the National Parks

Tourism in the Canadian national parks has increased nearly 50-fold over the past 40–50 years, bringing with it continual pressure for increased access and facilities. Banff National Park, the first in the present national park system in Canada, was established primarily to attract tourists rather than with any idea of environmental preservation. Only later did this concept creep in, and even after it was included in the 1930 National Parks Act, there was no clear understanding as to its implications, nor any policy for implementing it. Consequently, recreation dominated national parks management, and Banff and other townsites grew with almost no control (Bryan 1973). The 1964 National Park Policy attempted to correct this, stating, ". . . our obligation to protect the areas against impairment implies not only protection against private exploitation, but also guarding against impairment by overuse, improper use and inappropriate development" (Dept. of Indian Affairs and Northern Development 1969).

The commitment to environmental preservation and protection from exploitation has remained largely a paper one, despite a burst of enthusiasm during the 1970s, which in 1979 resulted in the current policy supporting this position. At that time, consideration was given to removing structures from the back country and managing much of it as true wilderness. Nevertheless, the front country, along the Trans-Canada highway, continued to blossom with new developments, especially in the townsites of Banff, Lake Louise, and Jasper.

In the early 1980s Parks Canada sought to deal with this increase by initiating the Four Mountain Parks Planning Program, the objective of which was to formulate a master plan that would determine the future of the four contiguous mountain national parks. A strong public participation program was included. Initially the public, including the environmental groups, participated hopefully and in good faith, but events along the way raised the fundamental question of Parks Canada's willingness to listen to and act upon public opinion. Following preliminary public meetings in 1982 and 1983, three management alternatives were drafted; they were presented to the public at open House sessions in June 1984 (Parks Canada 1984).

Option A, although allowing some development, was the most preservationist, favoring a limited response to visitor and recreation demands, and restricting new developments in both front and back country. Option B acceded to increased demand to a limited extent, allowing for some growth of services and facilities, along with increased ease of access; it most closely represents the existing management approach.

Under Option C the role of the four mountain parks as national and international tourist destinations would be actively encouraged by expanding existing facilities and providing new ones, in both the front and back country. It allowed for a 50% increase in tourist accommodation in the town of Banff, and 35% in Jasper, with expansion of town boundaries. Backcountry access would be made easier with new and upgraded roads, improved trails, more accommodations in commercial lodges and alpine shelters, and individual and group campsites, corresponding with a decreased priority on providing wildland opportunities. Numerous ideas have surfaced from time to time, some of which have received serious study; these include a monorail into the Tonquin Valley, now a favorite destination for fishermen, climbers, hikers and skiers; a funicular to the northeast ridge of Snow Dome, in the Columbia Icefields area; and a hostel style hotel at Lake O'Hara.

The public responded to these options with 3334 oral and written comments. Over half (52%) favored Option A, 32% Option B, and 16% Option C (Parks Canada 1985). The planning process seemed to be progressing satisfactorily until October 1984, when it was learned that prior to completion of public consultation, Parks Canada's steering committee for this program had drawn up a preliminary draft report recommending policies from Option C, a marketing management framework had been prepared, and some officials suggested that certain controversial items be removed from the plan (Patton 1985).

Not long afterwards, Suzanne Blais-Grenier, then Federal Environment Minister, promised to review any and all proposals for developments in the national parks, including those for resource extraction, long since phased out. So great was the public outcry that she soon retracted some of these statements, claiming she had been misunderstood and misquoted.

In trying to come to grips with Parks Canada's planning and policy formulations, it is difficult to know how seriously to take them, as they are written loosely and are subject to interpretation. Differences in perception and interpretation can be called upon to account for any discrepancies between what is stated and what is "ground truth." On the basis of what is actually happening over the long run, however, one can infer that the philosophy of Option C predominates, and that any heritage protection or environmental preservation receives a low priority.

Alberta's Tourism Planning

The Alberta government has expressed its intention to promote tourism by increasing visitation, length of stay, and visitor expenditures, and will help to fund projects which may require major amounts of public funds. This commitment is reflected in the activities of Tourism Alberta, Travel Alberta, a cost-sharing agreement for tourism development reached with the federal Department of Regional Industrial Expansion (DRIE), the *Tourism 2000* draft document (Alberta, Tourism and Small Business n.d.), and *A Policy for Resource Management of the Eastern Slopes, Revised 1984* (Alberta, Energy and Natural Resources 1984).

The original 1977 Eastern Slopes policy, developed after extensive public hearings, reflected the then-prevalent philosophy of environmental protection, giving primacy to watershed protection, and encouraging non-renewable resource development only where it did not conflict with the long-term goals of renewable resource management, observing the principles of conservation and environmental protection. Zoning was adopted to provide for compatibility of resource utilization within each zone, ranging from prime protection, where no development was permitted, to industrial and multiple use zones, where various resource extraction activities were the major features (Alberta, Energy and Natural Resources 1977).

The revised Eastern Slopes policy, developed with no public contribution, contained many changes. In the preface, Don Sparrow, Associate Minister for Lands and Forests, stated that the changes were considered necessary because of the realities of the economic situation. He pointed ut that the policy is sufficiently flexible that all future proposals for land se and development may be considered, and that zoning may be altered o permit developments which might not otherwise be allowed in a zone. Uses which would be permitted in specific zones were changed; for example, serviced camping, off-highway vehicles, and logging, formerly anned in the prime protection zone, may now be permitted; and serviced camping, mineral exploration and development, commercial development, and intensive recreation may be allowed in the critical wildlife zone. Water quality and the maintenance of natural stream flows are no onger considered priorities. The Integrated Management Plans for subregions have been made to conform with the new policy directions.

The transfer of Crown land to permit private ownership of recreational developments such as second homes and ski areas was also suggested; his is now starting to occur, even though the new policy regarding land ransfer is still officially in a draft stage. The lead article in the Summer/ Fall 1985 issue of *Landmark*, published by the Alberta Mortgage and Housing Commission, stated that developers would be able to buy, rather han lease Crown land under certain conditions (Bliss 1985).

Tourism Planning in British Columbia

A similar pro-tourism climate exists in British Columbia. In 1978 the provincial government entered into a cost-sharing agreement with DRIE, he Travel Industry Development Subsidiary Agreement (TIDSA), which s intended to serve as the catalyst for major tourism developments by providing master planning and capital cost assistance for key summer and winter resort developments. With this assistance, municipal governments and private investors were given the impetus for constructing hotels, restaurants, condominiums, and summer and winter sports facilities at an unprecedented rate. In the words of *British Columbia Mountain Resorts*, 'TIDSA investment in the ski industry has helped to make skiing in that province an international winner!'' (British Columbia n.d.) Since then, 1983 changes in the Municipal Act removing statutory Regional Planning power from Regional Districts and canceling all existing Regional Plans have given the government more control over developments throughout he province.

Conclusion

The cumulative impacts of the myriad development proposals, several of which were highlighted above, along with the pro-development stance of provincial and federal decision makers, is overwhelming. Many questions may be asked about what would happen if all were to become reality: how the landscape would be transformed, and how society would be affected, especially the local residents. One would also question what the role of government, environmentalists, and the average citizen should be. The underlying questions are, how much development is too much and what are the acceptable limits of change?

As long as individual development projects are perceived as being profitable, either alone or with government support, and landscape aesthetics and other environmental concerns are given little attention, there would appear to be no limits. The essentially technocentric value system held by most citizens supports this point of view. Examples from other parts of the world, such as the European Alps, provide ample evidence for this contention (Brugger 1984). On the other hand, if a desire for change exists, either because not all proposals are economically viable or because the costs of a few large ones are too high for the electorate to stomach, and alterations of the landscape are perceived to have transgressed acceptable limits, then the philosophical climate could shift towards an ecocentric mode, and change facilitated.

In a few cases, when enough people perceived that a problem existed and were willing to act, changes were brought about. In 1972, the overwhelming negative responses to a major development at Lake Louise led to its defeat, and in 1977 a coalition of environmental groups was successful in getting the government to adopt a low-growth option for the area. ALERT, a group centered in the small foothills community of Rocky Mountain House, was successful in its fight against the Odyssey project. The Valhalla Provincial Park in British Columbia was established to preserve the area from logging, after a long fight by local residents, backed by environmental groups. There are similar examples in the Alps: Obergurgl, Austria, and Silvaplana, Switzerland, have defined limits to growth, and the Austrian, German, and Swiss Alpine Clubs have moved from their former unqualified pro-tourism stance to one supporting "soft tourism paths" (Haszlacher 1984).

If the attempt to limit or control growth is to succeed, its proponents need to recognize how decisions are made within the political system and to use it rather than being used by it, applying constant pressure on politicians. The tourism industry is already making use of these techniques. The idea of multiple problems/multiple solutions, as opposed to a single problem/single solution needs to be pursued in terms of which areas should be protected and which developed, and whether development should be concentrated or dispersed.

Acknowledgments

Appreciation and thanks to Patricia E. Kariel for typing and editorial assistance.

19

Oases of the Karakorum

Evolution of Irrigation and Social Organization in Hunza, North Pakistan

Hermann J. Kreutzmann

Introduction

Irrigation systems have been the subject of cultural-geographical high mountain research nearly exclusively in the European Alps and especially in the Wallis canton of Switzerland (Chavan 1915; Lehmann 1913; Marietan 1948; Netting 1974; Rauchenstein 1908). In subtropical high mountain regions like the Himalaya Hindukush and Karakorum, studies mostly concentrated on the land use in different vegetation belts, *Höhengrenzen*, which were based on the geo-ecological zonation model of Troll (supra).

Only a few case studies were concerned with the exploitation of meltwaters for the irrigation of land in the desert steppes-zones and their cultural-geographical implications (Groetzbach 1969, 1972).

Researchers paid little attention to irrigation systems in the arid trans-Himalaya areas of Pakistan, which are not affected by the seasonal monsoon rains and where agriculture is only possible with irrigation. Other areas of Pakistan with the densest network of irrigation channels in the world—mainly concentrated in the Indus basin—are studied much more thoroughly and are well documented (Michel 1967; Scholz 1984).

Recently Mueller-Stellrecht (1978, 1980) published ethnographical material of D. L. R. Lorimer, a British colonial officer who collected valuable information between 1920 and 1935 about the valleys of Gilgit District (former Gilgit Agency) of the northern frontier of British India. They also contain the first details on the irrigation system found there. Charles's (1985) thesis concentrates mainly on the physical aspects of the relationship between man and glacier and on the use of meltwaters for irrigation.

Irrigation systems are treated preferably as static elements of high mountain societies for two reasons: on the one hand there is little source material available except in the best-studied European Alps and Pyrenees, and, second, their own dynamics as a reflection of the societal development are neglected.

In the mountainous Wallis canton of Switzerland where the yearly precipitation is 600 mm, irrigation is used as a supplement, whereas in arid regions like the Karakorum valley, agricultural activities depend totally on irrigation. The limitations of resource use are, besides water supply, cultivable land, manpower, and technical skills.

Of these factors only the construction, control, and maintenance of irrigation systems require a cooperative effort, while the others depend on individual initiative. The irrigation system of a given area and connected rights and duties, therefore, are taken as an object for study, in which the commercial management of communal water resources is regarded as an indicator for changes in a mountain society. The case study discussed herein was undertaken in the Valley of Hunza in the Northern Areas of Pakistan, the former Gilgit Agency of British India.

The Study Area

The Hunza Valley (Fig. 19.1) in the Karakorum belongs, according to Troll's Himalaya Classification (1967), to the dry, irrigated agriculture-dependent Indus-Himalaya, which is the westernmost part in this latitudinal classification.

Groetzbach (1982:15-16) characterizes the high mountain type Karakorum among others by the following criteria: overpopulation caused by century-long remoteness, which resulted in total exploitation of the different ecological zones; mixed agrarian and livestock economy; horticulture; subsistence agriculture, which does not produce the requirements of basic food items; non-agrarian job opportunities and out-migration.

The former principality of Hunza borders in the north upon the Afghan Wakhan Corridor, the Chinese Autonomous Province of Xinjiang, in the West upon Ishkoman, in the south and east upon Nager and Baltistan.

The territory of Hunza comprises 7900 square kilometers; out of this only 90 square kilometers form the area of permanent settlement (Mueller-Stellrecht 1978:1). In 1931, 13,500 lived in these irrigated oases and by 1985 they had 30,300 inhabitants, who consist of the ethnic groups of Shina, Burushaski, and Wakhi speakers (Census of India 1931; Jettmar 1973; Mueller-Stellrecht 1978; Lorimer 1938, vol. I). The Hunza River, a tributary to the Indus via the Gilgit river, breaks through the main ridge of the Karakorum. The riverbed is cut into the Pleistocene terraces in the form of a canyon with 100 m high walls, which makes it unfeasible to use these waters for irrigation. Low precipitation in the valley stations (Gilgit,

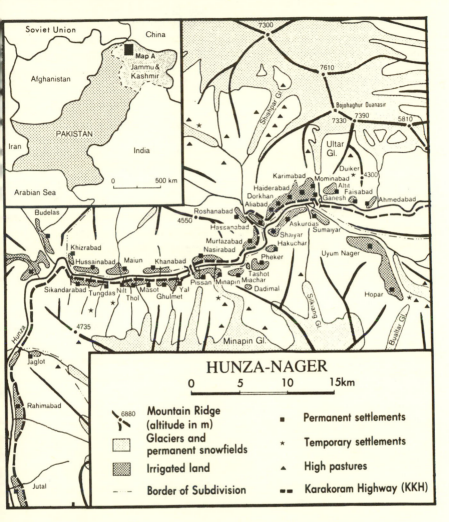

Figure 19.1   The Hunza Valley in North Pakistan

1488 m, 134 mm; Karimabad, 2300 m, 138 mm; Misgar, 3100 m, 100 mm)
gives no explanation for the enormous glaciation of the Karakorum with
28 to 48 percent ice-cover of its total surface. This is the highest outside
the Polar regions.

    The only reason for this phenomenon is a rapid increase in precipitation
with altitude, which was estimated as high as 2000 mm/yr. (Haserodt
1984:159; Schneider 1959; Paffen, Pillewizer Schneider 1956; Flohn 1969;
Batura Investigation Group 1979). This huge amount of water of the nival
zone plays the important role for irrigation purposes as meltwater during

the vegetation period. It is collected in gravity-fed leats and transported to the oases of the desert steppes and *Artemisia* steppes (Fig. 19.2). Haserodt (1984:132) gives the ratio of maximum to minimum flow of Hunza riverwater as 68:1, which demonstrates the variability of water availability.

Origin and Development of Hunza Irrigation systems

According to Barth (1956) and Staley (1969) there are, in northern Pakistan, two main distinctions between the different valley societies. Originally, independent and isolated principalities formed the political systems of this area. The principalities of the contemporary Swat and Indus Kohestan were conquered after the fifteenth century by invading Pashtuns (Pathans) from Afghanistan. They introduced their own acephalous society into these regions that were called republics in colonial times.

Hunza belongs to the principality-type. Staley attributes to the principalities intensified agriculture, sophisticated irrigation systems and total exploitation of the ecological zones. A higher level of cultivation distinguishes them from the republics, which are preoccupied with internal blood feuds and choose a common leader only in times of external threat. Agricultural undertakings are permitted only after communal consent is reached in a communal meeting (*jirga*), in which every participant has a right of veto. This proviso hampers communal activities.

The principalities used forced labor (Burushaski-*rajaki*) for land intensification. The rulers of Hunza, called Tham or Mir, and their prime ministers, Wazirs, became famous as hydraulic engineers to the whole

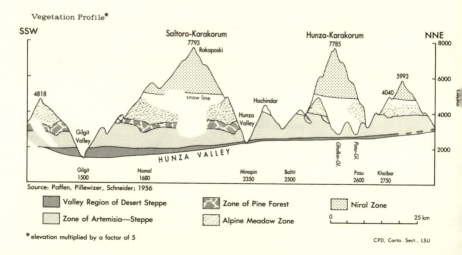

Figure 19.2   Troll's Biogeographical Classification of the Hunza Valley

region at the beginning of the nineteenth century. At this time, Tham Silum Khan III (1790–1824) returned from exile in neighboring Badakhshan with new techniques of leat construction which he introduced in Hunza.

Thus far Hunza had consisted of three nuclear settlements: Baltit (since 1983 Karimabad) Altit, and Ganesh, which were supplied with water by three leats named Balti-ill, Altitghotsil, and Hamachi. The increasing population pressure, on the available irrigated land was caused by increased wealth from raids on silk route caravans and slavetrading with Badakhshan. This pressure forced an exodus out of the fortified village (*Khan*) which had formed the dominant feature of settlement in this region.

During the reign of Tham Silum Khan III the completion of the Samarkand leat made water available for three new settlements, Haiderabad, Dorkhan, and Aliabad.

The construction of the new leat *(dala)* (Fig. 19.3, Table 19.1) included a

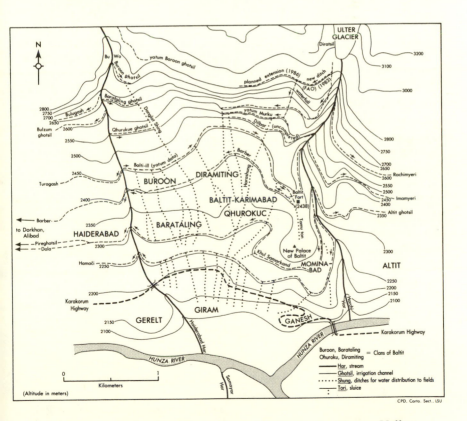

Figure 19.3   Irrigation Channels and Leats in the Hunza Valley

Table 19.1   Builder and Time of Construction of Hunza Irrigation Channels

Period	Institution	Engineer	Channel
—	—	—	Balti-ill
—	—	—	Hamači
—	—	—	Altitghotsil
1790–1824	Silum Khan III	Puno	Dala, Misgar, Ghujal
1824–1865	Shah Ghazanfar	Asadullah Beg	Barber, Murku
1865–1886	Shah Ghazan Khan	Asadullah Beg	Murtazabad, Khudabad
1886–1891	Safdar Ali	—	—
1892-1938	Muhammad Nazim Khan	Humayun Beg	Shishket, Sost, Alabad, Khanabad, Khizrabad, Reminj
		Shukrullah Beg	Oshikandas, Matum Das
		Zara	Danyor
1938–1945	Ghazan Khan	—	—
1945–1974	Famal Khan	Sajidullah Beg	Famalabad, Dilbar (uncompleted)
1982–	AKRSP-V.O.	Hussain Wali Khan	31 channel projects in different villages of Hunza (including widening and extension)

code for the distribution of the Ultar glacier waters: one share of the Ultar water is allocated to Altit village, one to Ganesh, and two to the new settlements *(thuankhanan).* The Bululo meltwater distribution cycle is 10 days for Baltit and 6 days for Haiderabad (the latter first set at 5 days) (Table 19.1).

After having provided the local Burushaski-speaking people with the fundamental installation for cultivating land, the Tham of Hunza extended his territory up to the headwaters of the Hunza River by expelling Kirghiz nomads and establishing a khan and irrigation leat in Misgar as the northernmost outpost of his territory. Wahki-speaking immigrants from the Wakhan Corridor were allowed to settle in the region of Ghujal by becoming dependents of the rulers of Hunza, who had built irrigation leats for their new settlements.

The successors of Silum Khan III expanded the irrigation network in central Hunza. An able wazir, Asadullah Beg, was responsible for the construction of the Barber and Murku leats. Only members of the Diramiting clan, to which the Wazirs belong, are eligible for the Murku irrigation waters. Also constructed at the same time were the irrigation leats for the new settlements of Murtazabad and Khanabad.

The Hunza military campaign of 1891 brought Hunza under British

Indian rule. A new Tham, Muhammad Nazim Klan, was installed, and, backed by the British Indian government, he exercised unlimited power in Hunza. During his reign (1892–1938) the strategy of creating settlements changed. In his early years the ruler continued the policy of his predecessors by developing land through leat construction in Shishket (now Nazimabad), Sost, Atabad, Khanabad, Hussainabad and Reminj. Migration was strictly prohibited and strict control of the borders enforced.

In 1917 with the grant of a tax-free gift of land in Rahimabad (Matum Das) by the Maharaja of Kashmir to the Mir, M. Nazim Khan, the construction of leats in Danyor and Oshikandas near Gilgit town allowed for the migration of Hunza settlers to the new settlements (Hassnain 1978:116–118; Snoy 1975:30–31). Several other Hunza colonies sprang up in the low-lying Gilgit and Ishkoman valleys. With the exception of the Jamalabad, near Morkhon, and the Dilbar leat in Baltit that was never completed during the time of Mir Jamal Khan (1945-1974), land extension and development in the Hunza Valley came to an end.

The Bhutto administration in Pakistan deposed the rulers of most of the principalities in 1972; however, the reign of the Mir of Hunza ended in 1974 because he was *de jure* representative of the Aga Khan, the spiritual leader of Ismaili Muslims, the dominant sect in Hunza. Bhutto sought counsel with the Aga Khan prior to any unilateral decision about the status of the Hunza princely chief. After the Mirs were removed a power vacuum occurred as the traditional institution for undertaking communal projects was not replaced by an adequate substitute.

It was only after the completion of the Karakorum Highway in 1978 that development agencies appeared in the Northern Areas. The Community Basic Services Programme of the Local Bodies and Rural Development Division was a service of the Pakistan government. A self-help "Drills and Dynamite Programme" of the Integrated Rural Development Project of UNDP/FAO provided technical support for repair and extension of irrigation leats to the villages. The most extensive development project in the Northern Areas, however, is the Aga Khan Rural Support Programme (AKRSP), which has operated since 1982. It developed a strategy to fill the above mentioned power vacuum by establishing cooperative Village Organizations (V.O.), representing whole village communities and distributing equal parcels of land to every household participating in land development. This program continues the tradition of channel building and furthers exploitation of unirrigated local barren land for the first time since the regime of Mir Muhammad Nazin Khan.

Out of 47 projects that are under way in Hunza tehsil, 31 are channel projects that either widen or extend current facilities. Financial expenditures total Rs 5.6 million. In the program area of the Gilgit District, leat construction accounts for 54 percent of the physical infrastructure budget

(AKRSP 1985). The revival of an uncompleted Aliabad channel fed from the Hassanabad glacier is part of the present scheme. If this proves successful, by 1986 the whole system of water distribution for central Hunza will have been changed.

Organization of Irrigation Facilities

As mentioned above, the owners of the oldest irrigation leats of central Hunza (Altitghotsil, Hamachi, Dala) have preferential water rights (Table 19.2). When these leats have been filled—normally around 21st June—the excess meltwater of the Ultar glacier is available for the other leats that are sequenced by time of their construction.

Consequently, double-cropping is possible only in the distribution area of the older leats, because they get water during the whole season of cultivation. The later developed lands are used mainly for orchards, meadows, and timber production and stand out against the lower areas of grain fields by having the older leats as their boundaries.

Hunza Irrigation Systems

A closer examination of the irrigation system shows a complex structure of water allocation. For example, there are special rights for the use of the Murku leats. Only the clan of the Diramiting, to whom the Wazirs as the hydraulic engineers belong, is eligible for Diratsil spring water. The water rights for Balti-ill were later divided between Baltit and Haiderabad. In both settlements the four clans of Baltit (Diramiting, Buroon, Qhurokutz, Barataling) live together; Haiderabad was populated by relatives of the people of Baltit and therefore exhibits the same clan structure. The four clans also share the snowmelt water of Bululo, which is distributed according to a complicated code. Contrary to Wallis canton in Switzerland, where there is a written schedule on wooden boards, in Hunza the code is passed on orally and is well known to everybody concerned. The four clans of Baltit take turns in their 10 days allocation of water comprising 2 days and 3 nights, and 3 days and 2 nights, sequentially. Each clan itself divides the water among the members.

Villages with relatively sufficient water, such as Altit and Ganesh, limit their organization of irrigation allocations to an annual lottery. By using this method, water allocations are made daily, instead of longer periods. On the other hand, in villages with meager supplies of water, like Baltit, there is a highly sophisticated system of water distribution to assure a just participation of every clan. Annually, they change the sequence of clans and the order of irrigation from west to east, from higher to lower fields, not by chance but through a system taking several years to complete full circle.

Table 19.2   Irrigation Facilities of Central Hunza

Channel	Year	Area	Water Rights	Number of Supervisors
Hamachi	—	Ganesh	1/4 of Ulter-Glacier meltwater	2
Altit ghotsil	—	Altit	1/4 of Ulter-Glacier meltwater	2
Balti-ill	—	Baltit, Haiderabad	10 days Baltit/6 days Haiderabad from Bululo Snowmelt water	1
Dala	1820	Haiderabad Dorkhan	1/2 day of Ulter-Glacier meltwater, 1 day Haiderabad, 9 days Aliabad (Dorkhan)	4
Barber	1824–65	Baltit-Aliabad	Only excess water from Ulter-Glacier in summer only daytime: Baltit; nighttime: Haiderabad-Aliabad	2
Murku	1824–65	Diramiting of Baltit	Spring and snow meltwater from Diratsil only for Diramiting	1
Imamyeri	1938–42	Altit	Excess water from Ulter-Glacier after filling of Barber in summer only	1
Dilbar	1958	Baltit	uncompleted	—
Rahim yeri	1973	Altit	Excess water from Ulter-Glacier after filling of Barber in summer only	1
Yatum Murku	1983	Diramiting of Baltit	Spring and snowmelt water from Dirabil only for Diramiting	1
Aliabad ghotsil	1986	Haiderabad-Aliabad	not yet decided	—

To sustain this complicated system a high degree of control is necessary: Supervisors (*yatkuin*) are appointed for each leat (Table 19.2) to maintain the irrigation canal headworks, to distribute shares equally , and to prevent leat disintegration. Second, the village communities entrust several representatives with the task of conveying the irrigation waters via steep connecting minor leats (*shung*) and sluices (*tori*) to the plots. They also have to inform the individual farmers about their time-table.

But in this case, time is not the criterion for distribution. One allocation is finished only when the parcel of land has sufficient water. As the amount of water available fluctuates with the seasons, water supply—not sequential timing—determines duration of allocation. Additionally, village communities monitor one another during water periods. For example, on the Barber leat every night during summertime, representatives of Haiderabad and Aliabad sleep next to the *tul* sluices that are used for the irrigation of Baltit fields and try to prevent people from stealing water. Watertheft is punished with the payment of a goat or a certain amount of money to the affected community. The irrigation supervisors organize the repair, maintenance, and clearing of the irrigation systems and are paid with grain (2 kg of wheat per household) at the end of the growing season. Each year these functionaries are elected in a village meeting.

During spring and autumn, seasons of extreme water shortage, village communities and their clans have to observe special regulations of irrigation. Each cycle of irrigation has its own name in the Burushaski language and permits the farmers to water certain crops: for example, in the beginning of spring only winter-sown wheat is watered. In the second phase, summer-sown barley, potatoes, and vegetables, the major food crops, get preference over orchards and grass and timber-plots. Disobeying these rules leads to punishment. The majority of cases that are brought to the attention of the religious Ismaili courts are water disputes. The shortage of water at the beginning of the growing season results in an extremely long cycle of first watering. It takes up to six weeks before each farmer has a chance to irrigate his wheat crop. This long period can delay and disturb the process of ripening of the first crops until second crops cannot be sown on time. A late wheat and barley harvest makes it impossible to grow maize and millets (*setaria, panicum*) as second crops. Only the inferior buckwheat (*fagopyrum tartaricum*) can ripen, provided there is sufficient sunshine until October. In a cold year, the second crops are adequate only for livestock fodder and do not add to the necessary amount of bread grain.

Problems of Irrigation

Irrigation in other valleys of the Karakorum faces the same uncertainties. Advancing and retreating glaciers often destroy the headworks of irrigation channels and cut off the essential water supply. The valleys southwest of the main ridge of the Karakorum depend solely on avalanche-fed glaciers without extended catchment areas, which respond sensitively to minor snowfall in winter and contribute to the overall uncertainty. Besides these physical aspects of constraints for irrigation, recent developments have changed the agricultural situation. An increasing population, division of inherited land, and reduced areas for new cultivation make subsistence farming impossible or at least difficult. Few households rely on agriculture alone. Because the average landholding per household is one hectare in Central Hunza (Saunders 1983:71–110) and a household membership is approximately seven, the importance of other sources of income is increasing.

Improved roads accessible by jeep, and especially through the opening of the Karakorum Highway, which linked the Punjab with China in 1978, permits easier out-migration and additional sources of income in government, transportation, tourism, and construction.

Despite the attraction of non-agrarian job opportunities, the intensity of irrigated cultivation did not decrease. The local agriculture still provides a significant portion of basic food items, but it has to cope with less manpower. As more and more children attend schools instead of herding cattle, as able-bodied men seek their fortune in the plains of Pakistan and abroad (principally in the Gulf States), the extra workload is a burden on the remaining men and women of the joint-families. This changing situation is rarely considered by the development agencies who are still concentrating their activities on improving the traditional form of agriculture. With methods known since the "green revolution" of the 1960s (introduction of improved seeds, chemical fertilizers, pesticides, and mechanization) they try to develop land on steep fans, flood-threatened terraces in the Hunza Canyon, and attempt to introduce cash crops such as seed potato production and fruit. The problem of increasing population and out-migration remains unsolved by these measures, as high mountain agriculture cannot compete with the huge irrigated canal colonies of the Punjab, from which subsidized wheat is exported to the Northern Areas to fill the gap of grain deficit.

Conclusion

Contrary to Wallis canton in Switzerland, where a neglected and decaying irrigation system is only a supplement for cultivation, the high mountain agriculture of Hunza is solely dependent on irrigation.

This case study demonstrates how the irrigation system evolved in Hunza. The reason for this expansion always has been a decreasing resource base for the nourishment of a growing population. Deficiency of water requires a high degree of social organization, which was formerly executed through the rulers of the principalities and lies nowadays in the hands of village communities.

The irrigation system of Hunza is still intact, in use, and is the vein for every form of cultivation. There are no indications of neglect and decay: on the contrary, new leats are being built and old ones extended and widened, although agriculture is no longer the only occupation of the people.

Acknowledgments

Fieldwork for this study is part of a larger research project of Fred Scholz of Free University of Berlin, financed by the Deutsche Forschungsgemeinschaft (German Research Foundation) during 1984 and 1985. Credit for the English translation of this manuscript is to Sabine Felmy, Berlin.

20
Adaptation to Frost and Recent Political Change in Highland Papua New Guinea

Bryant J. Allen

The highland valleys of Papua New Guinea are now permanently occupied by humans to an altitude of around 2,800 m. This chapter is concerned with the people who live at these high altitudes, their history of occupation and the major environmental hazard of this zone, frost. Although the highlands of Papua New Guinea may have been occupied by humans for 30,000 years, the high altitude areas have almost certainly been permanently occupied for only 400 years or less. The occupation of the higher areas of the Papua New Guinea highlands, the adaptation of its settlers to the conditions they found there and the rapid changes that these areas are presently undergoing as they become incorporated into a nation state and the world economy is a fascinating story in human ecology.

The Papua New Guinea Highlands

The major structural feature of the island of New Guinea is known as the New Guinea Mobile Belt (Loeffler 1977), a "spine" of metamorphic and instrusive rocks heavily faulted on a northwest to southeast trend. To the northwest and the southeast this belt consists of a series of extremely rugged mountain ranges with high, narrow, crested ridges and deep V-shaped valleys filled with coarse gravels and boulders. Between these two mountain ranges are a series of broad upland valleys separated by high plateaus of lesser relief and several very large, extinct, strato-volcanoes.

Although these valleys have a variety of geological origins, events during the Pleistocene have left them comparable in many ways. They have valley floors around 1,500 m to 1,600 m above sea level, and the most widespread soils are derived from a series of ash showers from volcanoes within the highlands and from some off the north coast.

Volcanism has also resulted in large laharic mud flows into the valleys, the disruption of drainage patterns, and the formation of large swamps.

Seasonal variation in temperature and humidity is not great in the highlands. Mean annual maximum temperatures are around 24 degrees C and mean annual minima 13 degrees C. Diurnal variation is much greater, however, and above about 1,500 m ground frosts are likely to occur, their incidence and severity increasing with elevation and locally conducive physiographic conditions (McAlpine et al. 1983:160–62).

The Occupation of the High Altitude Areas

Evidence for the history of human occupation of the highlands comes from archaeological and palaeobotanical studies. The examination of pollen in cores taken from bogs and small lakes in the western highlands suggests that about 18,000 years before the present, "more or less complete forest cover" existed in the main valleys (Powell 1982:29), but the earliest highlands occupation site is dated at 26,000 years. Evidence for well-developed horticulture 9,000 years ago has been found near Mt. Hagen at 1,600 m, and pollen analysis in the same area suggests significant changes in the forest (Golson 1977). Forest disturbance also occurred around Lake Ipea in Enga Province at 2,500 m around 5,000 years ago, but around 400 years ago both pollen records and sedimentation records suggest a sudden increase in the rate of forest clearance (Oldfield et al. 1980).

Based on this evidence and on ethnobotanical evidence that the present day staple of the highlands, the sweet potato *(Ipomoea batatas)*, was transported in the 1500s (Yen 1974), it is now widely accepted that the adoption of the sweet potato allowed a rapid "spatial and temporal expansion of food production" (Clarke 1977:161). It is not yet known what sort of technology was being used in the highlands prior to the introduction of sweet potato, but a form of swidden cultivation combined with intensive cultivation in drained swamps, using taro *(Colocasia esculenta)* as the staple seems most likely (Bayliss-Smith 1984). The new plant was more tolerant of declining soil fertility and of altitude. It allowed the permanent settlement of areas above 2,300 m, the approximate altitudinal limit imposed by taro.

Groups living above 2,300 m today have broadly similar oral accounts of their colonization of the upper valleys. At Murisoas, a Mai Enga group, the Pilyeni Yonope, recount how their ancestors lived at about 1,800 m in the Lagaip Valley and hunted up onto the broad interfluve where the group now live, at about 2,700 m. They discovered a salt spring in the forest and began manufacturing and trading salt from it to a wide area of the highlands, until around 150 years ago. Using genealogical reckoning (which may be foreshortened), the first permanent residences were established, based on new sweet potato fields cleared from forest on the edge of a swamp (Allen 1982). This group has now cleared almost 50 ha of forest and numbers around 230 persons. At Yumbisa, the Molopai people say their occupation began around 1800 when it was discovered, more or less by accident during a *karuka (Pandanus julianetti)* collecting and hunting expedition to the uplands, that sweet potato grew well in the new forest soils. Land was cleared along the edge of a large swamp and the drier, colluvial soils along the margins were drained. The Molopai numbered 318 in 1972 (Wohlt 1978).

A well-recognized pattern of forest clearing has developed during the expansion to higher altitudes. Forest along the edge of established fields becomes degraded through its utilization for firewood, timber, and pig foraging. When yields on existing fields have fallen to an uneconomic level, an area of degraded forest is stoutly fenced off and cleared. Pandanus trees are left standing as they are an important food source and are managed in large numbers in the forest. Sweet potato is cultivated together with a large number of mixed crops for up to three or four years,

Figure 20.1   Aerial view of a Murisoas Settlement at 2700 m in the Lai-Lagaiap Divide, Enga Province, Papua New Guinea. Cultivated land in fore- and midground is mounds and bed of sweet potato, intercultivated with vegetables and pyrethrum. A *Miscanthus* cane grass climax *(foreground)* is used for extensive pig grazing. Cultivated land in background, part of a potato project, has been ploughed with a tractor.

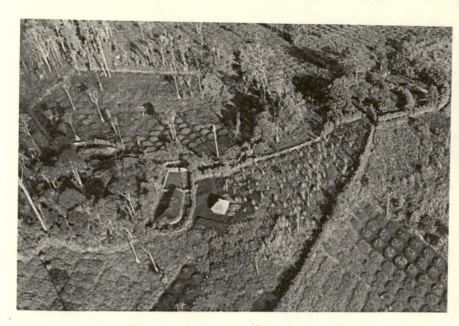

Figure 20.2   Dwellings on the Edge of the Forest at Murisoas. The larger building houses women and pigs, while the smaller building, in a nontraditional style, is a men's house. The buildings are surrounded by sweet potato mounds in all stages of cultivation. The gardens are heavily fenced against pigs with cordyline, which has sprouted to form a living barrier. The tall trees left standing in the gardens are *Pandanus,* important for their fruit. They are partially cultivated in the forest and are not felled when forest is cleared for cultivation.

while the new forest soils give high yields, and then the new field reverts to mainly sweet potato. This pattern maintains a steady upslope direction, leaving behind it large areas of *Miscanthus* cane grass. Pigs, fires, altered environmental conditions, and soil degradation combine to prevent the reestablishment of the forest. Most people say the grasslands are of no further agricultural use, although they do form important pig grazing areas (Bowers 1968).

Horticulture and Adaptation to Frost Hazards

Present horticultural systems in the high valleys are based on open fields of sweet potato, grown on composted mounds that are located on flatter land; slope gardens, which are sometimes cleared from forest or are on the forest-grassland edge, usually contain a greater range of crops than the open fields; and house gardens, grown around dwellings. This is an adaptation of a widespread system of highlands horticulture, which allows intensive cultivation of the main valleys and supports high human and pig populations (Brookfield 1971).

The composted mound is an innovation that probably developed following the introduction of sweet potato. In the main valleys the mounding system is designed to permit continuous cultivation of the soil. The Raiapu Enga in the Lai Valley at 1,650 m repeatedly told Waddell, "we do not fallow this ground" (Waddell 1972: 44). The mounded field is brought into production with one or two preliminary cultivations, after which the soil is tilled and mounded over a bundle of old vines, weeds, and grasses. Sweet potato runners are pushed into the loose soil all around the mound, where they strike, take root, and produce tubers. Harvesting is also continuous, with gardeners taking large tubers from beneath the surface of the mound while leaving smaller ones to grow further. Women do most of the everyday tasks associated with producing the staple crop. Up to half of the crop may go to raising pigs, depending on the size of the herd at any particular time. When one crop is harvested completely, the mound is broken open, more green compost placed in the center, closed over, and replanted. Slope gardens in the main valleys are swiddens, often cleared from low secondary woody growth, and are used for growing taro, greens, beans, and bananas, as well as introduced crops such as maize.

At 2,700 m sweet potato mounds are smaller in diameter and taller and tend to have more sod included in the till than in the main valleys. Here sweet potato takes up to 12 months to mature, compared to five to seven months at lower altitudes, hence more land is required to support one person for one year than at lower altitudes. In addition fields are cultivated for shorter periods and are fallowed. A much reduced variety of mixed crops is grown in slope gardens, and, in many areas, a great deal more interplanting of greens and sweet potato occurs on the mounds in the open fields.

Although mounding was most likely devised to maintain production for long periods on ash soils at lower altitudes, it is also well suited to handle the single greatest hazard to food production at these altitudes, frost. The sweet potato, a succulent, is severely damaged by air temperatures below freezing. Vines are planted concentrically around the top of the mounds, instead of on the sides as is the fashion at lower altitudes, to raise them above the cold air, and villagers recognize that the position of the plant on the mound is very important. The mounds also probably serve to promote cold air drainage across fields (Waddell 1972:154–57). Other environmental adaptations employed against frost are the dispersion of gardens, with some up to one or two days walking away, while locally gardens are cultivated concurrently on slopes and flats, a recognition of the freakish nature of frost. Smoky fires and the covering of mounds with cut grass are well known but little practiced techniques, rarely used because of the

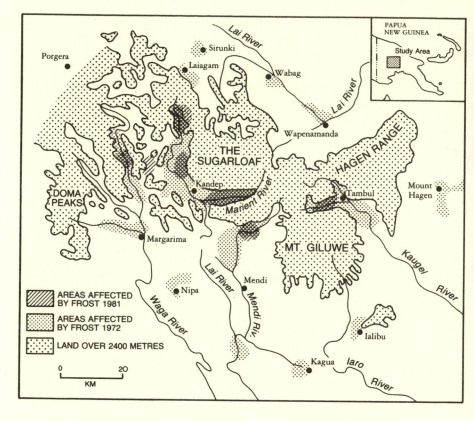

Figure 20.3   Areas Affected by Frost in 1972 and 1981

irregularity and unpredictability of the risk, and the inability of small groups to meet the very high labor demands of such practices.

Approximately every 10 years, regional climatic conditions associated with a reversal in the Walker Circulation across the Pacific (the El Niño phenomenon) raises barometric pressure in the western Pacific and brings with it lower than normal rainfall, clear skies, and increased risk of frost over the highlands of Papua New Guinea. Under these conditions severe frosts may occur three or four nights in succession, two or three times within six months. Oral accounts suggest such events have occurred around 1900 and 1920. In 1941 a recent famine associated with frost and widespread drought was described to the first foreigners to enter the high valleys. Between June and October 1972 a series of severe frosts occurred, causing food shortages for approximately 150,000 people in much of the western highlands, some of whom lived as low as 1,600 m. A similar but less severe event occurred in 1980 and 1981 (Fig. 20.3).

No amount of local adaptation can withstand a series of frosts some months apart. It was against such eventualities that people in the high valleys maintained their kinship, marriage, exchange, and trade links with people resident in the main valleys, where frost damage was likely to be minimal or non-existent. During good years they would contribute pigs, which thrive at the higher altitudes, to exchanges in the lower valleys, so that in a time of crisis, they could seek refuge there. Following a frost, mature and near mature tubers were harvested and consumed and some pigs killed. Before the family was weakened by lack of food, they would set out for their hosts' territory, leading pigs that they would use to support themselves during their stay. Almost as soon as they arrived they would begin bringing new sweet potato vines back to their home area to replant the gardens. When these gardens were ready to harvest, in 10 to 12 months time, they would return again to the high valleys, and take up where they left off.

Although it seems likely that the people who pioneered the high valleys were those who had been pushed there and who were the poorer sections of a society in which access to productive land was critical for the gaining of wealth and status (Bowers 1968), there were advantages to living in these areas. Many trade routes passed up these valleys and across the plateaus. In the high forests were the Pandanus nuts, birds of paradise, and fur coated animals, all of which were highly valued in the main valleys. In addition pigs grew exceptionally well in the swamps and forests of the high altitude zones. When outsiders entered these high valleys they found a pragmatic, highly adaptive and hardy race of people who they openly admired for their vigor.

Incorporation into the Nation State

The high valleys were first visited by foreigners in the 1940s, but the intervention of the World War II postponed the establishment of effective colonial control over many areas until the late 1950s. The Kandep Patrol Post, for example, was opened in 1960. By 1972 Papua New Guinea was internally self-governing, and by 1975, an independent nation. The people of the high valleys face particular problems in what are known as "less developed areas" within a developing country. Many of these problems are related to their isolation and their environment, and some to the nature of politics. Others are of their own making.

The Australian colonial government and the new Papua New Guinea government have invested in infrastructural development in the high valleys, using both local resources, particularly labor, as well as international funding. During the 1960s gravel-surfaced roads with timber bridges were constructed across much of this country. But compared to other parts of the highlands, where villagers began planting cash crops such as coffee in the 1940s, these areas remain disadvantaged.

Rural development in the Papua New Guinea highlands has been based firmly on the smallholder production of Arabica coffee for the international market. In 1984, this crop was worth K95 million ($91.2m in 1985) 25 percent of all overseas earnings, and 75 percent of it was produced by smallholders, mostly in the highlands. But coffee will not grow above about 2,100 m. In an attempt to provide high altitude dwellers with a means of earning cash, pyrethrum *(Chrysanthemum cinerariaefolium)* was introduced, and, after some setbacks, has become a successful smallholder crop. The flowers are cultivated intensively in beds for two to three years, in rotation with sweet potato, with the old flower clumps being used for composting material; a small amount of intercropping on sweet potato mounds and with other introduced vegetables can also be observed. The estimated income per household for this crop in 1981 was $75 (Carrad 1981).

A less spectacular but very important series of plant introductions has involved temperate vegetables such as Irish potato *(Solanum tuberosum),* cabbages, and carrots. All these crops are frost resistant to some degree and are in demand in the country's urban centers. Potato growing has become a very important activity and ranges from growing a few plants for household use to using machinery and inorganic fertilizers and growing for the urban market. In many highland towns the fast food industry is based on fried potato chips (French fries) and chicken, and much of the potato supply is coming from the high altitude areas.

These vegetables and traditional products such as Pandanus nuts and pigs form an important informal trade between the main valleys and the high altitude zones. Bird plumes and animal skins are also still important trade items, but salt has been almost completely replaced by the imported item. At local informal markets, people cook and sell deep fried dough, and a number of individuals and groups operate small retail shops selling imported foods such as Japanese tinned fish, Australian rice, tobacco, soap, salt, beer, clothing, matches, and tools such as knives, axes and spades. Store goods are transported in from wholesalers in the main valleys on Japanese pickup trucks, owned by individual entrepreneurs. Driving is not a well-developed skill in many owner-drivers; accidents are common, and vehicle life short on the rough mountain roads.

Cash has become an integral part of the exchange system and is required for many transactions, including bride prices, mortuary payments, and compensation payments, as well as for paying school fees for children, paying local taxes, for purchasing rides on vehicles to markets, and for personal requirements. It remains more difficult to earn cash in the high valleys than elsewhere in the highlands. For this reason many of the young of both sexes have left their villages to seek work elsewhere, many on coffee plantations in the main valleys. Almost one-third of the residents of Murisoas were absent from the village during a survey conducted in 1981, compared with an average 7 percent for the whole of the Province. Sixty percent of those absent were aged between 18 and 45 years.

Frost and Social Change

Incorporation has brought widespread social, economic and political change to the high valleys, but it has not yet changed the almost total reliance on the sweet potato by human and pig, nor has it reduced the risk of frost irregularly disrupting the production system. It has, however, affected peoples' ability to deal with the hazard. When frost struck in 1972, it was the eve of Australia relinquishing internal self-government to a government led by a political party of mainly lowlanders, against the wishes of most highlanders. Frost was a new experience to most Australian field administrators. The widespread destruction of sweet potato gardens shocked them, and they envisaged large scale social disorder in the wake of a famine. The Australian government reacted with a massive airlift of food into the highlands and prevented people from leaving their home areas by edict and by providing food for them there with helicopters.

Although later it was possible to say that nobody had died as a result of the frost and subsequent food shortage, as certainly was not the case in 1940, the ability of the high altitude people to deal with the problem was severely underrated. Rather than strengthening traditional means of coping, the relief program weakened them and increased the risk of their being unable to manage a subsequent event (Waddell 1974, 1975).

In 1980, following a series of less severe frosts, provincial and national politicians became involved in directing relief efforts, many unashamedly seeking votes in a forthcoming national election. People in areas not badly affected demanded to be included in the relief program, and some instances of thieving of relief supplies occurred. At first the high altitude people stayed, waiting for the helicoptered food they had experienced in the 1970s, but when it was not forthcoming in anything like adequate proportions, they reverted to traditional patterns and set out for friends in the main valleys. People expressed the fear, however, that as more and more transactions become monetized, they may soon be expected to pay cash for this hospitality (Wohlt et al. 1981). On the other hand, the increased introduction of Irish potatoes and the higher levels of cash earned in the high altitude communities has assisted them to make new adjustments to the problem of frost, partly by migrating temporarily, particularly to bring back unfrosted vines for replanting, partly by consuming a tuber that is less frost affected and partly by buying imported food.

The Future?

A greater threat than frost to the long-term stability of the high valley dwellers is that of land shortage. The practice of forest clearing in the face of falling yields is, in some areas, beginning to result in the deforestation of all cultivatable land. It is probable that the cane grassland can be satisfactorily recultivated with perhaps lower yields. What is required is some means of replanting at least some deforested land to provide building materials, fencing, and fuelwood, as well as food, a system of agroforestry that will enable these areas to be used permanently without environmental degradation.

Populations are growing more slowly in the high valleys than in the main valleys, partly as a result of migration and partly because of poorer access to health care and continuing high infant mortality. But when this situation changes, and more people remain at home, disappointed by the opportunities offered beyond the village, populations there will begin to grow. Before that happens, another wave of agricultural innovation is required, at least as comprehensive as that which first allowed people to settle these high valleys.

21

Nomadic Pastoralists and Sedentary Hosts in the Central and Western Hindukush Mountains, Afghanistan

Daniel Balland

Nomadization from the outside world represents one of the main cultural impacts experienced since the end of the antiquity in numerous South and Southwest Asian mountains (Planhol 1962:118). The process has been continuing for centuries until its contemporary decline. Its final episode took place in the westernmost portion of the South Asian mountain rimland (Afghanistan) during the past hundred years or so, at a time when it was already declining elsewhere.

Until this very late period, most Afghan mountains remained the exclusive home of various human communities whose subsistence economy combined sedentary agriculture, both irrigated (*abi*) and non-irrigated (*lalmi*), with some more or less mobile animal husbandry according to patterns that have been fairly well ascertained among the Tajiks (Groetzbach 1972:108), Nuristanis (Eldelberg and Jones 1979:50) and Wakhis (Shahrani 1979:62) of the Hindukush as well as among the Hazaras of Hazarajat (Ferdinand 1959:27; Denizot et al. 1977:59). In their stronghold of high mountains these isolated populations retained an autonomous life in terms of both cultural (religious, linguistic) and political status.

This situation came to an end in the course of the second half of the nineteenth century when all mountain communities were brought under political control by the Kabul amirs (Kakar 1971; Grevemeyer 1982). Broadly speaking, the process of mountain nomadization can be paralleled with the progress of the political unification of Afghanistan. Pastoral nomads very often became regular users of mountain summer pastures only after the latter's incorporation into the state. The current Afghan vertical style of nomadism that has been so frequently described was thus established quite recently. It consists of a winter (rainy season) dispersal of nomads in the more peripheral lowlands below 1000 m in the north and

1500 m in the south, with few local exceptions, and a summer (dry season) concentration in the central highlands that form the east-west backbone of the Afghan territory and cover nearly 50 percent of its surface (Humlum 1959:17). The lower limit of pastoral nomadic encampments thus lies in summer around 1000 to 1200 m, except in the north where it dips down to 400 m (Balland 1982:55).

However, the nomadization process has by no means been a uniform one, neither in its form and chronology nor in space and actors involved. It was formally achieved through different means such as partial or total transference of whole nomadic groups toward regions entirely new to them, accretion of new summer quarters to older migration routes (Balland 1982:61), and even transformation of peasants into nomads (Glatzer 1982). In the same space of time, former nomads frequently settled down or shortened their migration. The overall result being a tremendous territorial expansion of pastoral nomadism. None of the present-day 29 Afghan provinces lies off the dense network of nomadic routes. According to the unpublished 1978 Afghan Nomad Survey, out of 325 administrative units, 183 were reported to have a seasonal nomadic population either in winter or in summer, 68 had nomadic residents all year round, 37 were simply crossed over by nomads on their way to their seasonal quarters and only 37, that is, 11 percent of the total number of districts but no more than 8 percent of the country's surface, seem to be never visited by nomads. Incidentally, such a large spatial diffusion of nomads all over Afghanistan may well account for their frequent overestimation.

Chronologically, the nomadization process must be viewed as a multi-staged phenomenon with slow, continuous infiltration periods and crisis breaks. It came into being earlier in the much lower and easier to penetrate western half of the central highlands. In the beginning of the nineteenth century, Pashtun nomads from the southern lowlands already had access to summer pastures in the Siah Koh (Black Mountain) of southern Ghor (Elphinstone 1815:409). In eastern Afghanistan, mountains were then free of nomadic encroachments. Some of them still are: the nomadization wave remained aloof from the remotest mountain districts such as northern Darwaz and the upper drainage basin of the Kokcha River, east of Anjoman Pass, on the north side of the Hindukush, or the upper valley of the Bashgal River on its south face. Moreover, the nomads involved in the nomadization process belong to various ethnic groups. Besides the Pashtuns, who have been the most numerous, Arabs (Barfield 1981), Baluchis (Balland, de Benoist 1982), and others also took part.

The emergent picture of less than one century of the nomadization process in Afghanistan is a rather intricate one. It is still more complicated by the various adaptive responses that sprang out from the confrontation between pastoral nomads and their agro-pastoral host populations in the mountains. That point will be more fully treated below through the analysis of two very different cases: Gujar pastoralists in the Central Hindukush and Pashtun nomads in the Dasht-e Nawar area (southeastern Hazarajat) of the Western Hindukush. The material related to the former primarily comes from the unpublished files of the United Nations–sponsored Afghan Nomad Survey of 1978, while most data on the latter derive from the author's fieldwork performed in 1974.

Gujar in the Afghan Hindukush

For centuries the Gujars have been pastoral nomads wintering in the Panjab and Indus plains and moving up in summer on the southern slopes of the Himalaya (Fig. 21.1). Quite a number of them are still living in these regions (Uhlig 1973a:160; Shashi 1979:18; Rao, Casimir 1982). But the unprecedented progression of irrigated agriculture in their ancestral win-

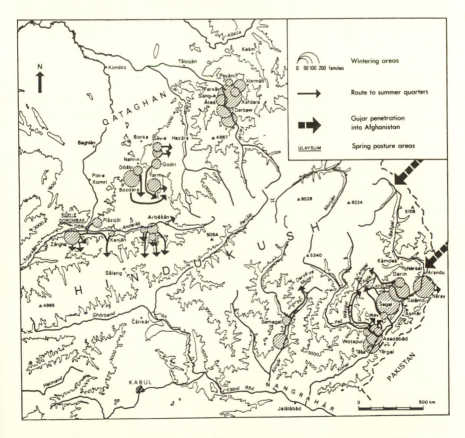

Figure 21.1   Gujar Nomads in the Afghan Hindukush, 1978

ter area since the second half of the nineteenth century forced many of them to settle down (Sarkar et al. 1982:65), while others, seeking alternative grazing lands, eventually penetrated into the Indus Kohistan (Biddulph 1880:40; Fautz 1963:45; Staley 1982:144), and thence into Afghanistan (Robertson 1896:297). Since the turn of the century, infiltration of Gujars into Afghan territory through the Durand Line has been steadily increasing, at least up to the 1960s (Lancaster 1946; Snoy 1965:119).

At first Gujars found habitation in the Konar River area by obtaining ex-Kafir alpine pastures after Amir Abd al-Rahman had conquered Kafiristan (now Nuristan). Later on, some Gujars were transplanted in Qataghan, on the north side of Central Hindukush. The exact circumstances of the transplantation remain unknown, but it was not yet initiated in the early 1920s as no Gujar population is mentioned in the careful survey of Qataghan conducted in 1922 (Koshkaki 1979).

Nowadays half of the 2270 Gujar families enumerated in 1978 (i.e., a total population of fewer than 15,000) belong to these north slope Hindukush communities. They make up three distinct geographical groupings with few contacts, if any, between them: the most numerous community (590 families) dwells in the Farkhar valley, southeast of Taloqan; the Nahrin heights (320 families) and the Andarab-Sorkhab trench (250 families) have smaller colonies. There is still further mention of northernmost Gujar communities in the districts of Keshm, Jurm, and in the Wardoj valley (Fischer 1970:49), but it remains to be seen if they were not only transitional locations.

The southern slope middle Konar region, along the Pakistani border, still has the major Gujar concentration in all Afghanistan (975 nomadic families). A few western outposts, numbering no more than 135 families, are located along the Alingar river. Still further west there is no trace of Gujar nomads, although small scattered colonies of sedentary Gujars are known to exist, for example in Kabul Kohestan, which seems to be their westernmost locality on the southern side of the Hindukush (Allan 1978:185).

Whatever the location, the migratory pattern of nomadic Gujar varies very little and stands distinctively from most Afghan nomads. It is a typical short-range intra-mountain semi-nomadism or transhumance with no relation at all with the large piedmont plains that stretch on both sides of the Hindukush (those of Kunduz-Khanabad and Baghlan in the north, of Jalalabad in the south). The migratory cycle may be very local, from the bottom of a valley up to adjacent hillsides, such as is the case in Farkhar, where high pastures are only one or two hours from the winter villages. Others migrate up and down one valley over a maximum distance of 50 km (or four days march). The Hindukush crest is never crossed in the course of the annual migration because Gujars have given up their efforts at controlling grazing grounds in the upper Munjan valley.

Winter settlements are located in low peripheral valleys between 800 and 1500 m; the highest ones reach 1800 m in the east of Nahrin (Say-e Hazara, Yarm). In summer, the altitudinal location of grazing grounds shows a sharp contrast between northern and southern Hindukush: while they always lie below 2500 m in the former, with a duration of less than five months (May-September, except in Farkhar, which is June-October), campsites are usually established up to 3000 to 3500 m, with a six to seven month occupation (April-October), on the Southern Hindukush. This difference accounts for the longer migration routes of southern Gujars (see Fig. 21.1). Spring camps are unusual: only 20 percent of the Gujars resort to them.

A second very specific feature of Gujar pastoralism is the virtual neglect of the tent in summer: fewer than 100 families from Nahrin and Andarab have been reported to have a tent. The most common summer dwelling is by far a kind of hut made up of wood, branches, turf, and dry grass raised above a crude and low stone-work basement. Such huts are called *kapa* all over northern Hindukush and *banda* (a Pashto word) on the south side.

In winter, only a minority of Gujars dwell in houses of their own. In the Alingar valley they use a mere hut of branches (Pashto *kudaley*). In Konar valley as well as in Andarab, many live in caves dug by hand in the loose alluvial terraces of the rivers (Persian *somoch*, Pashto *smatsa*). Still others are given a room in the house of some sedentary peasant in exchange for domestic services performed as *hamsaya* (client).

Precariousness is a third aspect of Gujar pastoralism. As latecomers in a mountainous region already densely occupied by permanent villagers and seasonal semi-nomads, territorial competition with occasional shootings and livestock rustlings has been perennial between them and Pashai (Petocz 1972:6), Safi (Dupree 1984:300), Munjani Tajik (Lancaster 1946; Snoy 1965:120), and above all, Kom Nuristani (Strand 1984). In the nineteenth century the Kafirs were already successfully fighting against Gujar encroachments (Robertson 1896:300). The Gujars could gain only access to alpine pastures, by paying a grazing fee in kind, because of the decimation of local herds during the Afghan military conquest of the region (Strand 1978:10). The reconstitution of the Nuristani herds was quick and revived the previous antagonism. In the 1940s there began a succession of armed conflicts known to the Kom as the "Gujar wars" (Strand 1984:84; Grjunberg 1980:103). They were to last, interrupted by short-lived truces, until 1978 when a coalition of Gujar and Pashtun nomads, backed by the new revolutionary Afghan government, conducted a fruitless military expedition against Nuristani who had just rebelled (Schneiter 1980:241; Strand 1978:89). The conditions of insecurity and precariousness over summer grazing ground use led some Gujar to try their chances elsewhere, for example in the upper Munjan valley, north of the crest-line, where they were finally driven out by the local Tajik villagers in the late 1950s and early 1960s (Snoy 1965:120), or in Laghman, where their penetration immediately followed their expulsion from Munjan (Petocz 1972:7). It is highly probable that their partial transplantation to Qataghan bears some relation with these continuous difficulties on the southern side of the Hindukush.

What is to be learned from this chaotic and little-known pastoralist evolution is the persistence of the highly volatile character of the location and migratory itineraries of the Gujars in the Hindukush. This is in contrast to the integration of Gujars into the eastern (Pakistan) Hindukush. In Swat (Barth 1956) and Gilgit districts, unoccupied ecological niches existed before their arrival that they were able to fill. Such niches also existed in Afghanistan, on the northern slopes of central Hindukush, owing to the depopulated state of the area in the early twentieth century (Groetzbach 1972:74). In fact the region still serves as a receptacle for fresh immigrants: in the Farkhar valley, the number of Gujar families increased from a mere 40 in 1963 (Groetzbach 1972:96) to near 600 in 1978. A further sign of distinctive access to pastoral resources on the two sides of the Central Hindukush is the number of summer camps compared to winter settlements. More than 20 winter localities are reported in the south compared to only 7 summer sites open to Gujars, while in Qataghan there are as many summer camps as winter settlements, a clear testimony that Gujar pastoralists could establish their seasonal migrations here almost without restraint.

The Pashtun Nomads of the Dasht-e Nawar (Southeastern Hazarajat)

A large, flat, enclosed volcano-tectonic depression at 3120 m above sea-level and some 60 km west of Ghazni, the Dasht-e Nawar (Fig. 21.2) is filled by a shallow playa (*nawar*) fed by snow melt that partly dries up in summer to form saline marshes with lush pasturages on its outskirts. It has thus always been a favorite grazing ground in the hot season (Burnes 1834 II:335; Masson 1842 II:221, 223). A thousand years ago the Ghaznavid army sent its horses there (India 1895:206), a practice still in use with the Afghan cavalry in the nineteenth and early twentieth centuries. Furthermore, long-range Pashtun nomads had by then found their way up to the Dasht-e Nawar and obtained grazing rights by paying a grazing fee (Persian *chara'i*) to the local Mohammad Khwaja Hazara (Fayz Mohammad 1333AH:714). According to local tradition these nomads belonged to the Mollakhel and Shinwari tribes and wintered in the Indus lowlands, which means their seasonal migration was 350 to 400km. Their penetration had not been an easy one: Ferdinand (1959:19) suggested that it could successfully take place only when good modern (i.e.,

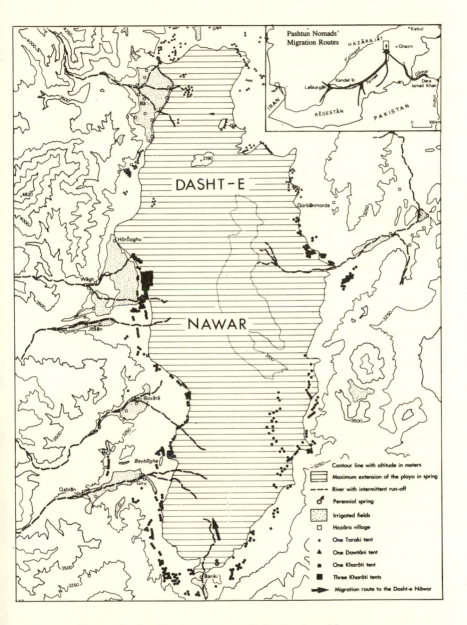

Figure 21.2 Pashtun Nomads in Dasht-e Nawar

English) rifles became available to the nomads, that is during the 1860s. Even then their presence remained as precarious as the one of the Gujars in Hindukush: in the late 1880s raiding parties of *yaghi* (rebel, unsubdued) Hazara were so frequent and murderous that nomads gave up moving up to Nawar as well as to the bordering districts of Behsud and Jaghori (Fayz Mohammad 1333AH:714). This is why they backed the army in the military campaign in Hazarajat, which was to soon follow. Not only did they hire out their pack-camels to help in transporting the army supplies, but twenty of their tribe also raised one levy out of each fifty men to join the regular invading troops (Fayz Mohammad 1333AH:715). After the final submission of the whole Hazarajat, their help was duly acknowledged by the Amir's grant of a *firman,* giving them large grazing rights on the state-appropriated pastures of the subdued and depopulated country (Kakar 1979:126). The Mollakhel were granted such rights in Daya (Ajrestan), in the territory of the Fuladi (also Polada) Hazara, west of Dasht-e Nawar. Most of them soon settled down in their new summer quarters where they are still traceable through the dense network of villages bearing names of Mollakhel lineages. This process was already underway in the 1930s (Robinson 1978:168) and has since steadily increased: the 1978 survey reported only 15 nomadic Mollakhel families in the area. The nomadic section of the noteworthy insubordinate Shinwari tribe (Kakar 1971:93), had been split up by Amir Abd al-Rahman. A part of the tribe was deported in 1891 to Turkestan (Herat News-letter 7 January 1892, IOR L/P & S/7/65:651), and their descendants lead a semi-nomadic life today in the vicinity of Aqcha and Maymana, while another part (110 families in 1978) was allowed to retain its ancestral *genre de vie* and is currently migrating between Behsud, north of Dasht-e Nawar, and the Shinkay Ghar, south of Ab-e Estada.

One result of these territorial transfers and accretions was the opening of the Dasht-e Nawar, then deserted by its former nomadic users, to a new wave of nomads previously unconcerned with Hazarajat, as they had their summer quarters in the plain around Ghazni or in the southern hills surrounding the Ab-e Estada lake. These latecomers, who are said to have obtained their pastoral rights in Amir Habibullah's time (1901–1919), still use the Dasht-e Nawar grazing grounds, for which they pay the state annual dues in kind. They belong to three Pashtun tribes who have been apportioned distinct grazing tracts: Kharoti are established in the east of the depression (155 tents in July 1974), Taraki in the south (223 tents) and Dawtani (also Daftanai) in the north (191 tents). They represent a total nomadic population of some 3,500 to 4,000 (Fig. 21.2).

Within each tribal grazing quarter a further radial, genealogical-based division into sectional patrilinear territories has been made so that every family should have free access to two different kinds of pasture-lands, in the bottom of the *dasht* and on the slopes of the surrounding mountains, respectively. This is a very important point, as there is complementarity between these two pasturages: the bulk of the flocks, consisting of ewes, gathered in collective herds under shepherds paid in kind, graze the *dasht* in day-time and the mountains at night, to avoid the nocturnal dew and not uncommon frost of the *dasht,* which is a very general herding practice among Central Asian nomads. Tani et al. (1980:27) describe a similar daily schedule among Pashtun nomads in Dasht-e Shewa, Badakhshan. The remaining rams and spring-born lambs are herded individually, never go in the mountain and spend the night at the campsite in the company of the pack-animals, which are mostly camels, donkeys, and still fewer horses.

The grazing periods in the Dasht-e Nawar barely exceeds two months (June-July). At altitudes above 3000 m, up to 3500 m, which is the uppermost limit of nomadic encampments in Afghanistan with the exception of Kirghiz (Balland 1982:58), night frost is the main limiting factor for nomads who, unlike Gujars, travel with dromedary camel, which is very sensitive to cold. The nomads' black tents are pitched for nine or ten frost-free weeks in the year. No week, however, is absolutely frost-free because at Obak, in the northern part of the Dasht-e Nawar, minimum temperatures as low as −4 degrees and −6 degrees C were recorded on 6 July 1971 and 25 June 1974.

The nomads' winter quarters are scattered in the lowlands between the Indus and Helmand valleys at distances ranging from 300 to 550 km from the Dasht-e Nawar. While the richest Dawtani go to Derajat, in Pakistan, others from the same tribe winter in the middle Helmand valley in southern Afghanistan. The Taraki spend the cold season in northeastern and eastern Regestan, along the Pakistani border. Going down as far as Garmsel, south of Darweshan, the Kharoti have the longest migration of all (Fig. 21.2, insert). Many routes were established only in the 1960s, after the closure of the Afghan-Pakistan border in 1961, which prevented Pashtun nomads from returning to their traditional winter quarters in Pakistan. Other routes were established earlier in this century, following a long-standing feud between Dawtani and Wazir (Balland, Kieffer 1979:85).

A strong tendency toward spatial instability in both migration routes and winter quarters characterizes the contemporary evolution of pastoral nomads travelling to Dasht-e Nawar for summer grazing. The situation contrasts sharply with the Gujar pattern in that summer quarters are stable. In the twentieth century the relationships between Hazara villagers and Pashtun tent-dwellers in the Western Hindukush (the mountains west of the Salang Pass Tunnel) lacked the severe conflict found in the Central Hindukush. Occasional clashes did occur and still do. Most of them originate by encroachments of Pashtun's herds on Hazara's fieldcrops. Few ever went beyond short-lived local disputes and none escalated into armed conflicts of the so-called "Gujar wars" type.

A fuller comprehension of the differences requires an analysis of carrying capacity of Gujar and Pashtun nomads and their respective host populations.

Nomads in the Wider Mountain Society

As a preliminary observation it must be stated that human pressure is very much alike in both cases: population densities do not significantly differ and similar symptoms of overgrazing are perceptible.

One difference lies in the juridicial context of the nomadic occupation of grazing lands. In the Dasht-e Nawar as in most of Hazarajat, Pashtun nomads hold official written titles to pasture. Collective access to the means of production, pasturage, is thus secured. It is all the more likely to be enforced, should a conflict burst out with the Hazara, that the latter, being Shia, are viewed with contempt by the Pashtun-dominated Sunni civil and military administrations.

Gujars, on the contrary, never received any official sanction for their presence on the southern slopes of the Hindukush. They always had to depend for grazing on individual, local, and tenuous contracts with the Nuristani. Moreover, while Nuristani and Gujar formally share the same Sunni faith, the former have strong advocates in Kabul, which the latter lack (Katz 1984:99, 107; Strand 1984:78). In a case of conflict this eventually leads to pro-Nuristani and anti-Gujar feelings in the government (Strand 1978:11). In the Central Hindukush the Afghan administration is partial to the sedentary villagers against the nomads. The reverse is true in Hazarajat.

A second, and more crucial, difference lies in the socio-economic relations established between external nomadic and local sedentary communities. Long-range Pashtun nomads succeeded in strengthening their presence in remote Hazarajat through trading and moneylending. This strategy was enacted by nomads who used to winter in British India, later Pakistan, and were integrated into a large-scale, international market economy. As a region without commerce, Hazarajat offered immense possibilities to dynamic nomadic traders until the 1960s when the motor vehicle revolution was induced by an active governmental road-building program and eventually led to the nomads' loss of their former trading monopoly. In the first half of this century, the constant resort to installment credit sales caused a progressive transfer of agricultural land from the Hazara debtors to their Pashtun creditors (Ferdinand 1959:20, 1962:131).

The Dasht-e Nawar is a good example of such an evolution. In the local context Taraki tribesmen have always been at a disadvantage owing to their older winter location inside Afghan territory (Robinson 1978:113) and summer location in an almost unpopulated part of the Dasht-e Nawar.

Land acquisition and trading were much less widespread among Taraki than among their Kharoti and above all Dawtani neighbors. The closure of the Afghan-Pakistan border in 1961 dealt a severe blow to local trading, and, ten years later, nomads' land holding suffered a sharp decline as a result of the 1970–71 drought (Balland, Kieffer 1979:83).

In Hazarajat, mutual hostility between Pashtun and Hazara was thus counterbalanced by mutual need. A symbiotic relationship was set up, working for the benefit of both villagers, who could have access to otherwise unobtainable articles—for example, clothes, sugar, and matches—and nomads, who could strengthen their control on their new summer quarters in Hazara areas. That the Hazara did not take advantage of the anti-Pashtun Saqawi movement of 1928–29 and welcomed Nader Shah's Pashtun restoration (Canfield 1973:104) is an indication of the weakening of their former anti-Pashtun feelings and of the emergence of an ambiguous form of solidarity between nomads and their host population.

This was not the case in the Central Hindukush. Being local nomads with no contact with any great urban bazaar, the Gujars were not in a position to establish trade partnerships with the Nuristanis: the function here was filled by Pashtun shopkeepers, not nomads (Katz 1982:212). Economic solidarity between Gujars and their host population was nevertheless achieved, but in the subordinate role of Gujars toward Pashtuns and much more in the winter area than in the summer one. Many Gujar are *hamsaya* (client) of a sedentary peasant or semi-nomad agro-pastoralist (Dupree 1984:273). In Andarab and Nahrin, daily casual labor as harvesters (Persian *derawgar,* Pashto *lawgar*) is a common practice among them before they travel to the summer pastures. Everywhere, but more commonly in Farkhar and Nahrin, some Gujars became agro-pastoralists through purchase or rent of small pieces of agricultural land. The only symbiotic relationship Gujars created in their summer quarters seems to be shepherding for Nuristani villagers (Edelberg, Jones 1979). This activity leads to greatly disputed political alliances with Nuristani (Strand 1978:11ff.). In the erstwhile princely state of Swat to the east, it has been suggested that a similar assimilation of Gujars by Pakhtuns occurred (Barth 1956), although this idealized model has been disputed (Allan 1985).

While Pashtun nomads were rapidly promoted to the rank of lords of the Hazarajat, Gujars always remained at the very bottom of social hierarchy in the Hindukush. Considered as unbelievers although they are Sunni Muslims (with Hindu gotras), they are easily distinguishable by their darker skin, dress, and specific language, Gujri, which nobody else would learn. Because of their entrepreneurial success as pastoralists, Gujars have an unfavorable reputation in conservative Pashtun dominated Afghanistan. Furthermore, Gujar women, their faces unveiled and tattooed, with their arms and necks festooned with bracelets and neck-laces, are viewed as rude interlopers by the reactionary *mullahs*.

The incursion of pastoral nomads into sedentary traditional mountain communities has often brought disturbing effects. Depending on the legal conditions of their intrusion and the socio-economic strategy adopted, very different results have been achieved. While fully "encapsulated" Pashtun nomads—to retain Fazel's (1973) terminology—emerged as a dominant strata in their Hazarajat summer quarters, marginally "encap-sulated" Gujar pastoralists failed to advance as a dominant ethnic pasto-ralist group in the Central Hindukush and had difficulty in maintaining geographical coherence. These two contradictory patterns clearly illus-trate how misleading it is to consider nomadization as a uniform process in the Southwest and South Asian mountains.

Acknowledgments

Fieldwork in Afghanistan was financially supported by Centre National de la Recherche Scientifique, Paris.

Bibliography

Aga Khan Rural Support Programme. 1985. *Progress Report*. Gilgit: AKRSP.

Aguiree Beltran, G. 1967. *Regiones de Refugio*. Ediciones Especiales, no. 46. Mexico City: Instituto indigenísta Interamericano.

Alberta Housing Corporation. 1983. *Canmore Northeast Benchlands*. Edmonton.

Alberta Energy and Natural Resources. 1984. *A Policy for Resource Management of the Eastern Slopes.*, 2nd ed. Edmonton: Resource Information Service.

Alberta Tourism and Small Business. 1981. *The Village at Ribbon Creek: Developer Package and Proposal Call.*

Alberta Tourism and Small Business. n.d. *Tourism 2000*. Mimeo.

Alberti, Giorgio, and Enrique Mayer. 1974. "Reciprocidad Andina: ayer y hoy." In *Reciprocidad e Intercambio en los Andes Peruanos*, Peru-Problema, no.12, edited by Giorgio Alberti and Enrique Mayer, 13–33. Lima: Instituto de Estudios Peruanos.

Alexander, Martin. 1974. "Environmental Consequences of Rapidly Rising Food Output." *Agro-Ecosystems* 1:249–264.

Allan, N. J. R. 1978. "Men and Crops in the Central Hindukush." *Dissertation Abstracts International*. Series A. 39/10:6332.

Allan, N. J. R. 1984. "Ecological Effects of Land Intensification in the Central and Eastern Hindu Kush." In *Beitraege zur vergleichenden Kulturgeographie der Hochgebirge*. Eichstaetter Beitraege no. 12, edited by E. Groetzbach and G. Rinschede, 193–212. Regensburg: Friedrich Pustet.

Allan, N. J. R. 1985. "Human Geoecological Interactions in Kuh Daman, A South Asian Mountain Valley." *Applied Geography* 5:13–27.

Allan, N. J. R. 1986a. "Accessibility and Altitudinal Zonation Models of Mountains." *Mountain Research and Development* 6:185–194, 205–206.

Allan, N. J. R. 1986b. "Deforestation et Agro-Pastoralisme dans le Pakistan du Nord." *Revue de Géographie Alpine* 74:389–96.

Allen, Bryant J. 1982. "Subsistence Agriculture: Three Case Studies." In *Enga: Foundations for Development*, edited by B. Carrad, D. Lea, K. Talyaga, 93–127. Armidale: Department of Geography, University of New England.

Anderson, C. Milton. 1975. "Food Crisis Forces Reform of Farm Policy in Ecuador." *Foreign Agriculture* 13/30:10–11.

Aquino, Francisco. 1967. "The Context of the Inter-American Bank's Activities." In *Agricultural Development in Latin America: the Next Decade: Round Table; April*. Washington, D.C.: Inter-American Development Bank.

Aulitzky, H. 1973. "Beruecksichtigung der Wildbach- und Lawinen-gefahrengebiete als Grundlage der Raumordnung von Gebirgslaendern." *100 Jahre Hochschule fuer Bodenkultur* 4/2:81–113.

Aulitzky, H. 1974. *Endangered Alpine Regions and Disaster Prevention Measures*. Nature and Environment Series, no. 6. Strasbourg: Council of Europe.

Bailey, F. G., ed. 1971. *Gifts and Poison: the Politics of Reputation*. Oxford: Blackwell.

Baker, P. T. 1979. "The Use of Human Ecological Models in Biological Anthropology: Examples from the Andes." *Collegium Antropologicum* 3:157–171.

Baker, Paul T. and Michael A. Little, eds. 1976. *Man in the Andes: a Multidisciplinary Study of High-Altitude Quechua.* Stroudsburg: Dowden, Hutchinson, and Ross.

Balland, Daniel. 1982. "Contraintes écologiques et fluctuations historiques dans l'organisation territoriale des nomades d'Afghanistan." *Production pastorale et société* 11:55–67.

Balland, Daniel and A. de Benoist. 1982. "Nomades et semi-nomades Baluch d'Afghanistan." *Revue Géographique de l'Est* 22:1–2, 117–144.

Balland, Daniel and Charles M. Kieffer. 1979. "Nomadisme et sécheresse en Afghanistan: l'exemple des nomades Pashtun du Dashte Nawor." In *Pastoral Production and Society* 75–90. New York: Cambridge University Press.

Barfield, Thomas J. 1981. *The Central Asian Arabs of Afghanistan: Pastoral Nomadism in Transition.* Austin: University of Texas Press.

Barth, F. 1956. "Ecologic Relationships of Ethnic Groups in Swat, North Pakistan." *American Anthropologist* 58:1079–1089.

Basile, David G. 1974. *Tillers of the Andes: Farmers and Farming in the Quito Basin.* Studies in Geography, no.8. Chapel Hill: Department of Geography, University of North Carolina.

Batchelor, P. 1984. *People in Rural Development.* Exeter: Paternoster Press.

Batura Investigation Group. 1979. *Investigation Report on the Batura Glacier in the Karakorum Mountains in the Islamic Republic of Pakistan, 1974–1975.* Beijing.

Bayliss-Smith, Timothy. 1985. "Pre-Ipomopan Agriculture in the Papua New Guinea Highlands above 2000 meters: Some Experimental Data on Taro Cultivation." In *Prehistoric Intensive Agriculture in the Tropics.* International Research Series no. 232, edited by I. S. Farrington, 285–320. Cambridge: British Archaeological Society.

Beck, Terry. 1983. "Mt. Allan and the 1988 Olympic Winter Games," Open letter dated February 15, 1983.

Bennett, John W. 1976. *The Ecological Transition: Cultural Anthropology and Human Adaptation.* New York: Pergamon.

Berger, P. and T. Luckman. 1967. *The Social Construction of Reality.* Garden City, N.J.: Doubleday.

Bernatzik, H. 1947. *Akha and Meau.* 2 vols. Innsbruck.

Berreman, G. D. 1963. *Hindus of the Himalayas.* Berkeley: University of California Press.

Bharati, A. 1970. "Pilgrimage Sites in Indian Civilization." In *Chapters in Indian Civilization Vol. 2,* edited by Joseph Elder, 83–126. Dubuque: Kendall/Hunt Publishers.

Bharati, A. 1970. "The Use of "Superstition" as an Antitraditional Device in Urban Hinduism." In *Contributions to Indian Sociology.* New Series, no. 4. Delhi: Vikas.

Bharati, A. 1978a. "Actual and Ideal Himalayas: Hindu Views of the Mountains." In *Himalayan Anthropology,* edited by J. F. Fisher, 77–83. The Hague: Mouton.

Bharati, A. 1978b. *Great Traditions and Little Traditions.* Varanasi: Chowkhamba Sanskrit Series.

Bharati, A. 1980. *The Ochre Robe.* Santa Barbara: Ross-Erikson Publishers.

Bhardwaj, S. M. 1973. *Hindu Places of Pilgrimage in India.* Berkeley: University of California Press.

Bhruksasri, W. and G. N. Oughton. 1970. "Research Priorities in Hill Tribe Development." In *Shifting Cultivation and Economic Development in Northern Thailand.* Bangkok: Land Development Department.

Biddulph, John 1971. *Tribes of the Hindoo Koosh.* 1880. Reprint. Graz: Akademische Druck und Verlagsanstalt.

Blache, Jules. 1933. *L'homme et la montagne.* Géographie humaine vol. 3. Paris: Gallimard.

Blankenship, J. C. and R. B. Thomas. 1977. "Demographic Impact of Introducing Modern Medicine to a Subsistence-level Agrarian Population: A Simulation." *Environmental Management* 1:401–417.

Bliss, Janet. 1985. "A New Slant on the Eastern Slopes." *Landmark* Summer/Fall, 4–7.

Bobek, H. 1962. "Ueber den Einbau der sozialgeographischen Betrachtungsweise in die Kulturgeographie." *Verhandlungen des Deutschen Geographentages* 33:148–165.

Bodley, J. H. 1975. *The Victims of Progress.* Menlo Park: Cummings.

Boehm, H. 1966. "Die gelaendeklimatische Bedeutung des Bergschattens und der Exposition fuer das Gefuege der Natur- und Kulturlandschaft." *Erdkunde* 20:81–93.

Boserup, Ester. 1965. *The Conditions of Agricultural Growth.* Chicago: Aldine.

Bowers, Nancy 1968. "The Ascending Grasslands: An Anthropological Study of Ecological

Succession in a High Mountain Valley of New Guinea." *Dissertation Abstracts International.* Series B. 29/8:2718.

Bowman, Isaiah. 1916. *The Andes of Southern Peru.* New York: Henry Holt.

Braudel, Fernand. 1972. *The Mediterranean and the Mediterranean World in the Age of Philip II.* 2 vols. New York: Harper and Row.

British Columbia. n.d. *British Columbia Mountain Resorts.* Ministry of Industry and Small Business Development.

Brookfield, Harold C. with Doreen Hart. 1971. *Melanesia: A Geographical Interpretation of an Island World.* London: Methuen.

Brown, Leslie. 1965. *Africa—A Natural History.* London: Hamish Hamilton.

Brugger, Ernst A., Gerhard Furrer, Bruno Messerli, and Paul Messerli, eds. 1984. *The Transformation of Swiss Mountain Regions.* Bern: Paul Haupt.

Brugger, O. and R. Wohlfarter. 1983. *Alpwirtschaft heute.* Graz-Stuttgart.

Bruneau, M. 1972. "Ray et Utilisation des Terres Hautes dans la Thailand Septentrionale." In *Etudes de Géographie tropicale offertes à Pierre Gourou.* Paris.

Bruneau, M. 1974. "Ethnies, Peuplement et organisation de l'espace en Thailande septentrionale." *Les Cahiers d'Outre Mer* 108.

Brunnschweiler, Dieter. 1971. "The Study of the Physical Environment in Latin America." In *Geographic Research on Latin America: Benchmark 1970.* Proceedings of the Conference of Latin Americanist Geographers, vol. 1, edited by Barry Lentnek, Robert L. Carmin and Tom L. Martinson, 220–231. Muncie, Indiana: Ball State University.

Brush, Stephen B. 1973. "A Study of Subsistence Activities in Uchucmarca, Peru." *University of Wisconsin Land Tenure Center Newsletter* 40:10–18.

Brush, Stephen B. 1974. "El Lugar del Hombre en el Ecosistema Andino." *Revista del Museo Nacional (Lima)* 40:277–299.

Brush, Stephen B. 1976. "Man's Use of an Andean Ecosystem." *Human Ecology* 4:147–166.

Brush, Stephen B. 1977. *Mountain, Field, and Family: The Economy and Human Ecology of an Andean Valley.* Philadephia: University of Pennsylvania Press.

Brush, Stephen B. 1984. "Agricultural Change and Genetic Erosion in the Andes." *Biology International* 10:24.

Brush, Stephen B., H. J. Carney, and Z. Huaman. 1981. "Dynamics of Andean Potato Agriculture." *Economic Botany* 35:70–88.

Bryan, Rorke. 1973. *Much is Taken, Much Remains.* North Scituate, Mass: Duxbury Press.

Budowski, Gerardo. 1968. "La Influencia Humana en la Vegetación Natural de Montañas Tropicales Americanas." *Colloquium Geographicum* 9:157–162.

Bunnell, Fred, et al. (pseud. Bubu Himamowa). 1974. *The Obergurgl Model.* Laxenburg: International Institute for Applied Systems Analysis.

Burchard, Roderick E. 1974. " Coca y Trueque de Alimentos." In *Reciprocidad e Intercambio en los Andes Peruanos.* Perú-Problema, no. 12, edited by Giorgio Alberti and Enrique Mayer, 209–251. Lima: Instituto de Estudios Peruanos.

Burke, Melvin. 1971. "Land Reform in the Lake Titicaca Region." In *Beyond the Revolution: Bolivia since 1952,* edited by James M. Malloy and Richard S. Thorn. Pittsburgh: University of Pittsburgh.

Burnes, Alexander. 1973. *Travels into Bokhara; Being the Account of a Journey from India to Cabool, Tartary, and Persia.* 1834. Reprint. Karachi: Oxford University Press.

Burnham, P. 1982. "Energetics and Ecological Anthropology." In *Energy and Effort,* edited by G. A. Harrison. London: Taylor and Francis.

Burton, Ian, Robert W. Kates, and Gilbert F. White. 1978. *The Environment as Hazard.* New York: Oxford University Press.

Butzer, Karl W. 1982. *Archaeology as Human Ecology.* Cambridge: Cambridge University Press.

Cabrera, Angel L. 1968. "Ecología Vegetal de la Puna." *Colloquium Geographicum* 9:91–116.

Caine, N., and P. K. Mool. 1981. "Channel Geometry and Flow Estimates for Two Small Mountain Streams in the Middle Hills, Nepal." *Mountain Research and Development* 1:231–243.

Camino, Alejandro. 1982. "Tiempo y Espacio en la Estrategía de Subsistencia Andina: Un Caso en las Vertientes Orientales Sur-Peruanas." *Senri Ethnological Studies* 10:11–35.

Canfield, Robert L. 1973. *Faction and Conversion in a Plural Society: Religious Alignments in the Hindu Kush*. Anthropological Papers, no. 50. Ann Arbor: Museum of Anthropology, University of Michigan.

Carlstein, Tommy. 1982. *Time Resources, Society, and Ecology*. Vol. 1. London: George Allen and Unwin.

Carrad, B. 1982. "The Economy." In *Enga: Foundations for Development*, edited by B. Carrad, David A. M. Lea, and K. K. Talyaga, 146–180. Armidale: University of New England.

Carter, William C. 1965. *Aymara Communities and the Bolivian Agrarian Reform*. Monographs in Social Science, no. 24. Gainesville: University of Florida.

Carter, William C. 1974. "Land in a Traditional Aymara Community." Paper presented at the 23rd Annual Meeting of the American Association of Anthropology in Mexico City.

Caudill, Harry M. 1962. *Night Comes to the Cumberlands: a Biography of a Depressed Area*. Boston: Atlantic-Little Brown.

Caudill, Harry M. 1973. *My Land is Dying*. New York: E. P. Dutton.

Census of India. 1931. *The Jummoo and Kashmir Territories*. Delhi: Superintendent of Government Printing.

Cernusca, A., ed. 1976. *Alpine Grassland Hohe Tauern*. Innsbruck: Austrian MAB Committee.

Cernusca, A., ed. 1978. *Ecological Analysis of Alpine Pastures*. Innsbruck: Austrian MAB Committee.

Champeau, Harold C. 1975. "Five Communes in the People's Republic of China." *Foreign Agriculture* 13/29:1–5; 13/30:7–9; 13/31:4–6; 13/32:10–13; 13/33:6–8.

Chapman, E. C. 1967. "An Appraisal of Recent Agricultural Changes in the Northern Valleys of Thailand." Paper presented to The 6th Academic Conference, Agricultural Economic Society of Thailand, Kasetsart University, Bangkok, Mimeo.

Chapman, E. C. 1970. "Shifting Cultivation and Economic Development in the Lowlands of Northern Thailand." In *Shifting Cultivation and Economic Development in Northern Thailand*. Bangkok: Land Development Department.

Chapman, E. C. 1973. "Villagers as Clients: A Study of Land Development in Northern Thailand." In *Studies of Contemporary Thailand*. Human Geography Publication, no. 8, edited by R. Ho and E. C. Chapman. Canberra: Research School of Pacific Studies.

Chapman, E. C. 1980. "Agricultural Intensification and the Role of Forestry in Northern Thailand." In *Conservation and Development in Northern Thailand*, edited by Jack D. Ives, S. Sabbasri, P. Voraurai. Tokyo: United Nations University.

Charles, Christian. 1985. "La Vallée de Hunza, Karakorum, Pakistan." Grenoble. Thèse de Doctorat de 3e Cycle.

Chavran, P. 1915. *Contribution´a l'échide de l'irrigation dans le canton du Valais*. Bern.

Chitman, V. 1980. "Land Use and Its Relationship to Agriculture in Pangsa, Chiang Mai: A Case Study." In *Conservation and Development in Northern Thailand*, edited by Jack D. Ives, S. Sabbasri, P. Voraurai. Tokyo: United Nations University.

Chomyn, Sharon A. 1985. "The Odyssey: A Proposed Resort Development at Cline River, Alberta." Calgary: Department of Geography, University of Calgary. Mimeo.

Clarke, William C. 1977. "A Change of Subsistence Staple in Prehistoric New Guinea." In *Proceedings of the Third Symposium of the International Society for Tropical Root Crops*, edited by C. L. A. Leakey. Ibadan: University of Ibadan.

Cole, John W. and Eric R. Wolf. 1974. *The Hidden Frontier: Ecology and Ethnicity in an Alpine Valley*. New York: Academic Press.

Collier, G. A. 1975. *Fields of the Tzotzil: The Ecological Basis of Tradition in Highland Chiapas*. Austin: University of Texas Press.

Conway, G. R. 1985. "Agricultural Ecology and Farming System Research." In *Farming Systems Research*. Hawksburg: Australian Council for International Agriculture Research.

Cooper, J. P. 1970. "Environmental Physiology." In *Genetic Resources in Plants–their Exploration and Conservation*. IBP Handbook no. 11, edited by O. Fraenkel and E. Bennett. Cambridge: Blackwells.

Cooper, P. J. M. 1979. "The Association between Altitude, Environmental Variables, Maize Growth and Yields in Kenya." *Journal of Agricultural Science, Cambridge* 93:635–649.

Coutu, Arthur J. 1969. *The Agricultural Development of Peru*. Benchmark Studies on Agricultural Development in Latin America, no. 4. New York: Praeger.

Credner, W. 1935a. *Siam, das Land der Tai.* Stuttgart.

Credner, W. 1935b. "Voelkerschichtung und Voelkerbewegungen im mittleren Hinterindien." *Geografiska Annaler.* 268–284.

Crowley, J. M. 1975. "Ranching in the Mountain Parks of Colorado." *Geographical Review* 65:445–460.

Cuatrecasas, José. 1968. "Páramo Vegetation and Its Life Forms." *Colloquium Geographicum* 9:163–186.

Cullingworth, J. Barry. 1984. *Canadian Planning and Public Participation,* Land Policy Paper no. 4. Toronto: Center for Urban and Community Studies, University of Toronto.

Curzon, George N. C. 1908. *Frontiers.* 2nd ed. Oxford: Clarendon Press.

Custred, Glen. 1973. "Puna Zones of the South Central Andes." Paper presented in symposium *Cultural Adaptations to Mountain Ecosystems* at Annual Meeting of the American Anthropological Association. Mimeo.

Custred, Glen. 1974. "Llameros y comercio interregional." In *Reciprocidad e Intercambio en los Andes Peruanos.* Perú-Problema, no. 12, edited by Giorgio Alberti and Enrique Mayer, 252–289. Lima: Instituto de Estudios Peruanos.

Degenhardt, Bodo. 1980. "Das touristische Potential des Hochgebirges und seine Nutzung." Ph.D. Diss. Berlin: Free University of Berlin.

Denevan, William M. 1980. "Latin America." In *World Systems of Traditional Resource Management,* edited by Gary Klee, 217–244. New York: Halsted Press.

Denizot, F., H. Haider and Xavier de Planhol. 1977. "Peuplement et mise en valeur de la vallée de Golak (Afghanistan central)." *Revue Géographique de l'Est* 17:1–2, 53–71.

Department of Indian Affairs and Northern Development, National and Historic Parks Branch. 1969. *National Parks Policy* Ottawa: Queen's Printer.

Dickerson, Mark O. and Thomas Flanagan. 1982. *An Introduction to Government and Politics.* Toronto: Methuen.

Dickinson, III, Joshua C. 1971. "Research on Forests and Man in Latin America." In *Geographic Research on Latin America: Benchmark 1970.* Proceedings of the Conference of Latin Americanist Geographers, vol. 1, edited by Barry Lentnek, Robert L. Carmin and Tom L. Martinson, 215–219. Muncie: Ball State University.

Dobbin–Cochrane Group. 1985. *Imagine Mountain Star,* Calgary: Mountain Star Resorts Ltd.

Dollfus, Olivier. 1981. *El Reto del Espacio Andino.* Lima: Instituto de Estudios Peruanos.

Donkin, R. A. 1979. *Agricultural Terracing in the Aboriginal New World.* Viking Fund Publications in Anthropology no. 56. Tucson: University of Arizona Press.

Dorsey, Joseph F. 1975. *A Case Study of Ex-hacienda Toralapa in the Tiraque Region of the Upper Cochabamba Valley.* Land Tenure Center Research Paper, no. 65. Madison: University of Wisconsin.

Dow, Vicki, Mischa Plam, and Jack D. Ives. "Mountain Hazards Mapping: The Development of a Prototype Combined Hazards Map, Monarch Lake Quadrangle, Colorado, U.S.A." *Mountain Research and Development* 1:55–64.

Dupree, Louis B. 1984. "Tribal Warfare in Afghanistan and Pakistan: A Reflection of the Segmentary Lineage System." In *Islam in Tribal Societies. From the Atlas to the Indus,* edited by A. S. Ahmed and D. M. Hart, 266–286. London: Routledge and Kegan Paul.

Dupuis, J. 1975. "Les Montagnes Rocheuses du Colorado: milieu naturel et vie humaine." *Les Cahiers d'Outre Mer* 28:305–325.

Eckholm, Erik P. 1975. "The Deterioration of Mountain Environments." *Science* 189:764–770.

Ecosign Mountain Recreation Planners Ltd., 1983. *Jumbo Glacier: Glacier Skiing Resort Feasibility Study.* Report prepared for Jumbo Glacier Skiing Ltd., Invermere, B.C. Whistler, B.C.: Ecosign Recreation Planners Ltd.

Edelberg, Lennart, and Schyler Jones. 1979. *Nuristan.* Graz: Akademische Druck-und Verlagsanstalt.

Elphinstone, Mountstuart. 1969. *An Account of the Kingdom of Caubul.* 1815. Reprint. Graz: Akademische Druck-und Verlagsanstalt.

Ellen, Roy. 1981. *Environment, Subsistence, and System: The Ecology of Small-Scale Social Formations.* Cambridge: Cambridge University Press.

Ern, H. 1966. "Die dreidimensionale Anordnung der Gebirgsvegetation auf der Iberischen Halbinsel." *Bonner Geographische Abhandlungen* 37:1–136.

Fautz, Bruno. 1963. *Sozialstruktur und Bodennutzung in der Kulturlandschaft des Swat*

(Nordwesthimalaya). Giessener Geographische Schriften vol. 3. Giessen: Wilhelm Schmitz.

Fayz, Mohammad. 1333 AH. (1914 CE) *Seraj al-tawarix*. vol. 3. Kabul: Matbaca-ye horufi.

Fazel, G. R. 1973. "The Encapsulation of Nomadic Societies in Iran." In *The Desert and the Sown. Nomads in the Wider Society*. Research Series no. 21, edited by C. Nelson, 129–142. Berkeley: Institute of International Studies, University of California.

Ferdinand, Klaus. 1959. *Preliminary Notes on Hazara Culture*. Historisk Filofiske Meddelelser udgivet af Det Kongelige Dansk Videnskabernes Selskab vol. 37, no. 5. Copenhagen: Munksgaard.

Ferdinand, Klaus. 1962. "Nomadic Expansion and Commerce in Central Afghanistan. A Sketch of Some Modern Trends." *Folk* 4:123–159.

Ferroni, Marco A. 1980. "The Urban Bias of Peruvian Food Policy: Consequences and Alternatives." *Dissertation Abstracts International*. Series A, 41/1:331.

Fischer, D. 1970. *Waldverbreitung, baeuerliche Waldwirtschaft und kommerzielle Waldnutzung im oestlichen Afghanistan*. Afghanische Studien vol. 2. Meisenheim am Glan: Anton Hain.

Flach, E. 1965. "Klimatologische Untersuchung ueber die geographische Verteilung der Globalstrahlung und der diffusen Himmelsstrahlung." *Archiv Meteorologie, Geophysik, Bioklimatologie*. Series B. 14:161–183.

Fleuret, A. and P. Fleuret. 1980. "Nutrition, Consumption, and Agricultural Change." *Human Organization* 39:250–260.

Flohn, H. 1969. "Zum Klima und Wasserhaushalt des Hindukusch und der benachbarten Gebiete." *Erdkunde* 39:250–262.

Flores Moncayo, José. 1965. "Objects of Agrarian Reform in Bolivia." In *Agrarian Reform in Latin America*, edited by T. Lynn Smith, 129–130. New York: Alfred A. Knopf.

Flores Ochoa, Jorge. 1968. *Los pastores de Paratia*. Serie Antropología Social, no. 10. Mexico: Instituto Indigenísta Interamericano.

Flores Ochoa, Jorge. 1975. "Sociedad y Cultura en la Puna Alta de los Andes." *America Indigena* 35:297–319.

Fonseca Martel, Ceasar 1972. "Nutrition, Consumption, and Agricultural Change." *Human Organization* 39:250–260.

Fonseca Martel, Ceasar. 1974. " Modalidades de la minka." In *Reciprocidad e intercambio en los Andes Peruanos*. Peru-Problema, no. 12, edited by Giorgio Alberti and Enrique Mayer, 86–109. Lima: Instituto de Estudios Peruanos.

Forman, Sylvia H. 1972. "Law and Conflict in Rural Highland Ecuador." *Dissertation Abstracts International*. Series B. 34/1:34.

Freitag, U., and Banlang Kamasundra. 1976. *Mapping the Population Characteristics of Developing Countries: Thailand as Example*. Bangkok: Royal Thai Survey Department.

Frutiger, H. 1980. "History and Actual State of Legislation of Avalanche Zoning in Switzerland." *Journal of Glaciology* 26/94:313–24.

Fuerer-Haimendorf, Christoph von. 1975. *Himalayan Traders: Life in Highland Nepal*. London: John Murray.

Gade, Daniel W. 1969. "Vanishing Crops of Traditional Agriculture: the Case of Tarwi *(Lupinus mutabilis)* in the Andes." *Proceedings of the Association of American Geographers* 1:47–51.

Gade, Daniel W. 1970. "Ethnobotany of Cañihua *(Chenopodium pallidicaule)*, Rustic Seed Crop of the Altiplano." *Economic Botany* 24:1–61.

Gade, Daniel W. 1972. "Chaquitaclla: the Native Footplough and its Persistence in Central Andean Agriculture." *Tools and Tillage* 2:3–15.

Gade, Daniel W. 1975. *Plants, Man and Land in the Vilcanota Valley of Peru*. Biogeographica 6. The Hague: W. Junk.

Gams, H. 1956. "Die Tragacantha-Igelheiden der Gebirge um das Kaspische, Schwarze und Mittellaendische Meer." *Veroeffentlichungen des Geobotanischen Institutes Ruebel in Zuerich* 31:217–243.

Geist, Valerius. 1983. "The Problems." Paper submitted to the Olympic Organizing Committee 1988. Mimeo.

Glaser, G. and J. Celecia, 1981. "Guidelines for Integrated Ecological Research in the Andean Region." *Mountain Research and Development* 1:171–186.

Glatzer, B. 1982. "Processes of Nomadization in West Afghanistan." In *Contemporary*

Nomadic and Pastoral Peoples: Asia and the North. Studies in Third World Societies, no. 18, edited by Philip C. Salzman, 61–86. Williamsburg: College of William and Mary.

Golson, J. 1981. "New Guinea Agricultural History: A Case Study." In *A History of Agriculture in Papua New Guinea: A Time to Plant and a Time to Uproot,* edited by D. Denoon, and C.Snowden, 43–54. Waigani: Institute of Papua New Guinea.

Gomez-Ibanez, D. A. 1967. "The Rise and Decline of Transhumance in the United States." M.A. thesis, Department of Geography, University of Wisconsin.

Gorfer, A. 1975. *Die Erben der Einsamkeit.* Trient.

Gottman, J. 1943. "Bugeaud, Gallieni, Lyautey: the Development of French Colonial Warfare." In *Makers of Modern Strategy: Military Thought from Machiavelli to Hitler,* edited by E. M. Earle, 234–259. Princeton: Princeton University Press.

Goudie, Andrew. 1982. *The Human Impact: Man's Role in Environmental Change.* Cambridge: MIT.

Grabherr, G. 1982. *Influence of Summer and Winter Tourism on the Alpine Vegetation,* Innsbruck. Mimeo.

Grabherr, G., E. Maehr, and H. Reisgl. 1978. *Oecologia Plantarum.* No. 3. Innsbruck.

Grevemeyer, J.-H. 1982. *Herrschaft, Raub und Gegenseitigkeit: Die politische Geschichte Badakhshans 1500–1883.* Wiesbaden: Otto Harrassowitz.

Grjunberg, A. L. 1980. *Jazyk kati.* Moscow: Nauka.

Groetzbach, Erwin. 1969. "Junge sozialgeographische Wandlungen im Afghanischen Hindukusch." *Mitteilungen der Geographischen, Gesellschaft Muenchen* 54:115–134.

Groetzbach, Erwin. 1972. *Kulturgeographischer Wandel in Nordost-Afghanistan seit dem 19. Jahrhundert.* Afghanische Studien, vol. 4. Meisenheim am Glan: Anton Hain.

Groetzbach, Erwin. 1976. "Ueberlegungen zu einer vergleichenden Kulturgeographie altweltlicher Hochgebirge." *Verhandlungen des Deutschen Geographentages* 40:109–120.

Groetzbach, Erwin. 1980. "Die Nutzung der Hochweidestufe als Kriterium einer kulturgeographischen Typisierung von Hochgebirgen." *Arbeiten aus dem Geographischen Institut der Universitaet des Saarlandes* 29:265–277.

Groetzbach, Erwin. 1981. "Zur raeumlichen Mobilitaet der Bevoelkerung in einer peripheren alpinen Region: Osttirol." *Mitteilungen der Oesterreichischen Geographischen Gesellschaft* 123:67–91.

Groetzbach, Erwin. 1982a. *Das Hochgebirge als menschlicher Lebensraum.* Eichstaetter Hochschulreden no. 33. Munich.

Groetzbach, Erwin. 1982b. "Yayla Erholungsverkehr im oestlichen Pontischen Gebirge (Nordost-Tuerkei)." *Mitteilungen der Geographischen Gesellschaft Muenchen* 67:91–124.

Guillet, David G. 1983. "Toward a Cultural Ecology of Mountains: The Central Andes and the Himalaya Compared." *Current Anthropology* 24:561–574.

Haffner, W. 1965. "Nepal Himalaya." *Erdkunde* 19:89–103.

Haffner, W. 1974. In *Geooekologie der Hawaii-Inseln,* Erdwissenschaftliche Forschung, vol. 9 edited by Ingrid Henning, 1–153. Stuttgart: Franz Steiner.

Haffner, W. 1979. ed. *Nepal-Himalaya: Untersuchungen zum vertikalen Landschaftsaufbau Zentral-und Ostnepals.* Erdwissenschtliche Forschung vol. 12. Stuttgart: Franz Steiner.

Hardin, Garrett. 1968. "The Tragedy of the Commons." *Science* 162:1243.

Hartke, W., K. Ruppert, eds. 1964. *Almgeographie.* Forschungsberichte, vol. 4–Deutsche Forschungsgemeinschaft. Wiesbaden.

Harrison, G. A. 1982. *Energy and Effort.* London: Taylor and Francis.

Haserodt, Klaus. 1984. "Abflussverhalten der Fluesse mit Bezuegen zur Sonnenscheindauer und zum Niederschlag zwischen Hindukusch (Chitral) und Hunza–Karakorum (Gilgit, NordPakistan)." *Mitteilungen der Geographischen Gesellschaft in Muenchen* 69:129–169.

Hassnain, F. M. 1978. *Gilgit—The Northern Gate of Indian.* New Delhi: Sterling.

Hasslacher, Peter. 1984. *Sanfter Tourismus: Virgental.* Innsbruck: Austrian Alpine Club.

Heath, Dwight B. et al. 1969. *Land Reform and Social Revolution in Bolivia.* Praeger Special Studies in International Economics and Development. New York: Frederick A. Praeger.

Henning, Ingrid 1972. "Horizontale und vertikale Vegetationsanordnung im Ural-System." In *Geoecology of the High Mountains of Eurasia.* Erdwissenschtliche Forschung vol. 4 edited by Carl Troll, 17–35. Stuttgart: Franz Steiner.

Henning, Ingrid. 1974. *Geoekologie der Hawaii-Inseln*. Erdwissenschaftliche Forschung, vol. 8. Stuttgart: Franz Steiner.

Hewitt, Kenneth. 1972. "The Mountain Environment and Geomorphic Processes." In *Alpine Geomorphology of Western Canada*, edited by Olav Slaymaker and Harold J. McPherson, 17–36. Vancouver: Tantalus.

Hewitt, Kenneth. 1976. "Earthquake Hazards in the Mountains." *Natural History* 85:5:30–37.

Hewitt, Kenneth. 1983. "The Idea of Disaster in a Technocratic Age." In *Interpretations of Calamity*, edited by Kenneth Hewitt, 3–32. London: George Allen and Unwin.

Hewitt, Kenneth. 1984. "Ecotonal Settlement and Natural Hazards in Mountain Regions: The Case of Earthquake Risks." *Mountain Research and Development* 4:31–37.

Heyduk, Daniel. 1974. "The Hacienda System and Agrarian Reform in Highland Bolivia: a Re-evaluation." *Ethnology* 13:71–81.

Hinton, P. 1970. "Swidden Cultivation among the Pwo Karen of Northern Thailand: Present Practices and Future Prospects." In *Shifting Cultivation and Economic Development in Northern Thailand*. Bangkok: Land Development Department.

Hinton, P. 1967. "Introduction." In *Tribesmen and Peasants in North Thailand*. Chiang Mai: Tribal Research Centre.

Hobsbawm, Eric J. 1974. "Peasant Land Occupations." *Past and Present* 62:120–152.

Hofstadter, Richard. 1959. *Social Darwinism in American Thought*. Rev. Ed. New York: George Braziller.

Hofmeister, Bruno. 1958. "Die Transhumance in den westlichen Vereinigten Staaten von Amerika." Ph.D. Diss. Free University of Berlin.

Hofmeister, Bruno. 1961. "Wesen und Erscheinungsformen der Transhumance." *Erdkunde* 15:121–135.

Holling, C. S., ed. 1974. *Modelling and Simulation for Environmental Impact Analysis*. Laxenburg: International Institute for Applied Systems Analysis.

Holtmeier, F.-K. ed. 1974. *Geooekologische Beobachtungen und Studien an der Subarktischen und Alpinen Waldgrenze in vergleichender Sicht*. Erdwissenschaftliche Forschung, vol. 8. Stuttgart: Franz Steiner.

Hourcade, Bernard. 1978. "Migrations de travail et de loisir dans l'Elbourz de Téhéran." *Revue de Géographie de Lyon* 53:229–240.

Howard, M. and P. Paret, eds. 1976. *Carl von Clausewitz on War*. New Jersey: Princeton University Press.

Humboldt, Alexander von, and Aime Bonpland. 1807. Reprint 1955. *Essai sur la Geographie des Plantes; Accompagne d'un Tableau Physique des Regions Equinoxiales*. Mexico City: Editorial Cultura.

Humlum, Johannes. 1959. *La géographie de l'Afghanistan*. Copenhagen: Gyldendal.

Huntington, Ellsworth. 1945. *Mainsprings of Civilization*. New York: Wiley.

Hustich, I. 1953. "The Boreal Limits of Conifers, Arctic." *Journal Arctic Institute of North America* 6:149–162.

Hymowitz, Theodore. 1969. "The Soybeans of the Kumaon Hills of India." *Economic Botany* 23:50–54.

India, 1895. *Gazetteer of Afghanistan*. vol. 4, "Kabul," 3rd ed. Calcutta: Government Printing.

Inntrec Group Ltd. 1981. "Analysis of the Development Potential of the former Canmore Mines Property near Banff, Alberta." Report prepared for Patrician Land Crop. Ltd. Calgary: Inntrec Group Ltd.

Inntrec Group Ltd. 1982. "Area Structure Plan for ECHO." Report submitted to Improvement District no. 8. Calgary: Inntrec Group Ltd.

International Union for Conservation of Nature and Natural Resources (IUCN). 1968. *Proceedings of the Latin American Conference on the Conservation of Renewable Natural Resources*. IUCN Publications New Series no. 13. Morges: IUCN.

Instituto Veterinario de Investigaciones Tropicales y de Altura. 1972. *Investigaciones del IVITA en camelidos sudamericanos*. Boletín de Divulgación, no.10. Lima: Universidad Nacional Mayor de San Marcos.

Isbell, Billie Jean. 1974. "Parentesco Andino y reciprodidad; Kuyaq: los que nos aman." In *Reciprocidad e Intercambio en los Andes Peruanos*. Perú-Problema no. 12, edited by Giorgio Alberti and Enrique Mayer, 110–152. Lima: Instituto de Estudios Peruanos.

Ives, Jack D. 1980. "Highland-Lowland Interactive Systems in the Humid Tropics and Subtropics: The Need for a Conceptual Basis for an Applied Research Programme." In *Conservation and Development in Northern Thailand,* edited by Jack D. Ives, S. Sabbasri, P. Varaurai. Tokyo: United Nations University.

Ives, Jack D. and Roger G. Barry, eds. 1974. *Arctic and Alpine Environments.* London: Methuen.

Ives, Jack D. and M. Bovis. 1978. "Natural Hazards Maps for Land-use Planning, San Juan Mountain, Colorado, U.S.A." *Arctic and Alpine Research* 10:185–212.

Ives, Jack D. and Bruno Messerli. 1981. "Mountain Hazards Mapping in Nepal. Introduction to an Applied Mountain Research Project." *Mountain Research and Development* 1:223–230.

Ives, Jack D. and Bruno Messerli. 1984. "Stability and Instability of Mountain Ecosystems: Lessons Learned and Recommendations for the Future." *Mountain Research and Development* 4:63–71.

Ives, Jack D. et al. 1976. "Natural Hazards in Mountain Colorado." *Annals of the Association of American Geographers* 66:129–144.

Ives, Jack D. and R. P. Zimina, eds. 1978. "Mountain Geoecology and Landuse Implications." *Arctic and Alpine Research* 10:.

Janetschek, H. I., et al. 1976. In *Proceedings of the 15th International Congress of Entomology.* 185–207.

Jennings, P. R., and J. H. Cook. 1977. "Centres of Origin of Crops and their Productivity." *Economic Botany* 31:51–54.

Jentsch, Christoph. 1977. "Fuer eine vergleichende Kulturgeographie der Hochgebirge." *Mannheimer Geographische Arbeiten* 1:57–71.

Jettmar, Karl. 1979. "Forward." In *Materialien zur Ethnographie von Dardistan (Pakistan).* Bergvoelker im Hindukusch und Karakorum, vol. 3, part 1, "Hunza," edited by Irmtraud Mueller-Stellrecht, v-ix. Graz: Akademische Druck-und Verlagsanstalt.

Jochim, Michael A. 1981. *Strategies for Survival: Cultural Behavior in an Ecological Context.* New York: Academic Press.

Johnson, Allen W. 1972. "Individuality and Experimentation in Traditional Agriculture." *Human Ecology* 1:149–159.

Johnson, Kirsten, A. Olson, and S. Manandhar. 1982. "Environmental Knowledge and Response to Natural Hazards in Mountainous Nepal." *Mountain Research and Development* 2:175–188.

Jorgenson, Harold T. 1971. "Basic Issues in the Process of Development in Latin America: Food–Land–Employment–Income–Environment." In *Geographic Research on Latin America: Benchmark 1970.* Proceedings of the Conference of Latin Americanist Geographers, vol. 1, edited by Barry Lentnek, Robert L. Carmin and Tom L. Martinson, 402–411. Muncie: Ball State University.

Judd, L. C. 1964. "Dry Rice Agriculture in Northern Thailand." Southeast Asia Programme Data Paper, no. 52. Ithaca: SUNY College of Agriculture and Human Ecology.

Kakar, H. K. 1971. *Afghanistan. A Study in Internal Political Developments 1880–1896.* Kabul: Punjab Educational Press.

Kakar, H. K. 1979. *Government and Society in Afghanistan. The Reign of Amir Abd al-Rahman Khan.* Austin: University of Texas.

Kariel, Herbert G., and Patricia E. Kariel. 1984. "Human Activities in the Canadian Cordillera." In *Beitraege zur vergleichenden Kulturgeographie der Hochgebirge.* Eichstaetter Beitraege no. 12, edited by Erwin Groetzbach and Gisbert Rinschede, 265–283. Regensburg: Friedrich Pustet.

Katz, David J. 1982. "Kafir to Afghan: Religious Conversion, Political Incorporation and Ethnicity in the Vaygal Valley, Nuristan." *Dissertation Abstracts International.* Series A 43/4:1214.

Katz, David J. 1984. "Responses to Central Authority in Nuristan: The Case of the Vaygal Valley Kalasha." In *Revolutions and Rebellions in Afghanistan: Anthropological Perspectives,* edited by M. N. Shahrani and R. L. Canfield, 94–118. Berkeley: Institute of International Studies, University of California.

Kawakita, J. 1956. "Crop Zone." In *Land and Crops of Nepal Himalaya: Scientific Results of the Japanese Expeditions to Nepal Himalaya,* vol. 2, edited by H. Kihara, 67–93. Kyoto: Kyoto University Fauna and Flora Research Society.

Kienholz, Hans. 1977. "Kombinierte geomorphologische Gefahrenkarte, 1:10,000 von Grindelwald." *Geographica Bernensia* 4:1–204.

Kienholz, Hans. 1978. "Maps of Geomorphology and Natural Hazards of Grindelwald, Scale 1:10,000." *Arctic and Alpine Research* 10:169–84.

Kienholz, H. 1980. *The Use of Aerial Photographs for Natural Hazard Mapping in Medium Scales for Planning Purpose on a Regional Level in Not Very Accessible Mountain Areas from Experience and Mapping Experiments in the Colorado Rocky Mountains.* Klagenfurt: Forschungsgesellschaft fuer vorbeugende Hochwasserbekaempfung.

Kirkby, A. V. T. 1973. *The Use of Land and Water Resources in the Past and Present Valley of Oaxaca.* Memoirs of the Museum of Anthropology, no. 5. Ann Arbor: Museum of Anthropology.

Klempin, A. 1978. *Contribution of State-Directed Settlement to Agricultural Development.* Heidelberg: South Asia Institute.

Knapp, Gregory. 1984. "Soil, Slope and Water in the Equatorial Andes: A Study of Prehistoric Agricultural Adaptation." *Dissertation Abstracts International.* Series A, 45/ 1:300.

Knapp, Gregory and Luis Canadas. 1986. "The Vulnerability of Marginal Indigenous Farming Communities to Climate Changes in the Ecuadorian Sierra." In *Assessment of Climate Impacts on Agriculture,* vol 2, *Semi-Arid Regions.* Reidel: in press.

Knapp, Gregory and William Denevan. 1985. "The Use of Wetlands in the Prehistoric Economy of the Northern Ecuadorian Highlands." In *Prehistoric Intensive Agriculture in the Tropics.* International Research Series, no. 232, edited by Ian Farrington, 184–207. Oxford: British Archaeological Society.

Koshkaki, M. B. K. 1979. *Qataghan et Badakhshan.* trans. M. Reut. Paris: CNRS.

Krippendorf, J. 1975. *Die Landschaftsfresser: Tourismus und Erholungslandschaft-Verderben oder Segen.* Bern: Beratende.

Kunstadter, Peter. 1967. "The Lua and Skaw Karen of Maehongson Province. Northwestern Thailand." In *Southeast Asian Tribes: Minorities and Nations,* 2 vols., edited by Peter Kunstadter. Princeton: Princeton University Press.

Kunstadter, Peter. 1970. "Subsistence Agricultural Economics of Lua' and Karen Hill Farmers of Mae Sariang District, Northwestern Thailand." In *Shifting Cultivation and Economic Development in Northern Thailand.* Bangkok: Land Development Department.

Kunstadter, Peter. 1980. "Implications of Socio-economic, Demographic, and Cultural Changes for Regional Development in Northern Thailand." In *Conservation and Development in Northern Thailand,* edited by Jack D. Ives, S. Sabbasri, P. Varaurai, 13–27. Tokyo: United Nations University.

Kunstadter, Peter. and E. C. Chapman. 1970. "Shifting Cultivation and Economic Development in Northern Thailand." In *Shifting Cultivation and Economic Development in Northern Thailand.* Bangkok: Land Development Department.

Kunstadter, Peter, S. Sabhasri, and T. Smitinand. 1978. "Flora of a Forest Fallow Farming Environment in Northwestern Thailand." *Journal of the National Research Council* 10.

Kyselak, J. 1825. *Skizzen einer Fussreise durch Oesterreich, Steiermark, Kaernthen, Salzburg, Berchtesgaden, Tirol, Baiern nach Wien, unternommen 1825.* Vienna.

Lamb, Michael. 1984. "Westcastle Resort Approved." *Lethbridge Herald.* June 15, 1984.

Lancaster, A. S. 1946. "General Report on a Tour in North-East Afghanistan." R/12/1/154. London: Indian Office Records.

Landplan Group. 1984. *Mount Allan Ski Area Master Plan.* Report prepared for Alberta Tourism and Small Business. Calgary: The Landplan Group.

Larcher, W. 1977. "The IBP Project." In *Zwergstrauchheide Patscherkofel,* 301–371. Vienna: Austrian Academy of Sciences.

Lauer, Wilhelm. 1952. "Humide und aride Jahreszeiten in Afrika und Suedamerika und ihre Beziehung zu den Vegetations-gurteln." *Bonner Geographische Abhandlungen* 9:9–98.

Lauer, Wilhelm. 1959. "Klimatische und pflanzengeographische Grundzuge Zentralamerikas." *Erdkunde* 13:344–354.

Lauer, Wilhelm. 1968. "Problemas de la división fitogeográfica en America Central." *Colloquium Geographicum* 9:139–156.

Lauer, Wilhelm, et al. 1973. "Arbeiten des Mexiko-Projekts der DFG: Klima, Geomorphologie und Vegetation des zentral-mexikanischen Hochlandes." *Erdkunde* 27:161–234.

Le Bar, F. M., G. C. Hickey, and J. K. Musgrave. 1964. *Ethnic Groups of Mainland South-East Asia.* New Haven: Human Relations Area Files Press.

Le Bar, F. M. 1967. "Miang: Fermented Tea in North Thailand." *Behaviour Sciences Notes.* vol. 2. New Haven: Human Relations Area Files Press.

LaBaron, A. et al. 1979. "An Explanation of the Bolivian Highlands Grazing-Erosion Syndrome." *Journal of Range Management* 32:201–208.

Lehmann, L. 1913. *L'Irrigation dans le Valais.* Paris.

LeRoy Ladurie, E. 1979. *Montaillou: The Promised Land of Error.* New York: Vintage.

Leser, H. ed. 1971. *Landschaftsoekologische Studien im Kalaharisandgebiet am Auob und Nossob.* Erdwissenschaftliche Forschung vol. 3. Stuttgart: Franz Steiner.

Levins, Richard. 1966. "The Strategy of Model Building in Population Ecology." *American Scientist* 54:421–431.

Lewald, A. 1835. *Tyrol vom Glockner zum Ortler und vom Garda- zum Bodensee.* Munich.

Lichtenberger, E. 1975. *The Eastern Alps.* Problem Regions of Europe. Oxford: Oxford University Press.

Lichtenberger, E. 1979. "Die Sukzession von der Agrar-zur Freizeitgesellschaft in den Hochgebirgen Europas." *Innsbrucker Geographische Studien* 5:401–436.

Llaurado, J. Prats. 1968. "Forestry and Agrarian Reform." In *Proceedings of the Latin American Conference on the Conservation of Renewal Natural Resources.* IUCN Publications, New Series No. 13, 401–411. Morges: IUCN.

Lliboutry, L. et al. 1957. "Les glaciers du Désert Chilien."*Congres International de Geophysique Comptes Rendues Assemblée Générale de Toronto* 4:291–300.

Loeffler, E. 1977. *Geomorphology of Papua New Guinea.* Canberra: Australian National University Press.

Loehr, L. 1971. *Bergbauernwirtschaft im Alpenraum.* Graz-Stuttgart.

Loetsch, F. 1958. "Der Einfluss des Brandrodungsbaus auf das Gefuege des Tropenwaldes und die Wasserfuehrung der Stroeme, untersucht am Beispiel Nord-Thailands." *Erdkunde* 12:182–205.

Lorimer, D. L. R. 1938. 3 vols. *The Burushaski Language.* Instituttet for Sammen-liguende Kulturforschung Oslo. Series B, vol. 29. Wiesbaden: Otto Harrassowitz.

Lowey, Mark. 1985. "Parks May Be Turned Into Tourist Meccas," *Calgary Herald* June 14, 1985.

Lutz, W. 1981. "Das High Country der Suedinsel Neuseelands. Entwicklung und Struktur eines Hochgebirgsraumes." *Frankfurter Wirtschafts-und Sozialgeographische Schriften* 36:269–326.

Lynch, Owen. 1969. *The Politics of Untouchability.* New York: Columbia University Press.

MAB. 1974. *Final Report. Working Group on Project 6: Impact of Human Activities on Mountain and Tundra Ecosystems.* MAB report Series, no. 14. Paris: UNESCO.

MAB. 1975. *Draft Report. Regional Meeting on Integrated Ecological Research and Training Needs in the Andean Region.* MAB Report Series, no. 23. Paris: UNESCO.

Mackintosh, Sheila C. 1981. "Second Homes in the Calgary Hinterland," M.A. thesis. Department of Geography, University of Calgary.

Manndorff, H. 1967. "The Hill Tribe Program of the Public Welfare Department, Ministry of Interior, Thailand: Research and Socio-Economic Development." In *Southeast Asia Tribes, Minorities and Nations,* edited by Peter Kunstadter, 525–552. Princeton: Princeton University Press.

Marietan, I. 1948. *Les bisses: La Butte pour l'eau en Valais.* Neuchatel.

Marlowe, D. H. 1967. "Upland-Lowland Relationships: the Case of the S'kaw Karen of Central Upland Western Chiang Mai." In *Tribesmen and Peasants in North Thailand.* Chiang Mai: Tribal Research Center.

Marriott, McKim. 1955. "Little Communities in an Indigenous Civilization." In *Village India,* edited by McKim Marriott. Chicago: Chicago University Press.

Marshall, E. 1985. Personal Communication, March 1985.

Masson, C. 1975. *Narrative of Various Journeys in Balochistan, Afghanistan, and the Panjab.* 1842. Reprint. Graz: Akademische Druck-und Verlagsanstalt.

Masuda, Shozo, Izumi Shimada, and Craig Morris. 1985. *Andean Ecology and Civilization.* Tokyo: University of Tokyo Press.

Matzat, W. 1973. "Einige Besonderheiten des Reisanbaus in Nord-Thailand." In *Verglei-chende Kulturgeographie der Hochgebirge des Suedlichen Asien,* edited by C. Rathjens, C. Troll, and H. Uhlig, 117–121. Stuttgart: Franz Steiner.

Matzat, W. 1976 "Genese und Struktur der Dorfsiedlungen des Lawa-Bergstammes (Nord-thailand)." In *Verhandlungen des Deutschen Geographentages* 40.

Matznetter, J. 1958. "Das alpine Elementarereignis Wesen und Begriff." *Mitteilungen der Geographischen Gesellschaft Wien* 100:67–76.

Mayer, Enrique. 1971. "Un Carnero por un Saco de Papas: Aspectos del Trueque en la Zona de Chaupiwaranga, Pasco." *Revista del Museo Nacional (Lima)* 40:301–330.

Mayer, Enrique. 1979. *Land Use in the Andes: Ecology and Agriculture in the Mantaro Valley with Special Reference to Potatoes.* Lima: Centro Internacional de la Papa.

Mayer, Enrique, and C. Fonseca Martel. 1979. *Sistemas Agrarios en la Cuenca del Rio Canete.* Lima: Impresos ONERN.

Mayfair Place Ltd. 1980. *Panorama, Invermere, B.C. Development Plan.* Calgary: Mayfair Place Ltd.

McAlpine, J. R., G. Keig, and R. Falls, 1983. *Climate of Papua New Guinea.* Canberra: Australia National University.

McKinnon, John, and Wanat Bhruksasri. 1983. *Highlanders of Thailand.* Kuala Lumpur: Oxford University.

McRae, Stephen D. 1979. "Resource Allocation Alternatives in an Andean Herding System: A Simulation Approach." *Dissertation Abstracts International.* Series A. 40/6:3429.

McRae, Stephen D. 1982. "Human Ecological Modeling for the Central Andes." *Mountain Research and Development* 2:97–110.

Mehta, Gita. 1980. *Karma-cola: the Marketing of the Mystic East.* New York: Simon and Schuster.

Mercon Engineering Ltd. et al. 1980. *Fairmont Hot Springs Resort Conceptual Develop-ment Plan.* Fairmont Hot Springs, B.C.: Fairmont Hot Springs Resort Ltd.

Messerli, Bruno and Paul Messerli. 1979. *Schweizerische MAB- Information.* Bern.

Messerli, Bruno, et al. 1972. *Tibesti–Zentrale Sahara: Arbeiten aus der Hochgebirgsregion.* Hochgebirgsforschung/High Mountain Research, vol. 2. Innsbruck and Munich.

Michel, Aloys A. 1967. *The Indus River.* New Haven: Yale University.

Miller, D. M. and D. C. Wertz. 1976. *Hindu Monastic Life.* Montreal and London: McGill/Queen's University Press.

Miller, Keith J. ed. 1984. *The International Karakoram Project.* 2 vols. Cambridge: Cambridge University Press.

Millones, O. J. 1982. "Patterns of Land Use and Associated Environmental Problems of the Central Andes." *Mountain Research and Development* 2:49–61.

Milstead, Harley P. 1928. "Distribution of Crops in Peru." *Economic Geography* 4:88–106.

Mitchell, Clyde, and Jacob Schatan. 1967. "The Outlook for Agricultural Development in Latin America." In *Agricultural Development in Latin America: the Next Decade; Round Table; April.* Washington, D.C.: Inter-American Development Bank.

Mitchell, W. P. 1976. "Irrigation and Community in the Central Peruvian Highlands." *American Anthropologist* 78:25–44.

Momsen, Jr., Richard P. 1971. "Mapping Spatial Factors for Development Planning." In *Geographic Research on Latin America: Benchmark 1970.* Proceedings of the Conference of Latin Americanist Geographers, vol. 1, edited by Barry Lentnek, Robert L. Carmin and Tom L. Martinson 379–401. Muncie: Ball State University.

Moran, Emilio. 1979. *Human Adaptability.* North Scituate, Mass.: Duxbury.

Moran, Emilio, ed. 1984. *The Ecosystem Concept in Anthropology.* Boulder: Westview.

Moser, Walter. ed. 1972. *Obergurgler Zirbenwald.* Innsbruck.

Moser, Walter. 1975. in *International Workshop on the Development of Mountain Ecosys-tems,* edited by Klaus Mueller-Hoehenstein. Munich: German Foundation for International Development.

Mote, F. W. 1967. "The Rural 'Haw' (Yunnanese Chinese) of Northern Thailand." In *Southeast Asian Tribes, Minorities and Nations,* edited by Peter Kunstadter, 487–524. Princeton: Princeton University Press.

Mueller-Stellrecht, Irmtraud.1978. *Hunza and China, 1761–1891.* Stuttgart: Franz Steiner Wiesbaden.

Mueller-Stellrecht, Irmtraud. 1980. *Materialen zue Ethnographie Dardistans (Pakistan).* Part 2/3, "Gilgit,Chitral,Yasin." Graz: Akademische Druck-und Verlagsanstalt.

Murra, John V. 1968. "An Aymara Kingdom." *Ethnohistory* 15:115–151.

Murra, John V. 1970. "Current Research and Prospects in Andean Ethnohistory." *Latin American Research Review* 5:3–36.

Murra, John V. 1975a. "El Control Vertical de un Máximo de Pisos Ecológicos en la Economía de las Sociedades Andinas." In *Formaciones Económicas y Políticas del Mundo Andino,* 59–115. Lima: Instituto de Estudios Peruanos.

Murra, John V. 1975b. "Un Reino Aymara en 1567." In *Formaciones Económicas y Políticas del Mundo Andino,* 193–223. Lima: Instituto de Estudios Peruanos.

National Academy of Sciences. 1975. *Plant Studies in the People's Republic of China: A Trip Report of the American Plant Studies Delegation.* Washington: National Academy of Sciences.

Negi, P. S. 1981. "Impact of Money Order Economy on Socio-Economic Development of Garhwal Region." *National Geographer* 16:71–76.

Netting, Robert McC. 1974. 'The System Nobody Knows: Village Irrigation in the Swiss Alps." In *Irrigation's Impact on Society,* edited by Theodore E. Downing and McGuire Gibson, 67–75. Tucson: University of Arizona Press.

Netting, Robert McC. 1976. "What Alpine Peasants Have in Common: Observations on Communal Tenure in a Swiss Village." *Human Ecology* 4:135–146.

Netting, Robert McC. 1977. *Cultural Ecology.* Menlo Park: Benjamin/Cummings.

Netting, Robert McC. 1981. *Balancing on an Alp: Ecological Change and Continuity in a Swiss Mountain Community.* Cambridge: Cambridge University Press.

Nietschmann, Bernard. 1971. "The Substance of Subsistence." In *Geographic Research on Latin America: Benchmark 1970.* Proceedings of the Conference of Latin Americanist Geographers, vol. 1, edited by Barry Lentnek, Robert L. Carmin and Tom L. Martinson, 167–181. Muncie: Ball State University.

Nigh, R. B. 1976. "Evolutionary Ecology of Maya Agriculture in Highland Chiapas, Mexico." *Dissertation Abstracts International.* Series A. 36/12:8155.

Noe, N. 1869. *Tyrol vom Glockner zum Ortler und vom Garda zum Bodensee.* Munich.

Oldfield, F., P. G. Appleby, A. Brown, and R. Thompson. 1980. "Palaeo-ecological Studies of Lakes in the Highlands of Papua New Guinea, part 1: the Cronology of Sedimentation." *Journal of Ecology* 68:457–477.

Olympic Secretariat and Carson–Mulloch Associates Ltd. 1984. *Canmore Nordic Centre Master Development Plan: Summary Report.* Edmonton: Alberta Recreation and Parks.

Orlove, Benjamin S. 1973. "A Mixed Agricultural-Transhumance Economy and Techniques of Microenvironmental Variation in the Andes." Paper presented in the symposium on Cultural Adaptations to Mountain Ecosystems, at the Annual Meeting of the American Anthropological Association, New Orleans.

Orlove, Benjamin S. 1974. "Reciprocidad, Desigualdad y Dominación." In *Reciprocidad e intercambio en los Andes Peruanos.* Peru-Problema, no. 12, edited by Giorgio Alberti and Enrique Mayer, 290–321. Lima: Instituto de Estudios Peruanos.

Orlove, Benjamin S. 1976. "The Tragedy of the Commons Revisited: Land Use and Environmental Quality in High-Altitude Andean Grasslands." In *Hill Lands* 208–214. Morgantown: University of West Virginia Press.

Orlove, Benjamin S. 1977. *Alpacas, Sheep, and Men.* New York: Academic Press.

Paffen, K. H., W. Pillewizer, and H.-J. Schneider. 1956. "Forschungen in Hunza–Karakorum." *Erdkunde* 10:1–33.

Parks Canada. 1984. *Planning Options, Four Mountain Parks, Jasper, Banff, Kootenay, Yoho.* Calgary: Parks Canada, Western Region.

Parks Canada. 1985. *Public Response Report, Planning Option Stage, The Four Mountain Parks Planning Program,* Calgary: Parks Canada, Western Region.

Parsons, James J. 1985. "On 'Bio-Regionalism' and 'Watershed Consciousness.' " *Professional Geographer* 37:1–6.

Patton, Brian. 1985. "An Immodest Proposal." *Equinox* 4:108.

Peattie, Roderick. 1936. *Mountain Geography: a Critique and Field Study.* Cambridge: Harvard University.

Penz, Hugo. 1978. "Die Almwirtschaft in Oesterreich." *Muenchner Studien zur Sozial-und Wirtschaftsgeographie* 15.

Penz, H. 1984. "Entwicklungstendenzen der Oesterreichischen Almwirtschaft." *Wiener Geographische Schriften* 59/60:142–148.

Petocz, R. G. 1972. "Report of the Laghman Markhor Survey." Kabul: UNDP.

Pharis, Vivian. 1985. "Viewpoint." *Environment Views* 8:17.

Pitt, David C., ed. 1978. *Society and Environment: the Crisis in the Mountains.* Working Papers in Comparative Sociology, no. 8. Auckland: University of Auckland.

Planhol, Xavier de. 1962. "Caractères généraux de la vie montagnarde dans le Proche-Orient et dans l'Afrique du Nord." *Annales de Géographie* 71:113–130.

Planhol, Xavier de. 1968. "Pression démographique et vie montagnarde (particulièrement dans la ceinture alpino-himalayenne)." *Revue de Géographie Alpine* 57:531–551.

Planhol, Xavier de. 1975. *Kulturgeographische Grundlagen der islamischen Geschichte.,* Zurich/Munich.

Prebble, J. 1963. *The Highland Clearances.* Harmondsworth: Penguin.

Price, Larry W. 1981. *Mountains and Man: a Study of Process and Environment.* Berkeley: University of California.

Pulgar Vidal, Javier. 1946. *Historia y geografía del Perú. vol 1. Las Ocho Regiones Naturales del Perú.* Lima: Universidad Nacional Mayor de San Macros.

Radvanyi, Jean, and P. Thorez. 1976. "Le tourisme dans le Caucase." *Annales de Geographie* 85:178–205.

Radvanyi, Jean, and P. Thorez. 1980. "Une expérience socialiste dans une montagne traditionnelle: Le Caucase." *La Pensée* 212:80–93.

Rao, Apurna, and M. Casimir. 1982. "Mobile Pastoralists of Jammu and Kashmir: A Preliminary Report." *Nomadic Peoples* 10:40–50.

Rathjens, Carl. 1966–69. "Neuere Entwicklung und Aufgaben einer vergleichenden Geographie der Hochgebirge." *Geographisches Taschenbuch* 199–210.

Rathjens, Carl. 1972. "Fragen der horizontalen und vertikalen Landschaftsgliederung im Hochgebirgssystem des Hindukusch." In *Geoecology of the High Mountains of Eurasia* Erdwissenschaftliche Forschung, vol. 4 edited by Carl Troll, 205–220. Stuttgart: Franz Steiner.

Rathjens, C. 1982. "Vergleich und Typenbildung in der Hochgebirgsforschung."*Erdkundliches Wissen* 59:1–8.

Rauchenstein, F. 1908. *Les bisses du Valais.* Sion.

Reclus, Élisée. 1881. *Histoire d'une montagne* Paris: J. Hetzel.

Reitz, L. P., and J. C. Craddock. 1969. "Diversity of Germ Plasm in Small Grain Cereals."*Economic Botany* 23:315–323.

Rhoades, Robert E., and Stephen I. Thompson. 1975. "Adaptive Strategies in Alpine Environments: Beyond Ecological Particularism." *American Ethnologist* 2:535–551.

Rich, William. 1973. *Smaller Families through Social and Economic Progress.* Overseas Development Council Monograph, no. 7. Washington: Overseas Development Council.

Rinschede, Gisbert. 1976. "Die Transhumance in den franzoesischen Westalpen und in den Pyrenaeen." *Verhandlungen des Deutschen Geographentages* 40:803–830.

Rinschede, Gisbert. 1978. "Die Rindertranshumance in den franzoesischen Alpen." *Mitteilungen der Oesterreichischen Geographischen Gesellschaft* 120:74–95.

Rinschede, Gisbert. 1979. "Die Transhumance in den franzoesischen Alpen und in den Pyrenaeen." *Westfaelische Geografische Studien* 32:

Rinschede, Gisbert. 1981. "Die saisonale Nutzung des Hochgebirgsraums der westlichen USA durch Viehwirtschaft und Tourismus." *Frankfurter Wirtschaftliche und Sozialgeographische Schriften* 36:173–212.

Rinschede, Gisbert. 1983. "Die Transhumance der Rinder in den spanischen Pyrenaen." *Zeitschrift fuer Wirtschaftsgeographie* 27:92–103.

Rinschede, Gisbert. 1984. "Wanderviehwirtschaft im Vergleich: Alpen/Pyrenaeen—Hochgebirge der westlichen USA." In *Beitraege zur vergleichenden Kulturgeographie der Hochgebirge.* Eichstaetter Beitraege vol. 12, edited by Erwin Groetzbach and Gisbert Rinschede, 285–304. Regensburg: Verlag Pustet.

Rinschede, Gisbert. 1985. "Transhumanz." *International Geographical Glossary, Deutsche Ausgabe* edited by E. Meynen, 1175. Stuttgart: Franz Steiner Wiesbaden.

Robertson, George S. 1974. *The Kafirs of the Hindu-Kush*. 1896. Reprint. Karachi: Oxford University Press.

Robinson, J. A. 1978. *Notes on Nomad Tribes of Eastern Afghanistan*. 1935. Reprint. Quetta: Nisa Traders.

Rowe, P. R. 1969. "Nature, Distribution, and Use of Diversity in the Tuberbearing Solanum Species." *Economic Botany* 23:330–338.

Ruppert, K. 1982. "Die deutschen Alpen-Prozessablaeufe spezieller Agrarstrukturen." *Erdkunde* 36:176–187.

Sabhasri, S. 1970. "Effect of Forest Fallow Cultivation on Forest and Soil Productivity." In *International Seminar on Shifting Cultivation and Economic Development in Northern Thailand. Chiang Mai 1970*. Bangkok: Land Development Department.

Sabhasri, S. 1980. "Research and Training in Southeast Asia in Relation to Priority Areas of the Programme on the Use and Management of Natural Resources." In *Conservation and Development in Northern Thailand*, edited by Jack D. Ives, S. Sabbasri, P. Varaurai. Tokyo: University Nations University.

Said, Edward. 1978. *Orientalism*. New York: Random House.

Sanchez, Rodrigo. 1976. "The Model of Verticality in the Andean Economy: A Critical Reconsideration," *Actes du XLIIe Congrès International des Americanistes* 4:213–231, Paris.

Santa Cruz, Hernan. 1967. "Future Development of Latin American Agriculture." In *Agricultural Development in Latin America: the Next Decade; Round Table; April*. Washington: Inter-American Development Bank.

Sarkar, R., V. Sarkar, and M. K. Raha. 1982. "The Gujjars and their Society." In *Nomads in India*, edited by P. K. Misra and K. C. Malhotra, 65–74. Calcutta: Anthropological Survey of Indian.

Saunders, Frank. 1983. "Karakorum Villages." Gilgit: FAO/UNDP. Mimeo.

Schneider, H.-J.1969. "Minapin—Gletscher und Menschen im NW–Karakorum (und Karte 1:50 000)." *Die Erde* 100:266-286.

Schneiter, V. 1980. "La guerre de libération au Nouristan (juillet 1978-mars 1979)." *Les Temps Modernes* 408/409:237–244.

Schoepf, A. J. 1855. *Das 91-jaehrige Leben und Wirken des Fruehmessers vlg. Hoeflichkeit-sprofessors Christian Falkner*. Salzburg.

Scholz, Fred. 1969. "Zum Feldbau des Akha-Dorfes Alumn, Thailand." In *Jahrbuch des Suedasien-Instituts der Universitaet Heidelberg*. vol. 3. Stuttgart: Franz Steiner Wiesbaden.

Scholz, Fred. 1984. "Bewaesserung in Pakistan: Zusammenstellung und Kommentierung neuester Daten." *Erdkunde* 38:216-225.

Schumacher, E. F. 1973. *Small is Beautiful*. New York: Harper and Row.

Schweinfurth, Ulrich. 1956. "Ueber klimatische Trockentaeler im Himalaya." *Erdkunde* 10:297–302.

Schweinfurth, Ulrich. 1957. "Die horizontale und vertikale Verbreitung der Vegetation im Himalaya." *Bonner Geographische Abhandlungen* 20:1–372.

Schweinfurth, Ulrich. 1962. "Studien zur Pflanzengeographie von Tasmanien." *Bonner Geographische Abhandlungen* 31:1–61.

Schweinfurth, Ulrich. 1966. *Neuseeland, Beobachtungen, und Studien zur Pflanz engeographie und Oekologie der antipodischen Inselgruppe*. Bonner Geographische Abhandlungen no. 36. Bonn: Ferd. Duemmlers.

Schweinfurth, Ulrich. 1972. "The Eastern Marches of High Asia and the River Gorge Country." *Geoecology of the High Mountains of Eurasia*. Erdwissenschaftliche Forschungen vol.4, edited by Carl Troll, 276–287. Stuttgart Franz Steiner.

Schweinfurth, Ulrich. 1982. "Der innere Himalaya. Rueckzugsgebiet, Interferenzzone, Eigenentwicklung." In *Beitraege zur Hochgebirgsforschung und Allgemeinen Geographie*. Erdkundliches Wissen, vol. 59, edited by E. Meyner and E. Pelwe, 15–24. Stuttgart: Franz Steiner.

Schweizer, G. 1969. "Buesserschnee in Vorderasien." *Erdkunde* 23:200–205.

Schweizer, G. 1972. "Klimatisch bedingte geomorphologische und glaziologische Zuege der

Hochregion vorderasiatischer Gebirge (Iran und Ostanatolien)." In *Geoecology of the High Mountains of Eurasia*. Erdwissenschaftliche Forschungungen, vol. 4 edited by Carl Troll, 221–236. Stuttgart: Franz Steiner.

Scott, Christopher D. 1974. "Asignación de Recursos y Formas de Intercambio." In *Reciprocidad e Intercambio en los Andes Peruanos*. Peru-Problema, no. 12, edited by Giorgio Alberti and Enrique Mayer, 322–345. Lima: Instituto de Estudios Peruanos.

Senegacnik, J. 1984 "Veraenderungen der slowenischen Almwirtschaft im letzten Jahrzehnt." *Muenchner Studien zur Sozial-und Wirtschaftsgeographie* 27:77–85.

Senn, F. 1870. *Jahrbuch des Oesterreichischen Alpenvereines*. Innsbruck.

Shahrani, M. N. 1979. *The Kirghiz and Wakhi of Afghanistan. Adaptation to Closed Frontiers*. Seattle: University of Washington Press.

Shantzis, S. B., and W. W. Behrens. 1982. "Population Control Mechanisms in a Primitive Agricultural Society." In *Energy and Effort*, edited by G. A. Harrison. London: Taylor and Francis.

Sharp, W. Curtis. 1970. "New Plants for Conservation." *Economic Botany* 21:53–54.

Shashi, S. S. 1979. *The Nomads of the Himalayas*. Delhi: Sundeep Prakashan.

Sherbondy, Jeanette E. 1982. "The Canal Systems of Hanan Cuzco." *Dissertation Abstracts International*. Series A. 43/3:858.

Sinner, K. 1978. *Obergurgl Chronik*. Innsbruck: Alpin Forschungsstelle Obergurgl.

Skalnik, P. 1978. "Uneven and Combined Development in European Mountain Communities." In *Society and Environment: Crisis in the Mountains*. Working Papers in Comparative Sociology, no. 8, edited by David C. Pitt, 123–154. Auckland: University of Auckland.

Ski Action Alberta. 1983. "Minutes of a public forum held 24 February 1983." Mimeo.

Skinner, Reinhard J. 1976. "Technological Determinism: a Critique of Convergence Theory." *Comparative Studies in Society and History* 18:2–27.

Slaymaker, Olav, and H. McPherson, eds. 1972. *Alpine Geomorphology of Western Canada*. Vancouver: Tantalus.

Slotkin, R. 1985. *The Fatal Environment: the Myth of the Frontier in the Age of Industrialization, 1800–1890*. New York: Atheneum.

Snoy, Peter. 1965. "Nuristan und Munjan." *Tribus* 14:101–148.

Snoy, Peter. 1975. *Bagrot: Eine Dardische Talschaft*. Graz: Akademische druck- und Verlagsanstalt.

Soffer, A. 1982. "Mountain geography—a New Approach." *Mountain Research and Development* 2:391–398.

Srinivas, M. N. 1952. *Religion and Society Among the Coorgs of South India*. Oxford: University Press.

Stadel, Christoph. 1982a. "Mountain Regions—Their Nature and Problems."*Geographical Perspectives* 49:26–33.

Stadel, Christoph. 1982b. "The Alps: Mountains in Transformation." *Focus* 32:1–15.

Stadel, Christoph. 1985. "Environmental Stress and Human Activities in the Tropical Andes (Ecuador)." *Revista del Centro Panamericano de Estudios e Investigaciones Geográficas (CEPEIGE) (Quito)* 15:33–50.

Stadel, Christoph. 1986."Altitudinal Patterns of Agricultural Activities in the Patate-Pelileo Area of Ecuador." *Mountain Research and Development* 6:53-62.

Staley, John. 1969. "Economy and Society in the High Mountains of Northern Pakistan." *Modern Asian Studies* 3:225–243.

Staley, John. 1982. *Words for my Brother. Travels between the Hindu Kush and the Himalayas*. Karachi: Oxford University Press.

Stefansson, V. 1922. *The Northward Course of Empire*. New York: Harcourt, Brace.

Sternberg, Hilgard O'R. 1973. "Development and Conservation." *Erdkunde* 27:253–265.

Stewart, J. I. and C. T. Hash. 1982. "Impact of Weather Analysis on Agricultural Production and Planning Decisions for the Semi-arid Areas of Kenya." *Journal of Applied Meteorology* 21:477–494.

Stouse, Jr., and A. D. Pierre. 1970. "The Distribution of Llamas in Bolivia." *Proceedings of the Association of American Geographers* 2:136–140.

Strand, Richard F. 1984. "Ethnic Competition and Tribal Schism in Eastern Nuristan." In

Revolutions and Rebellions in Afghanistan: Anthropological Perspectives, edited by M. N. Shahrani and R. L. Canfield, 77–93. Berkeley: Institute of International Studies, University of California.

Surarerks, V. 1975. "Agrargeographische und sozial-oekonomische Struktur in Nordthailand (unter besonderer Beruecksichtigung der Pachtverhaeltnisse)." Ph.D. Diss. Giessen.

Tani, Y., T. Matsui, and S. Omar. 1980. "The Pastoral Life of the Durrani Pashtun Nomads in Northeastern Afghanistan." In *Preliminary Report of Field Survey on the Agrico-Pastoral Peoples in Afghanistan, 1978*, edited by Y. Tani, 1–31. Kyoto: Research Institute for the Humanistic Studies, Kyoto University.

Tansley, A. G., and T. F. Chipp. 1926. *Aims and Methods in the Study of Vegetation*. London.

Tappeiner, G. 1979. Paper presented at UNESCO/MAB International Journalist Seminar on "Mountain Development: For Whom and What Purpose?" Obergurgl, Austria.

Tendler, Judith. 1975. "A.I.D. and Small Farmer Organizations: Lessons of the Ecuadorian Experience." Washington: Office of Development Programs of the Latin American Bureau, Agency for International Development.

Thiesenhusen, William C. 1974. "What Changing Technology Implies for Agrarian Reform." *Land Economics* 50:35–50.

Thomas, R. Brooke. 1973. *Human Adaptation to a High Andean Energy Flow System*. Occasional Papers in Anthropology no. 7. University Park, Pa.: Pennsylvania State University.

Thomas, R. Brooke. 1976. "Energy Flow at High Altitude." In *Man in the Andes*, edited by Paul Baker and Michael A. Little, 379–404. Stroudsburg, Pa.: Dowden, Hutchinson and Ross.

Thomas, R. Brooke. 1978. "Effects of Change on High Mountain Human Adaptive Patterns." In *High Altitude Geoecology*, edited by Patrick J. Webber, 139–188. Boulder: Westview.

Thomas, R. Brooke, Bruce Winterhalder, and Stephen D. McRae. 1979. "An Anthropological Approach to Human Ecology and Adaptive Dynamics." *Yearbook of Physical Anthropology* 22:1–46.

Thomspon, W. F. 1964. "How and Why to Distinguish Between Mountains and Hills." *Professional Geographer* 16:608.

Tosi, Jr., Joseph A. 1960. *Zonas de Vida Natural en el Peru. Memoria Explicativa Sobre el Mapa Ecológico del Peru*. Boletín Tecnico, no. 5. Lima: Instituo Interamericano de Ciencias Agrícolas de la OEA; Zona Andina.

Tripathi, B. D. 1978. *Sadhus of India*, Bombay: Popular Prakashan.

Troger, E. 1960. "Ban-Pae-Lungar." *Mitteilungen der Oesterreichischen Geographischen Gesellschaft*, 102.

Troger, E. 1963. "Contribution to the Study of the Demographic Situation of a Yao Village in Northern Thailand." *Anthropology and Social Sciences* 3.

Troll, Carl. 1939a. "Luftbildplan und oekologische Bodenforschung." *Zeitschrift der Gesellschaft fuer Erdkunde Berlin* 241–298.

Troll, Carl. 1939b. "Das Pflanzenkleid des Nanga Parbat." *Wissenschaftliche Veroeffentlichungen des Deutschen Museums fuer Landeskunde zu Leipzig* New Series, 7:149–193.

Troll, Carl. 1941. "Studien zur vergleichenden Geographie der Hochgebirge der Erde." *Bonner Geographische Mitteilungen* 21:1–50.

Troll, Carl. 1942. "Buesserschnee *(Nieve de los Penitentes)* in den Hochgebirgen der Erde." *Petermanns Geographische Mitteilungen* Supplement, 240:1–103.

Troll, Carl. 1943a. "Die Frostwechselhaeufigkeit in den Luft- und Bodenklimaten der Erde." *Metereologische Zeitschrift* 60:161–171.

Troll, Carl. 1943b. "Die Stellung der Indianer-Hochkulturen im Landschaftsaufbau der tropischen Anden." *Zeitschrift der Gesellschaft fuer Erdkunde Berlin* 93–128.

Troll, Carl. 1943c. "Methoden der Luftbildforschung," *Sitzungs-Bericht europaeischer Geographen, Wuerzburg* 121–146.

Troll, Carl. 1943d. "Thermische Klimatypnen der Erde." *Petermanns Geographische Mitteilungen* 241: 81–89.

Troll, Carl. 1943–44. "Strukturboeden, Solifluktion und Frostklimate der Erde." *Geologische Rundschau* 34:545–694.

Troll, Carl. 1947. "Die Formen der Solifluktion und die periglaziale Bodenabtragung." *Erdkunde* 1:162–175.

Troll, Carl. 1948a. "Der asymmetrische Aufbau der Vegetationszonen und Vegetationsstufen auf der Nord– und Suedhalbkugel." *Jahresbericht des Geobotanischen Forschungs-Institutes Ruebel in Zuerich fuer 1947:* 46–83.

Troll, Carl. 1948b. "Der subnivale und periglaziale Zyklus der Denudation." *Erdkunde* 2:1–21.

Troll, Carl. 1949. "Schmelzung und Verdunstung von Eis und Schnee in ihrem Verhaeltnis zur geographischen Verbreitung der Ablationsformen." *Erdkunde* 3:18–29.

Troll, Carl. 1951. "Tatsachen und Gedanken zur Klimatypenlehre." *Geographische Studien* 184–202.

Troll, Carl. 1952. "Die Lokalwinde der Tropengebirge und ihr Einfluss auf Niederschlag und Vegetation." *Bonner Geographische Abhandlungen* 9:124–182.

Troll, Carl. 1955a. "Der jahreszeitliche Ablauf des Naturgeschehens in den verschiedenen Klimaguerteln der Erde." *Studium Generale* 8:713–733.

Troll, C. 1955b. "Die Klimatypen an der Schneegrenze." *Actes du IVe Congrès Internationale du Quaternaire Rome–Pisa 1953:* 820–830.

Troll, Carl. 1955c. "Ueber das Wesen der Hochgebirgsnatur." *Jahrbuch des Deutschen Alpenvereins* 80:142–157.

Troll, Carl. 1957. "Forschungen in Zentralmexiko 1954. Die Stellung des Landes im dreidimensionalen Landschaftsaufbau der Erde." *Deutscher Geographentag Hamburg 1955:* 191–213.

Troll, Carl. 1958. "Tropical Mountain Vegetation." *Proceedings, IXth Pacific Science Congress Bangkok 1956* 20:37–46.

Troll, Carl. 1959a. "Die tropischen Gebirge. Ihre dreidimensionale klimatische und pflanzengeographische Zonierung." *Bonner Geographische Abhandlungen* 25:1–93.

Troll, Carl. 1959b. "Zur Physiognomik der Tropengewaechse." *Jahrbuch der Gesellschaft der Freunde und Foerderer der Universitaet Bonn fuer 1958:* 1–75.

Troll, Carl. 1961. "Klima und Pflanzenkleid der Erde in dreidimensionaler Sicht." *Die Naturwissenschaften* 48:332–348.

Troll, Carl. 1962. "Die dreidimensionale Landschaftsgliederung der Erde." In *Hermann von Wissmann-Festschrift*, 54–80. Tuebingen.

Troll, Carl. 1966a. "Oekologische Landschaftsforschung und vergleichende Hochgebirgsforschung" *Erdkundliches Wissen* 11:2–12.

Troll, Carl. 1966b. *Landscape Ecology.* Publications ITC-UNESCO Centre for Integrated Surveys no. 4. Delft: ITC-UNESCO.

Troll, Carl. 1967. "Die klimatische und vegetationsgeographische Gliederung des Himalaya-Systems." In *Khumbu-Himal.* Ergebnisse des Forschungsunternehmens Nepal Himalaya, vol. 1, Series 5, edited by Walter Hellmich, 353–388. New York: Springer Verlag.

Troll, Carl. 1968a. "The Cordilleras of the Tropical Americas: Aspects of Climatic, Phytogeographical and Agrarian Ecology." *Colloquium Geographicum* 9:15–56.

Troll, Carl. 1968b. "Landschaftsoekologie." In *Pflanzensoziologie und Landschaftsoekologie*, 1–21. Den Haag: Mouton.

Troll, Carl. 1969. "Die Lebensformen der Pflanzen. Alexander von Humboldt's Ideen in der oekologischen Sicht von heute." In *Alexander von Humboldt: Werk und Weltgeltung*, 197–246. Munich.

Troll, Carl. 1970a. "Das 'Baumfarnklima' und die Verbreitung der Baumfarne auf der Erde." *Tuebinger Geographische Studien* 34:179–189.

Troll, Carl. 1970b. "Die naturraeumliche Gliederung Nord–Aethiopiens." *Erdkunde* 24:249–268.

Troll, Carl. 1970c. "Landschaftsoekologie (Geoecology) and Biogeocoenology. Eine terminologische Studie." *Revue Roumaine Géologie, Géophysique, Géographie, Série de Géographie* 14:9–18.

Troll, Carl. 1971. "Landscape Ecology (Geoecology) and Biogeocoenology. A Terminological Study." *Geoforum* 8:43–46.

Troll, Carl. 1972a. "Geoecology and the world-wide differentiation of high-mountain ecosystems."In *Geoecology of the High Mountains of Eurasia*. Erdwissenschaftliche Forschung, vol. 4, edited by Carl Troll,1–16. Stuttgart: Franz Steiner.

Troll, Carl. 1972b. "The Upper Limit of Aridity and the Arid Core of *High*-Asia." In *Geoecology of the High Mountains of Eurasia*. Erdwissenschaftliche Forschung, vol.4, edited by Carl Troll, 237–243. Stuttgart: Franz Steiner.

Troll, Carl. 1972c. "The Three-Dimensional Zonation of the Himalayan System."In *Geoecology of the High Mountains of Eurasia*. Erdwissenschaftliche Forschung, vol.4, edited by Carl Troll, 264–275. Stuttgart: Franz Steiner.

Troll, C. 1973a. "High mountain belts between the polar caps and the equator. Their definition and lower limits." *Arctic and Alpine Research* 5:19–27.

Troll, Carl. 1973b. "Rasenabschalung (Turf Exfoliation) als periglaziales Phaenomen der subpolaren Zonen und der Hochgebirge." *Zeitschrift fuer Geomorphologie* New Series, Supplement 17:1–32.

Troll, Carl. 1973c. "The Upper Timberlines in Different Climatic Zones." *Arctic and Alpine Research* 5:3–18.

Troll, Carl., and R. Finsterwalder. 1935. "Die Karten der Cordillera Real und des Talkessels von La Paz (Bolivien) und die Diluvialgeschichte der zentralen Anden." *Petermanns Geographische Mitteilungen* 81:393–399, 454–455.

UNESCO. 1974. *Working Group on Project 6: Impact of Human Activities on Mountain and Tundra Ecosystems. Final Report*, Man and Biosphere Programme, no. 14. Paris.

Uhlig, Harald. 1969. "Hill Tribes and Rice Farmers in the Himalayas and South-East Asia." *Transactions, Institute of British Geographers*, 47:1-23.

Uhlig, Harald. 1973a. "Wanderhirten im westlichen Himalaya. Chopans, Gujars, Bakerwals, Gaddi." In *Vergleichende Kulturgeographie der Hochgebirge des suedlichen Asien*. Erdwissenschaftliche Forschung, vol. 5, edited by C. Rathjens, C. Troll and H. Uhlig, 157–167. Wiesbaden: Franz Steiner.

Uhlig, Harald. 1973b. "Zelgenwirtschaften und mehrgliedrige Siedlungs und Anbausysteme (Kulu/Mandi, Himachal Pradesh, und Langtang, Nepal)." In *Vergleichende Kulturgeographie der Hochgebirge des suedlichen Asien*. Erdwissenschaftliche Forschung, vol. 5, edited by Carl Rathjens, Carl Troll and Harald Uhlig, 10–22. Stuttgart: Franz Steiner.

Uhlig, Harald. 1975. "Le remplacement de la culture itinérante sur brulis." In *Travaux et documents de géeographie tropicale*. Centre National de la Recherche Scientifique Publications no. 20. Paris: CNRS.

Uhlig, Harald. 1976a. "Bergbauern und Hirten im Himalaya: Hoehenschichten und Staffelsysteme—ein Beitrag zur vergleichenden Kulturgeographie der Hochgebirge." *Verhandlungen des Deutschen Geographentages* 40:549–586.

Uhlig, Harald. 1976b. "Die Agrarlandschaft im Tropenkarst—Beispiele ihrer geo-ökologischen Differenzierung aus Java und Sulawesi." *Geografski Glasnik* 38:313–335.

Uhlig, Harald. 1978. "Geoecological Controls on High Altitude Rice Cultivation in the Himalayas and Mountain Regions of Southwest Asia." *Arctic and Alpine Research* 10:519–529.

Uhlig, Harald. 1984. "Die Darstellung von Geo-Oekosystem in Profilen und Diagrammen als Mittel der vergleichenden Geographie der Hochgeibirge." In *Beitraege zur vergleichenden Kulturgeographie der Hochgebirge*. Eichstaetter Beitraege vol. 12, edited by E. Groetzbach und G. Rinschede, 93–152. Regensburg: Friedrich Pustet.

Ulmer, F. 1935. "Hoehenflucht. Eine statistische Untersuchung ueber die Gebirgsentsiedlung in Deutsch-Tirol." *Schlern Schriften* 27.

Vallée, Lionel. 1971. "La Ecología Subjetiva Como un Elemento Essencial de la Verticalidad." *Revista del Museo Nacional (Lima)* 37:167–173.

Van Roy, E. 1966. "Economic Dualism and Economic Change among the Hill Tribes of Thailand." *Pacific Viewpoint* 7:151–168.

Vayda, A. P., and B. J. McCay. 1975. "New Directions in Ecology and Ecological Anthropology." *Annual Review of Anthropology* 4:293–306.

Veyret, P. and G. 1962. "Essai de definition de la montagne," *Revue de Géographie Alpine* 50:5–35.

Vidal de la Blache, P. 1926. *Principles of Human Geography*. London: Constable.

Vojvoda, M. 1969. "Almgeographische Studien in den slowenischen Alpen." *Muenchner Studien zur Sozial- und Wirtschaftsgeographie* 5:9–50.

Voraurai, P. 1980. "Review of Current Research on Agriculture in the Highlands of Northern Thailand." In *Conservation and Development in Northern Thailand*, edited by Jack D. Ives, S. Sabbasri, P. Varaurai. Bangkok: Land Development Department.

Waddell, Eric. 1972. *The Mound Builders: Agricultural Practices, Environment, and Society in the Central Highlands of New Guinea*. Washington: University of Washington.

Waddell, Eric. 1977. "How the Enga Cope with Frost: Responses to Climatic Perturbations in the Central Highlands of New Guinea." *Human Ecology* 3:249–273.

Waddell, Eric. 1975. "The Hazards of Scientism: a Review Article." *Human Ecology* 5:69–76.

Wade, Nicholas. 1975. "Boost for Credit Rating of Organic Farmers." *Science* 189:777.

Webber, Patrick J., ed. 1979. *High Altitude Geoecology*. Boulder: Westview.

Weber, K. E. 1969. "Shifting Cultivation among Thai Peasants." In *Jahrbuch des Suedasien Instituts der Universitaet Heidelberg*, vol. 3.

Webster, Steven S. 1971. "An Indigenous Quechua Community in Exploitation of Multiple Ecological Zones." *Actas y Memorias del XXXIX Congreso Internacional de Americanistas* vol. 3, 174–183.

Webster, Steven S. 1973. "Native Pastoralism in the South Andes." *Ethnology* 12:115–133.

Weinstein, D. A., H. H. Shugart, and C. C. Brandt. 1983. "Energy Flow and Persistence of a Human Population: A Simulation Analysis." *Human Ecology* 11:201–225.

Werthemann, A. and A. Imboden. 1982. *Die Alp- und Weidewirtschaft in der Schweiz*. Langnau.

Westing, A. H. 1980. *Warfare in a Fragile World: Military Impact on the Human Environment*. London: Taylor and Francis.

Wetering, H. Van de. 1973. "The Current State of Land Reform in Peru." *University of Wisconsin Land Tenure Center Newsletter* 40:5–9.

Whiteman, P. T. S. 1985a. "Mountain Oases. A Technical Report of Agricultural Studies in the Hunza, Ishkoman and Yasin Valleys of Gilgit District, Pakistan." Rome: United Nations Food and Agricultural Organisation. Mimeo.

Whiteman, P. T. S. 1985b. "The Mountain Environment: An Agronomist's Perspective with a Case Study from Jumla, Nepal." *Mountain Research and Development* 5:151–162.

Whiteman, P. T. S. 1986. "Learning the Constraints of Mountain Farming in Northern Pakistan." *CERES*. in press.

Wichmann, H., ed. 1972. *Die Zukunft der Alpenregion*. Munich.

Wilken, G. C. 1976. "Surface Geometry." *Studies in Resource Management in Traditional Middle American Farming Systems*. Report No. 5, Parts 1 and 2.

Wilken, G. C. 1977. "Manual Irrigation in Middle America." *Agricultural Water Management* 1:155–165.

Wilken, G. C. 1979. "Water Management." *Studies in Resource Management in Traditional Middle American Farming Systems* Report No. 8, Parts 1 and 2.

Winterhalder, Bruce, Robert Larsen, and R. Brooke Thomas. 1974. "Dung as an Essential Resource in a Highland Peruvian Community." *Human Ecology* 2:89–104.

Winterhalder, Bruce, and R. Brooke Thomas 1978. *Geoecology of Southern Highland Peru: A Human Adaptation Perspective*. Institute of Arctic and Alpine Research, Occasional Paper no. 27. Boulder: University of Colorado.

Wissmann, H. von. 1943. "Sued-Yunnan als Teilraum Suedostasiens." *Schriften zur Geopolitik* 22:5–30.

Wissmann, H. von. 1960. "Stufen und Guertel der Vegetation und des Klimas in Hochasien und seinen Randgebieten." *Erdkunde* 14:249–272, 15:19–44.

Wissmann, H. von. 1972. "Die Juniperus-Gebirgswaelder in Arabien. Ihre Stellung zwischen dem borealen und tropische-afrikanischen Florenreich." In *Geoecology of the High Mountains of Eurasia*. Erdwissenschaftliche Forschung, vol. 4, edited by Carl Troll,157–176. Stuttgart: Franz Steiner.

Wohlt, P. B. 1978. "Ecology, Agriculture and Social Organization: The Dynamics of Group Composition in the Highlands of New Guinea." *Dissertation Abstracts International*. Series A. 39/9:5600.

Wohlt, P. B., Bryant J. Allen, A. Goie, and P. W. Harvey. 1982. "An Investigation of Food Shortages in Papua New Guinea, 24 March to 3 April 1981." *IASER Special Publication* vol. 6.

Wolkinger, F. ed. 1977. *Natur und Mensch im Alpenraum*. Graz.

Yen, D. E. 1974. *The Sweet Potato and Oceania: an Essay in Ethnobotany*. Honolulu: Bernice P. Bishop Museum Bulletin.

Young, G. 1962. "The Hill Tribes of Northern Thailand." Monograph no. 1. Bangkok: The Siam Society.

Young, Walter D. and J. T. Morley. 1983. *The Reins of Power: Governing British Columbia*. Vancouver: Douglas and McIntyre.

Zwittkovits, F. 1974. *Die Almen Oesterreichs*. Zillingdorft/Niederoesterreich.

Contributors

NIGEL J. R. ALLAN is associate professor of geography at Louisiana State University. A native of Scotland, he has conducted field research in the Scottish Highlands, Alps, Rocky Mountains, Tien Shan, Tibet, Himalaya, Karakorum and the Hindukush Mountains. His research interests are about mountain societies and habitat.

BRYANT J. ALLEN is research fellow in human geography in the Research School of Pacific Studies at Australian National University. A native of New Zealand, his principle interests focus on human ecology and agricultural development in Papua New Guinea and the Pacific.

DANIEL BALLAND is maître de conférence in the Department of Geography, University of Paris, Sorbonne. He has conducted extensive field research in Afghanistan under the aegis of the Centre National de la Recherche Scientifique, Paris, and is the author of *Nomades et Sémi-Nomades d'Afghanistan*.

AGEHANANDA BHARATI, professor of anthropology at Syracuse University, is the author of eight books, including *The Ochre Robe, The Tantric Tradtion,* and *Hindu Views and Ways and the Hindu-Muslim Interface.* His professional interests include cognitive systems and South Asian and Tibetan society and culture.

STEPHEN B. BRUSH is academic administrator of International Agricultural Development Programs at the University of California, Davis. An anthropologist by training, he is the author of *Mountain, Field and Family.* His more recent research includes conservation of mountain crop germ plasm and crop evolution in the Andes.

SYLVIA H. FORMAN, associate professor of anthropology at the University of Massachusetts, has a primary interest in the problems and processes of Andean rural development. Her applied research includes studies on food practices, nutrition, demography and migration.

ERWIN F. GROETZBACH is professor of cultural geography at the Catholic University of Eichstaett, Federal Republic of Germany. He has published extensively on the cultural geography of high mountains, especially the Alps, Hindukush, Himalaya, Karakorum, and Pontus Mountains of Turkey. In addition to writing on tourism, recreation, land use, and settlement, he has contributed to theoretical and methodological issues in mountain studies.

KENNETH HEWITT is professor of geography at Wilfred Laurier University, Canada. Trained in England as a geomorphologist with field experience in the

Karakorum, he has conducted extensive research on hazards throughout the mountain world, and lately has devoted a considerable effort to documenting human-induced hazards, as demonstrated in his most recent book, *Interpretations of Calamity.*

JACK D. IVES is president of the International Mountain Society and professor of geography at the University of Colorado. He is the founder and former editor of *Arctic and Alpine Research* and is founder and editor of *Mountain Research and Development* and co-author of *Arctic and Alpine Environments.* He has conducted field research throughout the mountain world and has participated extensively in UNESCO's Man and the Biosphere Program in alpine environments.

HERBERT KARIEL is professor of geography at the University of Calgary, Canada. A native of Germany, he has conducted field research in New Zealand, Himalaya, Alps, North Africa and the Rocky Mountains. He is the co-author of *Explorations in Social Geography* and conducts mountain research in recreation and tourism, and environmental conservation.

GREGORY W. KNAPP, assistant professor of geography at the University of Texas, specializes in the traditional and prehistoric adaptations of Andean South America, especially in the highlands of Ecuador. His forthcoming book, *Andean Ecology: Adaptive Dynamics in Ecuador,* examines the relatively high carrying capacity of the Andean highlands.

HERMANN J. KREUTZMANN is a research fellow in the geography department, Free University of Berlin, Federal Republic of Germany. He has conducted field research in the Southern Alps of New Zealand and the Snowy Mountains of Australia as well as the Karakorum of Pakistan.

ELISABETH LICHTENBERGER is professor of geography at the University of Vienna, Austria. Much of her work focuses on regional planning of Alpine regions in Europe, including eastern Europe. In addition to *The Eastern Alps* she has published extensively on migrant workers and agricultural land use in the Alpine countries.

WALTER MOSER is professor of botany at the University of Alberta, Canada, and Counsellor of the International Mountain Society. While at the Alpine Forschungsstelle Obergurgl in Austria, he coordinated the Man and the Biosphere activities in Austria's highest village. The survival of mountain plants and environmental education are among his research interests.

HUGO PENZ is lecturer in geography at the University of Innsbruck, Austria. A native Tyrolean, his field research documents the changes in the traditional mountain peasant livelihood caused by urbanization, recreation and tourism.

JEANNIE PETERSEN is an editor-in-chief of *Ambio,* the journal of the Royal Swedish Academy of Sciences.

GISBERT RINSCHEDE is a geography professor at the Catholic University of Eichstaett, Federal Republic of Germany. Culture and land use of the western United States complement his interests in the mountain geography of the western Alps and the Pyrenees. He is the author of two monographs on transhumance in Europe and the United States.

CHRISTOPH STADEL, born in Germany, is professor of geography at Brandon University, Canada. Fieldwork in the tropical Andes of Ecuador has resulted in publications on the concept of verticality in mountain agriculture and rural life and on environmental stress in tropical highlands.

R. BROOKE THOMAS is a physical anthropologist who is professor of anthropology at the University of Massachusetts. For the past twenty years his research has focused upon biocultural adaptations of high Andean human populations to a variety of stressors and limiting factors, including hypoxia, cold, malnutrition, and disease.

CARL TROLL was the pre-eminent mountain geographer of this century when he died in 1975. As professor of geography at the University of Bonn he was the founder and editor of *Erdkunde* and had published on mountains throughout the world. He is especially noted for his efforts at organizing international symposia on mountain regions that helped to focus the attention of scholars from diverse fields. His 1975 *Geographische Rundschau* article is translated by Christoph Stadel and reprinted in this volume as a testimony to his lifetime effort on mountain geography.

HARALD UHLIG is professor of geography at the University of Giessen, Federal Republic of Germany. He has devoted much of his life's work to the enumeration of complex agrosystems in the Eurasian mountain world. A particular research emphasis is on rice cultivation in the high mountains of Asia and on the vertical zonation of mountain agriculture.

PETER T. S. WHITEMAN was trained as a botanist and tropical agronomist in England and the Caribbean and has worked for the last two decades in tropical and subtropical agriculture, especially in upland and highland regions. His applied research has dealt with the environmental variables in mountains and the cropping options that mountaineers face in their everyday life.

Index

ablation forms of snow cover, 38
adaptive dynamics, 132
adverse habitats, 14
Afghan Hindukush, 26
Afghan Nomad Survey, 266–67
Afghan-Pakistan border, 273, 275
Afghanistan, 16, 17, 30, 216, 217, 265, 268, 270, 275; Wakhan Corridor, 244
Africa, 37, 39; highlands, 57
Aga Khan Rural Support Programme, 249
agrarian carrying capacity, 30
agrarian reforms, in Nunoa, 179
agricultural: development, 137; extension work, 149, 152; intensification, 113; land, loss of, 160; methods, 174; planning, 117; practices, 116; production, 139, 142; research, 145; small-scale, 152; society, 225; technology, 139; values, 200
agriculture, 58, 170, 172, 211, 221; calendrical patterns, 149; commercialization of traditional, 124; ecological aspects of, 219; equitorial mountain, 59; intensification of, 126; and transportation, 25
air photo archaeology, 36
Akademie der Wissenschaften und der Literatur, 42
Alberta, Canada, 229, 235, 240, 241
Alberta Business Development and Tourism Department, 236
Alberta Mortgage and Housing Commission, 241
ALERT, 242
Almora, 85
almwirtschaft, 108, 109, 111, 112, 114
alpaca, 142, 143, 169, 176, 178
alpine: cultural landscape, 33; elemental events, 25; environment, equilibrium between humans and, 203; foothills, 15; pasture, 97, 111, 112, 113, 209; ski-ing, 25; tundra, 101; use of terminology, 51; villages, 201
Alpine Club of Canada, 229
Alpine Research Station, 204
alpinification, 20
Alps, 15, 26, 32, 55, 104, 105, 106, 109, 155, 163, 204, 215, 218, 221, 222, 223, 225
Alps Maritimes, 104
altiplano, 47, 118, 169, 175, 176, 179, 182, 183; human-environmental system, 172
altitude: and relief constraints, 25; and humidity, 12; and warming rate, 65
altitudinal: belts in human geography, 26; differences, 24; ecological niches, 112; vegetation zones, 6; zonation, 28, 130
Amazonas lowlands, 15
anabatic winds, 71
Andes, 15, 37, 44, 46, 54, 57, 120, 124, 134, 156, 183; development, 136, 141; ecological integration, 135; ecology, 133; ecosystem, 136; high civilizations, 50; human population, 167; indigenous kingdoms, 141; nations, 133, 137; rural development, 140
animals: in Canadian rockies, 229; production of, 170
anthropological fieldwork, 84
anti-pollution issues, 139
applied-mapping methodology, 160
arid lands, 9, 16
ascending humance, 102
ascending transhumance, 98
Atlas mountains, 17, 99
atmosphere, dynamic models of, 22
Australia, 261, 263; agricultural project, 188
Austria, 113, 114, 157, 201, 204, 215, 224, 225, 242
Austrian Alps, 45, 223, 227